The ASPCA Complete Guide to Pet Care

No other book offers such detailed information about a wide range of domestic animals and the issues faced by pet owners. From common to uncommon house pets—cats, dogs, and birds to ferrets, snakes, lizards, and toads—this essential guide puts the facts you need right at your fingertips.

Discover:

- What to consider when choosing a pet—and what to do if an adopted pet isn't working out
- How to make your home safe for a pet—and making a pet safe for your home
- How to match the right pet to the right child
- Best bets for traveling with your pet—whether by car or by plane
- What you need to know about boarding your pet at a kennel
- The pros and cons of pet sitters
- How to keep your pet healthy—from finding a veterinarian to getting to know your pet's medications, to coping with an older pet
- The facts about pet insurance
- The ABCs of grief
- Health care tips for keeping your dog in top physical condition
- Common bird ailments
- How to maintain the health of your fish . . . and much, much more!

DAVID L. CARROLL is the author of more than thirty books and numerous screenplays, including an Emmy Award–winning production for *Hallmark Hall of Fame*. He lives in Tappan, New York.

The ASPCA®

Complete Guide
to
Pet Care

DAVID L. CARROLL

A PLUME BOOK

PLUME
Published by the Penguin Group
Penguin Putnam Inc., 375 Hudson Street, New York, New York 10014, U.S.A.
Penguin Books Ltd, 27 Wrights Lane, London W8 5TZ, England
Penguin Books Australia Ltd, Ringwood, Victoria, Australia
Penguin Books Canada Ltd, 10 Alcorn Avenue, Toronto, Ontario, Canada M4V 3B2
Penguin Books (N.Z.) Ltd, 182–190 Wairau Road, Auckland 10, New Zealand

Penguin Books Ltd, Registered Offices: Harmondsworth, Middlesex, England

First published by Plume, a member of Penguin Putnam Inc.

First Printing, November 2001
10 9 8 7 6 5 4 3 2

PHOTO CREDITS: **1:** *Kuno the ferret,* owner Jessica Lynn Peretti; photo by Uncle Nicholas DeVivo.
25: *Ashley the cat,* photo by Kendra Grega. **41:** *Franklin the turtle,* photo by Christopher Laird.
59: *Louie the rabbit,* photo by owner Jennifer Howse. **78:** *Miss Scarlett Belle Crane the dog,* caretaker and companion Stephen V. Crane. **108:** *Brownie the guinea pig,* photo by Teresa Hellstrom.
128: *Watson the dog,* owner Emily O'Neil; photo by Lane O'Neil. **179:** *Whitaker the cat,* owner
April M. Woodruff; photo by Bob Farrington. **230:** *Jerry Jr. the hamster,* owner Evan Moser, photo
by Phil Stokoe. **284:** *Ziggy and Zuka the birds,* photo by Nicole Dorame. **324:** *Seaking the goldfish,* photo provided by Saundra Kuchinski. **362:** *Iggy the iguana,* owner Leigh Mcneill.

REGISTERED TRADEMARK—MARCA REGISTRADA

LIBRARY OF CONGRESS CATALOGING-IN-PUBLICATION DATA:
Carroll, David.
    The ASPCA complete guide to pet care / David L. Carroll ; introduction by Stephen Zawistowski.
      p.   cm.
    ISBN 0-452-28272-1
    1. Pets.   2. Pets—Health.   I. Title.
  SF413 .C38 2001
  636.088'7—dc21

2001021958

Printed in the United States of America
Set in New Caledonia and Franklin Gothic
Designed by Eve L. Kirch

BOOKS ARE AVAILABLE AT QUANTITY DISCOUNTS WHEN USED TO PROMOTE PRODUCTS OR SER-
VICES. FOR INFORMATION PLEASE WRITE TO PREMIUM MARKETING DIVISION, PENGUIN PUTNAM
INC., 375 HUDSON STREET, NEW YORK, NEW YORK 10014.

Foreword

Most of us remember our childhood pets. They provided entertainment, diversion from boring homework assignments, and
companionship when there was no one else around who understood us.
In many cases, our fascination with animals followed us into adulthood
and we indulged ourselves, as more sophisticated hobbyists, by caring
for a more extensive and exotic selection of pets. For some very lucky
kids, this childhood interest became an exciting and rewarding career. I
am one of those lucky few.

One day, while exploring the back of the dictionary, I came across
the word *zoologist*—one of the first words I learned to spell—and it
quickly became a career goal. My very tolerant sister had the best cared
for collection of stuffed animals in the neighborhood. They endured
regular trips to the "veterinarian" for shots, splints and mysterious sur-
geries. My bemused parents simply watched as a live menagerie found
its way into most corners of our home, including the basement and
garage.

When I left home for graduate school it did not provide a total
respite for the family. My mother found a crayfish wandering aimlessly
around the basement about a year after I had gone. It had escaped from
an aquarium some time before and had taken up residence in a damp
corner. My father made sure it went back to the same creek where it
had been born.

My fascination with animals continues today, both in my personal and professional life, and I have discovered another important ingredient in a life full of pets—an understanding spouse. With great equanimity my wife has accepted and helped to care for an incredible variety of animals in need. Growing up, our son thought it was quite normal to have animals living throughout the house, and he learned to feed and clean like a professional.

Over the years I have also shared with others the disappointment of having a beloved pet die. While our family record with dogs, cats, and rabbits was quite good, some of the smaller creatures died from unknown causes in too short a time. For the most part, successes were based on trial and error, extensive research of a limited literature, and luck.

The past twenty years have seen a revolution in the quality of information available for pet owners. *The ASPCA Complete Guide to Pet Care* combines this new information into a single convenient package. Heavily salted with the experience and knowledge of ASPCA experts, it can help potential pet owners get started down the right path, skipping the trial and error stage so many people encounter when adopting and caring for a new pet.

If you are in the market for a pet, first and foremost be sure to pick the right critter for your home, family, and lifestyle. Time, commitment, money, and living arrangements should all play a role in choosing the right companion for you and your family. Use the *Guide*, its references and appendix, to develop a plan to select and then welcome this new member to your family. Work with your veterinarian and other experts to ensure that your new pet receives the best possible care.

Second, consider your local animal shelter or a rescue group as the place to go for a companion animal. In addition to dogs and cats, many shelters also find homes for rabbits, ferrets, birds, hamsters and other animals. If you Make Adoption Your First Option™ you can not only acquire a wonderful new pet, you can also give an animal a second chance at a happy life. In addition to visiting a shelter, you can look for a new pet on the internet by going to the ASPCA website (www.aspca.org) and accessing our Internet pet adoption partner, Petfinder. Thousands of shelters and rescue groups provide photos and other information on tens of thousands of pets available across the country.

Third, use the *Guide* as a reminder about all of the different things we so often forget about in the excitement of a new pet. How can I care for my pet when I go on vacation? How do I move with a pet? What about training? Since the life span of most pets is brief, the *Guide* also provides help on dealing with the death of a companion animal, especially for children.

Finally, and most important, remember to take the time to have fun with your pets. No fancy cage, collar, or toy can take the place of a gentle human hand and plenty of time for play. While there have been many wonderful innovations that make caring for our pets easier, it is still your voice and your touch that will make the relationship with your pet *complete*.

Stephen Zawistowski, Ph.D.
Certified Applied Animal Behaviorist
Senior Vice President and Science Advisor, ASPCA

Acknowledgments

The following ASPCA experts lent their knowledge and experience to this book:

Jacque Lynn Schultz
Lila Miller, D.V.M.
Stephanie LaFarge, Ph.D.
Sheryl Dickstein-Pipe, Ph.D.
Stephen Zawistowski, Ph.D., Certified applied animal behaviorist

Contents

The

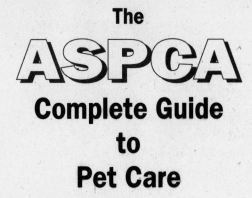

ASPCA

Complete Guide
to
Pet Care

The Big Choice:
Deciding Which Pet Is Best for You

Establishing Your Pet Compatibility Ratio

For many families deciding which animal companion to adopt is a major life decision.

Dogs and cats live ten to fifteen years, and other pets live even longer. Certain animals demand attention throughout the day. Others require handling and petting on a regular basis. All household creatures need to be fed, watered, cleaned, and cared for. You will be obliged to provide food, shelter, and love for your adopted pet 365 days of the year.

Bringing an animal companion into your home is thus not only an amusement and a recreation but a long-term commitment, one that requires the same thought and planning you might give to any of life's important decisions. Sharing your home with an animal is a form of partnership, one in which both parties, human and animal, must be comfortable with the accommodations. This, in fact, is the first rule of pet keeping: both pet and person must be happily adjusted to their role in the relationship.

What is the best way of determining which pet is best for you and your household?

There are three principal factors to take into account: personal preference, social compatibility, and living space.

Personal preference. First, there is the obvious matter of affinity and inclination. Which animal—or animals—do you like best? Which ones do you most enjoy having around? Which animal—or animals— would you most prefer to share your home and hearth with for the next X number of years?

Answering this question is, of course, a purely personal matter. If you grew up with malamutes as a child you may prefer them above all other pets. The same is true if you were raised with Maine Coon cats, or parrots, or white mice.

Or perhaps not. Our preferences in animals change through the years along with our tastes and personalities, and often these preferences take a more inclusive direction. Many is the animal lover today, for instance, who ends up keeping three or four pets at the same time, a dog, and a cat, a bird, some fish.

Remember, there is no rule that limits you to having a single pet. As long as there is room in your home, room in your wallet, and room in your heart, the sky's the limit.

Social compatibility. Second, there's the question of social fit: how comfortably will the pet adapt itself to the dynamics of your domestic life, your work habits, your financial situation, your daily schedule? How suited is the animal to living in harmony with the people in your household—your children, your relatives, your spouse, your significant other?

Living space and household logistics. Finally, there are logistical matters to consider: Will a dog or cat, fish tank or bird cage, fit into the physical dimensions of your house or apartment? Will the creature in question get along with your living room furniture and with the neighbor's rose garden? What size and shape pet does your residence most reasonably accommodate? How will such factors as noise, smell, dirt, hairs on the sofa, paw prints on clothes, and other by-products of the animal world affect you? How will it affect those who share your living space? How will it be welcomed by the people next door?

The answers to these questions differ from person to person and pet to pet, with endless variations on the theme. One good way to get a clear angle on your own special needs, and to help you decide which pet is best for you, is to determine your own personal pet compatibility ratio—that is, your overall personal and social affinity with whatever pets you are now considering. Establish this ratio and a clear picture of the animal (or animals) you're best suited to live with will emerge.

The section that follows contains a number of questions all related to pet compatibility. They will help you make your choice from a position of knowledge rather than guesswork.

What to Consider When Choosing a Pet

Which pet best suits your affections, needs, and personality?

Do you prefer an animal that greets you at the door when you come home from work each day? A pet that lies cozily on your lap while you watch TV? Do you envision a rollicking friend that jogs in the park with you or that plays games on your living room floor? Are you looking for a constant, loving companion?

Fine. Then you want a dog or cat. Dogs and cats are the most emotionally responsive of all domestic creatures, with the possible exception of certain large tropical birds.

On the other hand, perhaps you'd prefer an animal that requires occasional contact but that does not pine away for your company the moment you leave the house—a small, independent creature that you or your children can pick up and play with from time to time, feed, clean, and admire. End of story.

If this is the case, then gerbils, hamsters, mice, and guinea pigs are all solid bets. Or perhaps one of the friendlier small birds like a parakeet.

Alternately, you may wish for a more exotic creature, something off the beaten track. Not necessarily an animal to cuddle with, but one to enjoy and share your home with in more subtle ways. Reptiles and amphibians fill the bill nicely here.

Finally, you may simply be in the market for a creature that's wonderful to look at but not to relate to in any personal way. Tropical fish make ideal silent companions in this case. They can be watched and admired for hours by adults and children alike. Their colorful appearance and diverse behaviors fascinate observers, and bring a sense of peace and relaxation to any room.

A first step in finding the right pet, therefore, is to calculate the degree of emotional and physical involvement you wish to have with your animal; and equally important, to determine what kind of emotional response you expect in return.

Then act accordingly.

Which pet best fits the scheme and layout of your living space?

The human species dwells in a variety of habitats.

Some of us live in the city. Others live in the suburbs or the country. Some have a lawn behind their house, a terrace off the bedroom, a park up the block, a dog run in the neighborhood. Others do not. Some people inhabit a one-bedroom or studio apartment, a farm, or a twenty-room mansion. Others live with their families, with friends and mates, with an older relative, or a single child. Some of us live alone.

Each of these living arrangements places different demands on a person's lifestyle, and hence on the type of pet it's most appropriate to keep. For no matter how politely behaved or inconspicuous a pet may be, there are always challenges.

Dogs, for instance. They shed. They bark. They chew your bathrobe. They slobber. They smell. They track in mud. They jump up on visitors. They roll in manure. They burrow under the fence. They get sick. They eat a lot.

Minor offenses, no doubt, from a creature that provides us with so many major rewards. Still, be sure you're prepared to live with these annoyances. Or at least to spend the time teaching the dog manners.

Once a dog becomes your animal of choice, moreover, there's the fine-tuning to take care of.

The questions to ask yourself now are, What kind of dog best fits my lifestyle and my living space? Do I want an outdoorsy breed suited for backyard frolic or herding sheep? Or a less athletic animal that adjusts easily to sedentary apartment living? Am I looking for a big dog or a little dog? Long hair or short? Pure bred or mixed breed? A dog with a hair-trigger bark to scare away intruders, or a quiet dog that doesn't bother the tenants next door? What are the pros and cons? Large dogs are more expensive to feed and board. Small dogs can be restless and bark too much.

There's also activity level to be considered.

Great Danes, hulks that they are, actually make rather good apartment pets because of their constrained temperaments. The diminutive Jack Russell terrier, on the other hand, can be a nuisance in cramped quarters because of a jumpy, hyperactive nature.

Here a bit of homework on the different breeds will help. The chapters ahead on dog raising will answer most of your questions in this regard.

A similar evaluation, with appropriate modifications, can be applied to cats.

Do you prefer a longhair cat or short? Do you care if your cat is a mixed breed or purebred? Is there anyone in the house, an elderly person, or a young child, who is shaky on their feet, and who might trip over a tabby sleeping in the doorway or on the staircase? Are you thinking of adopting a Siamese? Know in advance that these delightful creatures express their affections with loud and continuous meows. This can be charming or annoying, depending on your tastes. Be prepared too for trips to the veterinarian. Annual visits for maintenance, vaccinations, and checkups are all part of the program, along with those unpredictable (and often inconvenient) occasions when illness comes.

With cats there's the shedding issue, too. All felines, even those with short fur, sprinkle their hairs lavishly about on the bed and the furniture. Despite careful house cleaning on your part, these hairs tend to accumulate, eventually building up to a critical mass. At this point these hairs not only pose a cosmetic problem but a medical one as well.

Why?

Because when cats clean themselves the saliva from their tongues dries on their fur and turns into tiny, invisible flakes. Certain proteins in this dried saliva are anathema to allergically sensitized humans, and can trigger reactions in minutes, causing sneezing, runny nose, skin rashes, even wheezing and shortness of breath for asthmatics. If you sneeze and sputter a lot when you're around a friend's cat this can be a red flag. A number of people suffer from allergies to cat dander.

Similar logistical considerations apply to other household pets.

Thinking of fish? Is there room in your home or apartment for a twenty- or thirty-gallon tank? Is the table or shelf you intend to place the tank on strong enough to support the weight? Thirty gallons of water is a lot of water. And if you're really enjoying it and keeping a much larger tank, 120 gallons, say, how strong are your floor joists? This is not a joke. A hundred and twenty gallons is something like having a baby elephant in the middle of your room. And what will you do if you want to move the tank someday?

Are you particularly noise sensitive? Will the low level bubbling from the aquarium filter annoy you or another family member? Is there a clear route from the fish tank to the sink, so that when you change the water you can empty the buckets of dirty water without stumbling over furniture?

As far as small animals go, hamsters, gerbils, rabbits, mice, and guinea pigs, all are potential sources of allergy, just like cats. Some furry animals also have distinctively gamy odors. Though these odors can usually be managed by frequent cleaning, smell-sensitive people should nonetheless keep this fact in mind.

Is there enough space in your apartment or house to comfortably house a cage? Will the noise of a hamster racing round and round its revolving wheel in the middle of the night prevent you and your children from sleeping? If you plan to give your new rabbit the run of the house, check first that all lamp wires and telephone cords are concealed. Rabbits love chewing wires and cords.

Thinking of a bird? Be sure you're not allergic to bird feathers first. Do you mind that your canary scatters gravel all over the dining room floor? Or that the finch's feathers drift onto the rug? Where will the cage hang? Near a window? If so, will it block the light or expose the bird to drafts? Near a radiator? Think about overheating. Near the door of the room? Will people bang their heads on the cage when they enter the room? In the children's room? Will the kids try to handle their little feathered friends every time you are looking in the other direction? If you adopt a bird that talks or sings, a parrot or a canary, say, are you prepared to hear warbling and talking sounds for ten to twelve hours a day? Some people love these avian vocalizations. Others do not. What's your preference?

A good way to plan ahead logistically for a pet is to tour all the possible rooms in your home where an aquarium or cage or dog bed might go. Quiz yourself concerning the feasibility of housing a pet in each of these places. Make a circuit through the house and evaluate the pros and cons of each location. Use stuffed animals or small cardboard boxes to simulate where a pet will sleep, or where you will place the cage and litter box. The right room for the right pet will quickly become evident.

How much does the pet cost?

There are two areas of concern when it comes to figuring out how much a pet is going to cost: the short term and the long term.

First, the short-term.

Here the primary thing people think of when adopting an animal is how much an animal will cost at the pet store, animal shelter, or breeder. Often that's *all* they think about.

Out-of-pocket expenses don't stop here, however, not even in the short run.

Why?

Because once you get the animal home a new series of expenses begins that can add up with amazing speed. The best way to cushion yourself against this second round of expenditures is to know about them ahead of time, and to include them into your overall pet cost estimate.

Small animals, for example, require a cage, bedding, feeding equipment, accessories.

Dogs and cats must have their vaccinations, collar, license, ID, leash, food bowls, litter box, toys.

Birds need a cage, seed, gravel, perches, accessories.

Reptiles and amphibians will require a tank, food, rocks, gravel, and perhaps a filter and heating unit.

Freshwater fish may cost only a few dollars apiece at the pet store. But the twenty- or thirty-gallon tank that comes with it plus the filter, charcoal, heater, gravel, rocks, and thermometer can cost several hundred dollars. And if you intend to establish a saltwater tank plan to spend in the high hundreds or perhaps even the low thousands.

All these cash outlays will be made within the first week or two after the animal enters your home, and should be considered short-term expenditures. Once these are buttoned down, it's time to turn your attention to the long term.

Any pet you keep must, of course, be fed and maintained. If you leave town for the summer or take frequent business trips, boarding expenses and pet-sitting fees must be paid. Aquarium filters constantly need replacement, and electrical bills are affected. Changing the bedding in an animal cage or the litter in a cat box are ongoing affairs. Turtles and frogs need their supply of insects, snakes their frozen mice, and for other animals, especially the large birds and mammals, medical costs loom, sometimes large ones. It has been estimated that the average dog and cat owner spends between two hundred and three hundred dollars a year on veterinary bills.

How much time can I and others afford to spend with a pet each day?

Another vital determinant for choosing a pet is the number of hours you're prepared to spend each day in the animal's company.

Here it comes as no surprise to learn that dogs are the number one attention cravers, and that having a dog should not even be *considered* unless owners are prepared to spend long stretches of quality time with their animal. Leaving dogs alone in a living room or tied up in the backyard for hours a day will make the animal neurotic and perhaps destructive as well. Many are the gnawed chair legs and gaping holes in the lawn that are due not so much to a hound's wayward nature as to the fact that he was so terribly lonely and bored.

Are all dogs equally in need of attention?

Not necessarily.

Within the canine kingdom there are some variations, and certain breeds do better than others in a solitary setting.

Shitzus, for example, are relatively comfortable staying by themselves for a number of hours each day. So are Pekinese. But be warned. These breeds will still expect you to compensate for your absence with extra helpings of love and attention the moment you walk through the front door.

In general, the rule of thumb is this: unless you or a member of your household are prepared to spend the time walking and exercising a dog each morning and evening, in addition to playing with her and grooming her, adopting a dog is probably not your best bet. Spending less time than this will make for an unhappy animal, and therefore an unhappy master. We will talk more about the attention needs of different canine breeds in the chapter on dogs.

Then there are cats.

Though these fascinating creatures are well known for their aloofness, it should be stated that felines have been given something of a bum rap in this department.

Cats are independent and self-sufficient, it's true, primarily because members of the cat family (with the exception of lions) live and hunt alone in the wild.

But a house cat is not a leopard or a puma. It's a cat. And like other favorite domestic pets she has a deep, if somewhat hidden, predilection for human beings.

Don't believe it? Just go a week without paying attention to kitty and watch how agitated she becomes. She rubs against your leg, walks under your feet in an apparent attempt to trip you, purrs a bit too often, and too loud, claws at the wallpaper—all to get your attention. Moral: if you intend to adopt a cat be sure you can give him the time and tenderness members of his tribe require.

What are the parameters here?

Cats can be left alone all day in a home or apartment without feeling much distress. They're generally better behaved and more at ease in this situation than dogs. Once you return to the premises though, be prepared to brush, comb, toss toys, tickle ears, stroke stomachs, and generally give Tabby the daily love workout she not so secretly craves. This not only turns on kitty's affection machine but gives her the exercise she doesn't get during the day. When confined to the indoors cats tend to sleep as much as sixteen hours a day.

And don't worry. Once she's received the appreciation and admiration she so royally deserves she won't be shy about dismissing you, either by walking away when she's had enough strokes or by gently pushing you away. Unlike dogs, a cat's desire for human affection has its limits and bounds.

What about birds?

Communal birds like finches and love birds keep each other company, and require a minimum of exchange with humans. Even parakeets are largely self-sufficient, especially if they share the cage with another parakeet. Fifteen or twenty minutes a day spent changing the bird's water and food is usually all that's necessary, plus the bird's presence in a room with human activity.

Larger, more intelligent birds are a different story, and these usually require a generous amount of human contact. This is especially true of tropical birds like cockatoos and macaws. Neglect a macaw and it quickly becomes neurotic. It may nip at your face, pluck at its feathers, hurt itself physically, or damage your apartment. Parrots left alone become nippers too, and almost as unpleasant, they squawk incessantly. This noise can drive you and your neighbors crazy and make it seem as if there's a twenty-four-hour-a-day *Tarzan* movie going on inside your living room. If you plan to purchase a larger bird, know in advance that it requires an hour or more a day talking to and playing with if it is to become fully human friendly.

In the small animals department, rabbits and ferrets require more attention than other furry creatures. It's common today for both rabbit and ferret owners to keep a hutch inside their homes, litter train their pet, then allow them the run of the house for most of the day. Though it is not widely known, guinea pigs can also be trained in this way, and with persistence a modest but real emotional bond can be forged with these gentle creatures. Like rabbits, guinea pigs enjoy chomping on electrical lines, but unlike rabbits, they are not repelled by the standard bitter apple sprays sold at pet stores that discourage most other animals from chewing up your household. If you do intend to litter train a guinea pig and allow it to run freely about your house, make sure all phone wires and appliance cords are out of harm's way.

Finally, there are fish and reptiles.

Fish are entirely self-contained, of course, and require only feeding and maintaining. Reptiles are much the same. While there has been a good deal of discussion through the years about whether or not snakes and lizards recognize their owners and grow attached to them, the scientific consensus is that with the probable exception of iguanas, they do not, and that they get along well without us, just as long as we feed them and keep them warm.

To this it should be added that many reptile owners, especially those who keep iguanas and snakes, will regale you with anecdotes about how their pet does, in fact, show real attachment and affection to them, and how their animal languishes if untended by its master. Whether or not such opinions are true or false will long be argued by zoologists and pet owners alike. The upshot is, if it works for you, who's to say differently?

Which pets are most appropriate for children?

The question of a pet's appropriateness for children depends principally upon a child's age.

Some parents purchase a dog for a very young child, only to discover that their little one is tormenting the newcomer, pulling ears and yanking tails. The dog, in turn, shuns the child, and perhaps even nips in self-defense.

The same scenario is acted out with other pets.

Cats are notoriously less patient with children than dogs. Though some rare felines are tolerant of being hung upside down or boxed on the ears, most are not. If you presently have young children it's a good idea to wait until they reach six or seven years old before letting them care for a kitten on their own.

The same is true for hamsters, gerbils, mice, rabbits, and, of course, fish and birds. With small children, large birds with their powerful beaks can become a danger.

An important point to keep in mind about introducing pets into a household is that as far as children are concerned, the first week of their arrival is the *crucial* week. This is true both in terms of making the animal feel at home and making the child's pet-care learning curve a successful one.

If a hamster cage is placed in a child's room the first week, for instance, the child will constantly stare into the cage and try to feed the animal at every opportunity. If it's a bird children will poke at it and try to play with it. If a puppy, children will pick it up and carry it around for hours, even when the animal is exhausted or sick.

During those first days when a pet is new to the house, therefore, the rules of thumb are easy does it, a step at a time, slow and steady wins the race, chill.

Scheduling is the best way to put this advice into action. In the first week tell children that they are going to learn how to feed the new pet. If they do this job attentively, the next week they can be allowed to walk the animal or play with it. In the third week they help out in its training. And so forth.

With small animals, plan ahead so that children can add a new toy or piece of equipment to the cage every week. With an aquarium, schedule the purchase of a new fish on a regular weekly basis. Reptiles can be touched the first week, taken out of the tank the next, and so forth.

Continue in this way following a schedule making the child's experience of the animal new and at the same time disciplined. Eventually young persons will learn to respect their pets as well as love them.

Will the new pet live inside the house or out?

Companion animals are members of the family. As such, they should be encouraged to have their own place and space within the household and to always live inside.

Dogs need their outings, naturally, and enjoy being in the great outdoors at least part of the day. Other pets—cats, birds, small animals, reptiles, amphibians—are better suited to household life. Indeed, many survive *only* if they live inside the house.

Does this mean that your pet should never be taken beyond the portals of the front door?

Not necessarily. Depending on where you live, there are ways of giving an animal the proper quota of sunshine and exercise.

You can, for instance, keep rabbits and guinea pigs on the lawn during the warmer months in a special screen tent made for the purpose. Directions for using these devices are given in the chapters on small animals. A gerbil's cage or a hamster's cage can be moved outdoors from time to time, weather permitting. Sometimes just putting a cage on the sill of an open window provides light and fresh air enough.

Cats especially are well disposed to in-house living, and it is strongly recommended that your feline friend live inside all the time. Statistically speaking, cats who spend most of their time out-of-doors have an average life span of between five to seven years. Cats who live in the house all the time last from fifteen to twenty years. That's a significant difference, and one well worth noting. Remember, every time Tabby walks outside on her own a formidable arsenal of enemies wait to pounce—cat-hating dogs (and cats), cat-eating coyotes, cat-unfriendly people, cat-killing diseases, cat-poisoning plants, cat-destroying gullies, pits, and abandoned basements.

Consider the alternatives. For apartment cats, bubble enclosures are available that bring a cat closer to nature but not into it. These ingenious contraptions fit snugly into the window space, and are cantilevered out and over the window sill far enough so that the cat has the illusion of basking in nature. Cat slings and hammocks perform a similar function.

Also consider placing a bird feeder near a window where a cat hangs out. This way Tabby can sit contentedly on her perch all day long eyeing her avian friends, and dreaming of a feathered banquet. In general, cats live happily inside the home all their lives and can never be the worse for it.

Walking an animal is an option too. More than ever, people are chaperoning cats and ferrets on a leash, and occasionally you'll see a rabbit in a harness. When animals are taken outside, it is recommended that they always remain in the company of humans.

Leaving a dog unattended in a fenced-in area is also discouraged. This practice may be convenient for the pet owner, but it often results in behavioral and psychological problems for the animal. Solitary penning causes dogs to become frustrated and wired as they run frantically back and forth all day. When left alone in a yard, a dog may be stolen or abused. If a rabbit or squirrel happens by, a reasonably athletic breed like a boxer or Labrador retriever can leap six-foot-high chain-link fences in pursuit without a second thought.

Most seriously, dogs grow surly when confined for too long a time, and their angry mood can have serious repercussions for children playing nearby. A typical scenario: A ball rolls into the dog's area from next door. A child runs to retrieve it. The chained-up or penned-up dog lunges. The child is badly bitten and sometimes even mauled.

Still another disadvantage of leaving a dog alone outside is that the dog gets into the habit of doing his business where and when he pleases. Soon he evolves his own schedule of bowel habits, and eventually this schedule starts to interfere with the housebreaking rules you have worked so hard to establish.

Result: you become dependent on the dog's timetable, rather than the other way around.

All in all then, dogs are better off kept inside the house or even in a kennel during the day, then walked and frisked with outside when household members are in residence. For many dogs, an hour a day of vigorous walking and playing is usually all that's needed to work off excess energy and to refresh his spirit. More athletic canines, however, require a good deal more romping and exercise.

Should adopted dogs or cats be pure bred or mixed breeds?

Unless you intend to officially show a dog or cat, or to breed them professionally, the fact is it probably doesn't matter a great deal—with a few significant exceptions—whether your pet is pedigreed or mixed.

What are these exceptions?

With cats, except for some minor personality differences, it doesn't make much difference what breed or mixture you adopt. A cat, it seems, remains always and everywhere a cat no matter what its heredity.

With dogs though the situation can be more challenging.

Before you adopt a hybrid dog, find out which breeds are in the blend. Certain combinations such as, say, a cocker spaniel–poodle mix, produce splendid dogs. But healthwise, others can be problematic. Dalmatians, for example, are prone to deafness and Labrador retrievers to hip dysplasia. Adopt a cross between these two breeds and you may get a deaf dog with a limp.

Be equally deliberate when adopting purebreds. Each breed has its own personality, its own outstanding characteristics, its own eccentricities. Terriers, bred originally for hunting small rodents, are congenial companions, but tend to be jumpy and barky. Collies, raised to herd sheep, are gentle and keenly intelligent, but grow restless and neurotic when cooped up in small spaces. Bred hunters like beagles are endlessly active, and will stray if not carefully supervised.

Several years ago an updated version of Disney's classic film, *A Hundred and One Dalmatians*, was released. The movie was viewed by millions of children across the country and, predictably, a sizeable number of these young people badgered their parents into buying them one of the black-spotted fantasy dogs they'd seen on screen.

Seemed like a good idea. Trouble was that after several months reports began to filter in from animal shelters across the country declaring a Dalmatian emergency: Thousands of families were abandoning their black-spotted fantasies or hauling them off to the animal shelter.

Why? Because the people who had seen *A Hundred and One Dalmatians*, then rushed out to purchase what they thought was a friendly, cuddly playmate, discovered that most members of this active and high-strung breed are demanding companions. The ensuing epidemic of abandoned Dalmatians ended up causing a number of these dogs to be euthanized.

Moral: If you're going to buy a purebred, find a breed that fits your lifestyle and your family's needs.

Are mixed breeds smarter and healthier than purebreds? Some experts think so; others claim the opposite is true.

Professional kennel owners, for example, attempt to breed out canine diseases and birth defects. This practice, some say, produces healthier pets. But others claim that like the intermarried royal families of Europe, too much controlled mating within a breed *produces* these hereditary diseases and congenital defects rather than eliminating them.

Whatever the case, the fact is that a dog is generally a dog no matter what the intermixing, and—if you follow the above caveats—you can't go wrong with either a pedigree or a mutt.

What are the best places to adopt a dog or cat?

Although it may seem an incidental matter, deciding where to get an animal is one of the most significant concerns that any pet owner faces.

Here it is recommended that if you are looking for a friendly and healthy animal companion, particularly a dog or cat, the best place to go is an animal shelter.

The emphasis on shelter adoption is founded on decades of shelter experience, especially in the many instances of questionable animal merchandising reported through the years—especially the "puppy mill"-style stores that thrive throughout the United States, stores that receive their stock from commercial breeding facilities.

What's wrong with a shop that specializes in merchandising of commercially bred animals?

With a few exceptions, a great deal.

Remember, pet stores are in business for one reason only: to make a profit. They are not especially interested in dogs' or cats' welfare, or good health, or what kind of home they will be placed in. Pet stores are concerned with the bottom line, and as such everything is geared to cut costs and maximize profits, often to the detriment of the animal.

To begin, breeding stock in pet shops are often billeted outdoors with little or no protection against inclement weather. When in their pens, pets walk around all day on wire floors that are painful to the touch and crippling to the feet and paws. Living quarters are cramped no matter how generous the cage size, and scant attention is paid to the quality of diet. Healthwise, there is usually little or no check made on the genetic history of animals before they are sold. You rarely know the bloodline of the parents, and you have no absolute guarantees that the animal is a purebred, should that be an issue.

Most critical of all, animals bred in puppy mills are shipped out when they are very young, at a period in their lives when they have had little contact with people. This lack of familiarity with humans can be a strong determining factor in the formation of a dog or cat's personality. Indeed, if you study the research on canine behavior, you discover that for dogs to mix well with human beings they require constant touch and contact for the first six to twelve weeks of life. Without this contact they may remain shy, indifferent, and even hostile to human touch.

At pet stores, moreover, dogs and cats often arrive when they are eight weeks or older, and are then incarcerated in a cage for twenty-four hours a day until they are sold. While in these cages animals are looked in on from time to time by busy human keepers who feed them, pull out the soiled papers, change the water, maybe give a pat or two, then move on, leaving the animal isolated for the rest of the day. In stores where pets are kept in conspicuous places on the floor for viewing, the reverse situation can also hold true: animals are put on display all day long where they are poked, picked up, put down, and generally mishandled without ever seeing the same person twice, and without being in one identifiable person's arms long enough to establish a relationship.

All this happens, moreover, during the most formative period in an animal's socialization curve. At a time when dogs or cats would normally be in contact with their mothers, their littermates, and their human keepers, they are spending their days pacing a sterile wire box alone and lonely. This lack of fraternization is crippling to an animal in a variety of ways, triggering problem behaviors that last a lifetime, and causing psychological scars that can never be entirely healed, no matter how affectionate and concerned a human owner may be.

What, then, are the preferred places to purchase a new dog or cat?

There are two: an animal shelter and a breeder.

First, shelters.

These are ordinarily staffed by caring, concerned men and women, many of whom are volunteers. Shelter staff are almost always sincerely anxious to place animals in homes where they will be safe, happy, and well taken care of. For pet shelter staff, this work is not only a job, it is a mission—and sometimes a calling.

Animal shelters are also a good deal cheaper than pet stores and breeders. As a rule, you can adopt an animal for minimal expense, and sometimes this price includes vaccinations and neutering. Compared to breeders and pet stores, pet shelters are a bargain.

Finally, there is that feel-good sensation one gets from adopting a homeless pet.

Remember, the animals in most shelters are there on a temporary basis. If they are not adopted within a certain period of time they are usually euthanized. By adopting an animal from a shelter you are not only providing a home, you are saving a life and providing an animal with a second chance. To this kindly notion, however, should be added the caveat that when visiting a shelter, it is wise policy *not* to let sentiment be the central impulse driving your choice, and to avoid emotional blackmail. You may, for instance, adopt a dog or cat purely out of pity, then get him home and discover he has a contagious disease. There are a thousand other variations on this same theme.

The best policy when choosing a pet from a shelter, therefore, is to allow the shelter staff to help you with your choice and to judge according to the standards you would employ in any pet-choosing situation: the standards discussed so far—how well the animal fits your lifestyle, your living space, your personal preferences, and so forth. It is all right up to a point to allow the rescue impulse to flavor your decision. Just be careful not to let it become the driving factor.

Finally, note that you can check on available pets at over a thousand animal shelters around the country on the Internet at www.petfinder.com.

Next, the second choice: responsible breeders.

The good news here is that breeding facilities are usually run by animal lovers who treat their pets in a kindly and careful way. Breeders tend to feed their pets properly, provide vaccinations, make sure they are properly socialized, and care for them with concern until they are of selling age. If you are looking for a pedigree animal, bloodlines can be officially authenticated by breeders. If animals do not work out at home, breeders often (though not always) take them back. Moreover, when you scrutinize the puppies or kittens offered by a breeder, the animal's mother and sometimes father are present. Genetically speaking, parents of a purebred dog or cat offer an excellent guide to their offspring's temperament. If the parenting animals are alert, intelligent, friendly, and free of congenital and hereditary disease, this usually means their offspring are the same. If the parents seem timid, unfriendly, frail, or too aggressive, it's best to find another animal. Some pet buyers refuse to purchase animals from a breeder until they observe the parents.

Most communities have people who specialize in raising and selling the more popular kinds of pets. Ask around and check with the local pet clubs.

Where's the best place to purchase animals other than dogs and cats?

Pet stores. While animal shelters may have facilities to house smaller animals like rabbits and hamsters, and while some shelters occasionally offer more exotic species like snakes and frogs, conventional pet shops usually provide the widest range of choice. Do be selective though, with the store you choose. When selecting a pet store, there are basic guidelines you can follow:

Is the store clean? Is it well swept and generally sanitary? Is the floor littered with shavings or gravel? Does the store give the appearance of being cared for? Or does it simply seem like a revolving-door operation?

Do the animals in the store appear to be lively and well cared for? Is their fur fluffy? Are their eyes bright? Are their cages clean, their litter fresh, their food plentiful and wholesome? Is there evidence in the cages that the animals are fighting or chewing on one another? This can be a sign of disease or overcrowding.

Do the animals appear to be intact? Do you detect any wounds on their bodies, any blood spots?

Is the store's staff knowledgeable about the pets they're selling? Are they willing to take the time necessary to help you make the right choices? Does the staff answer your questions with accuracy and authority? Do they ask *you* questions about your pet needs and then make appropriate suggestions?

Are the same salespersons in the store every time you visit? Some pet stores hire workers with a minimum of training and a poor knowledge of pet care. Such people can be dangerous as well as ignorant, making you spend hundreds of dollars before you realize you've been misinformed. Generally speaking, if you find an entirely different set of people behind the counter in a pet store every time you visit this is not a good sign.

How does the store smell? Any pet store will have various animal smells filtering through the air. That's to be expected. But if the atmosphere is heavy with the odor of rotting food, dirty litter, and feces, that's something else. Or alternately, if a pet store is clouded with the smell of air deodorizers, and if you see a lot of disinfectant canisters around, this can be a danger sign. Is someone trying to cover something up?

Check with others who have shopped at a certain pet store. Do they recommend it? Are they happy with their purchase? If you have friends who have recently acquired a nice aquarium setup or a friendly parakeet ask where they bought it.

In terms of individual species and breeds at a pet store, the following concerns are important:

Small animals. When choosing a mouse, hamster, rabbit, ferret, gerbil, and other small animals look at the eyes. They should be bright, inquisitive, and clear. Then check the quality of the animal's fur: sleek and fluffy usually means healthy. Pay attention to the area under the tail. If it's encrusted with feces or diarrhea chances are the creature is sick. The animal should be active and alert. (This can sometimes be difficult to tell with hamsters because they sleep a great deal. When they are awake they should frisk and play with the others in the cage.)

While you're in the pet shop study the environment as well as the animals. Is the bedding clean? Are there signs in the shavings of diarrhea or vomit? Male hamsters are quite aggressive and often fight one another. If a hamster (or other small animal) has been injured you will usually see blood spots on the shavings. What about the other animals? If the gerbil or rabbit you are interested in appears to be healthy but several of its cage mates are ailing, this could mean a viral or bacterial infection has been introduced into the group and is waiting to break out the day you take the animal home.

Birds. Again, check the eyes. Are they clear and bright? Are the birds perky? Sleek? Are their feathers well marked? Are they active, hopping from perch to perch and happily doing their bird things? Or do they seem lethargic and droopy? Check the ventral areas where the bird defecates. If you see damp, dirty under feathers this can be a sign of disease. The same is true if a bird is puffing up its feathers—it may be fevered and is attempting to warm itself.

What about the cage? Is it clean and well kept? Examine the water container. Pet stores that change their water infrequently are often slack in other areas too. Pay attention to the bird's legs, toes, wings, beak. No cuts or blood spots should be in evidence. Watch for feather picking: when birds are stressed or anxious they peck at each other and tear out each other's feathers.

Still another critical question to ask about birds, especially parrots, is whether they are bred domestically. Besides the fact that a federal law bans the importation of many species of foreign birds, birds captured in the wild tend to be untamable, unhappy, and diseased. If a bird's leg is banded this is an assurance that it is domestically bred.

Fish. Danger signal number one: a number of dead fish in the tank. Dead fish can mean disease or simply inattentive pet care. Is the filtration system adequate in each tank? Is the water clean and clear? Are the fish active and interested? Study them carefully. Their markings should be clear, and their fins should not be clamped tight against their bodies when they swim. Check the mouth and gills for fungus. Small white spots on the fish's body can be a sign of the deadly fish disease *ich*. One fish with ich can contaminate—and kill—every other fish in your aquarium.

One good way to check up on a store's aquarium-keeping standards is to arrive at the store when they open their doors in the morning. Are there dead fish floating in the tanks? Then worry. Ditto if you see a staff member plucking little fish bodies out of water at a rapid rate. Though every pet store has some attrition rate each day due to a list of unavoidable factors, if the number of deaths is excessive this can indicate inferior-quality fish and/or poor sanitation.

Reptiles. Since many reptiles and amphibians tend to move slowly and ponderously (when they move at all), it is often difficult to judge the health of a lizard or frog. Here you have to go by instinct. Does the animal look healthy and energetic? Are its eyes clear? Is it alert and responsive when touched or prodded? Is its skin clean, unscabbed, and vital looking? Are there any secretions dripping from its nose, mouth, or vent areas?

As far as exotic pets like snakes and iguanas go, you will want to ask the store's staff whether the animal has been bred in a foreign or domestic setting. Many reptiles cannot legally be brought into this country, and some carry disease. Boas and pythons were once imported from foreign countries by the crate load into the United States, but today they are mainly bred in captivity.

Perhaps the most problematic of all reptiles acquired from pet shops are turtles. Because they are so abundant in the wild and so easy to catch, turtles are easily scooped out of local rivers and swamps, then smuggled in as stock to pet stores. But beware: wild turtles are breeders of disease, especially salmonella, and should be avoided, especially by children who may handle pets then put their hands in their mouths. When purchasing a turtle from a pet store be certain that it is disease free, American born, and raised in captivity from birth.

Private breeders and hobbyists. Before you race off to the pet store to purchase any of the above animals, remember that you have several other options.

Consider private breeders and hobbyists. Fish hobbyists, for example, tend to be a dedicated lot. They breed fish with loving and expert attention, then sell or trade them on the side, usually for highly reasonable charges. The same is true for bird owners, rabbit fanciers, and ferret fanciers. Ask around.

In many towns you find clubs dedicated to one exclusive form of pet husbandry—fish clubs, rabbit-raising clubs, herp clubs (for herpetology—reptiles). At club meetings you meet like-minded hobbyists who breed their own animals and who are sometimes walking zoological encyclopedias. Since we all tend to like those who share our personal interests, pet hobbyists are usually thrilled at the chance to help you get started.

Still another possibility is to answer ads listed on school, store, or supermarket bulletin boards. When people move away from a neighborhood they often sell their aquarium, their cages, their hamsters and turtles, their pet equipment. Sometimes they even give them away free. Acquiring your pet this way allows you to check out the home the animal has been raised in and to talk directly with the owners. Refer to ads in the town or city newspapers as well.

Finally, there are local fairs, pet meets, swap shows, and 4-H Club gatherings. Though dedicated mainly to farm animals, people at these gatherings sometimes deal in household pets as well. If you live in a rural area these shows can be a great deal of fun, and you may find the pet of your choice in the bargain. Check newspapers and bulletin boards for listings.

What about adopting an abandoned animal off the streets?

No one should be discouraged from saving an animal that is abandoned and left alone to starve. This is an act of common decency. At the same time, potential conflicts should be well considered before people take an abandoned animal into their home.

The most obvious worry is disease. If you intend to adopt an abandoned dog or cat, it is advised that you first take these animals to a vet before bringing them home. Have the creature checked over for skeletal problems, injuries, worms, fleas, lice, and communicable diseases: feline leukemia, feline immunodeficiency virus (FIV), eye, ear, or skin infections, and more. Your vet will know what to look for.

If you have other dogs or cats at home, it's a good idea to keep new-

comers in quarantine for a few weeks before giving them the run of the
house. There are many tragic cases in which a stray is brought into a
home and immediately allowed to mingle. Unbeknownst to the owners,
the animal is incubating an infectious disease. Within several weeks
both the stray and all the other beloved household animals come down
with the disease.

If you already have a dog or cat at home, there's the turf-protecting
instinct to consider. Dogs and cats are strongly territorial, and any newcomer is automatically viewed as an invader. Alternately, if the new cat
in town is feral, or the new dog is a veteran of the streets, these animals
will perceive the permanent residents as antagonists to dominate and
perhaps as enemies to destroy. Consequence: growls, hisses, snarls, all
day long and sometimes raging claws and flying fur.

If you intend to introduce a new animal to a household that is
already ruled over by a resident dog or cat, the trick here is to do it
s-l-o-w-l-y.

To begin, have a veterinarian examine the animal before allowing
contact. Once taken home, keep the new animal isolated in a side room
for several days. This tactic allows your regular pets to get used to the
newcomer's smell. During the period of isolation, study the new animal's personality and habits.

Observe: How well is the animal socialized? Is the animal housebroken? Does the animal chew the couch or claw the rug? Does the
animal relate in a friendly way to other members of the household, especially to your children?

What about prey drive? Even if your probationary pet gets along
well with other dogs or cats in the house, does she go after the fish, the
rabbits, the mice, the frogs? This habit quickly loses its charm. What's
more, if children in the house are especially attached to these resident
mice or fish, the new animal's stalking habits can be a recipe for
heartbreak.

Another point to consider is the question of where the dog or cat you
are rescuing originally came from. If dogs and cats are docile, well
groomed, responsive, and friendly, chances are they come from a loving
home and just happened to lose their way. Indeed, their owners may
still be searching for them. Thus, before you give the new animal your
heart, call in a description of the pet to your local animal control agency
and animal shelter. Even better, take the animal directly to a shelter and
tell the staff members there that if nobody claims the animal within a
week or two you intend to adopt him yourself. Leave your phone number and address, then wait it out. Shelters are usually happy to make

such arrangements, and if the dog or cat turns out to be troubled or diseased this condition will show up during the holding period. This way you avoid adopting a problem animal, and at the same time act preventively to protect your other pets.

What about adopting a mature dog or cat from friends or previous owner? Can an adult animal bond with new owners?

In a vast majority of cases, yes.

For animals other than dogs and cats, such as rabbits, guinea pigs, and snakes, adjustment presents few problems. Parrots and big bird species, however, do tend to become attached to particular owners and must be given a great deal of attention and love during the transition period.

As far as adult dogs and cats go, animal shelters across the country have seen millions of animals adopted, usually with great success. Transition periods are needed, of course, but this is true for any of us, human and animal alike, who undergo a dramatic change of place.

With cats the challenge is to help the newcomer accustom itself to the new location, to let it sniff out the good hiding places, the comfortable sleeping nooks, the beds and perches, and the location of its litter pan. Usually a week or two is all that's necessary for an adult cat to feel at home.

With dogs it's more or less the same story, though with an added emphasis on the personal element. A dog who is particularly attached to its master will probably mope for a while, sometimes for weeks. But almost always it will come around. Just be patient and give the newcomer plenty of delicious food—this is a crucial factor—plus regular hugs, play, and attention.

What if elderly people live in the home? Are pets a danger to them?

Usually not. You will have to take certain commonsense precautions, of course. If you adopt a puppy and it jumps up on people (thereby threatening to knock grandma off her feet), be sure this habit is trained out of it early on. Make an attempt to place the animal's bed in a place that does not interfere with a senior's coming and going. Keep dog and cat toys out of the hallways and bathrooms, and so forth.

At the same time, numerous studies have been carried out to determine the psychological effects of dogs and cats on the elderly. These findings are almost unanimously positive—so positive that the ASPCA has recently helped push a bill through Congress that gives seniors in federal housing developments the right to keep a pet, even if local laws prohibit it.

Most research on the subject shows, for example, that pets can bolster an older person's sense of self-esteem; that it keeps seniors physically active and promotes mental acuity. Seniors who are hospitalized show faster recovery rates when a pet is waiting for them at home. Seniors who are depressed frequently experience a lightening of the spirit when a pet is introduced into their lives. Studies in nursing homes show that pets brought onto the premises encourage patients to exhibit more interest in socializing with others. Patients with chronic skeletal diseases such as arthritis and osteoporosis show greater joint flexibility when given a chance to play with a dog.

Animals, in short, and most specifically dogs and cats, are a great boon to the elderly in a variety of ways. Taking the proper precautions, they can help make an older person's life richer and happier. Today there are many programs throughout the country that encourage this exchange between the elderly and their pets and that sponsor volunteer programs that bring dogs and cats into nursing homes.

What to Do If an Adopted Pet Is Not Working Out

There are two kinds of situations in this regard: reconcilable problems and irreconcilable problems.

Does the puppy urinate on the living room rug? Does the cat spray? Is the rabbit chewing the telephone cords? Do the hamsters smell?

These are all remediable problems. The animal can be removed from temptation, trained, taught, challenged, changed.

If, on the other hand, a dog seriously bites your child; if you cannot stand the smell of the water the turtles sit in, even when you change it every few days; if the cat constantly leaps around the room acting menacing and unbalanced; if bird feathers give you allergies; if, after all, you simply do not like having the pet around—these are indications that it is time to rethink the situation.

The same is true when significant changes in a person's life make it impossible to maintain a pet—a death, an illness, a handicap. Sometimes there is nothing we can do in these situations but find the pet another home. When all is said and done, there is really no ultimate criteria for knowing when an animal is not working out. If it is not, chances are you will simply know it.

What does one do in such circumstances?

There are several options.

Perhaps a family member is interested in adopting the animal, or a friend in the neighborhood. What about your veterinarian? Might he or she know of someone looking for a pet? How about a senior citizen? The elderly are sometimes eager to adopt an older pet, one that is quiet, housebroken, and not likely to outlive them.

Meanwhile, get the word out. Talk it up; ask around. A well-placed advertisement in your local supermarket, school, veterinarian's office, or local paper featuring a flattering photograph of the pet sometimes catches the eye of the right family. The offer of a free, healthy animal for adoption is often all that is needed.

Finally, you can take the animal to a local shelter and work with the staff there to find the pet a good home.

Whatever you do, the first rule of pet ownership must always prevail: *both pet owner and pet must be happily adjusted to their role in the relationship.* And you as pet owner must be committed to making it happen.

2

Home Is Where Your Pets Are:

Living Comfortably with an Animal in a House or Apartment

Welcome Home

So now you've chosen your pet—or pets. You've brought it—or them—home.

The work and the play are about to begin.

The first few weeks a new pet enters a household are a particularly formative and developmental time in an animal's life. Your new companion is untrained, a kind of blank slate. The lessons you write on this slate right now remain emblazoned there for a lifetime; they determine your pet's temperament, personality, and its personal relationship with everyone in the household. The good things you do for your pet at this age to teach and protect it will be returned to you with compound interest throughout the rest of your pet's life.

Making New Pets Feel Wanted

The welcome wagon

Young animals are a peculiar combination of the very robust and the very delicate. Like children, they love to play and frolic, and like children they need proper supervision, care, and plenty of rest.

During the first few days at home introduce your pet to her new environment in gentle stages. Avoid overstimulation. Though your impulse, and even more your child's impulse, may be to spend every waking moment hovering over the new visitor, it's better for everyone to allow some breathing room.

During the first few days, for example, seasoned pet owners isolate a new pet in one room of their home. Sequestering a pet in this way allows her to acclimate to the new sights and smells of the household, and keeps her from running crazily from room to room, as baby animals are likely to do. If there are other companion pets in the household, quarantining the new animal for a few days is an excellent method for letting other animals become accustomed to the new sounds and smells.

Some pets should not be overhandled during the first week or so. Others require plenty of attention from the beginning. With a little experience you'll discover your pet's individual tolerance level for being handled. You'll recognize when she's tired, restless, hungry. Use these first weeks to get to know your pet's rhythms and habits. Every member of a species is different, every member has its own personality, behavior patterns, and eccentricities. Find out what these are and act accordingly.

Establish a positive feeding environment

An especially important task is to establish a positive feeding environment for the new pet. Few things make an animal bond to human beings faster than food.

Wholesome food should be given at regularly scheduled intervals during the day. If you have more than one pet, feed them all at the same time, but in separate rooms at first. This keeps food disputes to a minimum. If you want your new pet to bond to one person in particular, designate this person as the primary feeder.

As a general rule, it's best to feed new puppies after you finish your own meal. For ferrets, kittens, and small mammals the rule is to always keep the feeding dish far from the litter box. (If your pet is a picky eater and the litter box is close to the feeding bowl simply moving the food bowl may be all that's needed to improve the animal's appetite.) With reptiles be careful not to let their food sit too long in the cage; it easily becomes contaminated.

A feeding rule that is often overlooked is to make a gradual transition between a pet's previous diet at the breeder's or shelter and the diet you intend to give it in your home.

If, for example, you adopt a kitten from a shelter and know that his diet at the shelter consisted of kibble, it is best to avoid giving your new householder rich, wet foods and table scraps right away. Better to keep him on his regular kibble for a while (perhaps even indefinitely). If for whatever reason you wish to provide wet foods as well, introduce new foods a step at a time. A couple of weeks' transition is a reasonable period of time to accomplish this task. Going from kibble to fatty steak scraps overnight may be a treat for a new pet, but it can work havoc on their digestive systems, producing nausea, diarrhea, vomiting, and worse.

Make the new pet follow *your* schedule—not the other way around

Note that like human beings, animals form set routines then stick to them with great tenacity.

Cats, for example, are crepuscular by nature, which means that in the wilderness they hunt at dusk and dawn and sleep during the day. But cats are also adaptable, and as long as you accustom them to your daytime schedule at an early age they will happily adjust. On the other hand, there are also times when you must be flexible on your end as well and meet the developmental needs of your animal, even if it requires a little rearrangement of your own schedule. With a little time you will find the right balance.

Whatever you do in the habit-training department, do it early. Contrary to the adage, old animals *can* learn new tricks, but the fact remains that young animals learn them better and faster. The social and domestic habits you train into your pet now, at this early stage, will last a lifetime.

Making Your Home Safe for a Pet and Making a Pet Safe for Your Home

When a new pet enters your house the first thing to consider is personal safety, both your own and the animal's.

From day one, assume that any small, chewable object left on the floor automatically goes into an animal's mouth, be that animal bird, rabbit, dog, ferret, cat, or rat. In many ways the situation is comparable to when a toddler waddles through a living room and bedroom, grabbing everything in sight and putting it in its mouth. Whatever is within reach becomes fair game. It's the same with an animal.

The first order of the day, therefore, is to petproof.
Here's what to do.

Remove all chewables. Begin with the obvious. Start by getting down to the pet's-eye level in your home and scan the area for inviting chewables. If you have a pet that can stand on its hind legs on the floor or furniture, factor in this added distance. Working from a list can be helpful in this regard. Or compile one as you go along for present and future use.

Once you locate the dangerous items in the environment, remove them immediately. For example, keep your floors free of soft objects like slippers, shoes, socks, magazines, electric wires, children's toys, belts, hairbrushes, coins, panty hose, pencils, pens, plastic containers, and any other mouth-watering items. Out of sight, out of mind.

Unauthorized chewing can, of course, be as harmful to an animal as it is harassing to pet owners. Be watchful of small household objects: bottle caps, erasers, string, pens, matches. These and a hundred other bite-size items have all ended up in an animal's intestinal tract at one time or another.

Protect your breakables. If a new kitten enters your living space be assured he will climb on every table, chair, shelf, and ledge. When a new dog arrives his swishing tail will endanger the safety of every fragile object in sight. If a new bird is flying free around the living room, its droppings can ruin your day. Rabbits and other small mammals are notorious for nibbling at electric and phone lines, as well as at sisal flooring and wicker or rattan furniture.

As a protection against the above, move all precariously placed glass figurines, bowls, plates, pictures, display stands, and similar breakable items to a safe place, at least in the early days when your pet is learning the territory. Sometimes precautions can be as simple as putting a fragile item away for a few weeks, or setting it a bit higher up on the shelf. Take a walk through your home, look around for dangerously perched items, and make the appropriate adjustments.

Appliances. Watch those household appliances. A steaming iron left unattended on an ironing board is an invitation to trouble. A toaster oven can be a hot place indeed for a dog's nose. Computer printers are fascinating to animals, especially when they're printing.

Look through the rooms in your home, preferably before the new pet arrives, and place all potentially harmful appliances in a safe place. Also vulnerable are the various wires, cords, and cables that attach to appliances. Be certain that these wires are well tucked in and out of sight. See the section "watch those wires" below for more information on protecting cords and wires.

A child's room. Besides the fact that you don't want a parrot or ferret mangling your child's dolls or action figures, the usual assemblage of small toys left strewn around a child's floor fit quite snugly into animals' mouths and hence down their throats. Watch especially for rubber balls, marbles, figurines, doll clothes, blocks, plastic animals, and other bite-size items. If a child is not the meticulous type, and if your pet is young and teething, it's generally a good idea to keep the pet out of the child's room entirely. Close the child's door or use a child gate and discourage the animal from entering. No matter how well behaved a new pet may be, the temptation to chew everything in sight is too strong to resist. As the proverb goes, "What the eye doesn't see the heart doesn't yearn for."

Keep toxic household chemicals well out of sight

There are an amazingly large number of chemical poisons around people's homes these days, and it is imperative to keep them away from pets. Remember, for human beings the acrid chemical odor of a household cleaner is its own warning. But animals are different. They explore the world with their mouths as well as with their eyes and noses. For them sampling a box of laundry soap or bleach is not necessarily done out of hunger. It may be an attempt to familiarize themselves with the world around them. Don't assume that because a substance has an unpleasant odor or a strange appearance that these features will be a deterrent for your pet. They may not.

Keep the doors of your kitchen, bathroom, cellar, and garage cabinets shut at all times. Some pet owners secure cabinet doors with child locks. Others pin up signs reminding themselves and others to keep the doors closed at all times.

Check for toxic household chemicals. These are commonly stored under the sink in a kitchen, bathroom, cellar, workroom, plant shed, and garage. Assume that any product kept in these places is a potential poison.

The following household poisons should all be kept away from animals:

Medications: Certain substances that cure humans kill animals. Cats in particular have a body chemistry different from our own and are highly sensitive to medicinal drugs of any kind. Unless directed by your veterinarian, never give household pets human prescriptions or over-the-counter medications such as aspirin, ibuprofen, or cough medicine, no matter how sick they may be. Acetaminophen is deadly for cats. Be careful not to leave medicine bottles on the counter. Pets can chew open a pill bottle and swallow the contents in minutes.

Indoor plants: Certain houseplants are fatal if eaten by pets. Easter lilies, for instance, cause kidney failure in cats and sometimes death. Chewing on certain plants may result in severe irritation to the mouth and throat. Other plants, while not fatal, cause severe intestinal upset. It is best to know the names of the plants you keep around the house, and to place dangerous varieties out of reach. For more information on the subject, the ASPCA has compiled a sixty-seven-page publication indexing and describing toxic and nontoxic plants. (See the appendix for information.)

Outdoor plants: Many outdoor plants such as oleander, azalea, rhododendrons, and Japanese yew cause heart stoppage in dogs and cats. Other outdoor vegetation triggers stomach upset, vomiting, diarrhea, and mental disturbance. (See the paragraph above for the ASPCA's guide to poisonous plants.)

Flea and tick control products and insecticides: When you treat a house for fleas or ticks, read the product label first and follow all directions. These substances are quite toxic, especially if applied directly to a pet's skin or fur. If you have ant or roach baits around your house, make sure they are inaccessible to pets. Keep track of the baits and dispose of them when they've done their job. It's also a good idea to record the time the bait was put out and the brand of bait used. If your pet ingests this substance, you will then have a record of what it contains to report to a veterinarian or poison control center. For more information on flea and tick control, consult the individual animal chapters further on in the book.

Mouse and rat poisons: These substances are deadly and at the same time highly attractive to pets because of their appealing smell. Mouse and rat poison should be placed in a location well out of a pet's way. Record the date you set the poison out and the type and brand of bait used. Dispose of the poison as soon as it is no longer necessary.

Household chemicals: Many household cleansing materials are poisonous for pets and trigger severe intestinal upset and vomiting. Even seemingly harmless substances like dishwasher detergent can produce lesions. When mopping your floors or using household chemicals, keep your pet in another room. Rinse well when appropriate.

Gardening and lawn care supplies: Avoid using garden and lawn care chemicals around domestic animals. If you are sprinkling these substances on the lawn or garden, keep your pet in the house until they dry. The same should be done when using weed killers or insecticides. Pets should be kept out of areas where snail or slug bait is applied.

Automobile care supplies: As with indoor cleaners, car-cleaning compounds cause severe stomach and intestinal problems in pets. Antifreeze and windshield washer fluid are likewise harmful and sometimes fatal. Never allow a pet to drink water that has leaked from a radiator. Antifreeze is attractive to dogs, and they lick it up if given the chance. But be on the alert: even small amounts of this substance can be deadly.

Miscellaneous chemicals: During household construction projects keep pets away until all equipment and materials have been removed. Steer animals away from fresh paint, varnish, sealer, etc., until these finishes are dry. Particular favorites are drain cleaners (highly deadly) and commercial cleaning agents. Be especially careful of steel wool. Dogs and cats adore chewing on these springy metal fibers, especially if the steel wool has been used to scour fat off a skillet or pot. In such cases the wool lodges in the animal's digestive system, and the sharp fibers cause painful tissue damage. Once this situation occurs, the only way to remove the tangled metal residues is with surgery.

Watch those wires

A new source of temptation for your pet has come to the fore during the past fifteen years: the personal computer, with its ever-growing number of attachments and peripherals. Anyone who owns a computer, printer, scanner, modem, or fax knows just how many wires octopus out from the back of these devices and what unbelievably complex tangles result.

So be warned. Every pet that runs free in your house—this includes ferrets, rabbits, guinea pigs, dogs, cats, occasionally even free-flying birds—adore electric and phone wires, each for their own particular reasons.

Rabbits, ferrets, and guinea pigs, for instance, like to gnaw at them. Cats play with them. Dogs burrow into them and get tangled up. There are, in fact, cases where dogs have gotten caught in a nexus of wires, panicked, run, and pulled the computer and the printer along behind them. An even worse scenario occurs when these machines are pulled off a table and land squarely on a dog's head.

A similar danger spot is the home entertainment center with its TV, stereo, multiple speakers, and VCR. There may also be a cable box around, and a video game or two. All of these devices have wires attached, making them ever-present temptations.

The best way to avoid catastrophe is to visit a local computer or electronics store and purchase plastic sleeves made especially to hold and organize wires. The store personnel will know what you're looking for when you ask.

For do-it-yourself types, several strips of duct tape wound tightly round the wires will do the trick. Stuff the tangle into a single, compact bundle, or simply cut an appropriately sized length of PVC plastic pipe, and snake the wires through it. If you have an especially massive collection of cords and wires somewhere in your house (as most people do behind their computers), you may wish to keep them protected by running them through lengths of two- or three-inch-diameter flexible plastic hose, available at most hardware stores.

Households with pets and computers can also benefit from covering the computer keyboard with a plastic "skin" to protect it from the spills that are likely to happen when pets are around.

Windows and doors

It's not that your new pet wants to run away. It's just that an animal's nature is often to explore and roam. When pet owners get careless and leave front doors or cellar windows open, this can become an open invitation to the animal to stray.

Window screens make a perfect deterrent for all but the most determined critters. Kittens in particular, being natural climbers, are likely to walk precariously along high window ledges. (So many cats have fallen from window ledges that the term *high-rise syndrome* has been coined to describe typical injuries after a fall.) A full or accordion screen fitted into the bottom section of a window discourages this behavior.

As for doors, most unhappy incidents occur when pet owners (or more likely, their children) fail to close them securely. Storm doors in particular require careful attention when closing. If there is a large dog in residence it can easily pop open the handle with its nose or paw if it is left ajar. Pet owners are prone to leaving doors open when the weather turns warm. Be especially attentive during the spring and summer seasons. Sliding door screens can fall off their tracks when tugged or split open with a little pushing.

What about screen doors? They'll keep your pet contained most of the time but not all. Over the years pets can do skillful work clawing an exit hole in both the front screen door and the back. Rambunctious animals can poke and paw a screen to tatters. If you are going to rely on screen doors for protection, monitor them carefully throughout the warm months of the year.

Pet doors—yes or no. A word on doors made especially for letting pets in and out of the house. Extremely popular over the past few decades, the downside of these contraptions is becoming increasingly apparent, and in many parts of the country they are falling out of favor entirely.

What constitutes this downside?

Several things. First, it is better not to leave pets outside unattended. Having free run of nature is dangerous for domestic pets, and statistically it shortens their life span.

Second, if you are attempting to train your animal to a regular eating and sleeping schedule, there is nothing like a pet door to sabotage the process. Example: It's five o'clock, feeding time. But where is Rover? Outside chasing squirrels. Or another: It's 11:30 P.M. No sign of Tabby. And so forth.

Third, most pet doors are not airtight, and in wintertime they allow a great deal of cold air into the home. Even if you own a top-of-the-line insulated pet door, this expensive device cannot stop the gusts of arctic air from blowing in each time a pet enters or leaves the house, which can be several dozen times a day. Your heating bills will soon show the difference.

Finally, as the adage goes, the door swings both ways. Imagine your surprise on finding several neighborhood cats gorging themselves at your feline's dinner bowl. And this is not to speak of other hungry friends in the neighborhood such as racoons, skunks, and groundhogs, many of whom are not the least bit shy about entering your home when they smell food.

In short, pet doors cause more problems than they solve. Use them only in conjunction with a fenced yard or kennel. Otherwise keep your companion pet inside or in an outdoor enclosure.

Yard safety

Many pets, especially large ones, require frequent exercise and thus need to be outside for at least part of a day. To accommodate this need an enclosed backyard is the perfect compromise between household confinement and running free.

For safety's sake be sure that the fence surrounding your yard is secure all the way round. One hole or break in the wire can bring disaster. There should be no sharp posts or spikes around the yard, and no boards with nails protruding. If you plan to erect a fence, a chain-link fence with plastic inserts is a safe way to go. Wood stockade fence is also excellent, closing in the yard completely, shutting down visibility, and thus stopping dogs from becoming agitated every time someone walks by. Many people consider wooden fences aesthetically pleasing as well.

Finally, be aware that certain animals love to dig, and can burrow under fences in a matter of minutes. Your fence may have to be sunk into the ground at least a foot to foil this maneuver.

Ensuring the safety of other pets in the house

Cats eat birds. They also eat fish. Certain breeds of dog chase small rodents and cats. Sometimes they kill them. Certain birds hunt fish. Certain snakes hunt birds and mice. And so forth. You get the idea. If you have a multiple-pet household, take precautions.

A screen placed over a cage or box, for example, keeps larger pets from eating your rabbit or guinea pig. A lid over the top of an aquarium does the same. With the exception of certain canine breeds (like terriers) that are bred to hunt rodents and small animals, most dogs are relatively tolerant of small animals if raised with them. When a dog bumps a rabbit with its nose or bats a hamster with a paw—a situation you should not allow, by the way—this is not necessarily the predatory instinct at work. It may be an impulse to play. Or it may not; it's difficult to tell. From the small animal's perspective, however, this pawing is a life-threatening assault, and from your standpoint it is best avoided.

If you own pets that prey on birds, make sure the cage is suspended in an area of the room that can't be reached from a nearby shelf or even by a standing jump from the floor. Be careful not to place the cage on a low table or on any easily accessible resting place. While you're at it, avoid a mistake that novice pet owners sometimes make with birds: never place the cage on top of a steam radiator. Sounds obvious. But in this busy world one forgets. Steam radiators are often capped with shelves, and are conveniently located near a window with plenty of light and an outdoor view, a seemingly perfect spot for the cage. But beware: heat from radiators is too intense for most birds, especially smaller birds like finches and canaries. Your avian friend will literally be overheated in a matter of hours.

Finally, the knife cuts both ways. A large bird like a parrot can inflict a surprising amount of damage on a pesky cat or nosy dog. A large rabbit can bully a young kitten and sometimes inflict serious scratches. In most cases this and other cross-animal problems can be avoided by simply keeping your pets separated in different parts of the home or apartment.

Laying Down the Rules of the House

Rules for very young children

For children ages two through five the first rule of the house is no touching a pet unless a parent or grown-up is present. This means no picking up the guinea pig, no feeding the frogs, no playing with the kitten, unless mommy or daddy or perhaps an older brother or sister is supervising.

The second rule is that children should always behave gently around a pet, especially in the first few weeks when the animal and the child are getting to know each other.

This means no grabbing, no hanging by the tail or paws, no throwing in the air, no sudden yelling, and so forth through the lexicon of childish mischief. When agitated or startled, an animal's first response is to protect itself, and this usually means scratching or biting. Such reflexes are as common to gerbils as they are to kittens, as common to cockatiels as to poodles. Discourage all animal mishandling from the very beginning.

How?

First, by making sure children are not overexcited or overly aggressive when handling a new pet. Start slowly. Have children sit down and calm down. No yelling, flailing, fooling around. Animals are living things and must be treated with respect.

Let small children cup their hands if the pet is small. Let the animal crawl around in their hands or on their lap for a few minutes, then have them put it back in the cage or box. Repeat this procedure every day for a few weeks, gradually increasing the daily handling time.

Especially important is to teach children the proper way to pick up and set down an animal. For children ages two through five, tactile response is not yet fully developed, and they may inadvertently squeeze too hard. This, in turn, provokes the animal to bite.

Proper instruction and role modeling in the art of picking up, handling, petting, playing with, and putting down help avoid this reaction. Basic rules of the game are: no grabbing, no dropping, no abrupt movements. Master the picking-up technique yourself, then model it for the child and have the child imitate you. Repeat today and tomorrow until the lesson is learned.

In the beginning, limit the amount of time children handle a new companion animal to a few minutes each day, then gradually extend these periods. Teach children to release the animal when the animal indicates it no longer wishes to be held. Help them become familiar with their pet's body language. Through the weeks your children will learn to interact properly with the pet, and your pet will become more accustomed to the child. A majority of animals, even shy ones, eventually adapt to being held, and children eventually become more expert at holding them. Dogs and cats love to be loved, of course, but with proper training even shy, small mammals like guinea pigs, mice, and even certain reptiles come to enjoy human company and look forward to human touch.

One special concern for very young children is the possibility that the new animal will defecate on their hands or clothes. Evacuation, we know from studies in animal biology, is a common measure of anxiety among small animals. Scientists in the lab often gauge the level of an animal's nervousness by the number of defecations it makes per hour. To children this behavior can be a yucky and frightening surprise. They may react by tossing the pet in the air, dropping it, even throwing it across the room.

To avoid this situation prepare children in advance. Explain to them that small animals eliminate frequently when they are frightened, and that the new pet may do just this the first few times it is handled.

Tell children that when and if an accident happens it's no big deal. Tell them not to worry about the excrement. It comes off easily when the hands are washed and does absolutely no harm. Most of the time it doesn't smell very much either. Explain that it's all part of having a pet and making friends with a new animal.

A good trick for reducing the defecation problem is to place sheets of newspaper on a table top and allow the animal to run around on its own, occasionally picking it up and petting it. As the animal starts to feel comfortable being handled by humans, it relaxes and defecates less frequently. The child, meanwhile, gets used to the animal's behavior and doesn't get overexcited if it does have an accident.

Older children

For older children, house rules change in relationship to their level of attention and maturity.

Children over five years of age can begin to perform basic pet care duties, such as feeding and grooming. By age nine or ten most children are capable of doing a majority of the things an adult does for a dog, cat, bird, or gerbil. The important thing at all ages is to supervise children lovingly, making sure they discharge their duties correctly, carefully, and consistently.

House rules for your pet

Before a new animal enters the home members of the household should sit down and determine a list of house-pet rules. It is critical that everyone agree to the rules and that everyone do their best to enforce them. Inconsistency, studies show time and again, is the primary reason why pet training fails in the home.

What should these rules be?

It depends on your personal sensibilities and priorities.

Does it bother you that the cat sleeps on your bed? Discourage this behavior at the start before it becomes a habit.

Does a bird's early chirping wake people up? Place the cage in a part of the house away from the bedrooms.

Does your puppy beg at the table? Make it a house rule to keep her in another room when dinner is served or train her to stay in her place during mealtime.

Are you averse to feeding the fish? Before setting up an aquarium, make sure the designated feeder is chosen and willing.

Allergic to the dander in an animal's fur? Make sure everyone agrees to keep dander-carrying pets out of the bedroom.

Who will exercise the new pet? Agree on the designated walker or handler beforehand, then draw up a daily walking or exercising schedule.

What commands do you intend to teach your new pet? Decide, then write them down and become familiar with them.

Who will shop for the animal? Agree on this beforehand and make sure everyone is in accord.

What about cleaning up after the animal and caring for its sanitation? Perhaps more discord arises in pet-keeping families over this issue than any other, and it is a wise idea at the beginning to establish sanitation policies that everyone agrees on.

And so forth.

Every household has its own do's and don'ts lists. Establish them in advance, then—very important—be consistent.

Honoring an Animal's Rights of Privacy

Set off an area of your house or apartment that is totally a pet's own. Even if your pets sleep with you each night, they will also welcome a comfortable oasis where they can go when they're tired, and where they can be left alone. Animals require moments of privacy as much as humans do, and they clearly enjoy being solitary when the mood comes over them.

Honor this impulse by making your pet's private area as warm and accommodating as possible. Put down an old pillow or pile several towels in a box and place it where the pet can curl up undisturbed. Place a treat or two nearby. The animal will quickly get the idea and form positive associations with this part of the house. For cats, a natural log or sisal scratching post adds interest. This important piece of feline apparatus allows kittens to exercise muscles and remove old claw sheaths. It also diverts them away from couches and chairs.

A word of warning. Many animal beds today are stuffed with cedar or pine chips. Both substances give off a pleasing smell—pleasing, at least, to humans. That's the upside. The downside is that for small mammals like gerbils and hamsters, long-term exposure to the aromatic hydrocarbons in pine and cedar may cause liver problems.

Choosing the Right Toys

Purchase as many commercial toys as you like, but don't assume your pets will play with them. They may find a gum wrapper or a plastic hair clip more amusing to bat around than your ten-dollar rubber ball with the bells inside. Simple toys are often the most appreciated, especially ones that simulate the movements of prey animals. A Ping-Pong ball rolling along the ground excites a cat's instinct for chasing small running animals. A bell or mirror keeps birds entertained for hours. Rocks and plants in the aquarium make attractive swim areas for fish.

Choose toys for a pet in the same way you would for a child.

For example, stay away from toys that are potentially hazardous. The squeaker in a cheaply made toy can come loose after a little zealous chewing and become lodged in an animal's throat. A ball or rubber bone that is too small can end up getting caught in the throat or being surgically removed from an animal's stomach.

Examine the toy. How durable is it? How resistant is it to wear and tear? Can it splinter? Does it have offending dyes, coatings, sharp edges, spiky protrusions? If it's going into an aquarium, is it waterproof?

Pick it up and squeeze it. If it seems fragile, it probably is. What about toxicity? Most pet toys in the United States maintain a reasonably high standard of safety, but this is not necessarily true of toys made abroad. If you suspect that an animal toy is made from inferior or potentially poisonous materials, don't buy it. The rule of thumb is that if you have any hesitations about a toy's safety, even if there is nothing about it you can put your finger on, go with your hunch and avoid it. Generally speaking, it is recommended that you purchase animal toys at reliable pet stores or from a good pet supply catalog.

Finally, pets are like children: they become bored with a toy if it's available all the time. To maintain a high level of interest, try alternating your animal's toys, leaving them down for a week, then putting them away for several weeks. Then down again.

Experiment on your own. It's fun.

Protection in Times of Natural Disaster for Pets

For pet owners who inhabit parts of the country where natural hazards are rare, disaster protection for an animal may seem to be a low priority. But even if you don't live in areas prone to floods, fires, tornados, hurricanes, mud slides, and earthquakes, accidents do happen, and you are well advised to work out a care and rescue scenario for your pet just in case.

The first rule of thumb is, *in time of disaster, take your pet with you.* When disaster strikes people often decide to evacuate now, then come back later for their pets. But often there is no later on, and the animal is lost.

Better to plan ahead. Have a bag or two of food, a carrying case or crate, and a jug of water set aside in a closet or cellar for your pet in case a rapid exit is necessary. Keep extra medication on hand too, along with your pet's medical record, especially if your pet is taking a prescription drug. An animal first aid kit is also advisable.

Finally, keep a copy of your pet's vaccinations and licensing records in a nearby file or drawer. This way, should you need to place your animal in a shelter during times of emergency, you will have all the records you need on hand.

Most of All, Have Fun

Most of all, when a new pet enters your home welcome it in the same way you like to be welcomed: with affection, play, and happy times. Animals are not that different from human beings. They like to have fun. They like to make new friends. They like to explore and learn and take a look around. Most of all, they like to be valued and treasured.

When all is said and done, the best way to make your new dog, cat, rabbit, ferret, bird, or snake feel like part of the family is to treat them with caring, attention, good will, and lots and lots of love.

3

Children and Pets

Foremost Concerns

There are two critical notions for parents to bear in mind when children meet pets, and when pets meet children.

The first notion pertains to responsibility. Children may love the family critter in a seemingly boundless way. They may make heart-breakingly sweet attempts to care for it, and nurture it. Despite a child's good intentions, however, the ultimate responsibility for pet ownership lies with you, the parent.

Why?

Because experience shows that most youngsters under the age of fourteen or fifteen are simply not mature enough or experienced enough to attend to an animal's needs in a fully consistent, day-to-day way. Children make mistakes. They forget things—important things. They get distracted. They're bored. They're busy. No matter how well meaning they may be, there are going to be days when Jennifer or Billy neglects to feed the rabbit or to change the turtle's water. Such lapses simply go with the territory when one is young.

For this reason parents must as a matter of course assume that many of the pet-care jobs assigned to children will end up half-done or even undone. It then becomes the parents' job to correct their children's oversights and to chaperone the maintenance and nurturing of companion animals on a regular basis.

As children grow and mature through the years, moreover, their priorities change. At a certain point activities such as sports, studies, friends, music, and an expanded social life make their claims on a young person's time, and in the process the once dearly loved family pet becomes of secondary interest in the young person's eyes. When this process begins to happen, as it often does around puberty, parents must be prepared to step in and take over many of the pet-care responsibilities that once belonged to the child.

That's notion number one.

Notion two pertains to the question of whether or not a child should have an animal in the first place.

This seems an odd consideration in a book on pets. But the fact is that the popularity of companion animals in this country has generated its own peculiar half-truths, one of them being that pets and children invariably go together, and that all children desperately want and need a pet.

This belief is related to the understandable tendency on the part of parents (especially those who were pet lovers themselves when young) to assume that children will inevitably treasure the experience of animal care as much as they once did and that without a companion animal a child's youth is barren and incomplete.

This assumption is just that—an assumption.

Some children are simply not drawn to animals, and a few actively dislike them. Such youngsters find their pleasures elsewhere, in sports, in music, in reading—whatever. It's not that they are less caring or concerned than other children, only that temperamentally they are not animal people.

If a child shows no interest in animals and demonstrates no enthusiasm when the subject of owning a pet comes up, it's probably best not to force the issue. If a child seems decidedly set against the idea—very few are, as you might guess—let this be your guide.

One effective way of testing children's enthusiasm for pet ownership is to allow them to take the lead. If they have any interest in pet ownership at all, they will do just that. One day, for example, your daughter comes home excited over the fact that Katy's family has adopted a dog. It was cool playing with the new pet, she tells you. Can I have one someday?

Having a dog is a big responsibility, you say, not something to leap into without thought and planning. Why not first ask Katy if you can help her walk her dog and clean up after it. See how you like taking care of an animal. If you do, we can talk about it some more.

Perhaps you have a friend or relative who has a pet. Pay that person a visit and let your child interact with the animal for several hours. Observe the results. See how the child feels after the experience. Talk to him or her about it. Then act accordingly, remembering that while a vast majority of children are natural pet lovers, a few are not.

Finally, consider the fact that even if a child is not enthusiastic about animals, in many cases it is still appropriate to bring a pet into the house for other members of the family to enjoy. If you go this route, however, avoid assigning pet-care duties of any kind to the reluctant child. And do not assume that the animal and the child will eventually bond. They may not.

Matching the Right Pet to the Right Child

All this said, it may be added that a vast majority of children have an inherent love for animals, and with proper instruction almost any young person can become a loving and responsible pet owner. Pets serve as companions for children, as objects of affection, as playmates, and in certain ways, as teachers. For sick and convalescing children, pets are known to improve a child's healing time. Psychological studies show that a dog, cat, rabbit, or bird can help draw out a child who is depressed or emotionally disturbed. Even for the normal child, a companion animal feeds those emotional parts that need to be loved—and to love.

Pets, in short, are highly recommended for children, and in most cases they supply the kind of positive early life experiences that form glowing childhood memories. At the same time, pets are an ongoing obligation, and part of the challenge is to pick the right animal for the right child. This task revolves primarily around two concerns: a child's temperament and a child's age.

Temperament

As far as temperament goes, the decision falls primarily to the judgment and discernment of the parent.

Some children, for example, may be "cat children." That is, their nature is best suited to feline care. Others are "dog children" or "bird children" or "rabbit children."

At the same time, many young persons—most of them, probably—are "every-kind-of-pet children," meaning they are temperamentally suited to having any type of dog or cat, plus, say, some white mice, a rabbit, and a few fish thrown in. It is hard if not impossible to say exactly what determines such designations, and here parents must rely on their intuition.

After the question of predilection is established, the question of age becomes a central issue.

Here things can get complicated. For while children and animals mix splendidly, certain children of a certain age and certain animals of a certain kind do *not* mix. At least not well, or safely. It is in this area that foresight and planning are most important. The following program lays out a series of experience-proven suggestions for matching the right pet to the right maturational stage in a child's life.

Age

Infants

Newborn children will make visual contact with the family pet from day one, and this is a good thing. Infants of this age are, of course, far too young in their development to handle an animal (infants often grasp an animal's fur in their little fists, an action that causes animals a good deal of pain). Instead, simply let the baby look and the pet sniff.

Some infants are fascinated by pets. Others couldn't care less. As a general rule, neither child nor pet should be forced to interact if they prefer not to.

Many dogs are curious and interested when an infant is first brought home. Others are afraid. Cats may be standoffish at first and even frightened. Others try to mark new family members by rubbing against them. There are many possible reactions.

With dogs the goal is to keep their excitement level under control and to prevent them from pawing or licking the infant. With cats, the goal is to show them that the newcomer means them no harm. In both cases, parents will wish to acclimate the pet to the infant's smells and movements, and to accustom the child to the pet's appearance and ways.

Finally, be especially careful of dog behavior around newborns.

Newborns look, smell, and move differently than the larger human beings that dogs are familiar with, and a case of mistaken identity can cause dogs to assume that an infant is a separate species and thus fair game. Be especially careful of dogs that enjoy running after cars or pursuing squirrels in the backyard. This love of giving chase means that the dog has strong predatory impulses. Such an impulse can, if the dog is not properly trained and supervised, become overly aggressive toward small children.

Toddlers

Toddlerhood is the most problematic of all ages for children and pets. At this stage a child's motor skills are clumsy at best, and their cognitive abilities are not developed enough to understand the concept of giving and receiving pain. For this reason it is recommended that all interactions between toddlers and pets be carefully supervised by parents.

Care must be taken, for example, to keep toddlers away from pets during feeding time. Nothing riles animals more than being bothered at dinner. Some dogs may growl and even snap when their owners draw too near the feeding bowl. Imagine, then, the scenario when toddlers pick up the food dish and walk blithely away with it, or when they stick their hands in the kibble and scatter it around the room.

So much for when pets harm toddlers. What about the reverse situation, when toddlers harm pets?

To toddlers, everything in the environment is an object to touch and yank and try out. This is as it should be, except where animals are concerned. For a young child anything prominent about a pet can become a target—its curly tail, its floppy ears, its shaggy hair, its wet nose. A rabbit's ears may wiggle in an enticing way. But to the rabbit they are *his ears*. Hands off is the policy here. As children grow older, they often subject their pets to "experiments." Will my gerbil fit into a pillowcase? Will the goldfish like me if I pour a glass of milk into his tank? If I put a sock with a rubber band over Rover's nose will he still be able to breathe? Needless to say, such activities must be outlawed and, if discovered, appropriately addressed.

Avoid letting a toddler walk off with an animal's toys. If your dog is territorial or possessive, the theft of a favorite bone or rubber ring may provoke trouble. Be especially careful with dogs that are snappy and those that tend to be pushy.

With cats, stealing their food or taking their toys is not as problematic, though there are exceptions. In general, cats are more nimble than dogs, and can leap out of children's way in a split second. At the same time, cats are less tolerant with children than their canine counterparts and more irascible. Some are quick to scratch and claw, if for no other reason than to get away from a toddler's loving embrace. When a toddler surprises a cat or grabs at it from behind, real trouble can result. Be especially careful of the household litter box—to a toddler it looks a lot like a sandbox!

As far as small furry mammals and reptiles are concerned, biting and scratching are primary dangers. Children of toddler age are still developing their motor skills, and a grasp can easily turn into a squeeze. If unsupervised, toddlers often poke at small animals or drop them when distracted.

Up to the age of five it is thus suggested that parents keep interactions between small animals and children on the level of observation only. Ferrets especially should be carefully monitored in a household where there are infants. Reports of these pets nipping infants are not uncommon. As far as hygiene goes, reptiles can be carriers of salmonella, and children who habitually place strange objects in their mouths should be kept at a reasonable distance. Mandatory policy here, for adults as well as children, is to wash hands thoroughly after handling.

Ages three to five

Children of this age can be allowed to pet dogs and cats, perhaps help change their water, and tag along while parents take them for a walk. The main thing at this age is parental supervision. Children from three to five should *never* be left alone with an animal or *ever* be allowed to take an animal into their room unattended. Though a child's motor skills are more developed at this age, their attention span is still limited, and if left to their own devices they are likely to do only half the job or become distracted and leave the pet dangling, sometimes literally.

As far as small animals go, rabbits, gerbils, and the like, children of three to five can be encouraged to carefully pick up the animal, always with parental supervision, and to help in the feeding and cleaning chores.

The best small animal for the three-to-five-year-olds is a guinea pig. Extremely docile and slow to bite or scratch, keeping these South American imports in the house provides an excellent opportunity for introducing young children to companion animals. Guinea pigs sit quietly in a child's lap and appear to enjoy being petted. Rarely resistant to handling or play, their high-pitched whistling sounds are a constant delight to small children. Encourage your child to pet the guinea pig and to feed it carrot sticks. Avoid overfeeding, though, as it can easily make guineas sick. During warm months you can keep the guinea pig or any other small animal outside in an empty plastic wading pool. This way children can kneel by the side of the pool and play with the pet to their heart's content, always, of course, under parental supervision. The spaciousness of the pool provides room for the animal's toys, and allows it an area to stretch its legs and take its exercise.

A word about rabbits and young children. Though bunnies are gratifyingly cute and cuddly, these enticing creatures are more feisty than some people imagine, especially where young children are concerned. Being prey animals, rabbits' main instinct when children attempt to pick them up is escape. They attempt this maneuver by pushing off vigorously with their back feet, an act that may startle a child, and perhaps inflict scratch marks in the process. The child, in turn, may drop the rabbit, or otherwise injure it; indeed, if improperly handled a child can easily break a rabbit's back. Rabbits likewise tend to defecate when handled, and this can startle children, causing them to drop the rabbit or throw it up in the air in disgust. When fully grown, rabbits are extremely territorial around the house and have been known to scratch and even attack young children when mishandled. If you intend to bring a bunny into the house, it is recommended that you wait until a child is at least seven years old.

In matters of hygiene for children of this age, the rule as always is to wash your hands and the child's hands after handling an animal, especially if the animal is a reptile. Unwashed hands go into a child's mouth, creating the risk of contamination. Indeed, the mouth is a favorite target for all children in this age range, not only for their hands but for other odds and ends, such as Rover's dog food and Tabby's cat toy. Keep all sources of saliva-borne infection as far from children as possible.

Ages six to ten

Most children can now be trusted to perform a basic regimen of petkeeping chores, including cleaning the cage, feeding, watering, grooming, and playing with dogs and cats. Shelf pets such as goldfish begin to fascinate children at this age, and children can help out with feeding and cleaning chores. When allowing children to feed fish, measure out the day's portion into their hand, and let them drop the food directly into the tank. Never allow children to shake a fish food container directly into the aquarium. Even for adults it is difficult to gauge the right amount of food, and half the contents of the container can easily end up in the water.

Young people in this age category are well meaning, and their motor skills are adequate to the task. Still, they forget, they postpone, they get careless, and they sometimes simply shirk their duties. The best way to ride herd is to write out a schedule of chores, complete with check boxes and instructions, and tape this list on a bulletin board or onto the animal's cage. Ask your children to pencil in a mark after performing each feeding or cleaning. This way children learn to become accountable, and parents maintain control of the process. You will probably still have to remind children of their duties at this age, but by providing them with a well-designed chart they see the tasks spelled out in front of them, and this makes matters cut-and-dried. A chart should be simple, easy to follow, and should not include so many chores that the child feels overburdened.

A sample chart looks something like this:

Chores for the week
Check the day's box after doing each chore

	Mon	Tue	Wed	Thurs	Fri	Sat	Sun
Feed Tabby before school							
Feed Tabby before dinner							
Clean litter box							
Put down fresh water							

Ages eleven to thirteen

Most children at this age are ready to take on a full range of pet-care responsibilities, though you will still need to remind them of their duties from time to time. It is always important not to turn pet care into a burden for young persons or into something they come to resent. Here, it is all in the way you ask and tell.

For example, when a family is seated around the dining table a parent may bring up the subject of pet responsibilities, getting the point across in a casual or oblique way. Were you able to get that new cat food today? The parents ask. Did Buffy eat all his dinner when you fed him? How did Stumpy like those new shavings? How was the weather when you walked Red today? Did he pull at the leash like he always does? Do you think we should get him that new collar?

In other words, introduce the subject of pet care naturally during the course of conversation and let things flow from here. You will get the picture pretty quickly whether or not pet chores are getting done. During the conversation keep the tone light, nondirect, and do not scold or badger too much if a mistake is made. Give praise when the job is done properly, and let children know you appreciate the fact that they are taking responsibility and trying their hardest. Such dinner table conversations can become an exercise in positive motivation as well as a practical reminder.

Ages fourteen to seventeen

Children now are no longer really children. They are young men and young women who live in largely adult bodies, and who are mostly capable of taking over all the animal care chores in the household. The question is, will they?

And the answer is, Usually. Most of the time. Perhaps.

Even the most motivated teenager slips now and then, of course, and even at this age it's still the parent's job to ride herd. A few gentle reminders ordinarily do the trick. Parents should also remember that long-life pets such a dogs and cats acquired at this time will probably remain at home when or if the child goes off to college or moves away, and thus the responsibility for care will fall on their shoulders.

After age fourteen is also a good time in a young person's development to interest him or her in the formal aspects of animal studies—breeding, ecology, veterinary medicine, animal rights, zoology. Teenagers who show an inclination in this direction should be encouraged to read all they can about their favorite pets and to get involved in school projects that profile animal issues. Provide interested students with appropriate literature on the subject. Suggest that they join a pet club or animal breeding association. If a young person is interested in breeding fish or training dogs, direct them to experts in your community who specialize in this practice. Many professional animal people, zoologists, ecologists, and vets included, will tell you that their enchantment with animals began at an early age, but that their actual professional involvement evolved as a result of the encouragement and guidance they received from parents and mentors.

Helping Pets Deal with Children

The period of adjustment

Up till now the emphasis has been on teaching your child ways to deal safely and respectfully with the family pet. But every stick has two ends. Preparing a pet to deal gently with your child is an equally important issue.

Here the most common scenario is when a dog, cat, or other companion animal has long been the center of the household. Then one day, lo and behold, an infant human comes on the scene. Being territorial, the pet judges this new arrival as something of an interloper. The infant has its own set of smells, most of which do not resemble those of adult humans.

At the first sign of pregnancy, it is thus imperative to sign yourself and your dog up for an obedience class if you have not already attended. It is important that both the expectant mom and dad attend these classes together. Tell the trainer what the situation is and that you wish to emphasize a training regime that teaches pets respect and gentleness toward children.

Expectant parents usually have seven or eight months to teach dogs the essential lessons in these classes—commands like "sit," "stay," "no," "drop it." Dogs are pack animals, and are comfortable following a single leader. It's thus absolutely necessary that parents-to-be reestablish the fact that they, the human beings, are the leaders of the pack, and that the dog is the follower who must obey all household rules, including those rules that pertain to the new human child.

One of the first habits that must be trained out of a dog is the tendency to jump up or to mount. Even midsize dogs tower over children at the toddler stage, and in their enthusiasm to play they can knock little ones down and trample them. The remedy for this situation is to teach dogs to sit and stay at the training sessions before the child enters the home.

Other adjustments may also have to be made. In many cases, for example, the mother-to-be is the family member who ordinarily walks the dog. As her stomach expands, however, the mother-to-be will be less sure on her feet, and the father-to-be will have to take over walking chores. It is important at this point that the father knows the hows and whys of obedience commands and that he have full control of the dog on a leash.

Noises

Help your pet become accustomed to the noises your infant makes. These include crying and gurgling sounds that can upset and agitate animals when hearing them for the first time.

One way of introducing pets to these sounds is to take them for a visit to a friend or neighbor who already has an infant. Or, you can arrange for a friend to bring their infant to your home. When the child arrives, encourage the dog or cat to look at it, smell it, study it, get used to the strange sounds it makes, and generally accustom itself to the ways of newborn human babies. In cases where an infant is not available, pet owners sometimes make tapes of crying babies and play them back to the animal for extended periods of time in the home. Another method is to make a tape of the baby's noises and play them to the pet at pleasurable times of day, such as when the animal eats.

Spending quality time with the pet

In many childless homes a dog or cat is the center of attention and is accustomed to receiving huge doses of their owners' affection on a regular basis. Then one day the infant arrives, and suddenly the owners' affection machine is turned off, and their attention diverted. The pet, in turn, becomes correspondingly jealous and upset.

Avoid this situation by spending at last a half-hour of quality time each day with your pet during the first weeks after the infant's arrival. Be sure the infant is nowhere in evidence during these sessions. Walk, play, talk to your pet, and have fun in the way you did before the newborn came on the scene. Another approach is to reward the pet with food, play, and affection whenever the baby is in the vicinity. In this way the pet begins to associate the child's presence with rewards and pleasurable sensations, and a positive connection results.

Neutering

A final consideration to take into account vis-à-vis pets and infants is whether or not your pet is neutered.

Animals that are neutered or spayed tend to make better family pets in general than those that are not. They also tend to be healthier and happier. A dog that is unneutered may be inappropriately territorial. He may become dominant toward strangers and owners alike. Unneutered dogs are easily distracted, and this makes training problematic. Every time a bitch enters a heat cycle, moreover, she experiences hormonal changes that make her irritable and aggressive. The sexual frustration experienced by an unneutered pet, what's more, causes unpleasant behaviors. Dogs may howl inappropriately. They may mount or jump up. They may destroy valuable objects around the house. They may become overly protective of their possessions and of the home. They may snap and bite.

Having your pets spayed or neutered, in other words, not only makes them better with children. It also helps them live longer, healthier, happier lives.

Getting It Right: A How-to List for Children Taking Care of Pets

The following list includes a number of the basic pet-keeping tasks and activities for children that parents will need to concern themselves with. At the moment in time when a pet and child become comfortable with each other, they begin to establish their own special relationship. At this point children will want to become increasingly involved in overseeing their pet's welfare and in helping with day-to-day care. Each of these tasks brings its own challenges, and each has its own shortcuts and caveats. Knowledge of them can make life simpler, both for a parent and for a child.

Feeding

The most persistent problem young children face when feeding a pet is measuring out proper amounts.

Here parents can help. If children feed the dog, supply them with their own measuring cup or container. Let children fill the cup themselves and pour the food into the bowl.

When feeding a cat, a child of six or seven is old enough to pull the tab on a self-opening can, or pour the kibble into the measuring cup. Scooping out cat food and dropping it in the bowl is somehow intensely satisfying to children, and at the same time helps improve their hand-to-eye coordination. While near the feeding bowl you may also wish to take this opportunity to help children understand the concept of measuring—what a kilo and an ounce is, say, or the difference between liquid measure and distance measure. In this way pet-feeding time becomes an educational experience as well as a recreational one. Up to around the age of thirteen, feeding should always be done with the supervision of a parent or responsible adult.

Grooming

When children have enough dexterity to comb their own hair, usually around age seven or eight, they are also ready to give a dog or cat an effective brushing and combing. Adult supervision is necessary at the beginning, but after children learn the ropes they more or less manage on their own. For most pets, brushing and combing is a highly pleasurable experience, and the mutual loving contact that takes place during these sessions helps cement the human–animal bond. Here though, a word of warning. If your pet's coat or fur is especially thick, snarled, or matted, a child's inexperienced brushing may cause the animal pain. In such instances it's better to do the job yourself, or even to turn the task over to a pet-care professional.

Grooming is also an excellent way to help animal-shy children break the ice and experience the unique communion that can take place during a grooming session. One family, for example, keeps a separate set of grooming tools for each of their children, each brush and comb labeled with the child's name. Having pet-care tools of one's own increases a child's proprietary involvement in a pet's upkeep.

If you live in an area where deer ticks and Lyme disease are a problem, it is sound policy for a child (and for you) to groom pets outdoors, and to wear gloves, high socks, and a long-sleeved shirt in the process. As far as nail cutting goes, children are not ready to perform this task until they are in their early teens. Despite an eight- or nine-year-old child's best intentions, their manual coordination is still not steady or practiced enough to perform this potentially harmful task. And sensing a clumsy touch, most animals are likely to resist.

Walking

At one time dogs were the only pets walked on a leash. Today it is not unusual to see pet owners walking a cat, a ferret, even a rabbit.

Walking is one of the best of all pet-care activities for children and pets alike. Along with exercising animals it brings children into the out-of-doors as well. Besides helping the child and pet bond, pet walking is an ideal time for parent and children to be together, to discuss the issues of the day, to commune.

Do be careful, though, of entrusting too large a dog with too small a child. Even well-trained dogs sometimes sniff pleasure in a far-off hill or dale and yank small children along for the ride. Or, in another scenario, your child is walking her toy poodle when along comes an unleashed German shepherd looking for trouble. Before you know it, the child is in the middle of a dogfight with both her and the poodle on the losing end.

As a general rule, if you're going to let your child hold a pet's leash, it's a good idea to remain close by and, with children under seven, to hold their hand as they hold the dog. Children under seven years of age, moreover, should not be allowed to hold the leash by themselves. Use a double leash or confine walks with the child to a fenced-in yard.

Watering

If the job of watering falls to a child, make certain he or she attends to this seemingly small chore faithfully. Most pets require lots of fluids, and some become dehydrated in a day or so if a fresh water supply is not available. In the summertime keep a bowl of fresh water down at all times. Be sure that the pet's water bowl is washed several times a week.

Be especially careful of water contamination, both for the pet's sake and the child's. Children should wash their hands thoroughly after changing an animal's water. In fact, it's imperative that you make hand washing a mandatory part of the watering, feeding, and grooming routine. At the same time, make sure your pet's water comes from a clean source. Most animals are unconcerned with the purity of water they drink, and this lack of discretion causes infection and disease.

Cleaning

Cleaning a cage or tank is a complicated process, and most children are not up to the challenge until they are nine or ten years old. At the same time, younger children derive many benefits from helping grown-ups perform daily manual pet chores like scrubbing a turtle's tank, siphoning the gravel along the bottom of a fish tank, or replacing a gerbil's bedding.

Children have the remarkable gift of learning by observation as well as by doing. Simply watching cage- or tank-cleaning maneuvers over a period of time gives them a great deal of useful hands-on data. When the moment finally comes for them to take over these jobs they'll be ready.

Giving affection

Ordinarily you will have no trouble helping your child act in an affectionate way with a new pet. More often the problem is the opposite; the child wants to hug, kiss, feed, water, walk, and play with the new pet twenty-four hours a day, despite the fact that the pet is tired, hungry, or simply needs a little alone time.

If overhandling is a problem, encourage children to show affection in nonphysical ways. "I know you love puppy," a parent says, "but puppy is tired now. We need to let her rest for a while." At such moments children can be encouraged to talk to the animal rather than hug it. They can be prompted to sit next to it quietly, even to watch TV with it, or let it sleep on their lap. Pets should also have a place of their own to go when they want a bit of private time.

Practicing restraint in this manner helps children learn that they must give to an animal as well as take from it, and they learn that all living creatures, just like you and me, need their own privacy, rest, and personal space.

Arranging fun outings with an animal

Talk to children about activities the whole family can participate in together *including* the family pet. Make plans. Think up ideas for local adventures and fun activities. Be inventive. Use this opportunity to make it clear to children that your pet is part of the family, and that it has an individuality of its own. Message: the new pet is not a toy, a Barbie doll, nor stuffed bear. It is a living being with a name, temperament, and personality. It deserves to be treated with care and respect.

Keeping a pet journal

One of the most creative activities for children is keeping a written or oral journal about their pet-owning encounters. In their own private book or on a tape children record all that has interested, mystified, delighted, and even bothered them about their pet. An inexpensive spiral notebook or a tape recorder is all that's needed to get started.

The sky's the limit here. No ground rules. Just encourage children to write or record whatever facts and information they find pertinent about their pet, and to do so on a regular basis.

Start them off as soon as the new pet enters the house. A few simple observations will do:

"Hammy the Hamster is running on his wheels today."

"Tweety ate some gravel and then sang a lot."

"I gave Lucy a piece of apple and she ate it right down."

Children who are too young to write can dictate their thoughts to parents. The pet's growth rate, the games it plays, what it eats, where and when it sleeps, its daily disposition, a new collar, a new toy, a messy accident, a narrow escape, a romp in the park, a confrontation with another animal, a funny incident, all are potential subjects for the record. These and other similar observations made by inquiring young minds are the very stuff that helps children become dedicated animal lovers and, in some cases, launches careers as vets or zoologists.

A wonderful addition to the journal are children's own illustrations and drawings. Have a child draw and color a picture of the family rabbit while it eats from its bowl. Let children sketch one of the brightly colored fish in the aquarium. Encourage them to cut out pictures of animals and paste them into a "pet notebook." Photographs go nicely here too, and a combination of drawings, cutouts, and original photographs makes a really impressive project.

Such a journal allows children to monitor the development and maturation of their pet. It helps them appreciate the fact that each animal is an individual, different from all others of its species and kind. And on the day when a pet passes away, a journal helps children come to terms with this melancholy event. It shows them the rhythms of their beloved pet's life cycle, and allows them to witness the phases it passed through as the months and years of its life went by. The pictures and memories in this book, moreover, make it a tool both for helping a child cope with the animal's demise, and for learning more about life and death in the natural world in general. The complex matter of pet death and bereavement is discussed in chapter 6.

Recognizing When Children and Pets Aren't Working Out

Sometimes things just don't work out between a child and a pet.

The child, it turns out, does not care for the animal and may even dislike it. Or the animal is impossible to train. The new pet is unruly, destructive, mean. It may bite or have an uncontrollable need to tear up the furniture. The child may have a violent allergic reaction to the animal. The animal may shun the child.

There are endless variations.

One situation to be especially on the alert for is when a child wantonly mistreats a pet.

The difference between clumsy roughhousing and intentional infliction of pain is as apparent as night and day, and the latter should be immediate cause for concern on the part of parents. Any indication that a child is mistreating or tormenting a pet should be a danger sign.

What to do?

Immediately protect the pet, then seek the guidance of a mental health professional for the child. As a rule, children who delight—and persist—in inflicting severe pain on animals are bothered in other emotional ways as well, and they need help.

Finally, when and if it becomes apparent that things are not working out with the animal and child, and that they can *never* work out, several options are available.

First, are you certain you have looked into all the options for making the relationship between family and pet a viable one? Habits like biting, barking, or tearing up furniture can be addressed in training classes. Hostile behavior on the part of an animal can improve when love and attention are provided. Children who react negatively to an animal at first sometimes have a change of heart. Be sure you are not giving up too soon.

If you do decide to give the pet away, a friend or family member may be willing to provide a new home. Notices posted on bulletin boards at the veterinarian's office, a school, the post office, or supermarket often get results. Advertise in the newspapers. Bring the animal to your local pet shelter for adoption.

Any sign of aggression by your pet toward a child should be taken very seriously, especially with dogs. Consult your veterinarian, behaviorist, or trainer immediately.

Go with the Flow

The issue of bringing children and companion animals together is a complex one and requires both preplanning and forethought on the part of parents.

We all tend to have our assumptions concerning how children *should* react to the things that once delighted us as children. Too often we make the humbling discovery that our children are independent beings who act and react according to their own predilections, and who may or may not fancy the same kind of dog or cat or bird or hamster that was such an integral part of our own early years.

If this is the case, if your child reacts to a pet in diametrically opposed ways than you once did, needless to say, go with the flow, and let the child make his or her own discoveries. These discoveries may not be the same ones you made as a child. They may not bring the same delights. But they will be the child's own discoveries and the child's own delights, and this is what the experience of having a pet is all about.

Whatever you do, remember that children and pets are natural allies and inherent friends, and that though it may take time—and though some of the shenanigans on the part of the child and on the part of the pet may exercise your patience—there are few greater gifts you can give to your daughter or son than the joy of loving, training, and caring for a companion animal. In the long run, their joy will be your joy.

4

Traveling with Your Pet

This Chapter's Time Has Come

One hundred fifty years ago, in the age before planes, automobiles, and tickets purchased over the Internet, a chapter titled "Traveling with Your Pet" would be looked on as an oddity, and would serve little purpose. In our increasingly mobile society, however, events that were once unusual are currently the norm: extended business trips, moving to a new residence, weeklong vacations, and traveling to far-off corners of the world. Today we are a footloose society, and our animal companions have become footloose with us. The ins and outs of traveling with pets is now a major concern for millions of people.

There are, of course, right ways and wrong ways to travel with an animal. The right ways make life a lot easier both during and after the trip. The wrong ways can foster headaches and delays. In this chapter we will learn how to avoid the wrong ways and how to take full advantage of the right.

Preparation, Preparation, Preparation

When traveling for fun or for business, the only pets you will want to take with you, most likely, are your dog and, less frequently, your cat. Fish, gerbils, turtles, and the like make fine pets, but they are unlikely choices for traveling companions. Chances are the only time that travel will be an issue for small mammals, fish, birds, and reptiles is when you are moving from an old residence to a new. Otherwise, these pets remain happily at home.

This leaves dogs and, to a lesser extent, cats.

Being domestic and territorially inclined by nature, cats (with a few exceptions) make poor travelers and often require special coaxing and training to accustom them to new locations. Dogs, on the other hand, adjust relatively well to wayfaring, though again, exceptions are more frequent than might be expected. Fortunately, both dogs and cats can be taught to become comfortable travelers. The key term underlying these lessons is *preparation*.

Here are some time-proven methods for putting preparation into action:

Finding the right travel kennel for your pet

Start the process when your dog or cat is still young.

Purchase a roomy, well-constructed travel kennel. There are inexpensive models on the market, but these don't always hold up to the inevitable punishment such objects take on the road. For this reason, pet owners are advised to dig deep into their pockets and purchase a quality carrier. A good travel kennel lasts a pet's lifetime and sometimes several pets' lifetimes. If dogs or cats become familiar with a kennel while still young, they are more inclined to become accustomed to this den and to enter it without hesitation when travel time arrives.

Two styles of kennel are available: closed and wire.

The sides of a closed kennel are usually constructed of plastic walls with a small barred opening at the door and sometimes a small window. Wire kennels are fashioned of sturdy wire grating, allowing in more air and light than molded plastic, and providing animals with a wider field of vision.

Which type of kennel is preferable?

It depends on the animal's personality and the mode of travel.

Some pets prefer the cozy, secure feeling that closed kennels provide. Others like to look around as they travel and see what's happening through the open wire enclosure, and these work well for car travel. Note that for plane travel, closed kennels are legally mandatory, as well for all kennels placed in cargo holds. For small, carry-on pets, soft-sided luggage-type kennels that fit under the plane seat are allowed on most—though not all—commercial flights.

The art and practice of kennel training

After procuring a sturdy kennel, pack it with clean, comfortable padding. Old towels or blankets are ideal. Place a tasty food treat inside, then position it in a convenient part of the house. Encourage your dog or cat to enter the kennel and to just hang out there for a while. Leave the door open while the pet is inside.

Puppies and kittens are naturally curious and will start exploring the carrier the moment you set it down. Adult animals are more suspicious, though they eventually get around to liking the strange new box, especially if their food dish is placed inside. As a rule, animals find kennels to be private and accommodating places. At times pet owners may even have trouble getting them to come out.

After a week or so of this drill, start closing the kennel door for several minutes while the animal is inside. Never force the issue and always allow the animal to set its own pace. The critical thing to keep in mind during this training period is to establish positive connections in your pet's mind with everything that has to do with the kennel.

Go through this routine every day for several weeks, gradually extending the time your pet is inside the kennel (but always being careful not to push an animal beyond its developmental capacities). At the end of this time a puppy or kitten should be thoroughly comfortable with kennel logistics. Sometimes they may even adopt the kennel as their sleeping den or as a place to hang out in and be quiet. If this is the case, wonderful: mission accomplished!

After the kitten or puppy is comfortably at home with its kennel, take the next step. With the dog or cat safely inside, close the kennel door, place it in the backseat of your car, strap the kennel in with the seat belt, and take your pet for a short ride to the park or around the block.

Dogs usually take well to these abbreviated trips, especially if they are already familiar with cars. Kittens will be restive at first, so talk to them soothingly as you drive and make sure they are comfortable.

Repeat these test drives once or twice a week. After a month or so, both dogs and cats should be accustomed to the routine and may even look forward to it. An added benefit of this training, besides making travel easier for you, is that when the time comes to take your dogs or cats to the veterinarian, they won't bolt and hide under the bed when they see the kennel.

Travel preparation tips

Here are more steps you can take to be well prepared for travel with a pet:

- Tell your veterinarian that you will be traveling. Provide him or her with information on where you are going, how long you intend to be gone, which animals you are taking, and whether you are traveling by air, car, sea. Note, by the way, that Amtrak does not generally accept pets on their trains. Regional commuter trains do, on the other hand, as do some foreign train lines.
- If you are traveling in the United States, ask your veterinarian if the area you intend to visit is a danger zone for specific animal diseases—heartworm, worms, parasites, deer ticks. He or she may not always know the answer to these questions, but it's worth a try. If your pet has a tendency to motion sickness, ask your vet to provide proper medication in advance.
- If your pet has fleas or ticks, have these conditions treated before you leave. Fleas and ticks can infest a car or another residence just as easily as they infest the inside of your own home.
- Make certain that your pet's vaccinations are all up to date. During times of crisis or emergency when travel becomes imperative, pet owners are sometimes forced to board their animals. Be prepared for this contingency in advance by having copies of your pet's medical records with you and available at a moment's notice.
- Clip your pet's nails before leaving home. If a dog or cat becomes excited in transit, short nails do less damage to a car seat or to human arms than long nails.
- Never allow a pet to wear a choke, pinch, or training collar while traveling. A standard buckle with an ID is best for dogs. Cats should have an elastic collar with an ID.
- When traveling, bring along a recent photograph of your pet plus a written profile of the animal: name, sex, age, breed, weight, height, color, markings, birth defects, scars, and microchip or tattoo numbers. If your pet is lost this information will be vital in the search process.

A Word of Warning on Cats and Travel

If you plan to leave home for an extended period of time, chances are you will want to bring your cat with you. If your trip is short, say a week or less, it is probably best to leave your cat at home with a pet sitter or friends. There are exceptions to this rule, of course. People who maintain a weekend home frequently travel with their cats. Over time the animals become accustomed to both residences. On the other hand, people who are simply going on vacation for a week or two are advised to let Tabby stay put.

Why?

Because cats by nature are territorial creatures and tend to bond deeply with their local stomping grounds. While dogs thrive on adventure and visits to new places, cats experience the opposite reaction, becoming agitated and sometimes downright scared when plucked out of familiar surroundings and placed into unknown territory. Stress and hiding behavior can result. If repeated too many times, travel can have a detrimental effect on a cat's state of health as well.

Avoid these reactions by arranging to have someone stay with your cat while you're away. You can, for example, have a friend live in your home during this time, or have a neighbor look in on the cat during the day. You may wish to hire a pet sitter. Or boarding may be the most convenient solution. As a general rule, cats hate travel. Spare them this imposition whenever you can.

Traveling by Car

All this said—and assuming that it's still necessary to take a cat with you on the journey as well as a dog—the following car-travel techniques should be part of every traveling pet owner's repertoire.

Matching the right car to the right pet

All cats fit comfortably in a kennel while traveling.

The same is true for some dogs—but not all. Big canines can be a problem. A Newfoundland, for example, may not fit in the kennel, or the kennel may not fit the Newfoundland. Or both the Newfoundland and the kennel may be too large to fit in the backseat.

One way around the big dog dilemma is to ask your local pet supply store about seat belts for large dogs. Most of these units today buckle directly into a car's rear seat belts, and little or no installation is required.

The size of a vehicle is also a major factor when traveling, and here, if you have not yet purchased or rented your car, you may want to factor in your dog's size and temperament when making the decision. Certainly a van or utility vehicle makes toting a big dog (or several dogs at once) an easier job, and on long trips there is still plenty of elbow room left over for everyone. At minimum, make sure the vehicle you are interested in has a roomy backseat plus an interior that is high enough and wide enough to comfortably fit your pet's carrier.

Arranging feeding schedules while traveling

Pet owners are often advised to let their animals eat a meal three hours before departure time. This schedule, however, is not always feasible for people who must leave early or late in the day. In such instances, dogs and cats can be given light meals two hours before setting out, then fed at the end of the journey. If you are leaving in the morning, feed your dog or cat in the accustomed way the night before, then provide a light snack of kibble (not meat or soft canned food) several hours before setting out. Avoid feeding pets when a vehicle is in motion, especially those that are not seasoned travelers.

When making trips of five hours or less, some pet owners allow their animals to fast all day until reaching the destination, then they serve them a light meal. All-day trips with an overnight stop call for a light feeding in the morning before departure, then another feeding at night, plus at least one bout of exercise in between.

Creative pit stops

Plan to stop every two or three hours for pit stops, especially when traveling with a dog.

When pulling over, your canine will be keyed up from confinement and excitement, so be sure to slip her leash on before opening the car door.

Many turnpikes and highways now provide dog-walking zones in the rest areas. If you pull into a populated area use a regulation-size leash for walking. If you are in open country a fifteen- or twenty-foot lead line allows your dog plenty of romping room. You may wish to take both types of leashes with you on the journey.

Some pet owners let their cats out of the kennel during rest stops (but not out of the car), though this sudden freedom can confuse cats who may prefer to stay tucked into the carrier where the security lies. On the other hand, cats that are trained to a leash respond happily to short, brisk walks during stops. You may also wish to let your cat use the litter box within the confines of the vehicle at this time. Because of the excitement of the trip, a cat may not avail herself of this option, but it's worth a try. On long trips most cats will eventually comply.

At each pit stop offer your pet water. Cats are not great drinkers, but dogs get thirsty easily, especially when traveling. Be sure and bring along spare water in case it is not available at the rest stops.

Finally, when pet owners stop along a highway to eat or stretch their legs, under no circumstances should a dog or cat be left unattended in a car. This is especially true during the summer months when isolation in an overheated car for even a few minutes can cause heat stroke. If an emergency situation makes it necessary to abandon a car and leave a pet alone—a practice that is highly discouraged and should only be done under the most dire conditions—be sure the windows are cracked and that the animal is left with an adequate supply of water. Before you leave the car, park it in the shade or beneath an overhead shelter such as a bridge or underpass that stops direct sunlight from overheating the interior. Keeping a cell phone with you while on the road will make all of these maneuvers unnecessary.

Arming your pet with proper identification

Car journeys are stimulating events for animals, and they sometimes provide just enough excitement to make them do irrational things—like run away. Open the car door for a minute somewhere in the middle of nowhere with your dog or cat unattended, and in a microsecond they're gone. Or say you reach your destination. You're in a strange place with strange sights, sounds, smells. Your dog or cat has no intention of running away, of course. But while sniffing around and following a scent it inadvertently wanders into the woods and gets lost.

The best preventive against such contingencies, besides vigilance, is to leash and tag your dog and cat when you travel. The identification on these tags should include three vital pieces of data:

1. Your home phone number and address. If you have an 800 number include it. Otherwise have the words "call collect" written after the phone number.
2. The phone and address of your final destination.

3. The phone and address of a friend, family member, or neighbor who knows how to contact you while traveling. If your pet is lost then found by a stranger, your name and address is of no value if you are not home. Be sure to list an intermediary who is willing to handle the transfer and pickup details for the animal.

What kind of tag is best?

For identification, key tags make perfect temporary ID indicators. Be sure the tag holder is well secured to your pet's collar and enclosed in a plastic lining in case your pet is exposed to rain or snow. Engraved collars are good also, but tend not to hold as much information.

Controlling motion sickness

If your pet is prone to motion sickness, avoid feeding him before you leave. An empty stomach weathers jolts and bounces better than a full one.

Dogs tend to become motion sick more commonly than cats, though neither is immune. If your pet has a tendency in this direction, and if the condition does not go away after it logs a few travel miles, consult with a veterinarian. Do not, however, medicate a dog or cat on your own. Dosages and dosage schedules are critical, and mistakes can make your pet twice as sick.

Finding a hotel or motel that takes pets

If you know the motor route you are taking and where you'll be spending the night, save yourself a mountain of headaches by booking reservations before you leave. Many motels and hotels now accept pets, but many don't. You won't know which ones do unless you call ahead and ask. And you certainly don't want to take your chances in this department. There are few more frustrating experiences after a taxing day's car trip than spending several hours driving blindly around searching a strange town for a place that accepts pets.

Many of the larger hotel and motel chains today accept pets. (See the appendix for the 800 number you can call for further information.)

Some of these places have stipulations you will want to learn about ahead of time. Most good road travel guidebooks provide detailed information on a hotel or motel's pet-accommodation policies. Note, by the way, that while most states in the country have few laws regulating pet occupancy in hotels, one southern state, North Carolina, has a ban on animals of any kind staying overnight in a hotel or motel.

In the hotel room

Once in your hotel room, let your pet calm down and relax.

Exercise him, then give him some water and a light meal.

For cats, put a litter box in the bathroom, making sure the cat sees where you place it. If you bring your pet's favorite sleeping cushion, blanket, or pillow, place it in a convenient location and show it to the animal.

Some pet travel experts suggest that dogs and cats should sleep in the bathroom of a motel or hotel. While this advice is sound in theory, some dogs and cats do poorly when closed up in a small room, and you may end up listening to scratching and barking all night. In such cases it's better to simply place the bedding in your bedroom and let the pet spend the night near enough to where you're sleeping to feel secure.

Finally, when leaving a pet alone in a hotel room, consider placing a Do Not Disturb Sign on the door, even when the animal is crated. Also consider leaving your cat in the bathroom when you go out to dinner rather than allowing it to run free. Note, by the way, that some hotels and motels do not allow guests to leave their pets alone and unsupervised in the room under any circumstances, crated or uncrated.

Items recommended for traveling with a pet in the car

On any lengthy car trip with a pet the following items will all come in handy:

- A sturdy leash.
- An extra collar.
- An old blanket or sheet for the backseat of the car or wherever the pet's carrier is placed (for those times when the animal is let out of the crate).
- Two old sheets to cover bedding and furniture at your destination.
- Some of your pet's bedding.
- Food. If you're not sure you can find your pet's brand of pet food where you're visiting, bring a supply of this food along with you. If you feed your pet canned food, remember to take a can opener and serving spoon as well.
- Two gallons of drinking water.

- Food and water bowl set.
- Toys and chewy items. Food treats.
- All required medications and food supplements.
- Brush and comb. Lint and hair remover. Baby wipes or moist towelettes.
- A full litter pan for cats with extra litter, liner, and paper. Waste removal bags.
- Paper towels, odor neutralizer, and trash bags.
- First-aid kit. A flashlight for nighttime walks.

Traveling by Plane

For long trips and sometimes long vacations, travel by plane is often the most viable transport option for a pet. There are, however, important safety and logistical concerns, all of which should be taken into consideration when making your travel plans.

Making advance preparations

If you intend to fly with a pet be sure to book flight reservations well in advance. Almost all airlines accommodate pet travel, but each has its own regulations, some of which can be restricting.

A list of questions to ask when making airline reservations for yourself and your pet includes the following:

- What are the airline's general policies for pet air travel? Does the airline offer a brochure or printed material outlining these policies? If they do, this material is usually featured on the airline's website.
- Who takes care of feeding and watering the pet during flight time and/or when a pet is waiting in the cargo area?
- If a change of planes is necessary, how does the airline's baggage department make certain the animal is put on the correct flight?
- Does the airline supply a flight kennel for pets? Are pet owners obliged to use the airline's carrier or can they supply their own?
- If pets are small and docile enough, and if their kennel fits under the seat, can owners carry pets on the plane?
- Does the airline have a formal policy of limitation on size, age, species, etc., for pets? Note that federal law mandates that a pet must be eight weeks old before it can be put onboard a flight.

- If an animal is harmed in flight, is it insured? Does the airline offer special insurance for pets? Among commercial airlines approximately 1% of all pets are injured in flight. This sounds like a small number until you realize these figures translate out to five thousand injuries per year. The question of in-flight safety responsibility for pets is a murky one, and there is a great deal of pressure today by animal organizations to pass federal legislation that defines—and substantially increases—the parameters of airline liability.
- What are the costs involved for shipping a pet by plane? Is it a flat rate? Or is the cost calculated by the number of pounds the pet weighs?
- What pickup and delivery services does the airline provide for animals? Will they send a vehicle to pick up the pet from your home? From time to time in the past, airlines have offered this service.
- Upon arrival, is the pet unloaded and carried to the baggage claim area by hand? Or is it trucked out with the rest of the luggage and placed on the baggage carousel? Obviously, the first alternative is preferable. For some people, this criterion alone is cause enough to choose one airline over another.
- When traveling overseas, what are the quarantine laws of the country? Determine in advance the health requirements and vaccination certificates necessary in the country of destination. Call their embassy and inquire about current regulations in these areas.
- Upon arrival in a foreign country, does someone from the airline help the pet through the process of customs, immigration, and inspection? If not, how can you find out what must be done to expedite these formalities?

Finding the right flight kennel for your pet

If possible, purchase your kennel weeks or even months ahead of the flight. Before setting out let your dog or cat familiarize itself with its new home-away-from-home. The instructions given in the beginning of this chapter for helping a dog or cat bond with a new carrier apply here as well.

When shopping for a kennel let the USDA specifications be your guide. According to this guide, a travel kennel should have the following:

- A door that swings open easily with a strong latch.
- An interior that is large and roomy enough to allow a dog or a cat to stand up easily, turn around, and lie down.
- Sturdy construction materials, preferably plastic.
- Bumper guards, knobs, or rims at least three-quarter-inch high on the exterior of the kennel. These items ensure that baggage handlers do not press the container flush up against other pieces of cargo in the hold during the flight, cutting off a dog or cat's air supply.
- Strong handles on top or on the side of the kennel.
- Ventilation openings on at least two of the four walls of the carrier.
- The words Live Animal penned in clear, one-inch-high (or larger) letters. These letters can be written with black magic marker on at least one side of the kennel, and preferably on two. Most carriers come with stick-on signs.

Preparing the kennel for the flight

Make the kennel as homey and inviting as possible for your dog or cat's long trip. Place several layers of soft, absorbent material (such as shredded newspaper) on the floor of the carrier. Adding a blanket or cushion with familiar smells will also provide a sense of security during the trip. Be sure that before the animal enters its kennel it is wearing an identification tag on its collar. Finally, never place a leash inside a dog or cat's kennel. Leashes tangle easily and in the worst-case scenario can strangle an animal.

If you are carrying your cat on board a plane and are asked at the gate to remove it for a security check, request a closed room, and consider placing a leash and harness on the cat to maintain full control. Few things are more frustrating than removing a cat from the carrier for inspection at the security check and having it bolt out of your hands and into the terminal crowd.

Leaving instructions for airline baggage handlers

All feeding and watering instructions should be plainly written out on a tag, and conspicuously attached to the side of the kennel. Ironically, most animals do fine while the plane is in the air. If trouble occurs, it usually happens during the preboarding period when the kennel sits, sometimes for long periods of time, sometimes totally exposed to the elements, on the tarmac waiting for loading. If your plane is delayed, as planes frequently are, baggage personnel are obliged to keep a close eye on all animal passengers. Assuming that your instructions attached to the kennel are clearly marked, it is their responsibility to supply the animal with food and water in case of prolonged delay.

Monitoring health concerns during the flight

Federal regulations now state that an animal must have a health certificate signed by a veterinarian within ten days of the flight in order to fly. This law protects the airline, of course, but it's also a form of flight insurance for your pet. Travel by plane can be taxing and fatiguing, especially if a pet's health is already compromised. Older pets, very young pets, and pets who suffer from chronic illness often make poor candidates for plane travel. If you have any doubts along these lines consult with your veterinarian first before planning to send your pet by air.

To tranquilize or not to tranquilize

Should an animal be tranquilized before a flight or, for that matter, before any lengthy journey by plane, train, or car?

The answer is usually no.

Medically speaking, sedatives and tranquilizers are nervous system depressants. They slow down important physiological mechanisms such as respiration and heart beat. Since an animal's system is already strained in flight by pressurization in the cargo and a general state of excitement, a sedative adds insult to injury, depressing these functions even further. Tranquilizers and sedatives can also interfere with an animal's sense of balance and equilibrium.

On the other hand, now and then an animal comes along that is a chronically poor traveler. In such instances, when nothing else helps, a sedative may be in order to get the animal (and yourself) to where you're going in one piece. A word of warning though: some dogs and cats are sensitive to tranquilizers, and incorrect doses can produce harmful results. Others are relatively *insensitive*, leading to oversedation by owners. Sedation should always be done under the guidance of a veterinarian. He or she will want to know a number of variables about your pet, including weight, size, age, and breed, before writing a prescription. Under no circumstances should you attempt to sedate a pet on your own.

The best times to fly with a pet

If possible, try not to travel with a pet on three-day weekends or during high-traffic holidays such as Christmas and Thanksgiving. Delays are likely to occur at these times, which means that your pet may end up stranded in cargo storage or outside in a baggage holding area for hours at a time. Travel traffic is slowest and hence best for a pet during the middle days of the week. During the actual flight the temperature in a cargo hold is controlled, and this is fine. When a takeoff is delayed by high volumes of traffic, and a plane is forced to sit on the runway for hours at a time, its internal power is shut down, and so the air conditioning stops working. This experience is unpleasant enough for the passengers, but far worse below in the cargo area where temperatures soar above 100°F. If your animal is already overheated and excited, such an extreme of temperature can trigger heat stroke or worse.

Finally, to reduce the amount of time your animal spends in transit, be sure and book a nonstop flight. As far as animals go, the less time spent on a plane the better.

Retrieving your pet at the end of the flight

There are few times in the life of a pet when they are happier to see you than the moment you pick them up after a flight. If you and your pet are on the same plane, retrieval takes place at the baggage claim area along with other baggage. Your dog or cat will be delivered here (worst-case scenario) on the baggage carousel, or they will be hand carried by a member of the airport staff to a holding room in the baggage area (best-case scenario). Consult with the airline about their pickup policy. With some companies you may have to pick up your pet at a cargo area far from the passenger terminals. Other companies are more obliging. Again, policies differ from airline to airline and from country to country. Be sure to inquire about pickup policy in the beginning when making flight arrangements.

A last word of warning: after a flight don't take your dog or cat out of its kennel until you arrive at your final destination. Your pet will be nervous and keyed up from the trip and difficult to handle. Once at the final destination, they will be dehydrated from the flight, just like people, so make sure their water bowls are full. See to it that your pet is well exercised, fed, petted, fussed over, and then put to bed. It's been a long day.

Shipping a Pet

There may be times when it is unavoidably necessary to ship an animal alone by plane rather than take it with you. Shipping an animal can be a complex undertaking, and as a rule it's best to turn the process over to professionals who specialize in the task. Consult your local yellow pages for the name of a local animal shipper or give your veterinarian a call. Be sure and ask for references and recommendations before using a shipper's services.

Though each company does things a bit differently, the process basically works like this. After giving them all pertinent information, a member of the shipping company's staff comes to your home and picks up the animal, which presumably is waiting in its kennel. The shipping company then takes care of delivering the animal to the airline and seeing to it that it's loaded onto the plane. Some shippers, though not all, also arrange to send a member of their staff to the destination airport where they pick up your animal. Be sure and go over the entire procedure with the shippers beforehand, and take down all pertinent information including airline, flight numbers, pickup numbers, phone numbers, and addresses. Get all the procedures and guarantees in writing from them.

What about transporting animals other than dogs and cats such as birds, fish, reptiles, and small mammals like rabbits and gerbils?

Most animal shippers have facilities for sending these creatures. But note that such services may not always be necessary. Many airlines allow birds to be carried into the passenger cabin if kept in a small bird kennel. The same is true with small mammals. If you're traveling by car, aquariums can be placed in the backseat, and the fish specially packed in oxygen-inflated bags. Some pet stores provide this service.

Boarding Your Pet at a Kennel

At times it may be impractical to take a dog, cat, or bird with you while you're traveling. The trip may be too long or too short to warrant extra travel arrangements. Pets may not be allowed where you're going. Or your pet may simply be a poor traveler. Whatever the situation, when and if the time comes to place a pet in a boarding kennel, it's best to be well informed of your options ahead of time. In the past decades the image of boarding kennels has gone from dreary parking lots for abandoned animals to country clubs for pets. While it's true that at the high end of the kennel spectrum, facilities exist that offer animal guests their pick of carpeted private rooms, expensive fluffy toys, exercise courts, gourmet meals, television sets that play twenty-four-hour animal videos, and the like, a majority of kennels offer plain vanilla accommodations at decent and sometimes modest prices. If you live in an urban or suburban part of the United States, chances are you will have your pick of both extremes, with many degrees in between.

Before choosing a particular boarding facility visit several in your area and learn what's available. Tell the staff that you're thinking of boarding your animal, and that you'd like a tour of the facilities. Most kennels will be happy to oblige.

While you're making the rounds consider the following:

A good kennel should be well ventilated, clean, secure, and efficiently run. The overall impression a kennel makes when you first walk in should be a positive one. As far as pet-boarding facilities go, first impressions count.

A good kennel performs regular on-premises flea and tick exterminations. Fly populations are kept at a minimum.

A good kennel should have a smell that is mildly animal but not oppressive. If the odor of feces is prevalent and infiltrates the unit, this probably means the kennel is short-staffed on cleaning personnel, and that its general state of hygiene is poor. Similarly, be alert if the smell of deodorant is pervasive: management may be disguising foul odors with lilac and rose.

Living accommodations should be roomy, airy, and light. A dog or cat should enjoy enough elbow room to stand up, stretch out, turn around, and walk around. Avoid kennels that cram too many animals into one small area.

The animals at a kennel should appear to be comfortable and adjusted. A kennel full of constantly howling dogs and screaming cats is a danger sign. Certainly there will be some complaining in the swankiest of facilities. But if the noise output seems especially pained and frantic, this is probably a sign that the guests are especially unhappy.

A good kennel has staff members on duty who are constantly watching the facilities, along with personnel who regularly clean and maintain the premises. Any kennel that leaves animals unattended, even for short periods of time, is putting their guests into jeopardy. Don't tolerate this breach of trust.

A good kennel feeds pets a wholesome, plentiful diet. Inquire about how many times a day are pets fed? What does the feed consist of? Who does the feeding?

If your pet has special dietary requirements, ask the staff if they accommodate such needs. Is there an additional charge for this service? If they do not accommodate special dietary needs, will they allow you to leave your pet with a supply of its own favorite or special food?

The staff at a kennel should be friendly, kindly, polite, and willing to go the extra mile for you and your pet. Find out if staff members have any training in pet care, and whether they have the basic medical skills to deal with emergencies. If possible, watch the staff at work while visiting. Watch as they feed the animals and interact with them. If you like the men and women who work at a boarding facility, chances are your dog or cat will like them too.

A good kennel maintains ongoing liaisons with local veterinarians and animal hospitals. Find out which medical services are offered at the kennel and what procedures are practiced in times of emergency. Ask your own veterinarian's office if it offers boarding services, and if it does not, ask if it can make recommendations.

A good kennel provides animals with regular exercise sessions. Find out if the facility maintains an ample-size running area. Is the area secure? How often are the animals taken out of their living areas and allowed to move around? Twice a day? Once a day? Not at all? Are kennel runs provided? If so, how many times a day are the animals turned out into these runs? Are there other exercise options available for purchase as well, or as part of the package? Are animal guests supervised during exercise periods? Are pets exercised alone or with other animals? Since brawling and nipping is a problem in a yard full of animals that are unfamiliar with one another, it is preferable that pets be exercised alone.

A good kennel keeps dogs and cats reasonably well segregated. Ideally, facilities include an area for dogs and an area for cats, with plenty of space between them.

Ask whether grooming services are available at the kennel, and if so, what the costs are.

Many kennels require you to sign a contract before leaving your pet. Read this agreement carefully, looking for unreasonable disclaimers or hidden financial demands.

Before choosing a kennel, ask around about prices and get quotes from several facilities in your area. Also ask for references. If a kennel is accredited by the American Boarding Kennel Association this is a good sign.

Before you leave pets off at a kennel, be certain all their inoculations are up to date. Germ pools at even the cleanest boarding establishment are large and potentially dangerous if pets are not caught up on their shots. A bronchial condition in dogs known as *tracheobronchitis* is espe-cially prevalent at boarding kennels. Be sure your pets are inoculated against this disease before dropping them off.

Finally, be certain to leave all pertinent information about your pet with the kennel staff. Critical information includes the following:

- The address and phone number of where you will be staying dur-ing your period away from home.
- The name, address, and phone number of a neighbor or family member who is willing to serve as backup in case you can't be reached.
- The name and number of your pet's veterinarian.

Choosing the Right Pet Sitter

Boarding facilities often deliver top-notch pet care. But all things considered, leaving an animal in the comfort of its own home with a trusted pet sitter is better.

Fortunately, there are now a number of men and women in our soci-ety who make their living watching pets, and who come to the job with experience, expertise, and often an impressive portfolio of references, referrals, and bonding credentials. As a rule, pet sitters are extremely fond of animals—why else would they choose this vocation? Concur-rently, pet owners stand to benefit in a double way from hiring a sitter: first, because the owner has a professional taking care of their pets, and second, because they also have someone to watch over their house or apartment.

Make sure a sitter comes to the job with all the proper references and referrals. If a friend or relative was satisfied with a sitter in the past, chances are you will be, too. If possible, find someone who lives in your area. Even better, use someone you already know and trust. You might also consider asking your veterinarian, local humane society, or groomer for references and leads. As a last resort, the names of pet sitters can be found in the yellow pages. Some pet sitters also advertise on local bul-letin boards.

Once you've located a potential sitter, set up a meeting and get to know him or her. Watch how this person interacts with your pet. Do the pet and sitter seem to get along? Is there rapport? Does the sitter ap-pear to have good pet-handling skills and a winning way with animals? If sitters are hired to watch smaller animals such as small birds, gerbils, fish, and so forth, they are responsible for the same day-to-day maintenance tasks that you perform: feeding, watering, and/or cleaning the cage and aquarium. Ideally, a sitter should also be familiar with the signs of illness in the type of smaller animals he or she is watching over. If a sitter is staying at your house, these tasks will be part of the day's work. On the other hand, if you hire sitters to simply check up on a pet several times a day and perform maintenance duties, be sure to give them written directions before you leave on the trip, and to leave an extra copy of these directions in a conspicuous place. Instructions should include information on the following:

- Your pet's diet, eating schedule, location of food, etc.
- Exercise and walking routines (be sure and leave the leash in plain view)
- Your pet's grooming needs (set out the animal's brush and comb)
- Your pet's favorite toys (tell the sitter where they're kept)
- Medication schedules (give detailed dosage instructions, and be sure to indicate where the medications are stored)
- Your veterinarian's name and phone number
- The phone number of the place where you will be staying
- A neighbor or family member's phone number in case of emergency

Finally, if you are looking for pet sitter references and information, or if you want to speak with experts on the subject, the names and numbers of pet-sitter associations can be referenced in the Appendix.

5

Keeping Your Pet Healthy

Overseeing Your Pet's Health

The medical relationship between humans and animals is an ancient one, extending back in time tens of thousands of years. Anthropologists digging through prehistoric ruins have exhumed early medical devices, such as earthen casts for setting a dog's broken leg and surgical instruments used for animal operations. In some parts of South America trepaned animal skulls have been discovered, evidence, some experts believe, of early brain surgery. Among the ancient Egyptian priesthood, a system of medicine existed exclusively for the treatment of cat diseases.

The underlying theme of these discoveries is that human beings have been concerned with the physical well-being of their animals for millennia, and that the development of animal medicine and human medicine have paralleled one another over the centuries. Just as achieving good health leads to a roster of benefits in humans, such as heightened immune defenses, elevated energy levels, and an overall sense of well-being, keeping pets in top condition assures that they will live long and enjoy full lives.

Simple steps that can save your pet's life

The following steps are based on the principle that taking health precautions now will save you a lot of headache, heartache, and veterinarian bills later on. As with human beings, prevention, prevention, and prevention is the name of the pet health-care game.

Give your pet plenty of physical workout time during the day. Animals in the wild are accustomed to extended exertions. The very regularity of these activities keeps their whole physiology, as it were, well oiled.

When these same animals are domesticated, their daily activity rate drops, and many turn into the animal version of couch potatoes. This lack of movement can be seriously detrimental to an animal's health and should be compensated for on a regular basis with exercise.

Dogs vary in their need for exercise. Some get adequate physical stimulation by taking two or three good walks a day. Others require more strenuous activities. Cats can be encouraged in the exercise department by providing around-the-house props such as scratching posts, catnip toys to bat around, crawling tunnels, or another cat to romp with.

For small animals, such as gerbils, guinea pigs, mice, and hamsters, plastic tunnels and exercise wheels provide adequate activity, while rabbits and ferrets get their blood moving by running freely around the house. Adequate space in a cage or tank is the primary requirement for reptiles and amphibians. If you have a bird, make sure there's enough space in its cage for it to hop comfortably from perch to perch, and to spread its wings. For larger birds, time spent out of the cage moving around the room is helpful. Larger flight cages make excellent exercise spaces for certain varieties of birds, allowing them the elbow room they need to stay fit.

Getting proper nutrition. Like all of us, pets are what they eat. Be sure your animal companion receives a balanced diet and regular access to fresh water. Young animals have different nutritional requirements than middle aged and old, and a diet that's good for one may be nutritionally inadequate for another. (If you have questions concerning diet, see the chapters on individual pets that follow.)

Groom regularly. Grooming is a health aid for almost all furry creatures. Dogs and cats love it, of course, but so do smaller animals like ferrets and rabbits.

Grooming keeps animals clean. It removes debris from their coats they might otherwise ingest (or shed on your favorite couch). It stimulates blood circulation, opens pores, spreads natural oils, protects the insulating qualities of the coat, improves skin quality, and appears to create a state of well-being in the animal's disposition.

The key to successful grooming is consistency. No doubt you can get by brushing and combing your animal once or twice a month; but don't expect such infrequent sessions to bolster your pet's appearance—or temperament—to any degree. For certain animals, moreover, such as Persian cats, longhair dogs, and Angora rabbits, grooming is an absolute necessity. Without constant brushing and combing, both their coats and their overall state of health may suffer.

Generally speaking, grooming two or three times a week for periods of from five to ten minutes or more generates all the benefits mentioned above (the length of grooming time depends on the breed type in question—see the individual animal chapters for specifics). And don't forget the person-to-pet assets that accrue from this activity: grooming can provide a pleasant emotional experience for all parties concerned, building trust, providing a quiet moment, and increasing the mutual bonds of affection that exist between animal and human.

Supply your pet with a secure sleeping area. Make sure your pet's sleeping quarters are comfortable, away from drafts, in peaceful surroundings, and away from loud noises, busy feet, and tail-pulling toddlers. Placing a pet's sleeping quarters in a highly trafficked part of the house may be convenient for humans, but it can also interfere with the quality of an animal's sleep and ultimately with its health. Make sure too that your pet has a clean, comfortable pillow or pad to lie on. A once-a-week flea check is advisable in this regard, especially during the warm months, both for the animal's sake and your own.

Keep your pet indoors all the time. Many surveys show that pets, and dogs and cats in particular, live longer, more healthy lives when kept indoors.

Home safety does not mean denying nature entirely, of course, only that outdoor sessions on a leash or in a fenced-in area should be carefully supervised by humans. Unlike the interior of most human dwellings, the great outdoors—and here we include suburban backyards as well as fields and forests—is rife with potential dangers. Poisons, infectious bacteria, wild animals, heavily trafficked roads, neighboring pets, and unfriendly neighbors are just a few of the potential life-shortening and health-deteriorating threats that lurk.

Pet Poison Emergency Kit

Prepare for pet poisoning emergencies ahead of time by assembling the following kit, then storing it in a handy place for times of emergency.

- Bottle of hydrogen peroxide
- Pet carrier
- Saline eye solution to flush contaminants out of the eyes
- Thick gloves to use if a poisoned dog or cat's mouth must be forced open
- Muzzle to prevent a poisoned animal from biting at you in pain
- Mild detergent to wash contaminants off an animal's skin or coat

---

Keep dangerous household chemicals out of reach. This caveat has already been mentioned in an earlier chapter, but it doesn't hurt to repeat the theme.

Household chemicals can be harmful to animals as well as to people, and this does not simply include the more obvious chemical killers such as rat poison and plant or insect sprays. If a soap, polishing cream, or household detergent smells good, pets will usually try to eat it. At the same time, animals can become intoxicated by chemicals that to our sense of smell are repulsive. Every home has certain items on the shelves (such as hand soap) that if eaten by human beings are relatively harmless, but which make pets extremely sick. Finally, simply the odor from certain toxic chemicals can cause harm and even death to certain varieties of pet birds.

Thus a rule of thumb: If you have any doubts as to whether or not a particular household substance is poisonous to animals, err on the conservative side and keep it well out of reach. In fact, it is best to take the same precautions with household chemicals that you would for young children. Remember, neither young children nor pets can read labels.

Be mindful of climate control. Be certain that the heat and humidity in your pet's living area is carefully monitored and controlled. Tropical reptiles often require precise degrees of heat and dampness. Desert reptiles need a deep, dry heat to survive. In the wild, gerbils are desert animals and prefer a cage that is dry and warm, especially when they are young. Some pet fish thrive in room temperature water; others require artificial heating devices. If you have questions pertaining to climate control for your pet, consult your veterinarian.

Keep those checkups and vaccinations up to date. This is an obvious piece of advice, perhaps, but one that is all too often ignored. Most of us are pretty good about having a new baby ferret or puppy or kitten inoculated. But as the months and years roll on we get busy, and then we forget.

To avoid what one pet person refers to as "forgotten veterinarian syndrome," keep a record that lists all your pet's veterinarian visits and the type of health care received at each. A good deal more on the subject of receiving regular veterinary care will be covered in a section below.

Pay attention to health problems right away. Be alert for early signs of sickness. If your pet is shedding out of season, if he scratches constantly, if he becomes lethargic or uncharacteristically irritable, if he loses his appetite or seems out of sorts, don't ignore these signals. And don't assume they will go away on their own. They may not.

Getting a pet to the veterinarian at an early stage of illness can save your animal's life, and save you a lot of anxious hours. Better yet, be certain to bring your pet in for regular year-round checkups. Prevention, prevention, prevention.

Spay/neuter: Dogs, cats, ferrets, and rabbits all benefit from spaying or neutering. These practices also reduce or even entirely eliminate the possibility of some diseases.

Finding a Veterinarian

Visits to a veterinarian should start early in a pet's life. Indeed, it is recommended that you visit a veterinarian for a baseline exam within forty-eight hours after first obtaining your animal.

Following the initial exam, work out a schedule for regular follow-up visits. This way, when the time comes to seek serious medical help for your pet—and eventually the time *will* come—you will be dealing with a doctor that you know and who is familiar with your pet's personality and medical history.

What is the best way to find a good veterinarian?

Start by asking around among friends and associates. Do some detective work. Talk to local shelters, local veterinary associations, friends, and relatives. Sometimes regional shelters make veterinarian referrals. Local animal hobby clubs are a fertile resource for information and advice. Look around.

If access is not available for any of the above leads, your local yellow pages has plenty of listings. But use these untested sources *only* if all others fail. As with human medicine, word of mouth is the best way to find a doctor.

What to look for in a veterinarian

In many ways, the same benchmarks you might use when searching for a good physician can be applied to animal doctors as well. Ask yourself the following questions:

Does this veterinarian seem competent? Does he or she give the impression of being sure-handed, well informed, compassionate, patient, careful, professional?

Where did you hear about this veterinarian? From a friend or reliable source? From a professional referral? From a person you trust? What is the local word of mouth about this doctor's practice?

What fees does this doctor charge? Are they competitive with other veterinarians in the area? Be sure to ask about this on your first visit. Note, however, that it is not necessarily grounds for disqualification if one doctor's fees are higher than another's. Perhaps the more expensive veterinarian offers expertise, laboratory facilities, and medical specialties that the others are lacking. Whatever financial conclusions you ultimately come to, become familiar with a veterinarian's fee scale at the beginning, and use this information to help you make an informed decision.

Does the doctor seem hurried or overbusy? Is he or she overbooked? Is there an inordinately large number of people sitting in the waiting room? Are you and your pet forced to wait for long periods of time before entering the examining room?

Does the doctor take time to answer your questions? Does he or she ask *you* questions? Does he or she take a thorough medical history?

One of the really crucial things that will help you feel confident about a veterinarian is how well you and your veterinarian communicate. When visiting their offices, you should feel free to ask any questions that seem pertinent. Avoid doctors who make you feel hurried, ignored, or talked down to. You should also be able to understand the

---

Choosing a Veterinarian: A Quick Checklist

- Do you like the veterinarian and staff?
- Is the office clean, organized, pleasant to visit?
- Are you impressed with the veterinarian's knowledge and skill?
- Do you find the doctor easy to reach? Does he or she return phone calls? Is he or she covered after hours? Does he or she listen to what you have to say?
- What are the veterinarian's professional credentials? Are there specialists on the staff?
- Does the doctor handle your animal gently and with expertise? Does he or she give your pet a few moments to adjust to the strange surroundings before performing invasive tests and procedures?

---

answers you're getting back. You should be able to ask a question a second time if the first answer is not satisfactory.

Is the doctor's waiting room clean and well kept? Is there a foul odor when you walk in? Is there plenty of comfortable seating for people and their pets? How friendly and helpful is the receptionist? Does the office supply you with pertinent literature to help you understand your animal's problem? Does the doctor's staff perform adequate follow-up and booking for future appointments?

After several visits, do the doctor and receptionist recognize you? Does the doctor greet you and your pet by name? This last consideration may seem trivial, but it's not. A veterinarian who is familiar with a pet is also familiar with its personality and medical history.

Is this facility a full-service hospital? Which specific medical services does the veterinarian offer besides the basics? Are boarding facilities available? Grooming? Dentistry? Emergency treatment? Dietary counseling? Behavioral counseling? Ask about these services on the first visit.

On a personal level, do you like this veterinarian? Are you comfortable in his or her presence? Do you approve of the way he or she handles and relates to your pet? Does your pet respond positively to the veterinarian? Personal chemistry in the doctor's office is as important with animals as it is with humans.

How close is the doctor's office to your home? Do they offer twenty-four-hour service? Can you get there quickly in time of emergency? It's fine to use an out-of-the-area doctor for regular exams and vaccinations, but in time of accident or crisis it is reassuring to know that a competent veterinarian is just around the corner.

Some states have a local accreditation program. Does the veterinarian participate? What other significant affiliations does a perspective veterinarian have in the community? Inquire if the prospective veterinarian is affiliated with the American Animal Hospital Association (AAHA). The AAHA is a professional organization that sets guidelines for responsible veterinarian practice that all members are obliged to follow. If the doctor in question is associated with this organization that's a good sign.

Generalists and specialists

When a pet is sick your first stop is the generalist's office. If he or she is unable to diagnose the problem or to treat a particular disease, you may be referred to a specialist.

Note, by the way, that such referrals are not a sign of incompetency on the part of a veterinarian, only an indication of how complex and compartmentalized veterinary medicine has become over the years. Indeed, there are now almost as many fields of medical specialization for animals as there are for humans.

If your pet has a skin problem, for instance, referrals to an animal dermatologist may be in order. Loss of sight is best remedied by a veterinary ophthalmologist. Poor teeth require veterinary dentists; behavioral problems call for certified applied animal behaviorists or veterinary behaviorists. Equine veterinarians, reptile veterinarians, bovine veterinarians, veterinarians who specialize in the medical concerns of commercial enterprises such as salmon hatcheries and public aquariums, all are available when the need arises. The list of specializations in veterinary medicine is long and growing longer every year.

Veterinary medicine parallels human medicine as well in its use of technological advance. Like human medicine, it employs endoscopy, magnetic resonance imaging (MRIs), CATscans, ultrasound, electrocardiograms (EKGs), hormone assays, echocardiograms, sonograms, and more. Though most people do not realize it, some techniques regularly used today by modern medicine, such as hip replacement surgery, were first perfected in veterinary medicine.

Working with Your Veterinarian

When your pet shows signs of sickness, record all its symptoms right away. It is amazing how many important details you can forget by the time you reach the doctor's office, so be sure and write this information down on the spot. Animals do not always produce symptoms on demand, and unless certain behaviors are evident in the doctor's office your veterinarian may miss them.

Along with symptomatic information it is also a good idea to fill your doctor in on details of your pet's habits and home life. What noteworthy diseases or conditions has it suffered from in the past? What is its normal diet, including meats? If you own a cat, does it have a tendency to develop fur balls or to catch vermin? If a bird, are there signs that it compulsively plucks at its feathers? Is your animal neutered? When was it last in heat? How old is it? Is it delinquent on any of its vaccinations? Has it been acting in a strange way lately? If so, how?

Always keep your pet in a carrier or on a leash when visiting the veterinarian. Even if the animal is docile at home, the excitement of a new place, the presence of other animals in the waiting room, and the animal's compromised condition may conspire to produce fearful behavior. If your dog tends to snap or if your cat turns frantic in strange places, inform the veterinarian's assistant ahead of time so that suitable precautions can be taken. Or consider a veterinarian who makes house calls.

When medicines are prescribed, find out what each preparation is for, the best ways to administer it, and be fully informed concerning all dosage schedules. Even if a pet appears to be well after a week or more of treatment, be sure to continue complying with the dosage schedule. In a ten-day course of medication, missing even the last day can cause the condition to relapse. Before you visit a veterinarian ask whether urine or stool samples are required.

If you have questions, ask. If you want to know more while you're at home, call. A good working relationship between pet owners and veterinarians is a critical ingredient in helping animals get well and keeping them that way.

Financial Concerns and Pet Insurance

Veterinary services can be expensive, especially when the sophisticated medical treatments mentioned above are used. People accustomed to paying forty or fifty dollars for ordinary veterinary visits may suddenly find themselves looking at bills for several hundreds of dollars and sometimes thousands more when acute sickness or emergency strikes.

To cushion these financial shocks it is critical that you inquire about a veterinarian's rates *before* you decide to go ahead with any treatments and procedures. In cases where a specialist is needed, and complex, high-tech treatment is necessary, work out a payment schedule with your veterinarian ahead of time, if need be. A good veterinarian will explain the costs involved, and most are agreeable to designing monthly payment plans. Realize, however, that in many cases nothing more than a general estimate can be supplied, especially in cases where hospitalization is required.

As far as insurance and third-person payer plans go, in certain European countries pet insurance is a regular part of the landscape (57% of pets in Sweden are insured). Though only a small number of animal owners use this option in the United States, the idea is catching on, and there are more options available today than ever before.

Be aware, though, that pet insurance plans are not all the same. Some are excellent and cover a wide range of medical costs. Other are extremely restrictive and scarcely worth the cost. Before committing to a program read the prospectus carefully. Does the plan insure you for outpatient care? Surgery? Diagnostic tests? Medicines? Accident and emergency care? Neutering? Regular checkups and exams?

If the policy pays for a majority of these costs, does it cover them fully or partially? How partially? Some insurance plans advertise a wide range of coverage. But when (and if) you read the fine print, you discover that this coverage is less than 50 percent, or that it comes with an impossibly high deductible. Study and evaluate a pet insurance plan in the same way you would an insurance plan for yourself and your family. A representative list of pet insurance companies is provided in the appendix. Finally, ask your veterinarian about his or her experience with a particular insurance plan. Is this plan appropriate for you, your pets, and your veterinarian's care? Then decide.

The Warning Signs: When to Take Your Pet to the Veterinarian

When you or I get sick we report our symptoms to a physician.

Unfortunately, the only method animals have of describing their physical ailments is by means of body language and by their overt symptoms.

Happily, if pet owners learn to be on the alert for key behavioral patterns, these problems can usually be identified early on. Careful scrutiny helps us discern when our pets are healthy, when they are simply tired or stressed, and when they are seriously ill. These key patterns include activity level, appetite, bowel habits, vomiting, drinking, and urination.

Activity level

An animal's activity and energy level is the primary weather vane of well-being. If dogs, cats, ferrets, or rabbits begin to droop; if they move more sluggishly than usual; if they lose interest in the things that ordinarily excite and stimulate them; if they are apathetic to offers of attention, food, and play; if they frequently lie down and sleep more than usual; and if you observe dramatic changes in any of their basic behaviors, it is definitely time to take notice.

Appetite

Since most animals enjoy eating, a dramatic drop in your pet's appetite may be a behavioral red flag. The first signs of appetite loss are when pets fail to show up for meals at the regular hour, or when they sniff disinterestedly at their food and walk away. Be on the alert for abnormal increases in appetite. If pets frantically (and uncharacteristically) beg for food, or if they seem continually hungry, take note. They may have worms, or worse. Or the problem may be temporary stress. Keep the animals in question under observation until their normal appetite returns.

Bowel habits

Look for dramatic changes in an animal's bowel movements. A day or more of diarrhea or constipation may be a forerunner of disease. Blood in the stool is a potentially serious indicator. With smaller animals, pieces of feces constantly caking the anal areas often indicate trouble. Sick birds may display undue amounts of feces stuck to their feathers.

Vomiting

Though vomiting is an obvious sign that something is amiss, such behavior may simply be a sign that the animal has eaten something unsavory. Often the condition is temporary. If the vomiting continues for more than an hour or so, however, and if it seems particularly intense or if it becomes worse rather than better, be concerned.

Danger: Animal Diseases That Are Contagious for Humans

While most pet ailments are not contagious, a few are. Be especially careful of the following:

Salmonella.   Salmonella is a potentially serious bacterial ailment that causes food poisoning in humans. Many reptiles and amphibians carry the germ. Always wash your hands after handling.

Rabies.   One of the most lethal diseases known to man or beast, rabies is a viral infection carried in the infected animal's saliva. It is transmitted by a bite from the animal, or by contact with its saliva on an open wound. Report all suspected cases of rabies to local public health authorities immediately.

Cryptococcus neoformans.   A fungus found in the excrement of most pet birds, cryptococcus is harmless to avian carriers but can in a few cases cause meningitis and other serious diseases in humans. People with compromised immune systems such as those suffering from AIDS are especially vulnerable.

Leptospirosis.   Though rare, the spirochete bacterium that causes leptospirosis in dogs occasionally infects human beings as well through direct contact, causing fever, chills, and overall malaise.

Ringworm.   This annoying fungal skin disease is highly contagious and can easily be transmitted from animals to humans. Avoid contact with infected pets.

Intestinal parasites.   Under certain conditions (such as contact with the feces), roundworms, tapeworms, and hookworms can pass from pets to humans. Have all infected animals dewormed immediately, and keep your distance while they are infected. If children are in the house keep them well away from the animal's food and leavings.

Toxoplasmosis.   Though rare, this parasite can be transmitted to human beings through direct contact and is capable of producing birth defects in children in utero. Pregnant women should take all precautions.

Drinking and urination

Changes in an animal's drinking and urination patterns may signal ill health. Drinking too much or too little are both possible indications of disorder. The same if animals urinate with dramatically increased frequency or, conversely, if they seem to stop urinating entirely. Any major change in either of these patterns should be watched. If they persist for

more than a day or so seek help, especially if the animal has stopped urinating entirely, a potentially life-threatening situation.

The most effective way to spot any of these problems is to spend
time with your pet, and to become familiar with her personality, preferences, and eccentricities. Animals are creatures of habit. Even a small
deviation from their habitual daily rounds should be noted. If an animal
continues to show an abnormal pattern for more than a few days, seek
professional help. For a more specific list of symptoms see the specialized chapters.

Getting to Know Your Pet's Medications

Like all medications, animal drugs produce side effects.

A medication like steroids can sometimes cause increased urination.
Other drugs can induce malaise, skin rashes, vomiting, or diarrhea. The
list is long and sometimes dramatic. When such reactions occur pet
owners often think their pet is becoming sicker than before, when, in
fact, the vomiting is simply a reaction to the pill.

While at the veterinarian's office, make a point of asking about the
side effects and behavioral changes of a particular prescription or over-
the-counter drug. If your pet is already taking medication, inquire about
the possible complications of mixing more than one substance. Some
questions to ask include the following:

- Is the drug a sedative?
- Should you expect your pet to behave sluggishly for a few days?
- Is the drug a stimulant? A diuretic? Does it have narcotic proper-
  ties? Does it constipate? Does it reduce appetite? Does it cause
  nausea or vomiting or diarrhea?
- What are the typical drug reactions to look for?
- What should you do if they occur?

Some veterinarians will warn you about these responses in advance.
Others won't. It is best to simply ask. Likewise, become familiar with
the way your pet reacts to different delivery forms of medication. For
some animals, capsules are the most effective forms. Other animals tolerate pills or liquids best. If your pet has a bad reaction to a certain type
of delivery form, tell your veterinarian about this at the time of the visit.
It is entirely possible that another, equally effective form can be prescribed. If a pill or oral liquid must be given four times a day, but your

pet is a reluctant pill taker—or if the demands of life do not allow you to medicate on schedule—your veterinarian may also be able to prescribe a slow-release form of medication that cuts the number of doses in half. The same advice applies for poorly tolerated drugs. If your animal cannot keep a certain medication down, or if a medicine causes side effects, talk to your veterinarian about alternative solutions. In many instances another, equally effective drug can be used instead.

As far as helping a reluctant pet swallow medication, there are as many tricks as there are pets and pet owners. One of the most common methods is to place a pill or capsule into a pet's mouth, then briskly stroke its throat. Stroking stimulates the swallowing mechanism, and forces an animal to gulp. Another technique is to prepare animals long in advance for pill taking by rubbing their gums and mouth over the course of weeks and months. In this way, when the time comes for pets to take the medication, they are accustomed to having their mouth handled, and do not resist. A third option is to conceal medicines in a small, tasty treat. This process can be expedited by feeding pets a certain treat on a daily basis for some time. Pets grow accustomed to these rewards, and come to look forward to them. Then, when the day arrives for them to take their medicine, the pet owner hides the medicine in the treat, and the animal swallows it without hesitation. It is always a good idea to administer medicines in this way when the pet is especially hungry.

When liquids are prescribed, a syringe, eye dropper, or plastic squeeze bottle offers an ideal delivery system, and often helps solve the problem of clenched teeth. Some powders or granules can also be sprinkled or mixed into an animal's food, thus avoiding confrontations altogether. Check with your veterinarian to make sure that this method is appropriate.

Finally, as far as dosage schedules go, be sure and spread the times evenly throughout the day. This means, by way of example, giving a dose at eight o'clock in the morning, then at three o'clock in the afternoon, then at ten o'clock at night. If doses are grouped too close together during the day, this reduces their effectiveness.

Scheduling Regular Checkups

Different schedules for different pets

During the first year of life, human infants are taken to a pediatrician on a regular basis for shots and physical exams. The same routine should be followed for puppies, kittens, ferrets, and larger birds such as parrots.

After the first year pets are mostly grown, and checkups are advisable approximately once a year.

Finally, for older pets, especially those that suffer from chronic conditions, a physical examination is advisable every six months.

What about smaller pets?

With reptiles and fish, careful observation and proper husbandry provide the best medicine. Bird owners, especially those with exotic tropical specimens, will want to have their pet examined periodically by an avian specialist. While most pet owners do not take their gerbils or white mice to a veterinarian's office for regular examinations, some do. You may have to do some searching to find a doctor who specializes in your particular species of bird, reptile, fish, or small mammal.

Keep careful records

Most of us are busy people, and we often forget when and why we last brought our pets to the veterinarian. To keep this information current, it is suggested that you maintain a separate medical log for each pet in your household. No need to let this document become wordy or complicated. Simply record the basics of each visit: date, condition treated, vaccinations received, medication prescribed, recommendations made by the veterinarian, and so forth. Then store the log in a handy place.

While most veterinarians supply printed forms for the purpose, some pet owners like to have theirs tailor-made. To do this, create a template form, then make fifteen or twenty copies. Place these pages into a three-ring binder and label the binder. After each trip to the veterinarian jot down all pertinent information, using a new page for each visit. If you own several pets, compile a separate page for each animal.

A typical template page for recording visits to the veterinarian might look like this. It is suggested that you make several copies of this page and use it as part of your pet's medical records.

MEDICAL RECORD FOR _____

DATE OF LAST VISIT TO THE VETERINARIAN: _____

MEDICAL PROBLEM TREATED (IF ANY): _____

_____

_____

MEDICINES PRESCRIBED: _____

_____

_____

DOSAGE SCHEDULE: _____

_____

_____

VACCINATIONS: _____

_____

_____

DATE OF NEXT VACCINATION SCHEDULED: _____

SPECIAL DIETS RECOMMENDED: _____

_____

BOARDING INFORMATION: _____

_____

SPECIAL INSTRUCTIONS OR RECOMMENDATIONS: _____

_____

_____

DATE OF NEXT RECOMMENDED VISIT TO
VETERINARIAN: _____

NOTES:_____

_____

_____

Keeping track of vaccinations

When newly born, most mammals draw the immunological protection they need from the rich substance known as *colostrum* in their mother's milk. After weaning, the effects of this nourishing substance wane, and the wide world of infectious diseases now looms as a real threat. For this reason, pets should receive their initial series of vaccinations between the second and third month of life. The question of when to vaccinate, and for what, is based on an animal's specific risk ratio, which, in turn, is based on its age, medical record and health status, prevalence of local diseases, the geographical area inhabited, plus the veterinarian's own style of medicine.

Core and elective vaccinations

Puppies and kittens are considered fully vaccinated and immune at four months. For both dogs and cats there are two primary types of vaccinations: core and elective.

Core vaccinations provide vaccines that are medically necessary and in some states legally required.

Electives are given on an as-needed basis.

For a cat, core vaccinations come in a single broad-scope injection that includes feline distemper, rabies, and two upper respiratory diseases known as *rhinotracheitis* and *calicivirus*. Elective vaccines might include feline leukemia and feline infectious peritonitis (FIP). (See Chapter 8 for more information.)

For dogs, core vaccinations include canine hepatitis, canine distemper, parvovirus leptospirosis, parainfluenza, and rabies. Bordatella and Lyme vaccines are sometimes given as electives.

In general, veterinarians have different attitudes and philosophies concerning how often a pet should be vaccinated. Some prefer to vaccinate once every year. Others believe that a mature pet requires booster shots no more than once every three years. There are no absolutes in this area, and decisions must be made according to the variables of the pet's lifestyle. In some cases veterinarians will use an animal blood test to evaluate the level of disease-specific antibodies circulating in an animal's blood and will revaccinate if needed. With felines, for instance, it must be determined whether the cat is allowed outdoors on a leash or in a fenced-in backyard area, say, or whether it is exposed to other cats. Once such a profile is assembled and all the risks are evaluated, vaccination schedules can then be tailor-made to the animal's specific needs.

In general, therefore, it is best not to expect unanimity of opinion in the area of vaccination schedules. Because veterinarian number one suggests more shots, and veterinarian number two suggests fewer shots, do not jump to conclusions either way, thinking that veterinarian one is lax and two is greedy. Chances are they simply have different medical philosophies. The main point to keep in mind about vaccinations is that immunization technology is changing all the time, and that so many new vaccines are coming onto the market every year that it is increasingly difficult to be definitive. If you have any questions along these lines talk with your veterinarian directly.

The scoop on alternative medical therapies for pets

Once looked on with suspicion and even hostility by conventional doctors—and veterinarians—alternative therapies such as acupuncture, homeopathy, herbalism, acupressure, chiropractic, and others are today infiltrating the mainstream of Western healing on all levels. Many pet owners use these techniques not only as supplemental and elective resources but as first-line healing options.

Despite alternative medicine's growing popularity, however, a majority of pet owners have not availed themselves of alternative medicines, and many remain unconvinced. The questions they ask are, do alternate therapies really work? Can acupuncture really alleviate the symptoms of a dog's arthritis? Do herbal potions actually eliminate viruses in birds? Do chiropractic adjustments really cure hip dysplasia in dogs?

And the definitive, unequivocal, final answer is, It's difficult to say.

Why? Principally because funding for the study of alternate veterinary procedures is scanty, and to date few controlled experiments have been carried out to test their effectiveness. From a traditional veterinarian's viewpoint, it is risky business indeed to prescribe herbal remedies or acupressure touch therapy for an ailing pet, since these practices have not been clinically proven. The scientific principles behind such alternatives, they will also tell you, remain mostly unproven. Thus, for many veterinarians, the jury is still out as far as the effectiveness of alternative veterinary medicine is concerned.

On the other hand, anecdotal evidence celebrating the wonders of natural medicines abounds, and an increasing number of pet owners either combine natural therapies with standard therapies, or abandon the conventional fold entirely.

What then is the best way to proceed in the matter of alternative medicines?

With caution *and* an open mind.

As a broad rule, if you are receiving an inadequate response to medical care from local veterinarians, if one or more veterinarians have been unable to get to the heart of your pet's medical problem, and/or if you are chronically unhappy with conventional animal medicine in general, it may be time to give alternative therapies a chance.

Alternative therapies

Acupuncture. Acupuncture calls for the stimulation of certain points along an animal's "energy meridians." This stimulation directs and releases the energy flow, and thus helps the body heal itself. Among natural methods, acupuncture is probably the best known and most popular alternative method in use today.

Homeopathy. Homeopathy is based on what homeopaths call the law of similars: *like cures like*. What this means in a nutshell is that substances that produce harmful symptoms in a healthy animal can, when administered in microscopically small doses, cure this same set of symptoms in a sick animal.

Herbalism. The ancient art of herbalism has become extraordinarily popular in the past few decades. Most pharmacies now carry a range of these preparations, many of which are as useful for animals as they are for humans. Yet while some herbs do appear to cure sick animals, others can be harmful—even those that help human beings. It is therefore wise to consult with a veterinarian who practices herbalism before attempting home herbal treatment.

Chiropractic. The cause of most disease, chiropractors believe, both in animals and humans, is an incorrectly aligned spine. By "correcting" these misalignments and allowing inhibited nerve energy to move freely throughout the body, health is restored. Chiropractic is mainly popular today for use with horses, though it is applied to dogs and cats with increasing frequency.

Getting the most out of alternative therapies. Alternate therapies for pets are most valuable when used in conjunction with conventional medicine rather than in place of it. Though some natural medicine advocates take an all-or-nothing, this-or-that approach, the fact is that both healing systems have their place, and both can be of value in different situations. Rather than exclude one at the expense of the other, you may wish to avail yourself of both forms of medicine, and reap the double benefit.

For pet owners interested in taking the alternative medicine plunge, or at least in learning more about the subject, organizations that supply information, advice, and referrals are listed in the Appendix.

The ABCs of Emergency Care

Be prepared

There may come a time in the life of your pet when sickness or injury strikes, and when medical help is not immediately available. Though many pets live out their lives without encountering life-or-death situations, some do. It is best to be prepared for this event ahead of time, and to learn in advance which emergency steps to take until help is found.

The key to preparing for a medical emergency is knowing that the physiological systems of most mammals, such as dogs, cats, ferrets, and rabbits, work more or less the same way as our own. Like their human companions, mammals are warm-blooded. They have veins and arteries, digestive systems, hearts that pump blood, and lungs that breathe air. Thus, in times of emergency, many of the restorative procedures that work for human beings work for animals as well.

A severed artery spouting blood, for instance, can be controlled by applying direct pressure to the wound. An animal whose heart has stopped beating can be revived by cardiopulmonary resuscitation (CPR). An unconscious dog or cat responds to artificial respiration. A deep flesh wound calls for cleaning and bandaging. A broken limb heals better when splinted.

An important thing to remember in time of crisis is that if your pet is seriously injured, and you have no idea what to do, think human: perform the same life-saving procedures for the animal that you would perform for yourself or your family.

Making a first-aid kit for pets

The first step you can take to prepare for emergencies is to assemble a home medical kit, and keep it in a handy place at all times. The following items are all useful in time of emergency. Pick and choose the ones that seem most appropriate for your home situation and for your pet's needs:

Several sponges
A fresh washcloth
Three rolls of gauze wrapping
Several boxes of sterile gauze pads
Several rolls of different size adhesive tape—half-inch, one inch, two inches
Cotton balls, cotton Q-tips
Two Ace bandages
One bottle of hydrogen peroxide 3 percent (USP)
One bottle of alcohol
One bottle of mineral oil
One bottle of Kaopectate
One bottle of milk of magnesia
One container of activated charcoal tablets
One bottle of syrup of ipecac
Antibiotic ointment (ask your veterinarian for brand recommendations)
Ophthalmic ointment (ask your veterinarian for brand recommendations)
Tube of petroleum jelly
A good disinfectant soap
Sterile eyewash
Syringe or eyedropper (to give oral medications)
Styptic powder
Betadine solution
Rectal thermometer
Tweezers
Scissors
Muzzle
Vinyl exam gloves
Flashlight
Ball of twine
Jackknife

Place the above items in a box and keep them in a handy place. A large plastic Tupperware container makes an ideal storage kit, and can also be used to transport a small dog or cat in time of emergency. Do, however, make a point of remembering where you put the supplies.

There's nothing more daunting than carefully assembling a complete medical kit, then forgetting where you put it in time of crisis.

Dealing with common emergencies

The following emergency conditions require immediate first aid:

Poisoning
Stopped heart
Large, open wounds with much loss of blood
Deep bites
Broken limbs
Unconsciousness
Shock

Here, in a nutshell, is what to do for each of the above:

Poisoning

A recent survey shows that of all emergency situations among pets, poisoning is the most common. If you think your pet has ingested a toxic substance, do the following:

First, don't panic. Most poisons take a while to work.

Act purposefully and calmly. There is time to get help. A poison control center or your veterinarian will talk you through the process.

It is a good idea to locate the telephone number of a poison control center now, before an emergency occurs, then to keep it posted in a conspicuous place around the house. Bulletin boards or refrigerator doors are ideal. The ASPCA offers the following two poison control numbers for times of poison emergency:

1. **900-680-0000**—This ASPCA center does as many follow-up calls as are necessary for your situation, and at your request they contact your veterinarian.
2. **888-4ANI-HELP [888-426-4435]**—This ASPCA center does as many follow-up calls as are necessary in your situation, and at your request they contact your veterinarian. The center also faxes you specific treatment protocols and current literature citations when requested. Cost for services is forty-five dollars per call (calls to this number are charged to your credit card).

When calling a poison control center be prepared to provide the following information:

- Your name, address, and telephone number
- Generic or trade name of poison
- Information concerning the amount of poison ingested, the time it was eaten, and other significant circumstantial data
- The number of animals involved, and their species, breed, age, sex, and weight
- The symptoms your animal is experiencing
- Appropriate credit card information

Collect samples of the toxic substance the animal has eaten. Bring the container with you.

Cardiac arrest

If a pet's heart appears to have stopped beating, CPR clears airways and restores breathing as well for animals as it does for humans. Here's how to do it:

1. Lay the dog or cat on its side. Extend its head and neck, open its mouth, and check airways for blockage. Clear out any debris or lodged objects.
2. Close the animal's mouth and grip its muzzle firmly in one hand. Blow into its nostrils three times. Then push firmly on its chest with the other hand six times. In general, allow approximately two or three seconds to elapse between each push.
3. Alternate blowing into the animal's nostrils and pumping its chest at a rate of one breath per five chest compressions until normal breathing is restored.

Wounds and excessive bleeding

When wounded, even the most docile animal will bite, especially if you touch its wound or attempt to apply bandaging. Muzzling an animal is always appropriate when applying any type of first aid. If a muzzle is not available, gauze rolls or even panty hose will create a makeshift muzzle and keep the jaws tightly closed.

For smaller wounds, cut away all hairs around the wound if a pair of scissors is handy. Then flush with water and/or hydrogen peroxide.

Next, place a sterile gauze pad on the wound. Apply pressure until the bleeding stops or slows measurably. If the pad gets soaked through, place another on top. Do not remove the bottom pad; removing the pad may disturb the clotting process.

Wrap a roll of gauze around the pad over the wound several times, making sure not to pull the wrappings too tight. Secure the end of the wrapped gauze with tape, being careful not to let the tape stick to the animal's fur.

Seek medical attention immediately.

If an animal has a large wound with excessive bleeding, apply pressure to the wound with a sterile gauze pad. Pressure should be focused either directly onto the wound itself or several inches above it. As in human first aid, avoid using a tourniquet unless the animal is hemorrhaging severely. If a tourniquet is applied, it should be loosened for several seconds every ten minutes to avoid tissue damage (and even possible amputation) to the limb. Transport to the veterinarian immediately.

Bites

For severe bites, clean the wound carefully, trying not to hurt or startle the animal. At the same time, take precautions on your end to avoid being bitten or scratched. Muzzling an animal or swaddling it in a large towel are effective ways of keeping paws, teeth, and claws under control. If an animal's bite wound is especially deep, now is probably not the time to use ointment or disinfectant on the wound. Simply remove all obvious debris and contaminants from the damaged area, clean it, then take the animal to a medical facility. If there is profuse bleeding, apply firm pressure with a gauze pad until the flow is under control.

Broken limbs

Before transporting an animal with a broken bone to the hospital—but only if absolutely necessary—splint the wound. Incorrect splinting can make an injury worse, so be sure you know your animal first aid before attempting this technique.

If you do intend to splint a dog, first muzzle it. Then place the animal on the ground, positioned on the side opposite to the broken limb. Roll up two magazines or newspapers. Place one roll on either side of the broken limb, making sure to splint in the position the limb is found in. Cover the joints above and below the fracture site, then tape the entire splint from top to bottom, making sure the tape is secure but not too tight. Start the taping above the joint and work down until the entire limb is wrapped. Leave the animal's paw exposed.

Transport the animal to a veterinarian as quickly as possible.

Unconsciousness

If a dog or cat is unconscious, a number of causes may be to blame, including suffocation, a blow to the head, lack of oxygen, or electric shock. If, in fact, electric shock appears to be the cause of unconsciousness, check for wires that may still be in contact with its body first before touching and treating the animal.

Next, start applying artificial respiration.

Lay the animal on its side. Extend its head and neck, and make sure its airway is clear. Place your hands on either side of its chest and apply quick, firm, pushing motions.

Perform these motions approximately fifteen to twenty times per minute. Count to yourself as you push, allowing three or four seconds between each compression. A good trick is to match the number of compressions to the number of your own exhalations. Be careful not to push too hard. At the same time, push hard enough. A few practice strokes give you the feel.

If this manual method does not work, close the animal's mouth, hold it firmly shut with both hands, and blow air into its nostrils for three seconds. Stop for two seconds, then blow again for three seconds. Continue until the animal begins breathing. Seek medical care immediately.

If an animal has inhaled a large amount of water, hang it upside down, open its mouth, and allow the water to drain. Then begin CPR immediately. You will know the procedure is working when water and perhaps vomit dribble from its mouth, and when it appears to breathe regularly.

Shock

Immediately following a severe accident most animals, like most human beings, go into a state of shock. You can identify this condition by several important and obvious symptoms. These include the following:

- Low body temperature
- Dazed, apathetic behavior
- Pale whitish colored gums
- A glazed look in the eyes

- Disordered pulse (either too fast, too slow, weak, or thready)
- Panting or shallow breathing

As many animals die from shock following an accident as they do from the injury itself. The seriousness of this condition should not be minimized.

To treat shock, keep the animal quiet and comfortable. Cover it with a blanket or coat. Warmth is important. Talk reassuringly to the animal, but avoid excessive petting or handling. If the animal vomits, be sure it does not swallow or choke on the detritus. Avoid giving food and water, even if the animal appears hot, dry, or thirsty. Seek medical help immediately.

Methods of emergency transportation

It's a good idea to devise a transport plan in advance for home emergencies. If you have access to an automobile, transportation is usually not a problem. For those without access to a vehicle, a bit of thinking ahead may mean the difference between life and death.

First, determine if there is a local taxi service that takes pets.

Write the number down and keep it in your emergency medical kit.

Does a friend, relative, or neighbor own a car? Can you gain access to it on short notice? What about buses or subways? How often do they run? Do you have schedules? If not, get one and keep it with your first-aid kit. Though public transport is certainly not the ideal way to transport a pet to the hospital, sometimes it is the only option.

If a dog has been struck by a moving vehicle, place it on a blanket or towel as gently as possible. Make sure its airways are open, then transport it to emergency care. If a blanket or towel is not available, a flat board or even a piece of cardboard will do. With a small animal like a cat or rabbit, the large plastic container you store your first-aid equipment in makes an excellent medium for transportation. Tuck a blanket or towel into the container, place the animal inside, and carry it to the hospital. During the journey be sure that the animal is comfortable and that it is not moved unnecessarily.

Again, when handling a wounded animal, especially a dog, be wary of biting and snapping. The animal is in pain and stressed.

Finally, the most important step you can take in time of emergency is *do not delay*. Perform whatever on-the-spot first aid is necessary to keep the animal alive, then rush it to medical care. If possible, have someone call ahead to let your veterinarian know you are on your way with an emergency. As with human beings, minutes and even seconds are critical when a pet's life hangs in the balance.

If you have any question concerning whether an animal's condition is an emergency or not, opt on the conservative side and assume it is. Apply the appropriate first aid, then get medical help immediately. The least that should be done in such situations is to call a veterinarian and describe the animal's symptoms. At best this call will save your pet's life, and at worst it will save you an unnecessary trip to the veterinarian.

Pet Care for the Changing Seasons

Spring and summer

As far as fleas are concerned, the first thing to find out is whether they are a problem at all. Take your pet outside or position it near a window under a strong, direct light. Rub your hand across its fur, looking for crawling creatures, or for small, black, comma-shaped deposits on the skin (these are flea dirt and excreta). In a heavily infested animal you will see the tiny creatures scurrying along beneath the hairs. Another excellent method of flea detection is to place the animal on a piece of white paper and comb it with a flea comb. As you groom, check for flea dirt on the paper.

Fleas gather on the warm, protected sections of animals—the head, stomach, and especially on the back rear and the tail. An animal overrun with these creatures scratches, burrows, and itches so incessantly that bald patches eventually appear on the skin. Sometimes an allergic reaction may also set in. An abnormally large infestation, especially in a very young animal, causes lethargy, fever, and anemia, which may result in death. Though it appears minor, incessant itching is not a condition to ignore.

Flea collars are the most popular form of protection against infestation, but also the least effective. Some experts claim they are of no value at all. You can provide home treatment for fleas too, but you may go through several over-the-counter medications before you hit on one that works. Better to avoid the experimentation by seeking expert advice from the start. Your veterinarian can provide you with an arsenal of proven weapons against flea infestation, including dips, shampoos, pills, powders, oils, topical drops, and special combs and brushes.

During the warmer months certain animal diseases become especially rampant. If you live in an area where heartworm is a problem, start your dog or cat on heartworm preventive medication in the early spring. Like human beings, pets also develop allergies to plant products like grass, pollen, and flowers, with symptoms that include itchy skin, sneezing, and runny eyes. If your pet is prone to allergies, speak to your veterinarian concerning appropriate medication. Animals that are especially sensitive to allergens may be placed on a protective low-dose, alternate-day steroid program during pollen season.

Fall and winter

Walks should usually be brisker now, and at the same time shorter, especially for animals that are sensitive to the cold. Dry, cold weather combined with indoor heating systems have a parching effect on animals' skin. Check your pet's coat periodically for scaling and rashes, and check with your veterinarian to determine whether fish oil supplements are helpful for your pet's flaking skin condition.

Especially troublesome to dogs in the colder months are salt-based chemicals that are used to melt snow on sidewalks and roads. Be careful where and when you walk your dog, and if salt is unavoidable consider placing boots on your dog's paws. When you return home, wash your pet's paws to remove all traces of salts and chemicals. Many pet supply stores carry nonirritating snow melting products for home driveways and sidewalks. For shorthair, young, underweight, old, and sensitive dogs, outerwear may also be appropriate on cold days.

Special Health Concerns for the Older Pet

As your pet grows older and begins to develop the aches and pains that come with age, an increase in the number of routine checkups is in order. For an elderly dog or cat, which generally speaking is over ten years of age, at least two checkups a year are recommended, one in the spring, one in the fall. Health concerns that rarely affect younger pets now become major points of focus as the animal ages. Such factors as circulation, cardiac vigor, kidney function, blood sugar level, joint health, and cognition are central concerns. Keeping watch on these vulnerable areas is part of any good health-care maintenance plan.

As an animal matures look for signs of developing chronic or degenerative diseases. Changes in behavior may signal ailments that should be attended to now, while they are still in the manageable stage. If elderly animals begin to bump into the furniture or knock over the lamp, this may indicate eye problems, loss of sight, or impaired cognition. Frequent urination is often a sign of kidney problems, a very common condition in older pets. If dogs or cats make pained noises or show reluctance when climbing stairs or getting up from a nap, arthritis may be setting in. Lack of appetite or constipation often indicates digestive problems.

Stay alert to these behavioral signs and report them to your veterinarian when they occur.

When an older pet develops chronic ailments, adjustments to its living space help keep it out of harm's way. If a pet is wobbly on its feet from joint disease, add nonskid backing to your rugs and avoid using slippery waxes on hard floors. If a cat is having difficulty with bowel control, position several litter boxes around the house in areas it commonly frequents. This way the cat has a shorter distance to travel when the urge comes, and accidents are avoided.

An older animal with arthritis may need a softer bed to cushion its joints. A pet that shivers constantly will find relief in a sweater. An animal that is going blind needs to be walked on a short lead; it may also need a smaller space with food, water, and bed consistently located and within easy reach. While walking a dog with hearing problems, remember that it can no longer respond to your commands. Make the appropriate adjustments.

As a rule, older animals do not adapt well to change. If you are having a dinner party, or if numbers of people are visiting your home, the onslaught may be confusing and disturbing to an older pet. Avoid the situation by putting the animal in a separate room until your guests have left. On the other hand, if an older pet still thrives on interaction and attention, by all means, include it in your social gatherings.

Older dogs may also find walking difficult, and they quickly tire. When this occurs, shorten the length of the walks, and let the animal set their own pace. At the first sign of fatigue, head home. Never push an older animal to stretch its physical limits. The "no pain, no gain" philosophy clearly does *not* apply to older pets.

At the same time, a sensible exercise regimen is helpful for older animals, and it should be part of every elderly pet's routine.

Swimming is the ideal exercise for dogs, though finding a suitable body of water is not always an option. Otherwise, regular walks, chasing balls, romping with other dogs or cats, playing vigorously with toys, and leisurely jogs keep elderly animals fit. If your pet's joints are compromised, confine exercise sessions to soft, grassy areas, and keep away from hard-surfaced tarmacs, playgrounds, sidewalks, and paved areas. *Low-impact* is the watchword here.

As far as an older animal's diet goes, it is essential to keep them lean and trim. Statistically speaking, overweight pets have almost twice as high a chance of developing heart and kidney ailments as those that maintain their weight (once again we see the parallel between the animal world and the human).

Special foods for senior pets are available at pet supply stores. These contain lower fats and protein, and higher amounts of fiber, so that an animal's digestive organs have an easier job breaking down nutrients. There are also special mixtures for animals with kidney problems, heart trouble, diabetes, and others. Most of these special foods must be obtained directly through a veterinarian. Ask your doctor which diet best suits your older pet's needs.

Note also that if you switch pets to a special menu, it's best to ease them into it over a several-week period, unless directed otherwise. Sudden and dramatic dietary changes are upsetting to older animals' digestive tracts and can trigger nausea and vomiting.

An older pet may require extra vitamins, plus careful feeding. When young, dogs eat anything on the horizon and have no trouble getting it down. While their appetite may not languish in the later years, their stomach's ability to process rich foods does, and it's important not to feed them greasy, fatty, or sugary treats—ever. Foods that are high in fat can trigger pancreatitis in older animals, a potentially fatal ailment.

Older animals may spend a good deal of time by themselves, and they may remain sleeping or stretched out for long periods of time. They show less interest in meals and sometimes avoid them entirely. They hide under the bed. They sit hunched over much of the time. They seem to be in constant pain, displaying a wide-eyed look with their pupils slightly dilated. They even appear indifferent to your affections. At times, they snap when you come too near.

If elderly pets begin to behave in these ways, honor their needs. For many years your pet has been a faithful friend. Now the time has come for you to loosen the bonds and to say farewell. Help pets make the transition by rendering them as comfortable as possible in their last days, by being there when they need you, and most of all, by letting go gracefully when that saddest and most final of all moments finally arrives.

Saying Good-bye:
Grieving for a Pet

Grief: The Universal Human Emotion

The heartbreak we feel over the death of a loved one transcends all social and psychological boundaries. Anyone who has experienced it automatically understands this feeling in others. Grief, it turns out, comes as close to being a universal human emotion as any we know.

But are all losses the same? Does it hurt as much to lose a favorite dog or cat or bird as it does to lose a parent or spouse? Can we—should we even—make such a comparison?

The answer many people give to this question is a definite *no*. They tell you that sorrow over the death of a favorite pet and sorrow at the passing of a human companion are of an entirely different order. To compare these two experiences, they say, is frivolous, even irreverent.

This is how such a question might be answered by those on the outside.

But for those on the inside, those who have lived with a beloved pet for ten or fifteen years, and who now must say good-bye, the truth appears in quite a different light. These people know that the devastation felt at the loss of a close companion, whoever or whatever that companion happens to be, cuts across conventional distinctions and overrides emotional shoulds and should nots. Grief is grief, they know, no matter what the object of mourning happens to be.

And since grief is grief, many mental health professionals now recognize that the sadness felt at the death of a beloved companion animal goes deep indeed, and that it produces powerful and sometimes debilitating effects on mourners. Such emotions should by no means be minimized, bereavement counselors caution, either by those experiencing them or by that person's friends and relatives. These feelings are real and strong. They must be addressed with the same concern used for any other type of significant loss. They must be heeded.

And the first step mourners can take in this direction is to recognize the rhythms and sequence of the grief process itself.

Stages of Grief

The year 1965 saw the publication of Elisabeth Kübler-Ross's groundbreaking book, *On Death and Dying.* Originally written to define the stages terminally ill people pass through from the moment they learn they are terminal to their final moments of life, Kübler-Ross's work has been applied to many other charged situations since this time, one of them being the grieving process itself. Though experts have criticized Kübler-Ross's methodology, many professionals still consider it to be one of the most apt blueprints ever devised for understanding what people go through in a state of loss.

The following sequence of stages, based on Kübler-Ross's formulation, is common to the bereavement process in general and to grieving for a pet in particular. Though arranged chronologically, these stages must not necessarily follow one another in sequence, and it is perfectly possible to experience several of them at once. At the same time, there are few people who do not encounter one and often two or three of these reactions during the course of their grieving time.

The stages of grief, as defined by Elisabeth Kübler-Ross and applied to a pet loss scenario, are as follows.

Denial

When the moment of death comes for a pet something in us does not want to believe it. Rationally we know that the animal has left the world, that it will not pass this way again. But something in us refuses to accept this fact.

When taken to extremes, denial can be psychologically disruptive, not only to the person experiencing it, but to friends and family as well.

Yet though denial is a potentially troublesome trait, it has a protective function as well, especially for those who find the pain of death just too difficult to bear. In an act of emotional self-protection, these people temporarily "shut down," refusing to believe what their experience tells them is true. This temporary skewing of the truth helps cushion the blow, lessen the pain, and allows a person time to process what has taken place. Like all of the stages of grief, denial has a healing side as well as a withering one.

Anger

It isn't fair! It's not right! My pet still had years of life ahead of it! Why did this have to happen!

Or: "That stupid driver, if he'd been watching where he was going Rufus would be alive today!"

Or: "That idiotic vet, she bungled the whole operation!"

Anger at fate, at others, at the fact that a beloved animal companion has been snatched away from us in the midst of life, is a symptom of grief that can occur at any time during one's mourning process. Sometimes this anger can get out of hand. But usually it has a releasing effect, like opening the valves and letting off steam.

If and when anger comes, don't be surprised by its suddenness or dismayed by its intensity. It is a natural and inevitable reaction to loss, the ego's way of releasing negative energies that build up from too much sorrow and frustration. It is an inherent—and vitally necessary—part of getting it all out and getting better.

Bargaining

Bargaining takes place when an animal is sick and little hope remains for recovery. Stricken pet owners call on whatever higher force they choose—God, fate, their inner spirit—for more time, for a remission, for a miracle, for a cure. In return they pledge to improve their life, to donate money to a charity, to behave better to others.

Bargaining is a kind of rearguard action, an attempt to postpone the inevitable with prayers, petition, or sheer efforts of will. Though sometimes irrational, it is nonetheless a natural human response to the helplessness that sickness and death bring, an attempt to grasp a modicum of control in a powerless situation.

Depression

Depression often comes later on in the grieving process, after denial, fury, and negotiations with fate have failed to cure an animal or bring it back to life. In Kübler-Ross's terms, the bereaved person goes from saying, "Not my pet!" to "Yes, my pet!" It is as if all the trump cards have been played, and one has still lost the match. The depression that follows is a consequence of this undeniable loss.

Depression is perhaps the most common reaction to the death of a pet, and all mourners feel its effects in one form or another. On the other hand, if pet owners find themselves caught in a repeating cycle of anger and depression that lasts an inordinately long period of time, say several months or more, professional help may be in order.

Acceptance

Grief felt at death is a powerful emotion, probably the most powerful of *all* emotions we're ever forced to bear. When one is in its grips it feels as if the pain will simply never go away.

But eventually it does. Be assured: it does.

When this lessening occurs, a new and positive feeling of acceptance fills the space inhabited by our hurt emotions. Now at last one faces the fact of the pet's passing without undue sorrow or regret. A certain sadness lingers, and this is as it should be. But the sadness is no longer oppressive or debilitating. It is a memory now and a fine memory. It deserves a place in our hearts.

Each person grieves in a different way, and your own personal style may or may not include all the stages mentioned above. Still, the chances are strong that you will pass through at least one or more of these stages. When you do, know that they are all part of an identifiable emotional mechanism, and that each stage, in its own way, ultimately contributes to an ultimate sense of relief and release.

Giving Yourself Permission to Grieve

Pet owners feel an uncomplicated intimacy with their pets, a closeness they cannot explain but which other pet owners understand entirely. Free of the ego tensions that confound human relationships, a primal exchange of love flows between human and animal without barriers or defenses, transcending the boundaries of species and kind. Pet owners who experience this bond find that the death of their pet is also the death of certain unique feelings that somehow cannot be duplicated in the human world. The pain that results from this deprivation is great indeed.

Yet despite the immensity of these feelings, mourning an animal is not a socially sanctioned activity in our society, and it is thought by some to be maudlin and self-indulgent. "Get a hold of yourself!" one pet owner was told when crying over the death of her adored German shepherd. "Think of what people are going through who've lost their children, their spouse, their parents. They're the ones who have the real right to grieve!"

Yet as men and women have interacted with farm animals over the eons, a large part of their brains evolved that was specially dedicated to the human–animal bond. Animals have always been highly important to us not only for our pleasure but for our work, our food, our survival. Without them the human race might have perished. As a result of this relationship, there is a part deep in every man and every woman that is psychologically linked to our animal companions. The relationship between us and the animal kingdom is, some experts believe, wired into our brains.

In modern industrial society we do not depend on animals as much as we once did in past eras. As a result, we are socialized to ignore the human–animal bond in a way that might have surprised and even alarmed our ancestors. A two-year-old child thinks he can talk to a dog. Then his mother comes along and says, "No, Johnny, you can't talk to the dog. The dog does not understand what you're saying. It's only a dumb animal." Johnny then comes to think of his dog as stupid and unreachable, and in the process loses his chance to tune into the age-old human–animal kinship.

And yet, this animal–human bond still functions deep in our brains whether we're aware of it or not. For some people it is more accessible than others. These are the people who feel the death of the animal most profoundly. That deep evolutionary part in them is still very much alive. These are the people who really grieve and who *need* to grieve for a pet. No one should ever try to belittle their response or take their grieving away.

What advice do pet bereavement experts offer for dealing with the embarrassment and censure people sometimes feel when mourning a pet?

First, they suggest, realize that your "overreacting" is not an overreaction at all. The world is wrong about this. What you're going through is neither an overreaction nor an underreaction. It is *your* reaction, *your* feelings, *your* sadness over the death of *your beloved pet*. You have a right, even a mandate, to feel these feelings.

Realize also that grief has its own timetable, and that this schedule may not jibe with your wishes or even more, with the wishes of others. Let's face it, our grieving is often a bore to family and friends. Your children, your partner, your business associates will want you to have a good cry, a few days of sadness and then to get on with it. Especially since you are "only" grieving for a dog or cat, a bird or a ferret. Be prepared for this reaction. More than likely it is the response you will encounter from others.

Remember too that deep psychological loss is the equivalent of a physical wound. Like a major injury, this wound takes a great deal of time to stop bleeding, to close up, to heal, to scar over. Think of the months and even years it takes a massive body wound to get better. Then realize that there is a parallel between physical injury and the emotional injury felt at the death of a pet.

Finally, there is an especially difficult burden to endure when we feel guilt-stricken over the fact that we are grieving more intensely over the loss of a pet than we did, say, for our grandmother or even for our parents. This realization can be devastating. "What kind of person am I?" mourners ask themselves, "if I have more feelings for an animal than for my own loved ones, for my own next of kin? What's wrong with me?"

But again, things are not as they appear.

In such cases grief therapists often reassure people that as far as grief is concerned there is no graded hierarchy of feelings. There is no law that says you are supposed to feel X amount of grief for one type of death, Y amount for another. Such emotions cannot be measured and compared. If you try you will end up confusing and even tormenting yourself.

Therapists tell us that the animal–human relationship is unique, and that it is probably processed in a different part of our brains, in a different neurological substage. They tell pet owners that when a beloved pet dies they are likely to undergo a very strong emotional reaction, and that they should not be surprised if these emotions are more intense than those felt, for example, over the death of a parent or good friend. Such disparity of feelings does not mean one is a poor friend or a bad person. A relationship with an animal is less conflicted than a human relationship. It is easier to feel a direct kind of grief when an animal dies. Easier than it is to feel grief for the more complex and sometimes more conflicted relationship you might have had with a parent or a spouse.

And remember too: you don't measure how much you love a person by how much you cry at their funeral. Some people do not cry at all when someone close to them dies. They feel beyond tears, beyond overt displays of emotion. But inside they are crushed. That same person may mourn a pet with lavish displays of feeling. When the mourning is over, however, they are purged and get on with their affairs. The death of a parent or close friend, on the other hand, leaves impressions and a sadness that lasts forever. Whatever emotions you feel are okay. Just accept them, work through them. Then heal—and move on.

Ways of Saying Good-bye

Holding a formal ceremony

Psychologists and grief counselors generally agree that pet owners can draw a great deal of consolation by arranging farewell ceremonies for a deceased pet, and that in most cases, unless the animal is mutilated or decomposed, it is psychologically helpful to view the body before disposal.

Friends and relatives may, of course, disagree. They may tell you that viewing a pet's body will be too painful, especially for children, or that it's better to remember Spot as he was, healthy and whole.

Perhaps. The fact remains that when an animal companion passes away, those left behind require a sense of closure before they can begin to put the event behind them. Societies around the world have known for centuries that viewing a body is an effective rite of passage, a last moment of recognition that palpably helps the process of letting go. It doesn't matter what form these viewing rituals take, just as long as they accomplish their goal.

Viewing or not viewing at these sessions is, of course, an entirely personal choice. The human mind being what it is, however, a few days after seeing the corpse the mental picture of the dead animal fades and is invariably replaced by happier images.

In a number of cases, of course, traditional religions draw a line between humans and animals. They insist that from a theological point of view animals have no souls. Thus they should not be given death rites like humans. Yet at the time of loss, mourners may be deeply invested in the idea of an afterlife, and are comforted by the notion that someday they will be reunited with this pet in another world. Unfortunately, there is a social stigma in churches against voicing these ideas. Some congregations, it is true, are beginning to make reference to the grief that a member may be feeling over the death of an animal. A few churches in larger cities even have special days when animals are invited into the church for special services. But this is rare.

An alternative to church is holding a ceremony of one's own for the deceased animal. This ceremony can take any format you like—a memorial, a graveside interment, a full-blown funeral, whatever serves the purpose. Participants are encouraged to write a letter to the animal and read it during the proceedings. Children can draw pictures or make artwork to place in the grave with the animal. Music is welcome at such events. Refreshments afterwards are a good idea. During the ceremony someone may wish to speak about the pet, reminisce, share their memories, and help to close the circle. Such ceremonies are based on the same principles that inform any human funeral—people getting together, saying good-bye to a dear friend, and comforting one another.

Other grieving aids and supports

What other practices help mourners deal with the death of a pet?

Anything that provides a sense of comfort, security, and remembrance. Popular bereavement methods that are comforting to grown-ups and children alike include the following:

- Light a candle every day for a week or so in memory of the pet at a local church. Some pet owners keep a candle permanently lit in their homes, a kind of "eternal flame."
- Plant a tree in your backyard. Start a flower bed in the pet's name. Plant a vegetable garden.
- Give money in a pet's name to a favorite animal society or charity.
- Make a plaque commemorating your pet and keep it in plain view in your home or yard. A plaque can be made by carving initials in wood, crafting letters in ceramics, creating a page of calligraphy, and so forth.
- Draw a picture of your pet or frame a photo and keep it on display.
- Do volunteer work at a local pet hospital or animal facility in honor of the pet. Work at an animal shelter several days a week.
- Keep a journal during the mourning period recording feelings, thoughts, memories, and impressions.

- Start a scrapbook of pictures and mementos of your pet.
- Visit your pet's resting place on a regular basis. The International Association of Pet Cemeteries honors the second Sunday in September as National Pet Memorial Day. Make this visiting day an annual event.
- If you are religious, remember to include a prayer for your companion animal each time you pray.

Methods of Burial and Disposal

There are several alternative ways to dispose of a deceased animal.

Cremation

A local disposal company or animal shelter in your area (or a pet cemetery if you choose this option—see below) will take care of the details here. Staff members of these organizations come to your home, remove the body, and make arrangements with the crematory. Your vet or local shelter will guide you to a reputable agent. Arrangements can also be made with a disposal company to have the pet's ashes returned after cremation for keeping or scattering. This option usually entails further expense.

Most crematories dispose of a number of animals at once, which means your pet's ashes will be mixed with those of other animals. Unlike human cremation ovens, which are fired at an extremely high flame and which transform remains into a powdery ash, animals are burned at low temperatures, the result being that large bone fragments are mixed with the ashes. These fragments rattle and clatter noisily in the urn that holds your pet's "cremains." If children are involved, it is an excellent idea to warn them in advance of this potentially disturbing fact.

Burial

The second pet disposal option is burial, with the place of rest being any legal and accessible rural location. Place the animal's body in a wooden or cardboard box or a heavy-grade plastic bag. Some people prefer burlap or heavy cloth bags because they are degradable. The grave should be at least three feet deep to protect the body from animal scavengers. It should be placed at least ten feet away from a well or public water source.

The type of memorial used to mark a pet's grave is bounded only by a person's imagination. One family used a freshly cut log with the animal's name chiseled onto it. Another placed a small cement statue of a cat on the grave. Another made an attractive pile of rocks as a headstone. As far as marking a pet's grave goes, the choice is a personal one.

Pet cemeteries

Still another option is the animal cemetery. Once a controversial and even snickered at rarity, pet cemeteries are found in towns and cities across the country today and are becoming increasingly popular. For some people the trimmed lawns and tended sites provide an appropriate resting place for their beloved animal. Pet owners find visiting these parklike settings a great comfort.

Interment in a pet cemetery is done either by private plot or communal plot. In a private plot the animal's body is placed in a single grave or crypt. In communal interment, a number of animals, not necessarily of the same species, are buried together under the same headstone. Private plots are a good deal more expensive than group.

Make inquiries in advance concerning costs and services before committing to this alternative. Pet cemeteries are expensive, and the quality of grave upkeep varies from site to site. Be sure that the cemetery is located on "dedicated ground," which means the property can never be commercially developed or used for any purpose other than animal interment. Also inquire whether perpetual care is offered, or whether there is a time limit on the number of years (or months) the grass and plantings on your pet's site are tended. For further information on all aspects of pet cemeteries call the International Association of Pet Cemeteries at (800) 952-5541.

Rendering

Rendering is a term that describes the processing of an animal's body into commercial products such as fertilizer or food. We think of cows, pigs, and barnyard animals in this regard, but the bodies of dogs, cats, and horses also have their commercial and sometimes chemical uses. Pet owners who wish to see a pet's remains recycled and put to further ecological use may find this alternative to their choosing. Your veterinarian or a local animal shelter can advise you on the availability of a rendering program in your local area.

Taxidermy

Taxidermy is becoming a popular method of pet disposal today and is practiced widely across the United States, especially in the West. Pet owners availing themselves of this option are advised to make arrangements well in advance. This way, when the time comes, their pet's body does not have to be preserved for lengthy periods of time while owners search for available taxidermists.

The ABCs of Grief Work

What further steps can the owner of a newly deceased pet take to cope with the days and weeks of sadness that lie ahead? What practical means can be applied to work through the rigors of bereavement?

The following methods, based on techniques suggested by animal behaviorists and at grieving centers across the country, have helped countless pet owners in the past and are frequently suggested by counselors who specialize in the field of grief.

Take care of yourself physically during the mourning period

Studies show that men and women who live through the death of a loved one tend to become sick, sometimes seriously sick, more often than those who have not experienced loss. The reason for this reaction, experts believe, is that grief depresses our physiological functions, especially the immune system. Once this important line of defense is weakened, vulnerability to disease, to depression, and even to accidents and strange mishaps becomes heightened. Statistics show that people who are in mourning become ill more easily than nonmourners and recover from their illness far more slowly.

It is thus imperative that grievers think in terms of *wellness and prevention*. This means maintaining a proper diet, drinking enough liquids, watching one's weight, exercising regularly, taking a balanced regimen of vitamins and supplements, getting enough sleep, avoiding excessive use of intoxicants, tobacco, and sedatives, avoiding stressful situations whenever possible—the same measures one takes to stay fit in normal times. Remember, when you are in a state of mourning you are also in a state of heightened physical risk. Take precautions. Stay well.

Talk it out

Keeping strong feelings padlocked inside leads to side effects, both mental and physical. Avoid what one person referred to as "the ticking bomb syndrome" by giving verbal expression to your grief and by talking about the things you're thinking and feeling.

Find a sympathetic person to spend quality time with. Let it out. Get it out. Don't worry if you hear yourself telling the same story over and over. If it makes you feel better, do it. Your job now is to work through the grief in whatever ways you can. If others are willing to help, to listen, to suggest, to inform, let them.

The most helpful people to talk with are usually pet owners who have been through what you're going through and who understand the process from the inside. You will find that friends or family members are not necessarily the most effective supports at this time. Friends you thought you could rely on in time of emotional turmoil may be unwilling—or unable—to give you the advice you need and the support you crave. Instead, a neighbor up the street or a casual acquaintance at work turns out to have gone through what you're going through and to have a real understanding of how the process works. If this is the situation, fine. Use whatever resources you have at your disposal. Whatever you do, don't keep it bottled up. Talk it out and let it out as often as you can.

Avoid making major decisions for a few weeks

Although it may not be apparent, a person's judgment is often clouded during the early days of grieving. It's thus a good idea to refrain from making substantial life changes during the first few weeks after a pet's death and to postpone all important decisions: domestic moves, job changes, financial planning, and so forth. Wait a few weeks until your grief lessens and your head clears. Then proceed as usual.

Don't be alarmed if you lose interest in life for a while

During bereavement our passion for life becomes diminished and our spirits depressed. A similar process takes place in times of intense stress, in sickness, or when passing through difficult episodes of change. Don't panic. The passion for expressing yourself and enjoying yourself will return, probably quite soon. In almost all cases this condition is a temporary one.

Recognize that grief comes in waves

It's eight o'clock in the morning and you're feeling fine, ready to meet the day. You accept the death of your beloved pet, and are ready to get on with things. At ten o'clock you find yourself dissolved in tears. "I can never live without Smokey," you tell yourself. "I'll never see him again!" By lunchtime you're OK again. At three in the afternoon you go to the lavatory and have a good cry.

And so on.

If you find yourself on an emotive roller-coaster ride during the day, up one hour, down the next, don't think you're abnormal or that you're losing your mind. You're not. Grief comes in waves. Bear in mind also that when you're sad and grieving there is a tendency to think you will remain sad forever. Then when suddenly, inexplicably, the gloom lifts you think the sadness will never return. Human emotions know only the present moment. The fact of the matter is though, that during the bereavement period neither the sadness nor the relief are permanent fixtures. Both return in waves, then pass again. It's all part of the rhythm of grieving.

Give it time

Grieving takes time. There is no escape from this reality. When an animal that was an integral part of your life passes away, it may take weeks and perhaps months to make the appropriate emotional, psychological, and even social adjustments. Don't be impatient with yourself if you are still distressed after two weeks or a month or even several months. Your pet died in June and you find yourself mourning in September. Fine. This simply means you have been deeply touched, and that the process needs a good stretch of time to run its course.

Remember, your grief has a wisdom of its own. It knows how long it takes to finish the job, and what it must do in your unconscious mind to make things better. This grief is an ailment, it's true. But it is also a medicine. Your grief will make you sad, but it will also help you heal. Trust in the process.

Find a private place to grieve

In some cases family or friends do not understand how deeply the death of a pet has affected you. They think your grief is bothersome and gloomy. They wish you would stop.

When you find yourself surrounded by unsympathetic others it's a good idea to seek out a place where you can be private and at peace: find a place to think about the animal, remember the animal, cry over it to your heart's content, and say good-bye.

For the first few weeks after a pet's death set aside a period of time each day to be alone, a time when you are not needed elsewhere, and that is all your own. Use whatever private space suits your needs. Grieve there as you will: a cry in the bedroom, a meditation on the porch, a walk on the street or in the park. Let this period be entirely your own. Use it to grieve in whatever way you wish.

If the animal's props or mementos help, use them

Don't let a friend or relative come in and toss away your deceased dog's collar or dishes. Not right away. Not if these objects mean something to you. Instead, put them away for safekeeping. Some therapists even recommend making a "cry box"—a special container where a person keeps important mementos that belonged to their pet—a favorite toy or a leash. This box can be visited whenever one is feeling sad.

Though cherishing your animal's possessions may seem silly to some people, from time immemorial every human culture has drawn solace by looking at and touching objects that belonged to a departed loved one. Maintaining keepsakes and mementos, and giving them a special place in your home, is a natural human response to the mystery of death. If it helps you grieve for your pet, by all means do it.

Wait a reasonable period of time before getting a new pet

After an animal companion has passed away, many people feel the urge to go out immediately and replace it. Though there are no hard-and-fast rules, it is suggested that you wait at least a month before committing to a new pet. A month is usually ample time to work through grief and consider your options. Above all, avoid the error of adopting the first cute animal that comes along just to lessen your pain. Settling in this way can cause regret down the line: you wake up one morning and realize (1) I don't like this pet (2) I don't want this pet (3) I have no room or time for this pet (4) I'm stuck with this pet for the next fifteen years.

Better to wait until you're sure.

When the time does come to start the search for a new companion animal, pace yourself and avoid making decisions until you're sure you've found the right one. Take time to check out different animals. Look around. If you are a dog, cat, bird, or small animal fancier, look at a variety of breeds. If you are a dyed-in-the-wool Yorkshire terrier fan, wait until the right Yorkshire terrier comes along. Or perhaps you'll want to break rank and consider a different breed, even a different pet entirely—a cat, a bird, a ferret. Animal shelters offer a range of choices for prospective pet owners, and they allow you to pick and choose as you like.

One mistake many grieving owners make, and one you will definitely wish to avoid, is searching for a clone of the pet you've recently lost. Each animal is different. Each has its own personality and way of being. Try as you may, you will never find a duplicate of the one you've lost.

And why try anyway? Every pet has something different to offer, something new and fresh to bring to your life. This novelty and discovery is part of the fun. Stay open and let your instincts guide you. You may be astonished to find that in the middle of your search one animal in particular takes your fancy and speaks to your heart. It's OK to wait for this moment of connection to take place. It's worth the wait.

"One day my husband and I visited an animal shelter," a pet owner relates. "We weren't sure we really wanted a new pet just then. We had lost our beloved terrier a few months ago, and knew we could never replace her. So we were just sort of spending a few minutes browsing and reminiscing.

"We walked along looking at the large kennel full of puppies, all mutts, and all cute as can be, when we began to notice that one fuzzy little fellow kept following us back and forth, back and forth. He was yapping louder and harder than the rest, almost as if he was trying to tell us something. I asked the keeper to open the cage so I could get a closer look at him. Just for fun, you know.

"The moment the door swung open this little fellow literally leaped out of the cage and into my arms, then started to nuzzle up against my chest like a baby. The rest of the puppies kept milling around in their cage and paid us no particular attention. And so the decision was made by the dog himself. We had found our new pet—or more accurately— our new pet had found us."

When Mourning Becomes Too Painful

Though you won't find much mention of the fact in psychological literature, there are cases of pet owners becoming so disconsolate over

the loss of an animal that they develop physical symptoms and/or prolonged depression. Such reactions are uncommon—most people get
over grief for a pet in a few weeks. Yet there are more cases of grief
overload among pet owners than one might suppose.

How does one tell if the mourning process is becoming extreme
or even pathological? One or more of the following signs can be a
forewarning.

Development of adverse physical symptoms

Known to psychotherapists as *neuro vegetative signs*, these symptoms include insomnia, chronic diarrhea, loss of appetite, dramatic
change in weight, and a long-term loss of sexual interest. Having one or
more of these conditions may indicate severe depression.

Note that when speaking of depression, misconceptions often arise.
One of the most common is that depression is nothing more than a state
of feeling "down" or "blue." In fact, people can experience clinical depression by having one or more of the symptoms above, yet not feel particularly sad or melancholy at all. In this sense, many people are
depressed and don't know it. Identifying the above symptoms can be a
tip-off.

Extreme denial

Pet owners sometimes refuse to accept that their pet is dead. They
become angry at others who talk of the deceased animal in the past
tense, or who dare suggest that the animal will not return. A bit of denial is normal. A great deal of it over a prolonged period of time can signal trouble.

Zombielike behavior

Everyday activities are difficult for some to perform, and a sense
of grim futility surrounds everything they do. Although it is not unusual
for a person to behave in this way during the first days after a pet's
death, if the condition continues for months some type of pathology
may be present.

Inability to stop thinking about the dead pet

The person feels compelled to touch objects that belong to the pet.
They ruminate over details of its death. They are unable to control their

thoughts, which inevitably return to the memory of the animal or to morbid thoughts and fears of their own death. This condition is serious only if it continues for several months, or if it seems to be getting worse rather than better as time passes.

Abnormal grief reactions

Several symptoms separate a normal grief reaction from an abnormal one. A reaction that manifests in a violent way, for instance, either toward oneself or others, is a danger sign. If intense grief responses continue for a long period of time without abatement or change, something in the mourner is unresolved. If reactions are so intense that they interfere with normal functioning and daily activities, with a person's work or social life, this is a particularly worrisome sign.

If one or more of these conditions occur and do not improve after a reasonable amount of time, it may be necessary to seek professional help from a trained therapist or grief counselor.

Grief Counseling

There is a growing number of mental health professionals today who specialize in helping people recover from the death of a beloved pet. Your vet or a local animal shelter can make referrals. Animal bereavement counselors also advertise in the classified sections of pet journals, and their names are usually listed in the local yellow pages.

Before you make the commitment to visit a professional therapist, however, it is recommended that you first consult a pet loss support hotline. These helpful phone services are set up for people who find the grieving process a little more painful than they can handle. The services are almost always free and are staffed by sympathetic experts, many of whom are trained in animal sciences as well as bereavement counseling.

How does grief counseling help?

First, by crisis intervention. Occasionally bereaved pet owners feel as if they are losing their minds from grief. Breakdowns can follow. A good therapist knows how to recognize these conditions and how to apply appropriate therapeutic methods. As a rule, therapists are connected to a mental health facility and will contact them should intensive psychiatric help be needed.

Extreme crisis reactions, however, are relatively rare. For most people a trained and sensitive ear is all that's needed to get them through the pain. Sessions focus on the present problems and on the feelings of grief themselves. Counselors are not interested in learning about a client's childhood or their relationship with a significant other. Interventions are designed to address the mourner's state of mind in the here and now and to guide them through the current emotional swirls and eddies.

Besides providing crisis support, counselors also help bereaved patients deal with the logistics of everyday living. Getting enough sleep, eating properly, making it to work each morning, taking care of oneself physically—these are all essential elements if a person is to weather the storm.

When searching for a counselor or grief helper, make sure that the professional in question is both emotionally and physically accessible. You will want to find someone who is reasonably open about telling you their own experience with animal loss. You will want someone to speak with who understands what you are going through from a personal point of view. You will want someone who is a bit more active than the usual therapist is trained to be, someone willing to talk to you on the phone at odd hours or even come to your home if necessary. Credentials do not matter that much when choosing a competent counselor, except in the case where deep psychiatric help is required. Otherwise, simply look for someone you are comfortable with, who gives sound, practical advice, and who empathizes with your situation. Proper sympathy and support in this area go a long way toward helping a person accept the inevitable and then go on.

Helping Children Grieve for a Pet

Children grieve for pets in their own way and in their own time. A child who dearly loves a favorite dog or cat may appear entirely unbothered by its passing. Or conversely, a young one becomes inconsolable over the death of a gerbil or guinea pig that she scarcely noticed when the animal was alive. If there is one characteristic to expect from a young person's grieving, it is the unexpected.

When a pet dies, the best course is usually to let children find their own way through the sorrow and confusion, and in the process discover that most important and stinging of all lessons: that all living things must someday die. Death education is a kind of side benefit to keeping pets, and offers children an excellent introduction to the ways of nature.

Meanwhile, there are things parents can do to help.

The first and in many ways most important step, grief therapists are agreed, is to be as forthright about death as possible.

Telling children that Skippie has "gone on a trip," or that he is "visiting Grandma's house" may get parents off the emotional hook for a while. But young ones have a way of finding out what's really going on, especially when Skippie never does come back from Grandma's house. Such discoveries invariably make children feel deceived and betrayed. They may not mention their feelings directly, but they're there; be assured. As any mental health professional will agree, children can never be permanently injured by hearing the truth about a pet's death. They *can* be permanently injured by parents who avoid the issue or who lie about it.

What is the best way for parents to break the news of a pet's death?

Tell it as it is, with simple, basic facts.

Skippie doesn't need his body anymore. So he died. We're going to bury him in the ground tomorrow. In the backyard. We'd really like you to come to the ceremony we're planning for him. You can make Skippie a good-bye present if you feel like it: draw him a picture and put it in the grave. Or write him a story and read it at the funeral. We'll all be there with you, because we're feeling really sad too that he died.

Should children see the dead body of a pet?

Many grief therapists today believe that children of all ages should be allowed to see the body of an animal unless it's really a mess or mutilated from an accident.

They also tell us that children should be present for the euthanizing of a pet at a vet's office. If you have time to prepare children for what's going to happen during the euthanasia that's even better. Talk to your vet about this ahead of time. Bring this subject up at your first meeting with a vet. Find out if the doctor is open to having children at a euthanizing. If not, if the vet seems inflexible or unfriendly to the idea, you may wish to look elsewhere for your pet care. Today there are an increasingly large number of vets who are willing to come to people's homes to perform the euthanasia. In most cases if you're a good client, a vet will do this for you. Meanwhile, there are many books you can read to children to prepare them for the death of a pet, and to give them the message that you trust them to deal with this event when it occurs. This trust makes a child feel strong. It helps them deal with the actual death when it comes.

When a pet dies it's important for parents to contact a child's teachers, sports instructors, anyone who the child is in touch with on a daily basis. Inform these people about the pet's death. Ask them to be sympathetic and to give the child some acknowledgment of her loss.

If possible, help children prepare a show-and-tell about the animal in class. Alert other people that it will not be business as usual with the child for a few days. The child will need time to sort through the confusion and to work out his or her own grieving process. We must all be patient.

All in all, the message you want to send to children is that death is a natural part of life, and that's it's OK to feel sad when it comes. If parents exclude children from the mourning process or lie to them about it, the pet's death remains a disturbing mystery without rhyme or reason. This type of misunderstanding can be easily and entirely avoided— simply by telling it like it is.

7

People's Best Friend:
Caring for Your Dog

Origins of the Noble Dog

The noble dog. Long-time companion. Invaluable helper. Trusted friend of the human race. Where and when did such an unusual yet enduring partnership begin?

As far as scientists can tell, the dog's origins go back at least 55 million years, probably to the continent of Asia. The primal ancestor is known as *Miacoides*, a small, catlike creature that over millions of years developed into the genus we know today as *Canis*.

How did it all begin?

Huddled together on winter nights, speculation has it, kindly humans fling food scraps to canine scavengers that sniff curiously at their campfires and come ever closer. Before long early hunter-gatherers begin to realize that these fleet, intelligent creatures make excellent hunting companions and intimidating bodyguards. The bond is forged.

Though scientists do not know for certain when domestication began, evidence suggests around 14,000 to 12,000 B.C., most likely somewhere in the Northern Hemisphere and perhaps on several continents at once. By 6000 B.C. dogs are members in good standing of human households from Babylonia to China. Egyptian priests sanctify the species by awarding dog-headed gods a place in their pantheon. So highly regarded are these animals in Egyptian civilization that owners adorn their pets with embroidered cloaks, fitted shoes, and jeweled collars. Mastiffs are bred for the first time in Egypt, and greyhounds become the hunting dog of choice. At death, a favorite canine may be mummified the same way as her human master, and entombed alongside family members with full ceremonial honors.

It is not the first time—nor the last—that dogs will be highly honored by their human keepers.

A Primer of Canine Behavior

Dogs are social creatures that dislike solitary living and are most content in the company of human beings and other dogs. Most are highly territorial, as are their wolf ancestors, a trait that makes them faithful to the human home, over which they make intimidating guardians and guards.

The average life span of a dog is between ten to fifteen years. Just how old this is by human reckoning can be seen in the chart below.

Dog's age	Human's age
1 year	15 years old
3 years	28 years old
5 years	36 years old
7 years	44 years old
10 years	56 years old
13 years	68 years old
15 years	76 years old
18 years	91 years old
20 years	101 years old

Dogs are born in litters of from one to twelve or more puppies. Most breeds reach sexual maturity between 6 and 12 months. Adolescence lasts from 6 to 18 months, and social maturity is reached in $2^{1}/_{2}$ to 3 years. Toy breeds tend to mature quicker than other breeds and to age more slowly. Giant breeds also mature more slowly, but then age more quickly.

During their formative period dogs pass through four stages of maturation.

Stage one

First comes the three-week newborn period. During this most vulnerable period puppies are blind, deaf, and entirely dependent on their mothers. After two weeks they begin to open their eyes, sniff the air and each other, and explore the whelping area, though they remain delicate and defenseless.

Stage two

From three to seven weeks puppies grow physically and mature psychologically at an astonishingly rapid rate. A dog's primary probing mechanisms, smell and hearing, develop into what among human beings would be considered superhuman faculties. Certain breeds, for example, can smell through a one-foot wall of rock or twenty feet of snow. They can hear the sound of breathing fifty feet away. They also recognize the sound of the family car in traffic, even when the familiar vehicle is surrounded by two or three other vehicles of the same make and model.

During this three-to-seven-week period, puppies start to stray from the whelping area and begin exploring their environment with great curiosity and zest. Play is of crucial importance because through play the essentials of adult canine behavior are learned—hunting, mating, attacking, defending. Puppies who are raised with littermates throughout this stage also learn bite inhibition, an obviously important control if they are to mingle with humans.

After four or five weeks, weaning takes place, heralding the dietary transition from mother's milk to solid food. Puppies recognize littermates now and socialize in earnest, not only with other dogs but with human beings as well. Indeed, if puppies are not handled and played with during these formative months they are never entirely comfortable in the company of humans when they grow up.

Stage three

The seventh week to the twelfth mark the third maturation stage. During this time the human-dog bond is cemented, and a dog's allegiances are set for life. During the time they reach social maturity, from around two to three years old, it is not unusual for dogs, especially dominant breed types, to challenge for leadership (though this is not necessarily the case with certain breeds of dogs like chows and rottweilers). It is at this stage that human beings are best able to imprint the notion of themselves as "pack leader" or "dominant force" on the mind of a puppy. Unless mistreated in the most extreme ways, this lesson establishes a chain of command that a dog never rebels against for the rest of its life.

At some point in the third period, usually around eight to twelve weeks, dogs are also old enough to begin obedience training. For the next half-year trainers will put their pets through the paces, teaching leash training, housebreaking, an array of commands like sit, lie down, fetch, plus assorted stunts and tricks. Puppy kindergarten training classes can start at three months.

Stage four

In the last stage, between four and six months, dogs lose their first set of teeth and grow a second. Molars come in around six to eight months of age. A puppy's diet widens at this stage to include a full canine menu. Unlike cats, which are slow, sometimes fussy eaters, dogs scarcely chew their food, tending to swallow entire pieces whole, an instinctive throwback to the wolf pack mentality where competing members gobble frantically during feeding frenzies, tearing at the kill to insure getting their share.

Though at times dogs appear to think like their human companions, most authorities agree that the canine mind relies less on reason, memory, and a sense of the future than it does on associational thinking. The result is that a dog's problem-solving abilities are largely confined to the present moment. Its cognitive processes tend to be neither creative nor abstract.

Yet there is much to be said for associational thinking, which at times can produce marvelously complex and clever thought performances. For instance, when Rover sees a family member walking down the hall holding a leash, his thoughts quickly form a sequence, most likely arranging themselves something like this:

Ah, the leash! this means,
I'm going to be taken outside, which means,
I should run to the door immediately because,
standing by the door shows my walker that I'm ready to go, and since the door leads to the outside this means,
once my walker opens it I can get onto the street where I want to go to see other dogs and people, and relieve myself.

Some individuals are better endowed cerebrally than others. More significantly, different breeds are bred for different *kinds* of intelligence and for solving different types of logistic challenges.

The type of intelligence bred into a collie, for example, is a herding intelligence. The collie has the ability to think communally, to anticipate the way members of a flock will move, and to know which herding maneuvers must be made to keep all parts of a group together. A beagle, on the other hand, is bred with a hunting intelligence. It understands how to track, how to ferret out, how to pursue and corner. In a situation that calls for hunting intelligence, a collie is all but lost. In a herding situation, it is the beagle that appears deficient.

This is why, despite the prioritized charts one sees in books on dogs, it is difficult to rank breed intelligence. The fact is that different breeds are intelligent in different ways, and all dogs have their own special brand of mental savvy.

Dog Breeds in a Nutshell

As of the year 2000, 148 breeds of purebred dogs are officially recognized by one of the most authoritative of sources, the American Kennel Club (AKC). These 148 breeds have developed and changed over the years, so to keep them organized and to help tell the players apart, dog experts divide breeds into general groups based on fundamental canine qualities such as build, size, ancestry, and work duties performed. At the beginning of the last century, only two of these groups were recognized, sporting dogs and nonsporting dogs. Today there are seven. These include sporting dogs, hounds, working dogs, terriers, toys, nonsporting dogs, and herding dogs. Here follows a breakdown of each group, with a thumbnail sketch of the dogs included within each.

Sporting dogs

Function. Sporting dogs are bred for hunting, recreation, and, well, for sport—retrievers, spaniels, pointers. Their alternate name, *gundogs*, used in Britain and Australia, says it all. Endowed with a superior sense of smell and an uncanny aptitude for negotiating rough terrains at high speeds, hunting dogs are prized for their tenacity, stamina, and never-say-die spirit of pursuit. Unlike a group such as terriers, which is bred to pursue and kill, sporting dogs are best at locating a hunted animal, flushing it out, and when necessary, retrieving its body.

Personality. Sporting dogs are among the friendliest, most alert, and eager of all breed types. They are gentle with children and full of energy for play. A majority of breeds in this group are controlled barkers, a plus when they live with sleeping infants, convalescents, and people with sound sensitivities. They are cheerful, even tempered, easy to train, and make excellent travel companions.

Behavioral traits. Overfriendliness and an easygoing personality makes for poor watchdog ability. Sporting dogs are bred for action and grow restive when cooped up. Though some breeds make adequate apartment pets, members of this group tend to become nervous when hemmed in and usually require long, intense periods of exercise to compensate.

Representative Breeds. Types of breeds in the sporting class of dogs include:

German short-hair pointers   Cocker spaniels
Labrador retrievers   English setters

Hounds

Function. Specifically bred for hunting, hounds tend to have highly developed senses of sight and/or smell (hounds are, in fact, often spoken of as "scent hounds" and "sight hounds"), and have been bred for a variety of seek-and-find tasks. The dachshund, for example, is raised to hunt badgers and pursue them into their holes. The giant Irish wolfhound chases elk and wolves. Foxhounds chase the fox. And so on. Scent hounds mostly scent and hold, or drive back to the hunter. Sight hounds run down and dispatch. Scent hounds have perhaps the best sense of smell of all dogs; sight hounds have excellent vision, but a poorly developed smelling capacity.

Personality. Scent hounds usually make good natured, gentle, and friendly pets. They behave excellently with children, and make wonderful companions. Physically they are robust and are endowed with enormous long-term stamina. Sight hounds are more reserved, especially with strangers, and some breeds are better with older children than young.

Behavioral traits. Most scent hounds are loud barkers and bayers, especially when left at home alone. Males often stray far from home, especially beagle males, sometimes never to return. Hounds require a great deal of exercise, and so—with some exceptions like dachshunds, basset hounds, greyhounds, basenjis—do not always make ideal city or apartment pets.

Representative breeds. Breeds in the hound class of dog include the following:

Scent hounds	*Sight hounds*	*Dogs that are not true hounds*
Bloodhound	Greyhound	Norwegian Elkhound
Foxhound	Irish wolfhound	Basenji
Beagle		

Working dogs

Function. Over the centuries working dogs have been bred to help perform specific labors such as pulling sleds, hauling fishing nets, guarding a household, carrying messages, or saving lives. Sturdy and noble, these breeds are on the large and muscular side, and are known for their amazing feats of resourcefulness in time of danger and catastrophe. Many of the heroic tales one hears of dogs pulling children from fires, or running fifty miles to find help, involve breeds in this category.

Personality. Working dogs are resourceful, intelligent, loyal, and affectionate, though sometimes quite aggressive. They thrive on the companionship of their families, with whom they form an especially strong bond, but they may be aloof or wary with strangers. They are exceedingly loyal, either to a single person or to an entire family.

Behavioral traits. Two of the main virtues possessed by working dogs, loyalty and energy, can become problem behaviors under certain conditions. The fierce faithfulness of working dogs, for example, is channeled almost exclusively toward the dog's human family. But with certain breeds loyalty can turn to belligerent and sometimes even violent protectiveness. Many working dogs also require firm, consistent leadership to keep them in line. With a few exceptions, unless skillfully trained, they do not make ideal pets for first-time owners.

Representative Breeds. Types of breeds in the working class of dogs include the following:

Old English sheepdogs   German shepherd
Great Pyrenees   Doberman pinscher

Terriers

Function. Despite a disparity of size and appearance, there are basically two types of terriers: *bull and terrier* breeds, stemming from the bull-baiting and dog-fighting tradition, and *traditional* terriers. The dogs in both categories share many similar behavior patterns. Often divided into long hair, short hair, and rough hair, they possess a common British or Irish ancestry; hence the many English or Irish surnames: Welsh terrier, Irish terrier, Staffordshire bull terrier, Dandie Dinmont terrier. Terriers were first bred during the fifteenth century to hunt rats in barnyards and to chase foxes and polecats from their lairs. The very term *terrier* is derived from the French word for earth. Terriers are active burrowers and exhibit a ferocious hunting instinct. Some breeds are expert at chasing and killing small animals on the run such as foxes and badgers. Certain terrier breeds such as Airedales were used as police dogs in Germany, and as dispatch carriers during World War I and II.

Personality. Delightfully friendly and fun, terriers are curious, quick, independent, courageous, funny, and full of high-octane energy. They travel well, make wonderful companions for adults (be a little careful with them around children), and serve as alert, and for their size, ferocious watchdogs. They are popular show dogs as well.

Behavioral traits. Terriers are sometimes overly aggressive toward other dogs. They tend to be a bit mischievous and snappish, and many breeds are habitual barkers—yappers, really. They can be willful and stubbornly resistant to obedience training. They will learn all right—terriers are extremely intelligent—but only if firmly and intelligently (and persistently) tutored. Since they are bred to burrow, keep a close watch on the flower beds, yours and your neighbors'.

Representative Breeds. Types of breeds in the terrier class of dogs include the following:

American Staffordshire terrier   Jack Russell terrier

Toys

Function. In centuries past dogs were bred primarily as workers. But as civilizations around the world became more refined, breeders had the luxury of raising dogs purely as pets. Toys are the results, and are what the name implies, small dogs (usually less than ten pounds) bred primarily as playmates and family companions, and ideally suited to apartments and small area living. Toys are also popular show dogs. Some breeds were raised in a privileged hothouse atmosphere exclusively for the pleasure of kings and aristocrats, and did not join the ranks of the common dog until the twentieth century. Pekingese, for instance, were once the exclusive property of Chinese emperors and were bred to fit snugly inside the fluffy sleeves of royal concubines.

Personality. Toy dogs are cute, intelligent, curious, frisky, full of personality. They adapt easily to their living quarters, including small quarters such as city apartments, and make excellent if somewhat persistent alarm sounders when strangers appear. Less hardy than larger, stronger canine groups, such as working dogs and sporting dogs, a toy has the heart of a lion, if not the physique.

Behavioral traits. Toy breeds tend to be yappy, stubborn, and nervous. Some breeds are physically on the frail side, and their delicacy and touch sensitivity make them a poor choice as pets for young children. Some toy breeds have a tendency to become grouchy and eccentric in their later years. Others are stubborn and nippy. Toys are usually very people oriented, constantly looking for laps or a family bed to sleep on. Separation anxiety can be a problem with some toys if left alone. For this reason many toy owners keep more than one dog at a time.

Representative Breeds. Types of breeds in the toy class of dogs include the following:

Toy spaniels   Toy terriers   Bichons

Nonsporting dogs

Function. The term *nonsporting* includes a pastiche of breeds that fail to fit conveniently into any other group, or that possess characteristics of several groups at once. There is thus little continuity of size, shape, and temperament among these breeds; the spectrum runs all the way from the poodle to the dalmatian. When compared to their hardier sporting cousins, nonsporting dogs are often small in stature.

Personality. So many diverse breeds are lumped together into this category that it is difficult to generalize about nonsporting temperament and behavior. On the whole, dogs in this group are attractive, intelligent, and even tempered. They make good house or apartment dogs and good watchdogs, though their tendency to bark can be a mixed blessing in these conditions.

Eccentricities. Not all breeds in this category get along well with other dogs. Though most nonsporting dogs are good with children, a few breeds, such as the chow chow and dalmatian, are not. Inquire first before adopting if you have small ones in the house. Some breeds such as the Lhasa apso and poodle require elaborate and continuous grooming care.

Representative Breeds. Breeds in the nonsporting class of dogs include the following:

Bichon frise	French bulldog
Boston terrier	Keeshond
Bulldog	Lhasa apso
Chinese shar-pei	Poodle
Chow chow	Schipperke
Dalmatian	Tibetan spaniel
Finnish spitz	Tibetan terrier

Herding dogs

Function. Last of the dog groups to be named—this category was recognized by the AKC in 1983—herding dogs are mainly bred to shepherd domestic animals. Collies, sheepdogs, Australian cattle dogs, and others are all movers and organizers of livestock, mainly cattle, sheep, and goats. Many breeds in this group were originally bred in northern climates, hence their thick, rugged coats. Members of this group make excellent watchdogs.

Personality. Since hand signals and vocal commands play such an important part in the working relationship between a dog and its human handler, dogs in this category take to obedience training a good deal faster than many other breeds. Among the smartest of all canines (and actually of all creatures in the animal kingdom), these dogs tend to be friendly and alert. They should, however, be constantly engaged in work or other high-energy activities. Boredom brings destruction and sometimes aggression. Herding dogs are fiercely loyal, nimble, surprisingly inventive, great runners, and will labor until they drop to please their human keepers.

Eccentricities. Herding breeds need plenty of romping space and tend to grow restless when confined to cramped quarters. Some breeds shed profusely and require continual grooming. And don't plan on owning a herding dog unless you are prepared to give it a generous amount of love and attention. If puppies in this group are not handled by humans at a very early age they may become unpleasantly aggressive. Herders grow sullen and sometimes destructive when ignored. Some of the herding breeds are not suitable for the average family looking for an easygoing pet.

Representative Breeds. Types of breeds in the herding class of dogs include the following:

Cattle dogs   Shepherds
Collies   Corgies

A New Puppy in the House

Choosing a puppy

Of all pets, dogs seem to require the most work, the most attention, and the most love. And of all periods in a dog's life cycle, the puppy stage is the most demanding. If you are in the process of choosing a dog, check back to Chapter 1 for a list of buying and pet-keeping caveats. The following concerns should also be carefully weighed and considered when deciding which type of dog to obtain.

Appearance and temperament

Each breed has its own personality and temperament. Consider the options: do you want a dog that is playful? Reserved? Independent?

Funny? Offbeat? Noble? Gentle? Tough? Whatever? Then choose your breed type accordingly.

Appearancewise, a healthy puppy has bright, clear eyes and a friendly disposition. She takes obvious pleasure in being handled, is curious, her tail wagging, and shows no signs of cowering, whimpering, or snapping when you come near. She advances toward people and new situations with tail wagging, ears forward, and a relaxed, friendly facial expression. If her teeth are in, they are straight and gleaming white. Her gums are pink, not gray, white, or blue (except for the gums of a chow chow and shar-pei, which are naturally black). Her ears have neither a bad odor nor small black deposits inside them. There is no feces caked to her anus and no signs of diarrhea in the cage.

The puppy's fur is shiny and full; be concerned if clumps of hair come out when you gently pull at her coat. There is no sign of rashes, scabs, welts, abscesses, hairless patches, or other skin irritations. There are no tears or fluids dripping from her eyes or nose. When you run your hand over the puppy's belly, its surface is warm and smooth, with no lumps to indicate an umbilical hernia and no excess fat.

Age

Puppies are best purchased or adopted between the ages of seven weeks and four months. If younger, a dog may not yet be weaned. He may also be inadequately socialized in the litter and still needful of his mother.

Gender

Choice of sex in a dog is mostly a matter of taste. Male dogs are sometimes more social and loving than females, but this is a generalization, and there are plenty of exceptions. Unless spayed, females go into heat, which means owners must be prepared for the arrival of yelping, salivating suitors at their doorstep several times a year. During walks, on the other hand, males stop every few feet to lift their legs, and this can become tedious. Besides these and a few other minor concerns, there is not much difference between male and female canines. More important, really, is whether or not a pup is neutered. On the whole, neutered dogs tend to have fewer health and behavior problems than unneutered.

Dog size versus space in your home

If you live in a small home without a yard or in an apartment without a nearby park, you may prefer a smaller dog (under twenty-five pounds) that needs a minimum of walking and exercise. Have a look, for instance, at breeds in the toy group.

If you have plenty of indoor room plus outside exercise areas, a more active and larger dog (twenty-five pounds and over) may be appropriate. Small dogs eat less, take up less space, need to be walked less, and defecate less than big dogs. Though a few of the larger breeds such as Great Danes and greyhounds can accommodate themselves to small living spaces, most can't. The general rule of thumb is to look primarily at a dog's indoor and outdoor energy levels to determine the living suitability of that dog.

Grooming needs

Some people enjoy grooming and fussing over a dog's coat, others do not. Some dogs shed a great deal. Others shed very little. If shedding is a concern, factor this variable into your decision.

Purebred versus mixed breed

Popular wisdom has it that mixed-breed dogs are healthier than purebred, though this generalization appears to have as many exceptions as rules. Because they were originally bred for work purposes, purebreds tend to be more fixed in their behavior patterns than mixed-breed dogs. Such predictability can be an asset or liability, depending on your point of view.

The present age of children in the house

Up to the age of seven children are neither temperamentally fit nor developmentally ready to care for a puppy, especially a puppy under five months of age. Young children like to hit, pull, yank, and squeeze, often in the wrong places and frequently with too much gusto. These indignities hurt and often cause puppies to bite and scratch in self-defense. As often happens, the puppy then gets blamed, punished, and even given away.

Conversely, young dogs scratch and bite automatically when handled. It's done in the spirit of play, yet the scratches and bites hurt just as much. Young children have little savvy in dealing with a puppy's super sharp milk teeth, his unclipped claws, and his powerful, wiggly little body that even at four or five months old can knock over a toddler. If children under seven do play with the family canine, it should *always* be done under close supervision.

Likewise, it is cautioned that the parents of children under seven be wary of adopting toy dogs, especially the smaller members of this group such as Chihuahuas, pomeranians, and Yorkshire terriers. All these breeds have frail, fine-boned frames that take poorly to clumsy handling. Unless children are unusually gentle and careful, the better strategy is to adopt medium-to-large-size dogs over five months of age. Again, all interactions between the child and the puppy should be closely monitored.

The Puppy's First Few Days at Home

In those exciting days when a puppy first enters a home everyone, especially children, wants to handle the newcomer and play with him. This is fine, but only up to a point. Despite the fact that puppies seem like endless balls of energy, they actually tire easily, and too many people crowding round can be frightening and intimidating.

In the beginning it's best to portion out times of day for a puppy's activities: play, rest, sleeping, eating, and so forth. Think of treating a puppy the same way you would a child. Infant dogs require lots of rest, special foods, regular nap hours, wholesome toys that are appropriate for their age, and loads of attention and love.

Be as gentle and affectionate as you can in the beginning. During these delicate first days your pet is getting used to new sights, smells, and sounds. You can speed up the orientation process by talking to the puppy in soothing tones, stroking it, spending time with it, and generally making it feel like a welcomed guest.

If the weather is extreme, be especially careful. Dogs under three months are vulnerable to sudden drops in temperature and to high, cold winds. If your puppy enters the house during the warm months, be sure it doesn't overheat from too much play.

Designating the primary caretaker

The following excerpt from an ASPCA bulletin deals with the sometimes thorny question of primary caretaker:

Some parents bow to the pressure their children put on them to get a dog. The kids promise with tears in their eyes that they will religiously take care of this soon-to-be-best friend. The truth of the matter is, during the ten- to fifteen-year life span of the average dog, your children will be growing in and out of various life stages, and the family dog's importance in their lives will wax and wane like the moon. You cannot saddle a child with total responsibility for the family dog and threaten to get rid of it if the child is not providing that care. That is not fair to the child or the dog.

Choosing the family dog should include input from all family members with the cooler, more experienced family members' opinions carrying a bit more weight. The family dog should not be a gift from one family member to all the others. Doing some research and polling each family member about what is important to them in a dog will help pin down what you will be looking for. Books like Daniel Totora's *The Right Dog for You* or Bruce Fogle's *ASPCA Complete Dog Care Manual* can be tremendously helpful, and can warn you away from unsuitable choices for your family's personality.

Sharing responsibility

During a dog's infancy and puppyhood it is important that everyone in the family know the ground rules and, to the best of their ability— and if age permits—to help out. Schedule household discussions ahead of time during which family members agree on the following points:

- Who will walk the puppy?
- Who will feed the puppy?
- Where will the puppy eat and sleep?
- Who will clean up after the puppy?
- Who will oversee the puppy's health routines and bring it to the veterinarian for needed checkups?

Agreeing on commands

Agree ahead of time on a standard vocabulary of doggie commands that everyone in the household uses.

Say, for instance, that a puppy tries to jump up on family members. In response, Mom responds by yelling "Down," Dad by yelling "No," and daughter by shouting "Off!" Three different words for the same command confuse and confound. Or conversely, one family member says "Down!" when a puppy climbs up on the chair, and another says "Down!" when trying to teach a puppy to lie down.

"What are they trying to tell me?" the poor animal wonders.

Avoid this confusion from the start by agreeing to use certain established words for certain established commands. Write them down, then post the list for everyone to see and memorize.

Feeding a New Puppy

When you first pick up your puppy, find out what kind of food he has been fed and at what times of day. Once at home, provide him with the same menu at the same time for several days to avoid upset stomach.

If you wish to then introduce a different diet, take at least a week to make a transition from the old food to the new. Start by mixing one part of the new food together with three parts of the old. After two or three days switch to equal parts old food and new food. A few days later mix one part old food to three parts new. After a week or so put your puppy on the new food entirely.

During their first six to twelve weeks, puppies should be fed four times a day. For puppies aged three to six months, three times a day is adequate, while older puppies receive all the nourishment they need on two meals a day. After each meal, leash and collar your puppy and take him out to do his business. Praise him generously each time he eliminates in the proper place.

The amount of food provided at each meal depends on a puppy's size, age, and the type of diet. A three-month-old Newfoundland obviously needs more food in his bowl than a shih tzu of comparable age. Dogs of different size have different dietary requirements. If you have any questions in this area, consult with your veterinarian.

Why You Need to Crate and Isolate Your Puppy

Most dog experts agree that during unsupervised hours, encouraging a puppy to spend an hour or two each day inside a crate is sound operating procedure.

Why do this?

For several reasons.

To begin, allowing a mischievous, untrained puppy freedom to romp freely through your house all day is an invitation to disaster for rugs, couches, and floors, and perhaps for the animal's safety as well.

As pet owners who have made the mistake of giving dogs free run can testify, moreover, an unchecked canine soon starts defecating in several different parts of the house. Once this pattern is established and the dumping spots are chosen, it becomes extremely difficult to break the habit; so difficult, in fact, that some pet owners are forced to call in a professional for retraining. Why tempt fate?

Crating avoids these problems, and at the same time it is beneficial for both the dog and the household. Crating aids the process of housebreaking by reinforcing a dog's natural reluctance to soil its bed or resting area. It teaches puppies to be alone and self-sufficient. It allows them to get the rest and sleep they need. It helps build bladder and bowel control and introduces the concept of private territory. It accustoms pups to being crated and penned, an important lesson to know when traveling. And when traveling, it also helps travelers to secure rooms at hotels and motels, as management is far more likely to grant reservations to pet owners whose dog is crate trained. Finally, crating provides household members respite from a puppy's constant demands and persistent, sometimes relentless need to play.

Crates come in a variety of sizes. The most common are molded-plastic models used for shipping and open-wire models with metal or plastic trays on the bottom. Be sure the crate you choose is properly sized to accommodate your dog's particular dimensions. There should be enough room inside for Rover to stand up, turn around in a circle, and lie down. There should *not* be enough room for Rover to soil one end of the crate, then ramble over to the other and take a snooze. Not only does an oversize container encourage unsanitary conditions, it works against one of the implicit lessons of crating, which is to discourage dogs from soiling their own nests. If a crate is too large and there are no other alternatives, block part of it off with Masonite or plywood.

After choosing the crate, furnish it with several chewable toys plus a food and water bowl. Coax the pup inside the crate and keep him confined here for an hour or two during the day. Do not add bedding to the crate until you are sure he is capable of keeping it dry.

When training dogs to enter a crate, lure them inside with a treat. Open the door, and pronounce the command, "Go to your crate," and toss the treat inside. The pup will soon catch on. Once the crate becomes part of his daily routine, he will enter it on his own.

How long can you crate a puppy without being cruel?

A three-month-old puppy can be crated for a three-hour stretch.

A four-month-old puppy can be crated for a four-hour stretch.

A seven-month-old puppy can be crated for a seven-hour stretch. Any longer than seven hours and you are putting unfair expectations on a dog to keep his kennel clean.

Each crating session, moreover, should be preceded by aerobic exercise, the amount of exercise based on the size, age, and energy level of the breed type. An adolescent or young adult Border collie, for instance, or a terrier or sporting dog will need a considerable amount of exercise time. A breed such as a Pekingese will require a good deal less.

Before you leave your dog confined for a long stretch of time, make sure he is well accustomed to being kept in a small, confined area. Dogs not accustomed to confinement can become hysterical if left too long, and they may do damage both to the crate and themselves. Finally, never crate a dog while he is wearing a correction collar. These devices can get caught on the cage, and many dogs have choked to death in this manner.

Giving Your Pup Proper Daily Exercise

For most young dogs a walk of several city blocks or a ten-minute run around in the backyard is simply not enough exercise to last the entire day. Pups from the highly active sporting, herding, hound, and terrier groups, plus nearly all adolescents, require a more intense workout to burn off their oceans of energy. Such activities might include on-leash jogging, race walking, bicycle road working, and strolling several miles a day. Also consider playing frisbee with your pup if she likes to catch and retrieve. Throw a ball or bumper and let her fetch. Do road work with roller skates. If your canine is dog-friendly and she has all her vaccinations, let her romp with other pups in a dog run or fenced area for at least forty-five minutes a day.

It is also suggested that you base exercise sessions on the specific type of work your dog is genetically primed to perform. Most golden and Labrador retrievers, for instance, are naturals at retrieving tennis balls or rubber bumpers from the water. Corgis and Border collies are bred to herd, so naturally they love to herd basketballs or large balls made out of hard plastic. Bichon frises and Maltese delight in trick training. Beagles excel at biscuit hunts around your property.

Whatever activity you choose, remember that brisk daily exercise is even more important for the health of a dog than it is for a human being.

Step-by-Step Paper Training and Housebreaking

Although they are sometimes lumped together, paper training and outdoor housebreaking are two different processes. Some people speak of them as stages, implying that paper training logically leads to housebreaking, but this is not necessarily the case. In fact, some dog owners report that once a dog is trained to newspaper she gets to like it, and it becomes especially difficult to break her of the habit. Moreover, if you already have a fenced-in yard, there is no need to paper train in the first place.

For some pet owners, at the same time, paper training is all that is needed. An elderly or physically challenged person may be incapable of walking a dog, in which case layers of paper on the floor gets the job done.

Holding it all in

Generally speaking, puppies can control their toilet urges for approximately one hour for every month of age. This means a three-month-old pup can hold for three hours, a six-month-old pup for six, and so forth, up to around nine or ten hours.

At three-and-a-half to four months of age pups can usually stay clean for six or seven hours overnight, but tend to soil more frequently during the day. Three elimination walks morning, afternoon, and before bedtime provide adequate toilet time for most dogs that are eight months or older.

Paper training a puppy

Around nine weeks of age puppies generally begin to "place train" themselves. Under this age most puppies have neither the cognitive development nor the muscle control to be successfully paper trained. There is nothing wrong with introducing this concept early on, of course, but understand that most pups are simply not mature enough to master the task.

When the time does come for paper training, and your pup seems mature enough, here's what to do, step by step:

1. Use newspaper exclusively. It's cheap, absorbent, and expendable.
2. Decide on a specific room in your home. Plan on using *only* this room for paper training. Continually shifting paper around from

room to room confuses dogs and slows down their learning curve.

3. Cover a small area of the room with newspaper. A single sheet of newspaper is not always sufficient to stop leak through, so consider laying paper down two or three layers thick. As soon as the puppy finishes eating or drinking, playing, or sleeping—or if she simply shows signs of needing to eliminate—place her on the paper quickly after giving a toileting command, such as "Hurry up!" or "Do your business!" and keep her confined to the room until she goes.

   It is not unusual for a young canine to urinate and defecate eight or nine times a day. After a while you will recognize her body language when the urge comes as she sniffs, scratches, and lowers her tail. Note, by the way, that after a puppy soils the paper, some pet owners remove only the top layer, leaving the bottom layer intact so that the scent marks the spot for future use. This technique, with its inherent odor risks, works for some pet owners and not for others.

4. After your puppy becomes accustomed to using the paper in the training room, begin laying down less and less paper, and covering less and less of the floor area. Eventually you will want to limit your pup to a small papered spot in a corner of the room.

5. If your puppy has an accident, as she inevitably will, simply say "No!" then place her on the paper. Repeat this process each time a slip occurs. But do so *only* if you catch her in the act. Dogs know the present moment and nothing more. If you walk into a room and find a mess that was made an hour ago, then yell at your pup for her indiscretion, she will be incapable of making a connection between your yelling and her past mistake, and she will simply think you loud and unpredictable. Yelling and physical punishments like rubbing a pup's nose in her excrement are cruel and unnecessary, and tend to make a dog sneaky: instead of cooperating with you to learn proper paper training or housebreaking procedures she tries to outwit you, defecating in secret places when you're not around. Soon you find yourself locked in a fierce battle of wills. Keep paper training on a firm but pleasant and gentle level at all times.

6. Each time your puppy uses the newspaper give her lots of praise and a reward. Like human beings, dogs learn better by reward than by punishment. And remember, consistency is extremely

important in paper training. You are trying to build a habit and a routine. Repeat and repeat and repeat, then repeat some more and don't lose heart. Dogs are smart animals. They almost always get with the program.

Housebreaking a puppy to the outdoors

Although housebreaking seems a daunting task to pet owners, dogs' native intelligence plus their reluctance to soil their nests makes them quick studies. As with paper training, patience and consistency are the watchwords of success. Here's how to get the job done, step by step:

1. Choose an outside area within a half-block of your door where the dog can eliminate freely. The designated place can be a park, the gutter, a field, a backyard, wherever.
2. While he is being crated, observe your puppy carefully. Look for indications that he needs to eliminate. Puppies are most apt to go immediately after eating, drinking, playing, or sleeping. Signs that a dog needs to eliminate include whining near the door, pawing and scratching the floor or door, walking restlessly in circles, excessive sniffing, and lowering of the hind regions, as if about to squat.
3. When the time comes, leash your dog, say, "Out!" loudly and clearly, and take him outside to the designated walking area. Remain there until he goes.
4. Whenever the pup urinates or defecates, pet him fondly, and give him plenty of praise. After he finishes his business, reward him and let him play for a few minutes. Do not take the exercise or fun portion of the walk until the dog has soiled.
5. Take the same route every day to the soiling area. If you go to the park, follow the same series of pathways morning, noon, and night. If you use a field, go to the same rock or tree each time. If you live in a city, walk the exact same distance every time. Avoid varying this scheme one iota until your dog is thoroughly trained. Soon he will become accustomed to his routine, and he will come to look on soiling his own home with almost as much distaste as you do.

Dog Grooming 101

Human hair grows in continuous strands and falls out only when it is pulled or broken.

Dog hair, on the other hand, is designed to grow and die in cycles.

The first part of this cycle is marked by a strong growth spurt. It is followed by minimal, almost arrested periods of growth, then by a loss of hair, and finally by another spurt of growth. The length of these cycles varies from breed to breed, with an average time of between four to five months.

These bursts of loss and replenishment translate out in human terms into the dreaded word *shedding*. All breeds do it to some extent, though some do it far more dramatically than others. Shedding is one reason a dog needs grooming. Dogs with long, thick coats require more attention than short hairs. All dogs, however, profit from regular grooming.

To help you groom your dog successfully, a variety of tools are available at most pet supply stores. Some of these tools are mandatory if the job is to be done right, others are optional:

Mandatory grooming tools

Long-tooth slicker or wire brush (currycomb): Best for long-haired dogs. Slickers contain fine wire bristles designed to remove tangles and knots. A best bet for heavy shedders with thick undercoats.

Shedding blade: A flexible-tooth metal blade mounted on a handle, especially good for grooming long hairs. The blade goes beneath the outer hair coat to remove the dead underlayer (under hairs make up 95 percent of shed dog hairs).

Chamois cloth: For sleek, short-haired dogs.

Rubber curry brush: For short-haired dogs.

Flea comb: A fine-tooth comb especially designed for pets to remove fleas, lice, debris, insects, and insect eggs. For dogs with extra thick, long hair a wide-tooth comb will make combing easier, but it will not remove fleas, and should not be used in place of a flea comb.

Nail trimmer: These come in a number of sizes and styles, and sometimes as part of sets. Clipper and file are a must for keeping Rover's nails clean, short, and nonscratching.

Optional grooming tools

Mat breaker: This serrated blade mounted on a grip handle is used for dogs with especially thick and tangled coats.

Hair dryer: The warm, dry air from a dryer can be used to dry dogs after a bath or if they're caught in the rain.

Electric clippers: For dogs like poodles whose coats are frequently shaped and styled, cordless and electric models are available.

Shampoo: Conditioners, lusterizers, dry bath preparations, and grooming mists are all useful.

Pet bath hose with sprayer: This spray nozzle and hose attachment that clamps on the faucet is used for bathing pets. Most models come with aerators and a selection of settings on the nozzle.

Grooming glove: An abrasive glove with rubberized nubs on the palm. Grooming gloves fit on the hand and are run along the fur, collecting broken and fallen hairs. They are used more often with cats than dogs, but are useful for both.

Each breed and each dog requires different size and strength grooming instruments. Ask your groomer which type of brush, comb, etc., is best adapted to your dog's needs.

Basic grooming techniques

The following techniques apply to all dogs no matter what their breed or length of hair. Remember, grooming should be a pleasurable experience for both human and dog—a time to commune, to care for, to bond.

1. Start with a light brushing to pick off bits of debris, grass, twigs, dead skin cells, and other oddities that cling to the fur or are embedded beneath it. Examine the coat closely. It should feel dry, and appear glossy. A dull, dry coat may mean your dog's diet is deficient.

2. Do a spot check for ticks, lice, fleas, and other parasites. Also examine your dog's environment (such as his bedding) for infestation. If you see signs of vermin, apply appropriate medication, following instructions on the label carefully. If over-the-counter medication does not work, talk to your veterinarian about other options. (See the medical section of this chapter for more on ticks, lice, and fleas.) Although some vermin disappear during

the winter months, some don't, especially in warmer areas of the country. Do not automatically assume that because the weather is cold outside, ticks and fleas will all immediately die. They won't.

3. Like human beings, dogs enjoy a good massage. While you are running your hands over his body picking off debris and looking for infestation, spend a few minutes rubbing and kneading the dog's shoulders, back, neck, head, and the upper part of his legs. Massage as you would a human being with long, deep movements. Most dogs go into a kind of trance when rubbed this way. Massage treatment is therapeutic, stimulating blood and lymph circulation, working the joints, and producing a sense of overall well-being.

4. Check a dog's ears for redness, infection, irritation, wax buildup, and signs of ear mites such as small, black debris in the ear shell, and peculiar odors. Though mites are not always the cause of ear infections, they frequently are. Carefully wipe the ears of any extraneous matter with absorbent cotton.

5. Check the eyes for signs of foreign debris, scratches, or irritation. Clean the area around the eyes with absorbent cotton. Remove discharges and mucus buildup, paying special attention to the corners of the eyes. Note that the first signs of sickness often show up in a dog's eyes in the form of puffiness, redness, a glazed look, or excessive discharge.

6. Trim your dog's nails. Hold the paw firmly, trim the tips, avoiding the pink "quick" and veins. Cutting away too much surface area can sever the delicate veins networking throughout the nail. Next, smooth off any remaining sharp edges with a nail file. Work slowly and with care. Few dogs are comfortable in these sessions, and gentle patience on your part will be critical.

   A dog that spends lots of time outside wears its nails down naturally by contact with the pavement. Dogs that live indoors and/or on soft earth surfaces reap no such benefit, and will need a trim on a weekly basis. Start the trimming process while your pet is a puppy, and eventually the procedure will become a regular part of the maintenance routine. Dogs that do not have their nails trimmed at a young age often react to this procedure with fear and hostility when older. You may wish to get a lesson or two in this somewhat tricky skill from a good veterinarian or groomer before you begin. Keep some styptic powder on hand in case of bleeding.

7. Check your dog's teeth for chips, breaks, tartar buildup. A dog's breath should not be overwhelmingly unpleasant. If it is, make note and tell your veterinarian. His gums should be pink and healthy looking without any discoloration or signs of infection. You can shine up a dog's teeth using a toothbrush and an abrasive like baking soda. Pet supply stores carry specially formulated pet toothpastes.

8. Clean your dog's paws every day if possible, especially if he walks through (or rolls in) questionable places such as farmyards, grassy fields, tar roads, gravel beds, or city parks. Pay special attention to the area between the toes where debris tends to get trapped.

Grooming procedures for different types of coats

Short-haired coats. For short-haired dogs give the fur a thorough brushing with a curry brush, following the nap of the fur as you go. Be sure to groom the back, stomach, sides, legs, neck, and head. Trim off extra hairs with a scissors. After the curry brush work is finished go back over the coat lightly with a bristle brush. End the session by burnishing the coat with a chamois cloth.

Long-haired coats. For dogs with long-haired coats, such as cocker spaniels and Maltese, work over the dog's entire body including the back, stomach, sides, leg, neck, and head with a slicker brush and/or a pin brush. Follow the nap of the fur as you go, being sure to untangle all clumps and mats. Long-haired dogs that spend time outdoors or that are infrequently groomed will have many snarls and mats, and here you must proceed gingerly, being sure not to pull too hard or cause any pain during the process (you do not want your dog running away every time she catches sight of her grooming tools). Next, carefully run a wide-tooth comb over the coat, again going with the nap. Using your scissors, trim excess hair from the dog's hindquarters and in between her toes. Finish off with a brief combing with fine-tooth comb.

Silky coats. Silky-coated dogs such as Yorkshire terriers and Afghans require regular full-body brushing with a bristle brush or curry brush once a week, but not a whole lot more. Be sure to brush the back, stomach, sides, legs, neck, and head. Trim off extra hairs with a scissors, then follow up with a brief combing. Some pet owners add a shine to their dog's fur using a chamois cloth.

Curly-hair coats. For curly-haired dogs, such as terriers and poodles, apply general brushing with a slicker or pin brush. After the brushing is complete, go over your handiwork carefully with a wide-tooth comb. Most curly-hair coats require judicious trimming, preferably at the hand of an expert.

Bathing

Even if they have not rutted about in unseemly substances, many pet owners wash their dog at least three or four times a year on principle simply to clean away accumulated dirt and odors. Though dogs are relatively clean in their habits, their coats act as magnets for all manner of dirt and grit. Bathing often becomes the only solution.

Before bathing, groom out all snarls and mats. These snarls tend to become worse from washing, and after a bath they may become impossible to remove. Sometimes they must even be cut away.

Wash your dog indoors in a tub or large plastic container. Since he may wiggle a bit while being bathed, lay a perforated rubber mat on the bottom of the tub to avoid slipping. Keep the bath water tepid; a temperature of 68 to 72°F is ideal.

Soap the dog up, rub and massage his skin vigorously, and carefully rinse (a thorough rinsing is always essential). A good pet shampoo gets rid of smells and debris and rinses off easily. Dogs that are easily frightened by shower sprays can be placed in a bathtub and then washed down by pouring warm water over their bodies from a plastic pitcher.

After soaping and rinsing, pat the coat dry with a towel (or use a hair dryer). If it is cool or cold outside keep the dog in the house until thoroughly dry. When bathing facilities are scarce or when the weather is too cold—wet dogs catch cold easily in chilly weather—most pet supply stores carry dry bath preparations that can be used without water.

Feeding and Nutrition

Basic nutritional needs

Like human beings, dogs are omnivores, requiring foods from the three basic food groups: protein, fat, and carbohydrates. Their nutritional needs break down as follows.

Approximately 10 to 15 percent fat. Fat is contained in meat and oil. It promotes skin and coat health, keeps metabolism in equilibrium, provides energy, transports vitamins, and supplies essential fatty acids. Lack of fat in a dog's diet slows the healing processes and makes a dog nervous and weak.

Approximately 20 to 25 percent protein. Protein is found in meat, fish, eggs, dairy products, and to a limited extent in vegetables and grains. Protein helps build and repair tissue, bones, hair, hormones, and blood. It provides the essential building blocks of cellular growth. It also forms enzymes and hormones and strengthens the immune system. A diet low in protein produces a weak-boned, poorly formed dog. Despite the claims of manufacturers, dog food supplemented with protein does not necessarily increase a canine's get-up-and-go. Nutritionally speaking, protein builds and repairs tissue; it does not generate ready energy. This job is done by fats and carbohydrates.

Approximately 55 to 65 percent carbohydrates. These provide bulk and fiber, and act as a fundamental aid in the digestion and elimination process. Lack of carbohydrates can trigger a range of fertility, elimination, and digestion difficulties.

Water. Keep a bowl of fresh water out for your dog at all times, especially during the warmer months. Dogs need approximately three-quarter ounces of water a day for every pound of body weight, and more if they are sick, lactating, or living in a hot weather zone.

Vitamins and minerals

Also like human beings, dogs require a full range of vitamins and minerals to build strong bodies and to help transform the raw ingredients of their food into energy. Most important for dogs in the vitamin family are the following:

Vitamin A: Maintains a healthy coat, aids digestion, steadies the nerves, and keeps vision strong. It is found in grains, eggs, leafy greens, and carrots.
Vitamin B: Assists in body growth and metabolism. It is found in meat, fish, vegetables, milk, and yeast.
Vitamin C: A dog's precise needs for this vitamin have not yet been established.
Vitamin D: Promotes strength, bone growth, and increases calcium absorption. It is found in eggs, dairy foods, meat, and cod-liver oil.

Vitamin E: An antioxidant that is important in cell membrane function and for fertility. It is found in grains and green vegetables.

Vitamin K: Aids in blood clotting and wound healing. It is found in green vegetables, grains, and meat.

As far as minerals go, those required by dogs are surprisingly similar to the ones needed by human beings:

Calcium: For nerve health, bones, muscle function, and tooth formation. Found in dairy products and meat.

Cobalt: Helps in vitamin B_{12} processing. Found in meat and dairy products.

Copper: Helps in iron and hemoglobin processing. Found in meat.

Iodine: Maintains thyroid function. Found in fish, dairy products, and iodized or sea salt.

Iron: Used in respiration and blood production. Found in grains, eggs, meat, and green vegetables.

Manganese: Used in fat metabolism. Found in grains.

Magnesium: Aids in metabolism and bone and teeth formation.

Phosphorus: Builds bones and teeth, aids metabolism. Found in meat and dairy products.

Potassium: Controls acid-base balance in body, aids nerve function. Found in meat and dairy products.

Selenium: Aids in vitamin E synthesis. Found in grains, fish, and meat.

Sodium: Controls water balance and many body functions. Found in salt and grains.

Sulphur: Aids in amino acid production. Found in meats and eggs.

Zinc: Aids digestion and tissue repair. Found in meats and grains.

Tips on feeding dogs the right way

Commercial dog food comes in three forms: canned food, semimoist kibble (composed of 75 to 80 percent cereal and 20 to 25 percent water), and dry kibble (with 90 to 95 percent cereal and 10 to 5 percent water). Kibble is usually formed into meal, cakes, soft chunks, and hard chunks. For adult dogs a good commercial kibble supplemented with vitamins and minerals makes solid fare.

What brands of commercial dog foods are best?

First, check the label.

If a dog food claims to be "beef dog food," then by law 95 percent of the substance inside the can must be beef. The same if the label reads chicken, lamb, pork, and so forth. If the label bills the product as "chicken dinner" or "beef dinner," the product must be composed of at least 25 percent chicken or beef. A dog food that claims to be made "with beef" or "with pork" can have as little as 3 percent of the promised meat under the current standards. The rest of the contents is composed of vegetable and grain fillers.

Though some pet owners do not realize it, the parts of the animal used in dog food are considerably different from those we humans purchase at the meat counter. A "beef dog food" means that all parts of the steer are used in the mix including the viscera, blood, intestines, and even ground-up bones. The same with pigs, chickens, and so forth. This is not as bad as it sounds when you consider that dogs in the wild devour a prey's entire body after making a kill. Special "gourmet" dog foods claim to take their cuts from the better parts of the steer. These products tend to be expensive though, and it is conjectural whether or not they actually supply better nutrition for your dog.

More feeding tips

- An adult dog should be fed twice a day, once in the morning, once at night. Allow at least seven hours between each feeding.
- Although semimoist food is high on taste and easy to store, it is high on price as well and does not exercise a dog's teeth and gums in the vigorous way that dry food does.
- As a rule pregnant dogs do not require special diets until the last few weeks before they give birth. At this point increase their daily intake by 25 percent. Continue to increase the amount of food given daily, letting your dog set the pace. If she is hungry, feed her till she's full. As far as actually modifying the diet for pregnant dogs, many veterinarians discourage this and simply encourage allowing the dog to eat ad lib.
- When a mother dog is lactating double the amount of food you normally feed her each day. To help her build milk, supplement the protein supply in her food by adding eggs. Vitamins and mineral supplements are recommended, along with cooked whole rice, boiled carrots, and a sprinkle of corn oil and brewer's yeast over her food. Be especially generous to mother dogs if they are servicing a large litter.
- Dogs that eat a diet rich in wet foods require less water than those that eat predominantly dry. If your dog's meals are predominantly

composed of dry food, be especially careful to keep his water bowl freshly filled at all times.

- If your dog indulges in food or object guarding—canine possession aggression—this means he views you not as his feeder but as a potential thief of his food. Nip this tendency in the bud while he is still young. During feeding time make trips to his bowl with bits of food and encourage him to eat. Most important, avoid feeding the puppy alone. In the wilds, after the prey is brought down the alpha or top dog of the pack has the privilege of eating alone and uninterrupted until his appetite is sated. Only then are other dogs allowed to eat. If your dog is given this same perceived privilege, he will quickly think of himself as king of the hill and act accordingly.

Breaking Bad Habits, Teaching Good Ones

From time to time even the best dog errs, exhibiting habits that are annoying, destructive, and perhaps downright maddening. But take heart. Almost all the classic problems that dog owners face can be modified and corrected. The following section addresses the most common canine bad habits, providing time-tested helps and hints on how best to deal.

Mouthing

When puppies play together they simulate biting by mouthing each other in a harmless way. While romping with human beings they may replicate this same behavior. If allowed, the mouthing habit can turn into a kind of chewing as the dog matures, a process that is both annoying and potentially destructive.

Solutions: To break the mouthing habit wait until the puppy mouths you. Make a "hurt puppy" sound, then follow it with a firm command: "Stop biting!"

While you perform these actions allow your hand to remain in the dog's mouth. When the puppy releases the pressure, remove your hand, and offer the back of your hand to her for licking. If the dog obeys your commands, speak affectionately and stroke her.

By performing this routine you are both showing the puppy that your hand is a tender object not for biting, and as the one in charge here you expect signs of deference from your dog, such as licking rather than the more aggressive mouthing or biting.

Note, finally, that you should never offer your dog a toy, or worse, a bit of food when your hand is in her mouth. By so doing you are rewarding mouthing or biting behavior, and thus encouraging it.

Persistent barking

Next to biting, prolonged barking is usually considered the most serious of all dog misdemeanors. This problem arises for several reasons and is often related to breed. Among the canine family there are four types of problem barkers:

The genetically prone barker. Certain breeds such as Lhasa apsos, poodles, and schnauzers are genetically predisposed to yap and yip—to sound the alarm when the weasel raids the henhouse or the rat bores into the grain. If the same poodle or schnauzer happens to be in a city apartment and hears a noise next door, his yipping response comes naturally. As far as the poodle or schnauzer are concerned, they are simply doing their job.

Solutions: The best remedy for predisposed barkers is to train them to bark on command—and at no other time. This is not always easy to do, and with persistent cases a professional dog trainer may be necessary. Think also of finding a suitable place where your dog can bark to his heart's content once or twice a day to get the bark energy out of his system.

The territorial barker. These barkers often come from two groups: unneutered males and guard dogs. Like the genetically prone barker, guard dogs bark because that's what they are bred to do—protect your home, your henhouse, your kitchen sink.

Solutions: Neutering takes the territorial edge off a dog, which may in turn reduce his tendency to bark. Blocking the dog's view of property lines that may surround your home—for instance, installing stockade fence instead of chain-link—also helps. (If your dog can't see it she won't bark at it.) Also keep her away from the front and back door, and from places in the home where strangers congregate.

Monitor the territorial barker carefully. Don't permit her to bark at passersby. Set a precedent now, when you are home. Otherwise your dog will bark her head off when you're away.

The bored, underexercised barker. Dog groups such as hound, herding, and working dogs are bred to stay active and to spend a good deal of time on the run. To take a dog from one of these groups and coop him up in a two-room flat is asking for trouble.

Result: bark, bark, bark.

Solutions: At least two hours a day of vigorous aerobic exercise, and plenty of interesting toys to relieve the boredom. If you are gone more than six hours during the day, an hour of mentally challenging and physically active fun and games is mandatory. You should leave a tired-out, well-exercised dog behind when you leave for the day. If you do not have the facilities to exercise a hunting, herding, or working dog, it may be better to procure a dog from a less active group.

The fearful neurotic barker. A majority of dogs in this category are members of the smaller, fragile breeds, the miniatures and toys. The causes of this barking reaction are several.

Any size dog can, for instance, be transformed into a barker by being passed from home to home or by repeated neglect. If abruptly transplanted from the country to a small apartment, dogs quickly become candidates for nervous barking. In other instances a dog may suffer separation anxiety when left alone, and it complains to the world with a litany of continual howling. Overcoddling, mistreatment, long periods of isolation, and lack of socialization are all possible causes.

Solutions: The majority of nervous barkers need to be properly socialized to the world around them. Obedience work accompanied by plenty of praise builds canine confidence, yielding a more stable dog. When you leave your house, avoid dramatic good-byes—this can stimulate Rover and call attention to the fact that you're gone. In some instances, confining a dog to a crate also does the job. Kept in a small space with only a blanket and chew toy for company, many dogs calm down and curl up, apparently with real contentment. Note though that some nervous barkers exhibit severe anxiety reactions when crated. They shake, chatter, drool, and paw feverishly at the sides of the crate, and should be removed immediately. In such cases, it is wise to seek the advice of a qualified trainer or behaviorist. Without professional help this type of behavior does not change on its own.

Other ways to stifle the barking impulse include the following:

- Keep your dog in the quietest part of the house, away from the hubbub and noise of the outdoors or neighboring apartments.
- When going out for a period of time give your dog a special chew toy. Only use this toy when you leave the house. Consider giving your dog something spectacular in this instance—a sterilized beef

bone stuffed with canned dog food or cheese spread, say, or a fla-
vorful beef-basted knotted rawhide bone or a stuffed kong toy.
Give the treat to the dog just before walking out the door. Rub it
between your palms several times before you go, leaving your
scent behind.

- Create a dark environment for your dog. Pull the curtains. Put
  him in a room with few windows. Turn out the lights. Without visual stimuli dogs quickly quiet down.
- Leave a stereo or radio playing in the background when you go
  out. This method creates white noise to lull your pup into a quiet
  state. A turned-on TV also works.

Jumping up

Jumping up is not only annoying (and sometimes upsetting), but the
weight and force of a jumping dog is potentially dangerous for small
children and frail people. It can also be destructive to furniture and
fragile fabrics. Jumping up is likewise bad for the dog, giving her the
message that she can invade human space any time she wishes and
claim it for her own with impunity. Permission to behave this way soon
creates a discourteous pet.

Solutions: Greet the jumping up behavior with a firm "No!" or "Off!"
Repeat this command every time a dog jumps up. Don't delay, or the
command will be wasted. After shouting "No!" pivot so that only your
profile is facing the dog. Do not make eye contact—the dog will see this
as a challenge. Then give the command "Sit." When the dog obeys,
praise her and give her a treat.

Mounting

Mounting takes place when a dog attempts to simulate sexual mating
positions using human beings as their object. It is a disagreeable habit
that should be discouraged early.

Solutions: Male dogs are most likely to be the offenders here. It
often helps to neuter. When a dog starts his mounting motions greet
him with a firm "No!" and make him "Sit!"

Destructive chewing

Pet owners know in advance that they may take a few hits now and
then from the chewing habits of a new pup. It's part of the process. But

pups that chew and destroy every item in sight soon become a menace, especially as they age. Unless this problem is addressed early and with great consistency, your sweet little pet can soon turn into a household menace.

Solutions: Keep all chewy items out of harm's way, especially leather items (which are, after all, animal skin). To the list add slippers, socks, baseball mitts, leather belts, shoes, leather purses; all are perennial favorites. Also make sure your pup is well stocked with a hearty supply of chewable toys, especially the rawhide kind. When you catch her in the chewing act, say a firm "No!" and immediately give her a favorite chewy toy instead. Finally, besides teething, much chewing behavior is based on restlessness and boredom. Confining a dog to a crate is a good antidote here. Make sure to leave several chewables in the crate with the dog if you are going out. Nylabones and large rawhide knots are both good. Do avoid giving your dog old shoes, belts, and towels, however. This is equivalent to telling her it's OK to chew these items. And watch out for long, stringy rawhide rope or laces. Your dog can choke on them. Also be sure to secure electric cords to the wall away from the puppy's reach.

Digging

By nature many breeds of dog are burrowers. To this genetic tendency add several other possible causes for digging: boredom, lack of exercise, burying a bone (or digging one up), attempts to find a cool place, and the need to escape and join other dogs (i.e., to mate).

Solutions: Before putting your dog in the yard, take her for a good run. At least forty-five minutes of intensive and hopefully exhausting play tires out the burrowing impulse. (If she overheats during these sessions provide a kiddie pool in the yard for cooling down.) Dogs are also less likely to burrow after they've eaten. If you put your dog in a penned yard, feed her first, then supervise her when she is in the penned area.

The digging habit is likewise redirected by creating a special environment in your yard designed to accommodate the dog's burrowing instinct—a sand pit, a pile of topsoil, and/or a shallow hole. Finally, antidigging repellents and sprays are sold at most pet supply stores. These in theory create chemical barriers over the sprayed area, and/or interfere with a dog's sense of smell. In fact, there is some question concerning their true usefulness.

Feces eating

Why dogs eat stool is not entirely understood, though there are no lack of theories. From an evolutionary standpoint, animals that consume the widest variety of nutrients assure themselves the greatest chance of survival. Some animals in the wild also eat the feces of their offspring to avoid leaving scent trails for predators. Other theories for feces eating include boredom, overcorrection from housebreaking indiscretions, and parasites. Whatever the reasons motivating it, feces eating, known technically as *coprophagy*, takes several forms, each demanding a different solution.

Nutrition. Some believe feces eating is the dog's way of taking in nutrients missing in his ordinary diet. From this standpoint feces eating is nothing more than body wisdom.

Ecological Pet Waste Removal

When cleaning up after a pet, some people feel guilty that they are wasting all that wonderful fertilizer. Solution: an in-ground stool digester. These interesting contraptions are dug into the earth, special enzymes are added, and pet wastes are scooped up and deposited. Like any septic system, the stool digester slowly breaks down and finally liquefies the wastes, then returns them to the surrounding soil. Stool digesters can be ordered from any good pet supply store.

Solutions: A dog's diet should be carefully considered and perhaps reviewed by a veterinarian who specializes in canine nutrition. What's lacking from the menu? What foods should be added? Some veterinarians recommend that highly concentrated foods be served dogs who indulge in this unpleasant habit.

Competition. In some cases dogs ingest feces out of possessiveness and an impulse to compete with other dogs. "This feces is *mine!*" the dog is saying by its actions. "Keep away!"

Solutions: During exercise and outdoor periods, either isolate the dog in her own run, or redirect her possessiveness by giving her an attractive toy available as a substitute for the feces. Clean up all feces as soon as the dog soils.

Boredom. There is nothing else to do. Might as well pass the time by eating whatever's handy.

Solutions: If you are away much of the day, provide a food-dispensing device for your canine that allows him to eat when he feels the need. Also try increasing your dog's daily exercise quotient and award him with plenty of extra attention. If you are unable to give more of your time, ask a friend, family member, or dog walker to do it for you. A dog who eats feces out of boredom will continue this habit until the root cause of the boredom is addressed.

Refusal to come when called and to obey commands

You train your puppy to come when called and to obey all basic commands. He is an attentive student, and learns quickly. All's well. Then one day seemingly out of the blue he starts playing coy, sometimes coming when called, sometimes not, sometimes taking his own sweet time. This mutiny may soon turn into a blatant refusal to obey any commands whatsoever including the basic ones like "Sit!" or "Down!"

Solutions: The problem stems from the fact that your dog simply didn't learn his obedience ABCs well enough. The solution is go back to A and reteach him, using the same training tactics as before until the lessons are better learned. While you're at it, use positive reinforcement such as a treat, a favorite toy, lavish praise, or all the above to keep the experience enjoyable. Make retraining sessions brief, and end each with a romp to keep up the spirit of play. Remember, if you take away the fun, your dog will take away his enthusiasm and attention.

Note, finally, that disobedience may stem simply from a roving eye among male adolescents, especially if their training area is filled with distractions. See the next entry for details.

Sexual misconduct

Sexual frustration in a dog can produce a wide range of undesirable behaviors, the most prominent being roaming, intermale aggression, and sexually instigated mounting.

Solutions: Neutering usually takes care of these sexual problems (with the possible exception of mounting). Neutering nips undesirable sexual behaviors in the bud before they begin to express themselves. It also facilitates the retraining of a dog, which means that even if a dog forgets its basic training commands, neutering makes him more receptive to relearning them.

Separation anxiety

Some dogs become so bonded to their human master that when the master steps out of sight, even for a few moments, the dog becomes overly anxious and starts to pace, drool, soil, paw, bark, or chew household objects.

Solutions: Promote independence in your dog by teaching him to stay on his own bed when you leave the room or otherwise pass out of sight. Repeat for short durations, then build up to a length of time that the dog can tolerate. A gate placed between you and the dog also helps. Several family members (rather than one) should share in the walking, playing, and feeding sessions.

A dog's hysteria often takes place during the first hour after departure. Diffuse the emotion of your leave taking by heartily exercising the dog right after you wake up. Then, after feeding him, scale back your attention to the point of ignoring him during the last fifteen minutes before you leave. Turn off the lights and turn on the television, radio, or white noise machine—whatever you play most when you are at home. Then, with no more than a whispered "Be good," leave the house. For less seriously afflicted canines, presenting the animal with a toy stuffed with goodies can draw the focus away from your leaving.

In 1999 the Food and Drug Administration (FDA) announced that Clomicalm, a drug used to treat mental problems in humans, works relatively well for controlling separation anxiety in dogs. Since, legally speaking, any FDA-approved human medication can also be prescribed for animals if no veterinary drug exists to treat a problem, Clomicalm is now available in all clinical veterinarian practices. In the next few years we expect to see a proliferation of its use, a fact that is causing dog owners high hopes that otherwise fine dogs who are euthanized because of extreme separation anxiety will be able to live out their lives in a normal and adjusted way. If separation anxiety is a problem in your household, and environmental changes like the ones suggested above do not help, consult with an applied animal behaviorist who can design a treatment protocol for your dog that may include drug therapy. Note, however, that medications prescribed for problem behaviors in dogs should always be used in conjunction with behavior-modification training programs to be truly effective.

Possessiveness

You have probably seen a dog with a bone in her mouth growl menacingly at family members who come too close. The same reaction can take place when a dog has a ball or a toy. Known as "food and object guarding," this habit is best put to a stop when dogs are young and highly trainable. If not checked early, it can lead to biting and even to attacking.

Solutions: Accustom your dog at an early age to having his mouth touched and manipulated, so that when you place your hand in his mouth to remove an object he will not bite. Start the process when your dog is a puppy. Brush his teeth, rub his gums, play with his flews (the corners of the upper lip), open and close his mouth. Also, place one or two select doggie toys on the floor, keeping the others out of sight. During playtime start the session with a command for the dog to take the toy: "Take it." When you tire of the game tell the dog to drop the toy by saying, "Drop it." When he obeys, reward him with another toy in exchange, preferably one he likes better than the first (or if not with a toy, a favorite treat or activity). Gather the first toy and put it away. When dogs over six months of age show undue signs of possessiveness, it is often necessary to work with a professional trainer or behaviorist to rid them of this habit.

Maintaining Your Dog's Good Health

In Chapter 5 we discussed a range of health and emergency considerations for pets. Besides general wellness concerns, however, there are a number of pet-specific diseases and ailments that pet owners should watch for and know something about when they strike.

Your veterinarian is, of course, the one to diagnose and treat these ailments. But vigilance helps spot a health problem early in the game and gives you time to get your friend to the veterinarian's office before too much damage is done. Here, for instance, is a typical sickness scenario: Lassie walks into your room one day looking droopy and lackadaisical. Her eyes have no sparkle. You pick up her ball and roll it across the floor, but she ignores the invitation to play. Strange.

Dinnertime comes and goes, and her food remains untouched in the bowl. If she's not eating then where is she? Curled up on her pillow. Asleep? Not exactly. But not awake either.

That night you hear strange coughing noises. The next afternoon she uncharacteristically crawls under your bed to sleep. She whines when you approach her.

What's the problem? Hard to tell, but it's certainly something.

What are some of the possibilities? The following list includes the most common dog diseases. It tells you a bit about what they are, how they hurt, and what you—and your veterinarian—can do to prevent them and/or cure them.

Recognizing symptoms of illness in your dog

Generalized symptoms in dogs that indicate sickness include the following:

- A sudden loss or gain of weight; a marked decrease or increase in appetite.
- Chronic cough.
- Diarrhea or constipation for more than a day or two. Be especially careful of diarrhea and vomiting in puppies. At this age canines are easily dehydrated and can die from body fluid loss in a surprisingly short period of time. If a puppy shows signs of either condition take it to your veterinarian immediately.
- Lethargy and dramatically reduced activity level that lasts for more than a day or so.
- Constant itching, scratching, shaking of the head, licking of the paws, or digging into the skin.
- Gasping, heavy panting not caused by any apparent stimulation, heavy salivation.
- Lack of drinking or excessive thirst.
- Dramatic changes in skin or coat: rashes, welts, discolorations, thick dandruff, abscesses, or color changes.
- Swelling or inflammation, especially on the limbs and pads.
- Obvious signs of pain (e.g., a dog whines or makes small yelps when it stands up).
- Changes in urination, including excessive urinary straining.
- Blood in the stool, urine, or from other sources.
- Pale gums.
- Abnormal discharge from the eyes, nose, or ears.

It is commonly believed that a warm, dry nose in a dog is a sign of sickness. This is not necessarily the case. A dog's nose goes through many changes during the day, and dryness may be one of them.

Other symptoms of medical conditions in dogs include limping, an inability to stand or move about and play normally, worms or other living creatures found in the stool, open wounds, squinting, changes in consciousness, and lack of focused awareness of surroundings.

Common canine diseases and their symptoms

Parvovirus

Cause—Parvovirus is an extremely contagious and often fatal canine disease that mainly attacks puppies. It is spread from dog to dog via feces on the fur, paws, or other parts of the body. It can also be transmitted to animals from the clothes or shoes of human beings.

Symptoms—Symptoms begin from three to fourteen days after exposure. The main indication of parvovirus is bloody diarrhea, usually accompanied by fever, lethargy, vomiting, and loss of appetite.

Treatment and prevention—Once stricken with parvovirus a dog will require hospitalization, fluids, medication, and supportive care. In very young puppies the disease can be fatal. For this reason it is critical that your pup receives parvovirus vaccinations at around six weeks of age, followed up by booster shots every three weeks until twelve to sixteen weeks of age. Parvovirus vaccinations are 90% effective in adult dogs, but are somewhat less effective for puppies. If there is parvovirus in your neighborhood, and your dog is not fully vaccinated, keep her indoors and away from other dogs. The disease is spread via contaminants carried on clothes, fur, the bottom of shoes and paws, in a dog's crate or bed, and so forth. The parvovirus can survive in a friendly environment for months, and all steps should be taken to remove it from the home by means of thorough disinfecting. A dilute solution of bleach kills all traces of the virus.

Canine distemper

Cause: Canine distemper is caused by an organism similar to the human measles virus. An airborne disorder, it spreads easily among dogs and is common among animals in the wild as well such as racoons, ferrets, skunks, coyotes, and foxes.

Symptoms: The first symptoms of canine distemper appear three to five days after infection and are often mistaken for a cold. They include a fever of 103 to 105°F (normal temperature in dogs is between 101.7 and 102.2°F), lethargy, vomiting, diarrhea, and loss of appetite. A clear watery discharge from the eyes and nose appears, then turns yellow and clotted after several days. In the weeks that follow the brain and nervous system are affected, causing the dog to act crazy, running in circles, drooling, falling down, showing tremors and spasms, and shaking its head continually as if trying to clear its ears. Dogs in this advanced stage of distemper may or may not survive, and if they do many will have seizures or tremors for the rest of their lives.

Treatment and prevention: Distemper does not respond to antibiotics, though they are sometimes used (along with anticonvulsants, bronchial soothers, and antidiarrheals) to subdue secondary symptoms. The sooner the disease is diagnosed and treated, the better the chances are for survival. A highly effective vaccination is also available for distemper. The first shot is given around six to eight weeks of age, and a booster at twelve to sixteen months. Canine distemper is harmless to humans.

Rabies

Cause: This terrible disease, scourge to human beings and animals alike, is mainly spread by animals in the wild, especially the racoon, bat, fox, and skunk. The disease is caused by a virus that is spread through the saliva of infected animals. The virus enters the victim's body through any open wound, even innocuous wounds like a hangnail or chapped lips. Once inside the body, the virus directly attacks the brain. Though usually transmitted by the bite of an infected animal, contact with rabies-contaminated saliva or a rabies-contaminated wound can also transfer the infection.

Symptoms: The first symptoms of rabies can appear as early as three to eight weeks after infection, though incubation periods sometimes last as long as a year. Early symptoms include personality changes in the animal such as irritability, hiding, isolation, and antisocial behavior. The dog becomes restless, loses her appetite, and appears sensitive to light and touch. In the last stages she may drool, bite, foam at the mouth, lose muscle control, become delirious, and collapse.

There are two forms of rabies. The first is the "furious" form that causes aimless running, frenzy, convulsions, and the impulse to attack anything that moves. The second is the "paralytic" form. This produces slack tongue, drooling, poor locomotion, muscle paralysis, and reluctance to eat or drink (thus the name "hydrophobia"—fear of water).

Treatment and prevention: There is no cure for rabies, and no hope of recovery. If your dog (or a wild animal in your yard) shows signs of having the disease, *it is absolutely imperative that you notify your public health authority immediately.* Failure to report this event endangers both yourself and your family. Your local public health facility will respond quickly and will dispose of the diseased animal with dispatch.

Avoid all these difficulties by making sure your dog is vaccinated during the first three to six months of its puppyhood. Boosters are required every one to three years, depending on the vaccine used and on local regulations.

Heartworm

Cause: Like malaria or encephalitis, heartworm is transmitted by the bite of an infected mosquito. The larva from this contaminated insect burrows into a dog's skin where it goes through a three-month growth cycle, eventually turning into a small worm. Over time it makes its way to the dog's heart and surrounding vessels. Here it mates and produces more worms. The cycle continues until the effects of this massive population of worms destroys its host.

Symptoms: Dogs can harbor heartworm for several years before showing symptoms. When symptoms do appear their degree of intensity depends on how many worms are active and how effectively the animal's immune system responds. Possible symptoms include an uncharacteristic reluctance to run or play, constant coughing and labored breathing, weight loss (despite a strong appetite), swelling in the legs and abdomen, and general lethargy. After even short periods of physical exertion the dog appears to be weak and on occasion may even pass out.

Treatment and prevention: If you suspect heartworm, take your dog to the veterinarian immediately for an examination, X ray, and blood tests. If tests are positive, treatment protocols are available. With proper care and medication many dogs pull through. But some don't. There are no guarantees. The prognosis depends on how much infestation is present and how much organ damage has occurred by the time of hospitalization.

In the first stage of treatment, your dog will be treated with worm-killing drugs then released. For some time after treatment exertion must be kept to a minimum to avoid embolisms triggered by residues of dead worms. Three to six weeks later a second drug regime is employed to rid the dog's system of young or newborn worms. In serious cases of heartworm, surgery may be necessary to remove clusters of worms directly from the heart.

Prevention of heartworm consists in giving your dog a monthly medication to kill the offending larvae. For those who live in warm, mosquito-infested climates or in areas where heartworm is reported, this method is highly recommended. Year-round preventive medication should also be used if you travel with your dog through heartworm-infested parts of the country.

Kennel cough (tracheobronchitis)

Cause: The most common of all canine respiratory disorders, kennel cough is caused by a complex of viruses and bacteria. The ailment is highly contagious and is easily spread in crowded canine quarters such as kennels, animal shelters, dog shows, and pet stores.

Symptoms: The main symptom of kennel cough consists of a deep, loud, hacking and persistent cough. It appears five to ten days after exposure. As the disease progresses the cough may be followed by regurgitating or gagging sounds, plus the coughing up of a white frothy phlegm. Other than these conspicuous symptoms, the dog appears to be happy and healthy.

Treatment and prevention: Dogs infected with serious cases of kennel cough must be treated with antibiotics and rest. For mild cases, a good animal cough syrup keeps the coughing to a minimum until healing occurs. If you intend to board or show dogs, it is recommended that you have them inoculated against this pesky disease.

Leptospirosis

Cause: Leptospirosis is a bacterial disease transmitted through the urine of dogs. Contagion takes place when contact is made between an open wound and infected urine, or when a dog drinks urine-contaminated water. Leptospirosis primarily affects the liver and kidneys. This disease is also infectious for human beings, and it can be transmitted to humans by rats as well as dogs.

Symptoms: Because there are several types of leptospirosis that attack different organs of the body, not all cases present in a similar way. The most common symptoms include fever, loss of appetite, depression, vomiting, weakness, dehydration, intense thirst, and apparent pain in the abdominal regions. If the infection is in the kidneys, the dog frequently hunches herself up in an effort to relieve pressure on these organs. Her tongue often has a brown coating, and ulcerated sores may form around the mouth.

Treatment and prevention: Leptospirosis responds well to antibiotic treatment, and the prognosis is usually good. Hospitalization may be required. Note that the urine of a sick dog is infectious for up to a year's time, both for humans and for dogs. This is true even when all the dog's symptoms have disappeared. Talk to your veterinarian about ways to avoid contamination when handling your dog.

Coronavirus

Cause: First identified in 1971, coronavirus is a relatively mild and relatively "new" disease. It is spread through contact with infected dog feces or oral secretions, often in crowded dog conditions such as a ken-

nel, shelter, pet store, or dog show. The symptoms tend to be more serious in puppies than in adult dogs.

Symptoms: The hallmark symptom of this disease is diarrhea. Stools
smell foul, and they sometimes have a brownish orange color. Other
symptoms include depression, lethargy, loss of appetite, and vomiting,
sometimes with blood.

Treatment and prevention: Your veterinarian will treat coronavirus
by providing plenty of replacement fluids and medications to control
vomiting and diarrhea. Dogs rarely die from this disease, though it can
make them extremely sick. If you plan to place your dog in a kennel, or
if you intend to enter him in dog shows, a one-a-year vaccination for
coronavirus is recommended.

Infectious canine hepatitis

Cause: Infectious hepatitis is a highly contagious viral disease, in-
flaming the liver and attacking the kidneys and blood vessels. It is acquired by contact with sick dogs or with an infected dog's feces, saliva,
and urine. Though it strikes canines of all ages, puppies are most vulnerable and most likely to die from this ailment.

Symptoms: Symptoms include fever, lethargy, bloody diarrhea and
vomit, conjunctivitis, ocular and nasal discharge, reddened, bleeding
gums, and loss of appetite. Dogs sometimes become photosensitive if
their corneas become cloudy, squinting or looking away from even relatively dim sources of light. They may also develop bleeding and hema-
tomas, or walk in a hunched-up way to relieve the pain caused by the
swelling in the liver area.

Treatment and prevention: Infectious canine hepatitis can be detected by a veterinarian with examination and blood tests. Treatment is
complex, including antibiotic therapy and possible blood transfusions.
The prognosis depends on how advanced the disease is at the time of
treatment. Infectious hepatitis can be prevented by a vaccination given
in the first six to eight weeks of life, followed by a booster shot. Canine
hepatitis is different from the hepatitis that strikes human beings, and it
is not contagious to humans.

Brucellosis

Cause: Brucellosis is an infectious disease that produces reproduc-
tive failure in males and females and abortion in females. As might be
expected, it is especially dreaded by breeders. Transmission takes place
through an infected dog's semen, vaginal fluids, and discharge during
sexual contact.

Symptoms: Symptoms include generalized enlargement of the lymph nodes, especially in the groin and under the chin, spontaneous abortion, scrotal swelling, and infertility.

Treatment and prevention: Brucellosis can be detected at the veterinarian's office with lab testing. Once identified, the chance for cure is slight. Prolonged antibiotic treatment is required, and there is a high incidence of relapse. Experimental methods make an equally poor showing. Though not highly contagious, on rare occasions brucellosis can be transmitted from dogs to human beings, and vigilance is recommended when handling diseased dogs. Dogs who have suffered from this disease can never be bred.

Other Important Health Concerns for Dogs

Ringworm. Ringworm is a fungal skin disorder that takes its name from the sometimes ring-shaped rashes it produces. Ringworm is highly infectious, not only between dogs, but between dogs and humans and dogs and cats. If your canine is scratching himself frequently, put on a pair of rubber gloves and examine the scratch points. If you find round, red rashes with hair loss in the center, a visit to the veterinarian is in order. Oral medications taken for six-week periods along with fungicidal shampoos are usually required. Note that children are especially susceptible to the ringworm fungus, so keep them well away from infected animals during the healing process.

Intestinal parasites. Hookworms, tapeworms, and roundworms are the most common canine worms. Wiggly, prolific creatures that are surprisingly long, they make themselves at home in the dog's digestive tract, sometimes residing there for years. Puppies are especially vulnerable to infestation, so keep a look out for a potbelly in your pup, a probable sign that parasites have invaded. If worms are suspected, your veterinarian can determine exactly which variety of worm is present, then prescribe the appropriate medications.

Worms are a double danger: they infect human beings as well as dogs, usually via contact with an infected dog's feces or with objects that have touched the feces. To avoid worms and human infection entirely, worm your dog on an as-needed basis, pick up all his droppings immediately with a plastic bag or feces-scooping device, and keep both yourself and your children away from areas where dogs leave their daily deposits (children commonly develop worms by eating materials contaminated with infected fecal material).

Mange. Mange is caused by two types of microscopic mites that infect the dog's skin and/or fur, spread in all directions, cause fur to come out in small, ugly patches, and sometimes produce secondary infections such as impetigo. The two main offenders are *Sarcoptes* mites that burrow directly into the skin (especially around the ears), causing hair loss, itching, and sores, and Demodex mites that favor the hair follicles. Infection from Demodex mites causes little itching but produces nasty pustules over the dog's body. Since mange is difficult to cure at home and can be infectious to humans, treatment by a veterinarian is required.

Fleas. Not only do fleas suck your dog's blood, they are responsible for the spread of a wide range of human diseases from allergies to the black plague. If untreated they proliferate at lightning speeds, infesting an entire home. They are not to be trifled with or ignored. Severe cases can actually lead to an animal's hospitalization and death.

Constant scratching and self-biting are the primary symptoms. If your dog seems obsessed by a constant itch, slip on a pair of gloves and place your pet on a large piece of white paper. Gently brushing and parting her fur, search for vermin around those areas that are most likely to be infected such as the stomach, chest, anus, and tail regions. If fleas are present flea debris will fall to the floor, and show up against the white paper. Though minute, fleas are also plainly visible as they scurry away on the fur, or leap up in the air. They are especially conspicuous on a white fur background. You will also find their tiny, comma-shaped leavings deposited over irritated areas.

A number of commercial shampoos, powders, dips, salves, and sprays are available for treating fleas. Long-term antiflea treatments are also available directly from veterinarians. These are squeezed from a small dispenser directly onto the dog's skin or given orally. Each application does the job for at least a month. Some experts also claim that sprinkling brewer's yeast into a dog's food causes them to emit a smell that is unpleasant to fleas and encourages the fleas to abandon ship. It's worth a try—if your dog will eat it.

Contrary to popular belief, not only are flea collars considered an ineffective method of prevention by many pet-care experts, but once infestation begins they are more or less useless at stemming the tide. If you do use a flea collar, expose it to the air for at least three days before placing it on your animal and carefully follow all directions on the package.

Fleas constantly lay eggs on their victims and in surrounding areas, and these eggs hatch in rapid cycles. Treatment must be consistent and ongoing to be effective. If your dog becomes reinfested after each treatment the problem may be her environment. Make regular flea checks of your rugs (a favorite spot), blankets, and couches. Inspect your dog's sleeping area with special care, regularly washing blankets, pillows, and bedding. Flea bombs are available at most pharmacies and pet supply stores, and they are fairly effective for small infestations. If a flea population is allowed to spread unchecked for too long a period of time, however, a professional exterminator may be the only solution.

Ticks. Ticks fasten themselves onto the warm parts of animals, especially the neck, ears, shoulders, crotch, and between the toes. They proceed to drink the animal's blood until fully engorged. They then drop off five thousand or more eggs when finished before going their way.

The solution to this vicious cycle consists of putting on gloves, taking a pair of tweezers, and pulling the ticks off one at a time. Petroleum jelly can also be smeared over the ticks to suffocate them.

After ridding your animal of these creatures, check the bite areas for several days to make sure there are no signs of infection. If your canine is heavily infested, your veterinarian may recommend an in-office treatment with medicated dips.

Ear infections. If your dog starts scratching both ears violently and shaking her head, if you see small red or black waxy deposits clinging to the inside of her ears, and if an unpleasant odor emanates from these parts, chances are she has ear mites.

These microscopic pests can be eliminated, but you will have to be persistent. First, have your veterinarian make a positive diagnosis and prescribe the proper miticide. Apply this medicine faithfully or as directed. Be as diligent as possible in following the dosage schedule. Forgetting to apply the medicine even once may allow the eggs to hatch and ruin all your work.

Do not allow mites to get too dug into your pet's ear canals; it is a lot more difficult to remove them once they become chronic. It is also smart preventive medicine to give your dog's ears a thorough examination once a week. Dust them regularly with flea powder, avoiding the ear canals, and if there are other animals in the house make sure they do not become infected.

Dental care. If you handle a dog's mouth frequently while she is young she will become familiar with having human hands touch her tongue and teeth and will not balk at dental checks and teeth brushing when the time comes.

Many veterinarians suggest that you procure a child's toothbrush and brush your dog's teeth once or twice a week. This type of preventive maintenance helps avoid dental bills later on. Canine toothpaste should be used for the job, available from your local pet supply store. You may also wish to have a veterinarian check and clean your dog's teeth when necessary. Dental caries (tooth cavities), abscesses, malocclusions, and plaque buildup are all potential problems, just as in humans. Dogs also get periodontal disease. Here again, brushing helps.

One of the first symptoms of poor dental health is severe doggie breath. If this unpleasant condition is accompanied by raw gums and/or sores on the gums, a trip to the veterinarian is recommended. It is also a good idea to check your dog's teeth for plaque and tartar buildup. Plaque forms a kind of filmy deposit on the teeth at the gum line. Tartar is a calcified sediment that clings to the teeth like barnacles. These conditions are often accompanied by gingivitis (gum inflammation) and periodontal disease.

Brushing a dog's teeth every day discourages decay. Other preventive methods that maintain strong, white teeth include a diet that contains plenty of hard foods (such as kibble and biscuit), chewing on large, hard bones, rawhide toys, and a yearly cleaning and polishing at the veterinarian.

Tips to Keep Your Dog in Top Physical Condition

Avoid sugar. You are never helping your dog by giving him candy, sugar, ice cream, cake, or any other tasty but unhealthy treat. Do not even slip once in this area. By keeping sweets off a dog's menu entirely he never knows such foods exist, and he does not beg for them when they are on the table.

Exercise. Though it has been said many times throughout these chapters, the point cannot be repeated enough times: exercise, exercise, exercise. Statistically speaking, couch potato dogs live shorter lives and are prone to many more diseases than dogs that receive at least forty-five minutes to an hour of robust exercise every day. Even older dogs profit from physical workouts, though of course exercise sessions should always be suited to the dog's age and physical condition. Do not neglect this all important and relatively easy life-prolonging aid for your family companion.

Medications to keep on hand. Although there are many human medications that disagree with dogs, some really help. The following substances are all useful in time of sickness:

Charcoal pills—For stomach upset and diarrhea
Salt—To induce vomiting
Syrup of ipecac—To induce vomiting
Peroxide—To induce vomiting and cleanse a wound
Buffered aspirin—For pain relief: Give one-third of a 300-mg tablet per twenty-two pounds of weight every twelve hours
Kaopectate—For diarrhea: one teaspoon per five pounds of weight every four hours
Mineral oil—For constipation: one teaspoon per five pounds of weight once a day
Milk of magnesia—For constipation and stomach upset: one teaspoon per five pounds of weight every six hours

Check expiration dates on veterinary drugs: Veterinary drugs, like human drugs, go stale. After six months or longer they are often too weak to do the job. Always check expiration dates. As with human drugs, keep all pet medications out of reach of children.

Keep a first aid kit: If there is a dog in your house be sure and keep a home medical kit for emergencies. Instructions for assembling a pet medical kit are given in Chapter 5.

Keep older dogs warm: For aging canines, inclement weather can be harmful. During cold months let your elderly dog's walk be long enough for her to do her business. If she then appears to be uncomfortable, return home immediately.

Maintain a healthy weight: It is estimated that approximately one-third of all domestic dogs are overweight. When you consider that extra poundage contributes to a wide range of medical problems among dogs, including diabetes, fatigue, constipation, shortness of breath, joint disease, compromised liver function, heart attacks, strokes, and many more, you see why experts insist that canine obesity is no trivial matter.

As with humans, prevention is the best cure. Beware of overfeeding and between meal snacks. Don't sneak your dog extra tidbits or gorge him on rich table scraps. Better to determine the best diet for your dog's size, age, breed, and activity level, and then stick to it faithfully. Over the long haul, keeping a dog's weight steady is simply a matter of providing the right food in the proper proportions.

If your pup continues to put on weight after a period of sensible eating, a stricter dietary program may be in order.

First, have your veterinarian examine the dog thoroughly to make sure no systemic problems are producing the extra pounds. Then discuss a weight-loss program. Your veterinarian may or may not want to put the dog on a prescription weight-loss food. In some cases, a strict reduction in calories is all that is necessary. Combine the new diet with dramatically increased amounts of daily exercise, and follow this regime for as long as it takes to reach the target weight. Then keep the dog on the maintenance diet recommended by your veterinarian.

Periodically check your dog's vital signs. When checking your dog's vital signs, the following facts should be considered:

Breathing rate: A dog's breath rate varies from twelve to thirty-five breaths a minute, with fifteen breaths per minute being a normal approximate resting breath. When a dog is overheated or overexcited, make sure his breath rate does not go too far off this scale.

Normal resting pulse: The normal resting pulse for small dogs is around 130 per minute.

The normal resting pulse for medium-size dogs is around one hundred per minute.

The normal resting pulse for large dogs is around eighty per minute.

To take a dog's pulse, place three fingers on the femoral artery inside the hind leg midway between the knee and hip. Count the number of beats for fifteen seconds, then multiply this number by four. The result gives a fairly accurate pulse-per-minute count.

Temperature: The normal body temperature range for dogs is between 101.7 and 102.6°F. Anything much higher than this is considered a fever.

Beware of allergens. If your dog coughs, sneezes, and snorts constantly with a drippy nose, or develops eczema after rolling in the grass or lying under a blanket, allergies may be lurking. Like humans, some dogs are genetically susceptible to a range of antigens including pollen, leaf mold, mites, dust, aerosols, certain foods, and more. If your dog shows the classic signs as described above, your veterinarian can test for specific sensitivities and may be able to determine which antigens are causing the problem. Once you have isolated the culprits you can take steps at home to keep the dog and the source of the allergies apart. For persistent cases, weekly desensitization treatment is available, though this procedure is a long and costly process, and its rate of success far from 100 percent. In many cases, dogs, like humans, must simply learn to live with their seasonal sensitivities.

Give your dog plenty of care. Dogs, like people, are most healthy and happy when they live in a positive, loving environment filled with doting household members and wholesome living conditions. In the long run, the single most important factor in your dog's health is you— the home you provide, the care you lavish, and the quality of attention you give to your canine friend. Like you, like me, like all of us, a dog is at his best when he is most loved.

8

Caring for Your Cat

Your Mysterious Houseguest

Dogs were domesticated many thousands of years ago and for obvious reasons: they hunted and herded in the fields for their human masters during the day and guarded their homes at night. Their domestication makes practical sense.

Cats, on the other hand, arrived on the human doorstep around 3000 B.C., and under strange circumstances. They do not herd flocks. They do not pull sleds, flush out game, lead the blind, or guard the fences. True, they make excellent snake and rat exterminators, and our early ancestors clearly kept them around for this purpose. During the black plague in midfourteenth-century Europe, cities with large feline populations were known to have dramatically fewer outbreaks of pestilence than cities that chased away their cats (it was actually rumored in some cities that cats were the cause of the disease).

But another reason for the cat's domestication is more interesting and mysterious: many early cultures considered them holy.

Figures of cats embossed on protective amulets have, for example, been unearthed in early Chinese tombs and in Babylonian ruins. Among the tombs of the ancient Egyptians we see images of cats paddling boats, prowling the fields, sitting on thrones next to the pharaoh. They chase birds, strut on their hind legs, watch as the souls of the dead

march past them into the underworld, and, along with a few other chosen animals like the hippopotamus and the dog, heavily populate the art
and architecture of this ancient people. One of the greatest deities in
the Egyptian pantheon, the goddess Bastet, is portrayed with the head
of a cat.

What strange quality do these animals possess that makes us think
them so enigmatic and their presence so venerable? What makes us
open our hearts and homes to them so willingly, while they provide us
with so few practical services in return?

It is difficult to answer this question precisely, though people who
share their homes with a cat are always happy to give it a try. After all
the explanations are in, however, the theme that seems to predominate
above all others is this: we domesticated the feline species for one
simple reason—cats make wonderful pets.

So meet our friend, *Felis catus*—the common domestic house cat.

A Primer of Cat Behavior

Tiger on the blanket

As any animal expert will tell you, cats have one foot on the lace
blanket, the other in the jungle. This provocative combination of the living room and wilderness, the familiar and the inscrutable, is no doubt
what allows us to put up with cats' stubborn insistence on doing what
they want when they want—our needs and wishes notwithstanding.

Though well adapted to human family life, cats tend to be more solitary than dogs. Unlike dogs, ancestors of the cat did not live in struc-
tured social groups the way wolves do. The ethic of the pack, with its
group loyalties and devotion to a single leader, has never been part of
the feline operating system. Indeed, cats might well go their own way
from human beings entirely if not so seduced by our warm houses, our
tasty meals, and our tender affections.

Feline senses

Cats are *crepuscular* creatures by nature, which means they hunt by
dawn and dusk. This tendency is somewhat frustrated by the human
habit of rising by light and sleeping by dark. Nevertheless, a cat's five
senses are genetically engineered to operate in a twilight environment.

The feline sense of smell, for example, is one of the cat's most powerful nighttime hunting tools. Not only can cats smell and home in on prey in the darkness, but a small, pouch-shaped sensing mechanism on the roof of their mouths known as *Jacobson's organ* half smells, half "tastes" objects at a distance, allowing cats to determine their prey's level of palatability. The Jacobson's organ plays a part in the feline mating process as well.

Feline hearing is likewise a primary nighttime hunting weapon. It allows cats to discern noises several octaves above human range, especially such high-pitched sounds as the squeak of a mouse. A cat's ears are built to pivot in the direction of a sound, and their ability to form their ear into a kind of sound tunnel provides them with a remarkably effective feline ear trumpet.

Supplementing these highly developed senses are cats' facial whiskers and the hairs on the back of their front legs. Facial whiskers serve as measuring devices, guiding cats in the dark and telling them when a space is wide enough to squeeze through. Though to human beings a cat's whiskers seem nothing more than an endearing appendage, for a cat these hairs are vital, not only for navigating the world but as a tool of communication with other cats. The hairs on the forelegs, meanwhile, serve as delicate antennae helping them creep through the thickest brush undetected.

As far as sight is concerned, common wisdom has it that a cat's vision is underdeveloped in relation to human beings. This is not entirely the case. Cats do not see as well as humans in full light, it is true, but as compensation their eyes possess more rods and fewer cones, making their night vision more than twice as acute as that of human beings. Cats also have stereoscopic vision that allows them to judge depth, height, and distance with uncanny skill.

The hunting instinct

Cats are basically predatory, much to the chagrin of kindly cat owners who die a thousand deaths when their sweet little pussy cat proudly deposits the corpse of a dead mouse on the bed. If allowed outdoors for any period of time most cats will capture and kill a sample of the local wildlife. A cat's apparently senseless habit of "playing" with a captured animal before killing it is difficult to take for some pet owners, though some experts believe that by putting their prey through these tormenting gymnastics a cat is honing its hunting skills. (Experts also theorize that some cats play with prey because they were not taught to kill adequately by their mothers.)

Even small kittens exhibit these hunting and pouncing behaviors, sometimes to a harrowing degree. But be careful. Any attempt to alter the hunting urge or to train it out of the animal is not only futile, but a denial of a cat's most primal instincts. A better way to protect the small creatures in your yard is to simply follow the advice given by a majority of animal experts and keep your cat inside at all times.

Grooming

An aspect of feline behavior that is much admired is the cat's instinct to self-clean. Indeed, the first thing a cat usually does after waking, sunbathing, or having a meal is to groom herself, usually with great concentration and ceremony. Because of this tendency to groom, pet cats seldom need to be bathed.

Note that a healthy cat possesses a biological imperative to self-clean, and any feline that suddenly stops cleaning and lets her coat grow ragged should be carefully watched for signs of physical or mental disease or old age.

More interesting facts about cats

Most cats live from between ten to fifteen years, though a few hardy souls make it to twenty and even older. Cats mark any object they believe belongs to them, their owners included, and under certain circumstances they will fight to defend their turf. Every time you see a cat rubbing its head on the side of a house or against a human leg, that cat is not scratching himself. More than likely he is using the excretions that emanate from certain glands in his forehead and cheeks to anoint his personal property, and to make his ownership clear to all other cats in the neighborhood.

Extraordinarily playful by nature, especially during the kitten stage, cats are animals that seem to appreciate play purely for its own sake. Even older cats have spurts of amused interest when batting a shoelace or chasing a catnip ball. For this reason toys are a highly important feline resource, especially for cats that dwell in city apartments or in small living spaces. Cats are highly resourceful creatures, however, and if they are not provided with toys (and sometimes even if they are) they will play with ordinary household items found in their environment. Often these toys entertain them more than the store-bought variety.

Cat Breeds in a Nutshell

Among the cats of the world, only a small percentage, perhaps as few as 5 percent, lay claim to the title of purebred. Unlike dogs, cats are organized into relatively few breeds, the precise number of which differs according to the authority listing them. But like dogs, cat breeds are based on a variety of mental and physical characteristics, the main ones being size, body and head shape, coat color, hair length, temperament, and sociability.

Divided into two major categories, longhair and shorthair, the following list of cat breeds is meant to be inclusive but not exhaustive, a handy sampler to get you started in your search for the perfect cat. Though many cat owners take little interest in their pet's breed, some do, and a small number enjoy displaying their cats at cat shows.

For those whose preferences run along these last lines, there is a tempting variety of interesting and sometimes exotic breeds to choose from. The following list is representative.

Longhairs

Balinese

Appearance: Balinese have deep blue eyes and long, silky ermine-colored coat.
Temperament: Loving, sociable, intelligent.
Pros: Great indoor cat, talkative, active, affectionate.
Cons: May crave a little too much affection.

Birman

Appearance: Various shades of off-white, long, silky coat that forms a ruff around the neck. White feet with colored points.
Temperament: Outgoing, gentle, playful.
Pros: Great family cat. Elegant but full of fun. Adjusts well to indoor life.
Cons: Needs a lot of grooming.

Himalayan

Appearance: Long, thick, silky coat, much like a Persian in appearance, with Siamese coloring.
Temperament: Calm, live-and-let-live attitude, affectionate, a people cat.

Pros: Gets along well with other cats, agreeable and intelligent.
Cons: Coat needs continual grooming.

Maine coon cat

Appearance: Large cat with bushy fur, especially in the tail regions. Coloring varies from tabby to white (twenty-five different colors have been attributed to Maine coon cats)
Temperament: Affectionate, gentle.
Pros: Fond of people and families, very adaptable and agreeable.
Cons: Fur gets tangled easily. Needs grooming several times a week. Can be standoffish at times.

Persian

Appearance: Thick, fluffy, puffy fur in a variety of colors ranging from black to white to mixed grays and tans. Eye colors also vary widely.
Temperament: Elegant, sweetly sociable, refined, belle of the ball.
Pros: Friendly and fascinating, faithful, companionable.
Cons: Can be stubborn and demanding. Requires constant grooming. Often overzealous in their attempts to get (and keep) your attention.

Somali

Appearance: Lionlike orange-brown and ruddy coat with dense fur and tufts on the ears.
Temperament: Careful, shrewd, full of life, intelligent.
Pros: Interesting personality, high energy.
Cons: Can be mistrustful and shy.

Turkish Angora

Appearance: Silky, with long hair, bushy tail, often white though may also be silver, smoke, brown, blue, and bicolor.
Temperament: Poised, quiet, amiable, watchful, mysterious.
Pros: Good friend to have around. Interesting, offbeat personality.
Cons: Not always great with children or in a noisy, bustling household.

Turkish van

Appearance: Thick silky coat, usually white, though sometimes with traces of tan and orange, and often a ringed, reddish tail.
Temperament: Friendly, impulsive, responsive.
Pros: Happy temperament. Strong. One of the few cats that enjoys swimming and taking baths.
Cons: Needs frequent grooming.

Shorthairs

Abyssinian

Appearance: Thick, red, ruddy, blue, or fawn-ticked fur. This is the cat most frequently portrayed in Egyptian hieroglyphics.
Temperament: Extremely sweet and affectionate, agile, curious, bright.
Pros: A generally great all-round cat, nice to look at, easy to take care of, responsive to your needs. Can be trained to do a variety of tricks.
Cons: Sometimes shy.

American shorthair

Appearance: Large, muscular, with a round face and a thick coat that comes in a spectrum of colors from black to white and patterning.
Temperament: Active, affectionate.
Pros: A good family cat, likes children, very loyal and loving.
Cons: May go a bit stir-crazy if cooped up in small apartments without adequate exercise.

American wirehair

Appearance: Thick, curly fur that comes in a variety of colors.
Temperament: Active, inquisitive, much like the American shorthair in personality.
Pros: Affectionate, energetic, friendly companion.
Cons: Like the American shorthair, needs its running room and exercise. Does not do well cooped up for long periods of time.

Bombay

Appearance: Distinctive lustrous black fur, hefty, medium-size build, with penetrating yellow eyes.
Temperament: Even-tempered, individualistic, reserved, playful.
Pros: Faithful friend, easy to get along with, sensitive. An ideal apartment cat.
Cons: Not great around noise, confusion, and rowdy children. May dominate other cats in the household.

British shorthair

Appearance: Traditionally blue but also seen in other colors like white or black, with large glistening eyes and thick coat. Strong and sturdy body.
Temperament: Dignified, independent, affectionate, not temperamental.
Pros: Self-contained, clean, a good apartment cat.
Cons: Can be a bit lethargic and fussy.

Burmese

Appearance: Sleek brown, blue, or tan fur with yellow eyes.
Temperament: Playful, people-loving cat, vocal, active, intelligent.
Pros: Great household and family cat, friendly to kin and strangers alike. Adaptable to whatever living situation is put before it, including travel.
Cons: Can be loud, petulant, and pushy at times. Some Burmese tend to be troublemakers.

Chartreux

Appearance: Thick, velvety coat in a variety of gray shades with big, round copper to golden eyes.
Temperament: Sweet, adaptable, careful, friendly.
Pros: Gentle, all-round wonderful personality, great for kids and families.
Cons: Must brush and groom regularly.

Egyptian mau

Appearance: Thin, arched back, green eyes, silver with charcoal markings, beige with dark brown, smoke and black (and occasionally cinnamon and blue) fur, and long body. Has mascaralike

markings on its face, often with an "M" shape marking on the forehead.
Temperament: Very active, gentle, strong.
Pros: Interesting looks and personality.
Cons: Can be fussy and complaining when he doesn't get his way.

Havana brown

Appearance: Pantherlike, glossy chestnut brown coat, sleek, bright green eyes with a muscular physique.
Temperament: Outgoing, mischievous, playful, solid people cat.
Pros: Friendly companion, self-contained, often individualistic with an interesting offbeat personality.
Cons: Requires a great deal of attention and praise. Can be excessively (and continuously) vocal in its needs.

Manx

Appearance: Most conspicuous trait is its lack of a tail due to the breed's peculiar genetics. Its coat is thick, glossy, and double, and comes in a variety of colors from white to black, with practically all colors in between.
Temperament: Docile, intelligent, deft, busy.
Pros: Full of fun. Doglike in its willingness to play. A showpiece.
Cons: Can get edgy with children.

Japanese bobtail

Appearance: Large erect ears, black-and-white, red, and calico, with stumpy tail, medium-size and medium-length body, silky fur.
Temperament: Affectionate, curious, proud, full of play.
Pros: A good family cat. Wonderful personality.
Cons: Requires lots of attention from *all* family members. Can get hyper.

Korat

Appearance: Silver-blue thick coat, heart-shaped head, prominent green eyes, and muscular body.
Temperament: Obliging (learns tricks easily), snuggly, responsive.
Pros: Even temperament, intrepid, hardy.
Cons: Prefers the quiet and calm of adult owners. Can be a tough customer at times. Needs plenty of attention.

Malayan

Appearance: Short blue, fawn, or brown-colored fur, with round, wide-set yellow eyes, and a muscular, medium-size body.
Temperament: Friendly, gregarious, adventurous, resourceful.
Pros: Great family pet, very affectionate. Adapts more quickly than most cats to travel and changes of environment, making it a good bet for families that frequently move or travel.
Cons: Can be demanding. May become withdrawn if he doesn't receive the attention he feels he deserves. Uncomfortable in high-noise, busy urban environments.

Russian blue

Appearance: Silver-gray and blue, extremely thick coat (blues are cold-weather cats), long tail, and thin, rangy body.
Temperament: High-energy, affectionate, bright, stolid, shy.
Pros: Clean, undemanding, a good cat for families with children over ten.
Cons: Loves its family but tends to run from outsiders. A bit skittish at times.

Siamese

Appearance: Well-known thick, close-cropped beige with points in a variety of possible colors, blue, almond-shaped, sometimes slightly crossed eyes, and lean, svelte body.
Temperament: Highly intelligent, individualistic, alert, friendly, pushy.
Pros: Good family pet, extremely interactive; bright, playful, loving, and very partial to human beings. Among the most responsive, intuitive, and sensitive of all cat breeds.
Cons: Fickle moods, yowls a lot, even when happy. Can become overly attached to owner or to a single family member. Eccentric and demanding; can sometimes be a bit of a character.

Singapura

Appearance: Ivory coat tinged with brown ticking, small, strong body with short, stubby nose and large ears.
Temperament: Calm, affectionate, exploratory, friendly.
Pros: Undemanding, flexible, clean, makes an excellent pet for a quiet family or single adult owner.
Cons: Craves companionship.

Sphynx

Appearance: Exotic furless body covered with a soft down and strangely wrinkled skin. Long neck, large ears, and green or amber eyes.
Temperament: Bright, forward, confident, inquisitive, friendly.
Pros: Excellent for those who like novelty in a pet.
Cons: Catches colds easily, a bit skittish, needs plenty of attention and watching. A strictly indoor animal. Many people are allergic to the protein in its saliva.

Tonkinese

Appearance: Intriguing cross between a Burmese and Siamese. Blue eyes, beige and brown coat, with dark markings, long legs, long tail.
Temperament: Active, inquisitive, sociable, demanding.
Pros: Great family cat, very bright and loyal, with many of the best traits of the Burmese and Siamese breeds.
Cons: Strong willed, demands a great deal of attention and plenty of exercise.

Choosing the Right Cat

Where to look

If you are interested in acquiring cats of a particular breed or simply finding a congenial domestic shorthair, where should you look?

The best sources are shelters and breed and rescue groups. Kittens at animal shelters and rescue groups are well fed and usually free of disease. Adoption costs are minimal, and the fees you pay to a veterinarian for the mandatory neutering are sometimes reimbursable (if not done for free). Some shelters even neuter their animals before they are adopted and taken home. The people at shelters and rescue groups are avid animal lovers, and you can be sure that the animals they offer are well cared for and loved.

Finally, do be wary of the kittens you see offered for sale at commercial pet stores (not to be confused, by the way, with pet supply stores that sometimes offer cage space to local rescue groups or shelters for off-site adoptions). Though the animals at pet stores are usually displayed in an appealing and sometimes pathetic way (to arouse your sympathies), kittens from pet stores may be mistreated, sickly, and suffer from behavior problems. Shelters and rescue groups, on the other hand, are not in business for the profit, and are genuinely concerned with finding you a healthy, adjusted animal. If possible, take this route.

Choosing carefully and well

Which traits and features are most important to look for when choosing a kitten? Beauty is in the eye of the beholder, yes, but you will also want to apply some practical reality testing to the candidates for adoption before coming to a decision.

First, your Tabby should be physically appealing and healthy looking. She has a firm, muscular body with no obvious defects. She moves well without any limps. Her fur is glossy, unmatted, and silky. Her eyes are bright and inquisitive, with no discharge or discoloration at the corners. Her ears are flexible, alert, and their inner surfaces are free of specks, odors, or debris from ear mites. Her anus is clean and shows no signs of diarrhea, caked feces, or skin discoloration. Her nose is cool and has no discharge. Her teeth are straight and white, with gums a healthy shade of pink. Her tail moves with easy grace and has no crimping.

Behaviorwise, your cat is frisky, curious, friendly, and alert. Beware of felines that are overly timid or that scamper away when you attempt to fondle them. Cats that have been mistreated or poorly socialized may never lose their fear of people, and adopting a frightened animal can be a gamble.

Be aware also that a kitten will naturally nibble at your fingers in a playful way when you examine him. A bit of friendly mouthing is a natural impulse and nothing to worry about. Do, however, be certain that the cat in question is not oriented toward permanent attack mode. You can discourage the habit of nibbling, by the way, by redirecting the cat's attention to a toy.

What's your taste in cats? Frolicky or sober? Vocal or silent? Longhair or short? Large or small? Purebred or basic? The range of sizes and personalities among breeds is not as wide as among dogs, but it's wide enough to do some advance planning. If you are thinking about acquiring one of the more esoteric breeds like a manx or sphynx, prepare yourself for the fact that these rarities cost a good deal of money, require special handling, and must be acquired from a specialized breeder who may be located a good distance from where you live. It is also wise to educate and prepare yourself ahead of time for the health risks these purebreds may display. Talk to your veterinarian for the specifics.

After all these criteria are reviewed and you have the hard information at hand, let your feelings take over. If you are choosing from a litter of kittens, give each of the candidates a careful look. Then go for the one that sparks your affections and speaks most to your inner self. As with human beings, personal chemistry and emotional compatibility are critical elements when choosing a pet.

Strays: To adopt or not to adopt

What about taking home a stray you find on the street?

Adopting a stray, be it purebred or basic, is clearly an act of kindness and generosity. Homeless kitties rummaging through the garbage cans or shivering in the January air look so cute and woebegone that at times the impulse to take them home becomes overwhelming.

But consider the risks.

Stray cats are unknown entities. They may turn out to be happy, well-adjusted pets. Or they may be diseased or feral. One always takes a chance adopting a stray.

If you do decide to befriend a street animal, as a bottom-line precaution have the cat dewormed, vaccinated, tested for disease, and carefully checked over by a veterinarian before taking him into your home and life.

A New Cat in Your Home

Preparing in advance: Things to have on hand for a new cat

Before introducing a new kitten to your household it is a good idea to do some kittenproofing first and to stock all essential equipment. Be sure to have the following items at the ready as soon as your kitten frisks its way through the front door.

Food dish and water bowl. Food and water dishes should have a broad base and be stable enough to withstand tipping. Metal, stainless steel, ceramic, and glass all make excellent materials for a cat dish due to their sturdiness and ease of disinfecting. If plastic, be sure there are no scratches or cracks in the bowl that might harbor bacteria.

Be sure food and water bowls are located in a place where you won't trip over them, and where the cat can get to them easily. Some cat owners keep both receptacles on a plastic tray with a piece of newspaper or plastic mat underneath to absorb spillover. The kitchen is traditionally where a pet's food and water are kept, though this is not necessarily the best place in the house to put them. Some cats prefer to take their meals in private and are more comfortable when eating in a low-traffic area such as a porch or pantry. Others will only eat when people are around. Think the situation through, choose the best eating site, try it out, then go with the arrangement that works best.

Litter box. All cats need a clean and conveniently placed litter box. Remove all solids from the box at least once a day and empty the entire contents frequently, washing the box with mild soap and water, rinsing, and drying. A large slotted plastic spoon makes an ideal litter scooper and cleans easily.

If you allow too much waste matter to accumulate in a litter box your cat may seek out another, cleaner part of the house to soil or eliminate. Always keep a litter box in the same part of the home or apartment. Moving a box from room to room confuses cats and encourages them to make mistakes.

When training kittens to use the box, start by confining them to a small room for several days with the box in plain view. Once they begin to use the facilities and grow accustomed to them, station the box in its permanent location and don't move it again. With very young kittens you can speed up this process of familiarization by placing the kitten directly into the box after every meal.

Once cats begin defecating and, worse, urinating on a floor or rug, it is difficult to break them of the habit, as many cat owners have learned to their chagrin. Avoid this disastrous scenario by maintaining a clean, easily accessible box placed in a convenient part of the home. Handy places for a litter box include bathrooms, back hallways, utility rooms, basements, and enclosed porches. People who live in multistoried dwellings often place a litter box on every floor.

Note, finally, that while scented litter is a convenience for humans, cats often refuse to use it. Start your kitten off with plain unscented litter and, if you wish, use the scented variety later on when your cat is familiar with the daily routine.

Scratching post. Cats claw objects around the house to peel off old nail sheaths, to expose new nail, and to mark territory. If you wish to prevent your kitten from performing this ritual on your chaise longue, a scratching post is the best diversion. The post should be at least three feet high, constructed of a sturdy material like 4X4 pine, and covered with old carpeting (reverse it so the cat can claw the woven side) or other scratchable material such as sisal or burlap. Sprinkle a little powdered catnip over the scratching surface to pique or stimulate your cat's interest.

Identification tag. Even if your cat is not allowed outdoors it's important that he wear a collar and I.D. tag, be microchipped, or both. In case kitty bolts out a door or open window, a proper I.D. tag will help get him back. Safety collars made of stretchable materials or elastic are comfortable and allow cats to wiggle free if collars get caught on a branch or jagged surface.

Grooming tools. While all cats require some grooming, longhairs need a good deal more than short. Basic grooming instruments include the following: brush and flea comb, nail clipper, toothbrush, pet toothpaste, cotton swabs, and baby oil.

Begin grooming your new kitten the first week or so after she enters your home. These early sessions will get her used to the routine and accustom her to its benefits. Details on grooming a feline are provided later in this chapter.

Sleeping quarters. If your cat lived in the wilderness she would frequently hunt. But since domesticated felines do not forage for food, they spend a majority of their time doing the next best thing to eating: sleeping.

This means that your new kitty will require comfortable accommodations for her prolonged snoozes. Commercial cat beds come in all shapes and degrees of luxury, though a soft cushion and blanket tucked into an old drawer does the job quite well. Enclosed wicker baskets and cardboard boxes with a small entrance cut into them are appreciated, providing a sense of security for the cat and simulating one of their favorite sleeping places in nature, a cave. A bed placed by a sunny window also has a good chance of being used due to its combination of sun, heat, softness, and a view of the outdoors. At the same time though, be prepared: cats pretty much sleep where they like, just as long as the surface is soft, and your efforts to establish a primary sleeping area may come to naught.

Be sure and have kitty's bed waiting for her as soon as she arrives. Accustom her to its scent and appearance. This way she will bond to the sleeping area and spend less time shedding hairs on your bed and furniture.

Kittenproofing techniques. Kittens terrorize any object in their vicinity that hangs, dangles, swings, or for that matter, moves at all. A little kittenproofing is thus in order before your new visitor arrives.

Make the circuit of rooms in your home, tucking in exposed electrical cords, window sashes, hanging belts and ties, Venetian blind cords, and the like. If your favorite vase or bowl is precariously perched on a shelf or table, move it to a safer location.

Water in the toilet bowl fascinates kittens, and there are cases on record of cats falling in and drowning. Keep the toilet seat down and the lid closed at all times. Crevices, holes in the wall, tears in porch screens, doors that don't shut properly are all engraved invitations to sneak outdoors and get lost. Repair them as soon as you can.

What about windows? Might a kitten climb through a half-open window in a second-story apartment and fall? Absolutely. Cats are amazingly agile, yes, but even the most nimble lose their footing from time to time. To prevent this ghastly scenario, place screens on all your windows.

Basic Cat and Kitten Care

Love, love, love

The first few days of a cat's stay in a new home are especially formative to her psychological development. If these days are serene and fun, they set the mood for years to come.

As is always the case with pets, affection and attention are your primary resources. Snuggle with your kitty, talk to her, groom her, introduce her to other family members, carry her around the house, show her the sights. Let her know she's welcome. At the same time, give the cat space. If she does not seem interested in cuddling at the present time, don't force the issue.

Encourage exploring

After he's accustomed himself to his new environment, kitty will want to explore every nook and cranny in the house. Encourage this impulse. It's one of the ways in which cats exercise and learn.

At the same time, if your kitten is very young, avoid overstimulation. Kittens need constant supervision and should not be allowed to wander too far from the litter box if under twelve weeks old. Introduce him to the rooms in your home one at a time: the bedroom today, the living room tomorrow, the kitchen the day after that. If you have a cellar or crawl space it's a good idea to keep him away from this area until he learns the lay of the land. Be careful too of closets. Kittens wander into these small areas, fall asleep, and are inadvertently locked in, sometimes for days, when the closet door is closed.

The best way to pick up a kitten

Never pick a kitten up by the scruff of the neck. Mother cats know precisely how much pressure to exert with their teeth when they pick up babies by the neck and are experts at the task. Humans cannot duplicate this maneuver and should never try. The best way to pick up a cat is from beneath.

Do this by placing one hand under the cat's chest. Allow the cat's body to rest on your forearm, then use your other hand to support her rump and back legs. Perform this movement smoothly and gently, without abrupt or rapid movements.

Now lift.

Note that if cats feel off-balance while being picked up, or if they think their stomach is exposed, they will leap away in a flash, leaving scratch marks on your arms as a souvenir. They do the same if held with their stomach facing up. Be careful also of gripping too hard; cats interpret being squeezed as being captured, and they panic. When nestling in your arms cats should feel as if they are seated on a traveling pillow surveying the realm—head up, stomach down, paws free, in control, ready for action, with plenty of room to maneuver in all directions, and an unencumbered view.

Stroking, petting, caressing

There are certain areas of a feline body that feel especially delectable when stroked. These include the chest, ears, cheeks, forehead, base of the spine (especially for males), and stomach.

But be careful. Cats instinctively defend their vulnerable abdominal areas, and usually the only ones allowed to stroke them here are the humans they really trust. Some cats, moreover, simply hate having these areas touched no matter who is doing it. Hands off. Therefore, unless you have one of those rare cats in the house who rolls over and urges you to rub her stomach, it is best to avoid this area entirely and confine your stroking to the more tried-and-true regions of the head, chest, and back. Note, finally, that long, sustained strokes down the back can cause an aggressive response in a fair number of cats.

Playtime

When you see a kitten playfully banging and socking her catnip ball across the dining room floor what you're really witnessing is a rehearsal for attack. Cats are hunters, one and all, and toys symbolize prey.

Playtime is thus a vital part of feline development, even at a very young age. The most useful resources are toys that leap, jump, dance, and can be batted around—that is, items that move and look alive, and which in technical parlance are referred to as *interactive toys*. Possible inventory here includes a dangling piece of cloth on a stick, open brown paper bags, a catnip mouse, rolling bells, a tree branch waved above the cat's head, cardboard tubes, stuffed socks, Ping-Pong balls, cardboard cartons, feathers, and aluminum foil balls (especially recommended are the Cat Dancer and Kitty Tease toys).

Providing such interactive diversions has a side benefit also: it encourages kitty to pounce on her play items rather than on your toes. Here, moreover, a warning: Avoid making your hands and feet into objects of play. Fingers and toes temptingly wiggled in front of cats are fun for the moment, perhaps, but it causes cats to grow up thinking that biting and scratching human appendages is not only allowable but hilarious fun. Confine all cat play to interactive toys, and keep hands well away from a cat's teeth and claws.

It is also a basic principle of pet care to avoid toys that in any way endanger a cat's health or safety. Play items with appendages that can be chewed off, swallowed, and lodged in the throat, for example, or toys that can get snared on a cat's claws should be avoided. Be wary too of paper bags with handles. Cats can get tangled in them. Before giving your cat a bag to play with, snip off the handles first.

Be especially vigilant of potentially swallowable objects. If your cat seems determined to eat that coil of ribbon or piece of string rather than play with it, such objects should be kept well out of his reach. Commercial toys must also be screened before being deemed safe. Wands with a pompom of Mylar strips at the end are appropriate for cats who bat at them with their paws. But for cats who try to eat the Mylar, such toys are obviously off limits.

A word about catnip toys

While half of all cats respond to this minty herb, kittens are usually immune to its effects, and only start to feel the thrill after three months of age.

Biologically speaking, no one is sure why cats respond to catnip in such a daffy way. We know that it contains a chemical called *trans-neptalactone* that bears an olfactory similarity to a substance found in cat's urine. But that's about it. Effectwise, cats that are receptive to this herb appear for all intents and purposes to be delightfully drunk. As far as anyone can tell, catnip does no harm, and some cat watchers claim it is good for feline health. Certainly it keeps a cat active and exercised.

Take some catnip and rub it on your cat's scratching post. Or give your cat a catnip mouse. The physical effects of catnip appear to last up to a half-hour, after which the cat goes into a period of lapse, and no longer responds to the catnip taste or smell. Several hours later she's raring to go again.

Toys stuffed with catnip are highly recommended and are an excellent way to break the ice when a new kitten enters your home. But be advised: like most herbs, catnip goes stale after several months, and loses its magic. If your cat starts ignoring the catnip toy it banged around with such fervor last week, the problem is probably due to the fact that the herb has lost its zing. Time to replace the old toy with a new one.

Finally, you can avoid the staleness factor entirely, either by growing and picking your own catnip if you live in a rural area, or by purchasing a grow-your-own-catnip kit sold today at many pet stores.

Introducing a new cat to other household pets: A step-by-step plan

Almost invariably, in-residence cats resent the arrival of new cats. With the proper precautions trouble can be avoided.

First, realize that a certain amount of hissing, posturing, and chasing are to be expected when the new cat arrives. Be patient with this behavior and don't try to rush things along. In 90% of cases, time is all that's needed before cats make a truce and sometimes even an alliance.

When introducing cats, follow this step-by-step method to achieve the least amount of flying fur:

Step one. Place the newcomer cat into an isolated area, specifically a spare bedroom, utility room, or second bathroom. Be sure the room is equipped with all the cat necessities: litter box, food, water bowl, and bed. Isolation should last for 2 weeks to rule out incubating illnesses, and to allow the resident cat to become accustomed to the newcomer's scent.

Allow the newcomer cat to investigate and explore his room. Visit him several times a day. If he engages you, respond conservatively. But don't rush forward to lift and play with him. Stay with him for a while at each visit. Then leave without ceremony. Meanwhile, you will want to spend time with your in-residence cat, petting and playing with him. Don't be surprised if he hisses at you when you first come from visiting the new cat. You still have the newcomer cat's scent on your hands. You may also want to swap spaces between the cats, so that each cat leaves its scent in the other one's area.

Finally, let the resident cat prowl around the door of the room where the new cat is being kept. When the resident cat calms down and becomes accustomed to the newcomer's scent, it is time to take step two.

Step two. Allow the newcomer cat and the in-residence cat to see each other for a few minutes, but without body contact. Do this by placing each cat in an adjoining room. Then set up a mesh baby gate at the door between the rooms. Allow the cats to sniff and paw at each other for a few minutes. A certain amount of hissing and swiping is to be expected. If the cats leap over the doors—all can, but only some will—you may need to set up a screen door separation between rooms for the period of training.

Step three. When the cats seem relatively calm in each other's presence, take down the gate and allow direct contact to be made.

Do not make a big thing out of it. Instead, allow the cats to sort of "happen" upon each other while you remain on the sidelines trying not to interfere. Be sure to leave an escape route for either cat should a quick departure be needed.

What if a fight ensues?

There are several steps you can take. Try clapping your hands, for instance, or shouting and stamping, being sure all the time to keep your hands and feet well away from the battle zone. If none of these ploys work, a dousing with water sometimes ends the argument. Or try dropping a blanket or beach towel on the fighting pair to distract them.

Once separated, place the newcomer cat into isolation again and wait a few days before attempting to reintroduce them.

Accustoming cats to one another may take several hours if it is kitten-to-kitten, several months if it is adult male stray to resident adult male prima donna. Eventually, the chances are that hostilities will decline, that the felines will declare a truce, and that finally they will become household sharers, if not friends. At worst one cat will make the other cat's life a living hell. There are, of course, no guarantees that coexistence can ever be established between cats, though most of the time the outcome of such attempts is a positive one.

Feline Nutrition

Some cats—not all, as the myth goes—are fussy eaters, turning their noses up if portions are not fresh, aromatic, familiar, tasty, and served in a manner to their liking. In some cases cats will go hungry rather than accept food they consider beneath their standards.

How does one fulfill a cat's long list of eating requirements? The following steps guide you through the task:

1. *Feed your pet at the same time each day.* Cats prefer to dine at the same daily hour, and their digestive systems quickly become accustomed to this habit. Since cats are routine-loving creatures, they become stressed when their schedules are disturbed. Serving dinner at a standard time also assures that Tabby will be at the food bowl when you want her, ready to eat, and not sleeping in the hamper.

2. *Feed cats in the same place every day.* Keeping food and water in a fixed location gives cats a much needed sense of routine and security.

3. *Be consistent.* Because variety is not the spice of a cat's life, many cat owners feed their cats the same food every day. This means the same brand of cat food *and* the same variety (i.e., chicken, beef, liver). If your cat seems satisfied with the brand of food she is eating, why change?

4. *Make sure your cat's bowl is cleaned once a day.* Even a slightly dirty bowl causes cats to reject their meal. Frequent cleanings help eliminate unpleasant odors, food crusting, and insect invasions.

5. *Make sure all food is fresh.* Canned food and leftovers that sit in a bowl for more than two hours qualify as "old" for cats, and felines walk away from meat that is even slightly spoiled. While giving table scraps to your feline is not a very good idea in general, if

you must take this route be sure to wash off all the spices, ketchup, pepper, and Worcestershire sauce first before feeding, as cats detest the taste of those sauces and seasonings we so enjoy.

6. *Some cat owners leave a bowl of kibble down at all times.* This is acceptable if the cat does not have a weight problem (obesity), or if there are no litter box problems.

Pavlovian strategies

Some cat owners apply Pavlovian strategies at mealtime by ringing a bell or giving a distinct call every time food is served. This way humans avoid waiting around while their felines decide if they are hungry or not. And remember, while it may be gratifying to slip your friend a treat or two between meals, cats quickly come to expect these tidbits, and they factor them into what they consider to be their daily due.

Understanding your cat's nutritional needs

Omnivorous versus carnivorous. Some pet owners make the mistake of thinking that dogs and cats require the same diet. Nothing is further from the truth. Dogs are omnivorous. They love meat, of course, but they also have a fundamental need for grains, vegetables, dairy products, and even a little fruit.

Cats, on the other hand, are 95 percent carnivorous. They require approximately 40 percent protein per day, almost twice the amount needed by dogs. Since protein's main function in metabolism is the construction of tissue cells, kittens should receive more of this vital nutrient than adult cats.

Approximately another 55 percent of a cat's menu should consist of animal fats. Finally the last 5 percent includes cereal, eggs, plus a few carbohydrates for fiber and energy. Occasionally one comes across a feline who savors decidedly noncatlike foods such as pasta or bananas. But this is rare. The commercial cat foods on the market today supply all the nutrition a cat requires.

Choosing a commercial cat food. What steps can you take to assure that your cat receives top nutritional value from the food you give her?

First, read the label. Brands that have passed feeding trials conducted by the Association of American Feed Control Officials (AAFCO), a nonprofit federal organization, will state that "Animal feeding tests using AAFCO procedures substantiate that [this brand] provides complete and balanced nutrition." If the label contains the phrase, "formulated to meet AAFCO's nutrient profiles," this is also a significant endorsement.

If the AAFCO statement declares that a product is "for all life stages" then this guarantee is sufficient. The same is true for foods labeled "senior." The superiority of age-specialized foods has not been scientifically established, however, and special foods tend to be more expensive than regular commercial foods. Most critically, no federal regulations exist to govern the use of terms such as "senior," "processed," "fortified," "specially blended," and so forth. Result? Standards and definitions vary from pet food to pet food, and are often slanted to the manufacturer's advantage.

Wet food, semimoist, or dry? Which is better for your cat, wet food, semimoist, or dry?

Semimoist foods are higher than other types of food in sugars—not a good thing. They tend to be spongy, and at times downright soggy. And because they are soft, semimoist food provides little or no dental benefits when chewed by cats.

Dry food, on the other hand, offers substantial dental benefits, and may help reduce the tartar on a cat's teeth. Dry food is cheaper than canned food, neater to handle, and low on odor. It lasts longer in the bowl than canned as well. Many cats prefer a diet made up exclusively of dry food.

Canned foods, on the other hand, are more aromatic, which to a cat means tastier. They also contain a higher percentage of water, protein, and fat than dry food. For these reasons, cats often eat canned foods more willingly than dry and semimoist. Finally, canned foods usually contain all the water a cat needs at each meal, while dry and semimoist food have minimal moisture.

What's the verdict then?

The fact is that commercial canned food and commercial dry food both supply adequate nutrition for cats. Many pet owners prefer to feed their felines both the canned and the dry varieties. At the same time, each cat has her own opinion on the subject, and in the long run it becomes a question of which food, dry or canned, your cat enjoys most and thrives on most.

Special nutritional concerns. Older cats are less active than young, and hence less likely to burn calories and more prone to slowed digestion and constipation. It is best to feed them a diet specially formulated for seniors with decreased amounts of cholesterol, increased amounts of fiber, fewer calories, and more easily digestible nutrients. Make sure as well that senior cats do not overeat. Obesity is a major contributing cause to sickness and death in older cats.

Pregnant cats, of course, are eating for more than one, and require liberal nutritional additions to their regular diet. Once pregnant, a cat's gestation period lasts from sixty-three to sixty-five days. It is during the last trimester of this period, starting around the thirty-fifth day, that the mother-to-be requires the greatest amount of extra food—including 50 percent more protein and fat than usual. With pregnant cats it is thus a good idea to have their food bowl always out and filled, so that they can eat whenever the need arises.

Once the kittens are born, a lactating mother then continues to require more food than usual. Again, a diet rich in protein and fat is recommended. At this time, it is also wise to free feed, allowing the hungry mother to eat as much as she desires at each sitting.

Dealing with obesity. If your cats are grossly overweight you can take the following steps to help them drop those pounds. While on a weight-loss plan, however, it is important that each step be supervised by a veterinarian to avoid potentially serious health consequences.

Start by feeding your cat twice a day. Then gradually reduce the total amount of food he receives in increments of 10 percent a month for three months. Meanwhile, eliminate all free-choice eating, and make sure your cat gets at least twenty minutes a day of serious exercise.

Monitor your cat's weight every week. Make sure he doesn't lose more than a maximum 2 percent of his starting weight in a month. Easy does it. Remember to work closely with your veterinarian.

Further tips on cat nutrition

- Avoid feeding dog food to cats. A diet that keeps dogs alert and healthy over the long run is inadequate nourishment for a cat. It is missing essential vitamins and minerals such as amino acids that safeguard a cat's health.
- Although cats are relatively delicate eaters, they are still prone to choking on bones. If you feed your kitty fresh fish or chicken be sure to pick out all bones before serving.

- Your cat may enjoy a saucer of milk now and then, but before adding it to her regular diet make sure dairy products are well tolerated. Any signs of diarrhea or vomiting after she drinks a saucer of milk may mean that it isn't. In general, milk-based foods are not recommended for cats.
- Beware of feeding cats a diet composed entirely of home-cooked meats, cereals, and table scraps. A feline's nutritional needs exist in a delicate equilibrium, and even a small deviation from this balance can cause malnutrition. Commercial cat foods are scientifically blended to provide the exact mix of proteins, fats, carbohydrates, vitamins, and minerals necessary for a cat's well-being. Unless you are an expert in feline and animal nutrition, it is generally better to turn the job of dietary planning over to the pros. If you do decide to prepare a home diet, make sure to check first with your veterinarian to make sure the menu you concoct is balanced and 100 percent nutritionally complete.
- If you have more than one cat at home, maintain a separate bowl for each. If bickering is a problem at mealtime, some multiple cat owners feed each cat in a different part of the room or even the house.
- When preparing your cat's meal, try occasionally adding a spoonful of a good polyunsaturated oil such as corn oil, safflower oil, or peanut oil. These substances provide an array of useful vitamins and help to lubricate a cat's bowels. They also provide an excellent line of defense against constipation and impacted hair balls. If your cat is obese, it is probably best to skip this measure.
- Be careful of commercial food supplements. A cat's nutritional balance is a delicate one, and too much of a certain vitamin or mineral can be as harmful as too little. In general, it's a good idea to give your cat vitamin and mineral supplements only if he has a medically diagnosed deficiency in these areas. Check with your veterinarian for the details.

Secrets of Good Feline Grooming

All cats, no matter whether longhair or short, require some degree of grooming. Without this necessary nicety they soon begin to look ragged and unkempt. But make no mistake: grooming is more than just a cosmetic concern. A careful brushing removes debris and dead hair overlooked by your pet's own cleaning efforts. It helps distribute the natural oils throughout the fur, improves circulation, stimulates skin surfaces, and reduces matting. Lack of regular coat management, on the other hand, besides causing cats to look woebegone, actually contributes to various physical problems such as hair balls.

Grooming, in other words, is a central concern in cat care, important for health as well as appearance. It should be a basic part of every feline's maintenance routine.

To begin, grooming sessions should take place when both you and the cat are in a mellow mood. Once calm and settled, show your cat the brush and comb. Let her sniff the implements and play with them if she chooses. After a few minutes start gently brushing.

After a few sessions your cat will look forward to these exchanges and revel in them when they take place. In the long run, grooming not only helps cats stay fit and immaculate, it allows you and your pet to bond in a special way. Indeed, one can look at the grooming process as simply another way of showing affection for a cat and allowing her to show her affection in return. While grooming you are also closely examining a cat's coat and body for parasites, lumps, bumps, and foreign bodies. Grooming serves many purposes.

Mandatory grooming tools

Natural bristle brush: Used primarily for shorthair, low-shedding cats. A good all-around cleaner, brusher, debris remover, and circulation builder.

Long-tooth slicker, pin, or rubber curry brush: The pin varieties are best for longhair cats, though some find them useful for short as well. Slicker or rubber curry brushes are best for shorthairs. Wide-tooth metal combs are excellent for working on mats on longhairs.

Flea comb: A fine-tooth comb designed to remove fleas, lice, debris, insects, and insect eggs from dogs and cats.

Nail trimmers: These come in a number of sizes and styles. Sometimes they are bundled into a set. Nail clippers are a must for keeping a cat's claws short and manageable.

Optional grooming tools

Hair dryer: The warm, dry air from a dryer can be used to dry cats after a bath. If your cat is frightened by the noise of the machine, turn it off immediately and use a towel instead.

Pet shampoo: Shampoo is necessary for those times when a cat rolls in an unpleasant substance or the coat is dirty. Conditioners, lusterizers, dry bath preparations, and grooming mists are all useful.

Pet bath sprayer: A spray nozzle and hose attachment that clamps onto the faucet is used for bathing dogs and cats. Most models come with aerators and a selection of settings on the nozzle. Note that while some dogs seem to enjoy being sprayed, cats often panic. If you use a sprayer on your cat, start slowly and use a very low-volume spray. Gradually build up the intensity as your cat gets acclimated to the novel feeling of the spray.

Grooming glove: An abrasive glove with rubberized nubs on the palm, grooming gloves fit on the hand and are run along the fur, collecting hairs. Cats that balk at bristle brushes are often quite happy when you use a glove, perhaps because gloves provide a direct contact between you and the animal.

Basic combing and brushing techniques

Grooming a longhair cat. Longhairs require constant grooming if they are to be kept looking and feeling their best. Most breeds in this category, such as the Angora and Persian, need once-a-day care, while during shedding season at least two brushings a day may be necessary. Indeed, if a longhair is not regularly groomed her coat becomes hopelessly matted and tangled. In some situations only extreme solutions such as total body shaving can set things right.

Stage one: To groom a longhair place the cat in a comfortable position, either on your lap or in a familiar place on the floor. You may wish to put a sheet, towel, or piece of paper beneath her to catch the falling hairs, skin cells, and debris.

Brush your feline's coat in the direction of its nap. Use deep, firm, repetitive strokes. If you find signs of fleas, many powerful prescription remedies are available to combat this problem. See the section below, "Keeping Your Cat Well and Healthy," for more on flea and tick control.

When you come to a snarl or tangle don't pull at it violently. Pulling a cat's fur is tantamount to striking her; she will be off your lap and into the next room in seconds. Instead carefully work through each snarl, using short, abbreviated strokes until all tangles are gone. For particularly thick knots you may wish to do the untangling with your fingers, or use a hair mat cutter. When cutting out a mat be careful not to dig into the cat's delicate skin.

Continue brushing the back and sides in this manner, then work the underside. The hairs on the cat's tail, neck, legs, toes, and face should all be brushed.

Stage two: Combing. Start by combing your cat's back, side, and underbelly. Go with the lie of the fur. As you comb be careful not to pull or yank. If you hit a snarl, work it out by hand, then continue combing. Some groomers finish up their sessions with a final brushing to remove tenacious dead hairs.

You will also want to check your cat's nails at this point. If they are too long, clip them to manageable size. Clipping keeps nails blunt, which means that if cats scratch your furniture the damage will be minimal. Nail trimming, in other words, is an important part of cat grooming, and should not be considered an optional benefit. Untrimmed nails can cause infection and may eventually require medical care. Nip the problem in the bud by trimming your cat's nails on a regular basis at home. All pet supply stores sell nail trimmers.

Start by holding the cat on your lap. Stroke her and talk to her. When she seems calm take one of her paws and press the end gently so that the claws naturally protrude.

Examine each claw, making sure it is healthy, strong, and nicely curved. Then clip the dead white tip away, being extremely careful not to slice into the pink-colored quick. This area contains numbers of sensitive nerves and blood vessels. If violated it can cause a great deal of bleeding and pain.

Clip each claw on all four paws. During the session, and when it is over, you may wish to reward your feline with a treat. Rewards create positive associations with the clipping ceremony and help next time you clip.

Your cat's claws should be examined on a regular weekly basis, and/or every time you groom. On first sign of overgrowth, clip to a manageable size. For beginners, a consultation with a veterinarian on proper nail-clipping procedure is recommended.

Grooming a shorthair. Grooming a shorthair takes less time and energy than grooming a longhair. For most shorthairs, a once-a-week brushing is usually enough, though each cat has its unique needs.

As with longhairs, brush in the direction of the nap. Check for knots and snarls as you go. Even shorthairs develop them. Look for fleas, ticks, and other infestations.

Finally, give your cat a brief combing. Comb with the nap for several minutes. Some shorthair owners end grooming rituals by burnishing their cat's coat with a chamois cloth.

Other grooming concerns for cats

Teeth. From time to time you will want to brush your Tabby's teeth—if you can. Since this encounter is dreaded by both cat and human, it is suggested that you accustom your cat to the feel of the brush when he is still a wee kitten. A few months old is not too young to begin.

Use a small toothbrush for the job, use special pet brand toothpaste (available at most pet supply stores), and be sparing with the toothpaste; a little goes a long way with a feline. In the beginning you may want to dab a little of the toothpaste on the kitten's tongue to accustom him to the taste.

As you brush check the condition of your cat's teeth. A number of chipped or broken teeth in a young cat may be a sign he isn't receiving enough calcium or phosphorus in his diet.

Ears. If you see signs of wax buildup, clean a cat's ears immediately. Using a cotton ball soaked with baby oil, clean round the shell of the ear and into the earhole. Check for small pieces of dark debris—they may be an indication of ear mites.

Eyes. Give your cat's eyes a periodic check. Any discharge or tearing should be wiped away with a cotton ball. Needless to say, be careful when you do this and avoid getting any of the cotton fibers into your pet's eyes. If the discharge continues for more than a few days, see a veterinarian.

Bathing

Although regular baths are not recommended for cats, the time often seems to come in the life of an indoor feline when bathing becomes an absolute necessity. The causes may be infinite, ranging from preparing for a cat show to a general state of messiness.

If you approach your cat in the right spirit, baths should be no more traumatic to him than being combed or brushed. However, it is an extremely wise strategy to initiate him into the mysteries of water when he is a kitten, especially after he has been with you a few months and is part of the family. Introducing a mature cat to bathing is far more problematic.

Here's what to do.

First, have everything ready in advance: an empty plastic tub (or the kitchen sink), mild pet shampoo, washcloth, towel, and hair dryer (optional).

Stroke your cat, talk lovingly to him, and gently place him in the tub or sink.

At first he may balk. Keep talking to him in tender tones. Pet him. Calm him down. When he seems resigned to his fate, slowly start to pour lukewarm water over him, then soap him down with the shampoo, and rub him with a washcloth. Massage the shampoo into his coat with your fingers. After a few minutes cats usually understand there is no danger lurking, and occasionally they even start to enjoy themselves.

After soaping down, rinse thoroughly using pitchers full of lukewarm water or a pet bath sprayer. Squeeze water out of the fur with your fingers, lift him out, and towel dry. Some people use a hair dryer to finish the job. Whether or not this is a feasible option depends on your cat's tolerance for the dryer's noise and its dramatic blasts of hot air. After bathing be sure and keep the cat warm and dry, especially in the colder months. Cats are hardy creatures, but when wet they are vulnerable and can easily catch a chill.

Basic Training for Your Cat

A few hints before you begin

Cats are quite capable of learning a number of basic and sometimes sophisticated commands, and they're quite willing to learn, provided you go about the process in the right way. Note the following points of operating procedure before you begin:

Repetition. Once is not enough when trying to train a cat, and sometimes a hundred times is not enough. But on the 101st time you will see progress. That's how it goes with cats. Most are quick, intelligent animals, and after a while they get the picture. Just repeat and be patient. The rest will come, though on its own time. On the other hand, too many repetitions at one time will also bore a cat. The trick is to find the right balance, the right number of repetitions, and stick with it.

Teach with praise, affection—and food. Cats learn by reward, not punishment. Forget the notion of hollering at your feline when he misbehaves or hitting him. These tactics are counterproductive and cause cats to run from you in fear. Praises, kindness, stroking, grooming, affec-

tion, and food treats are the way not only to a cat's heart but to his rea-
soning mind and to his will. After your cat has made an effort and/or
learned a new behavior, always reward him with love—and tasty snacks.

Don't work a cat too long or too hard. When it comes to training,
the attention span of every cat, even the brightest, is limited to a few
minutes at best. Once attention strays, the learning curve drops to zero,
and any attempts at instruction are futile. It is therefore important to
know your cat's concentration span, and pack as much training as you
can into this window of opportunity. When the moment passes, end the
session immediately.

Pick the right time of day. Cats do not take well to training when
they are tired, restless, upset, on the prowl, or otherwise preoccupied.
During such times there's absolutely no point in even trying to get their
attention. Instead, choose those moments when your cat is mentally and
emotionally most receptive. For some cats this time occurs in the evening before bed. For others it comes on first getting up. Many cats are
particularly receptive to training around mealtime when their appetites
are up, and when they know that food treats will be given in reward. After a meal, on the other hand, tends to be a poor time for training. The
cat is sluggish now, wants to nap, and with a full belly is unreceptive to
food rewards. Experiment.

Housebreaking

Cats will use a litter box automatically if this practice is role modeled
to them by their mothers. When this training does not take place, don't
assume your feline's basic instinct for staying clean will automatically direct him to the litter. It may or it may not. Nothing guaranteed.

If your cat does not willingly use the litter box, there are several
steps you can take to correct the problem.

First, make sure the cat is spayed or neutered. Sexually active cats
mark their territory with urine and sometimes feces, and their territory
is rarely in the litter box. Note, by the way, that urination on flat surfaces
usually indicates an elimination problem—urination on vertical surfaces
indicates spraying.

Second, make sure the litter box is clean and the litter changed regularly. When wastes accumulate and smells grow strong, a cat may seek a
different environment similar to the cat box (such as an indoor plant or
tree) to do his business. Or he may simply soil the rug and floor. In

either case, the solution is easy: scoop the box at least once a day and change the litter frequently. Litter pan liners, available at pet supply stores, make the job easier, cleaner, and quicker. But beware: Many cats do not like the feel of litter liners. They may scratch holes in them, allowing the urine to pour through and create smells that are even worse than before.

Third, ask yourself, is my cat really litter box trained? Pet owners sometimes believe a cat is prepped to use a particular litter box when, in fact, he is simply accustomed to urinating and defecating in the area where the box is placed. When the box is removed the cat then continues to leave his deposits on this same spot. Moral: don't move the litter box if you can help it.

If you must move the box, accustom your cat to the change by moving the box a few feet each day in the direction of its new location, gradually, gradually, until it reaches the final destination.

Fourth, have you recently moved your residence? If so, your cat may be unsure where the litter box is now being kept. Confine him in a room with food on one side and a litter box on the other. Within a few days he will be comfortably adjusted to the new setup.

Retraining to the litter box

If a cat becomes inconsistent in his visits to the litter box, using it one day, ignoring it the next and soiling the rug instead, his problem may be stress; that is, he may be on anxiety overload.

Such a diagnosis sounds a bit trendy and human, perhaps. But in our harried world, cats fall victim to nerves as commonly as people, and their response may be to use your new oriental rug as a toilet.

The first step to take when soiling like this occurs is to make sure a physical ailment is not to blame. Once this possibility is ruled out, clean up the mess using an enzyme-based cleaner and odor neutralizer spray to banish all scents. Then visually change the soiled area by covering it with a chair or trunk, a wastepaper basket, a file cabinet—anything. The next time you see your cat sniffing confusedly at his old dumping ground, gently but firmly direct him to the litter box.

That's step one. Step two is to train or retrain him to use the litter box exclusively.

Begin by placing him in temporary confinement. Bathrooms are recommended for the job. They are small, private, and easy to clean. Arrange the cat's bed here, along with his toys and food, and position his litter box in a conspicuous place. While he's in isolation it's important to visit him frequently and give him plenty of attention. The retraining process should be instructive and supportive, not punitive.

Feed your cat two meals a day while in confinement, leaving the food down for approximately a half-hour each time. When you find that he is using the box, and the box alone, for two straight weeks, allow him access to other rooms in the house, one room at a time. Continue supervision until you are certain he is retrained.

A model method for teaching specific behaviors

Cats are capable of learning many useful tricks. You may, for instance, want to teach her to come when you call her. Here's what to do:

First, find a tasty meat tidbit, one you know she enjoys. Hold it out and call her name, "Midnight!"

When she comes and sniffs, give her the food.

Repeat this exercise two or three times every day, being sure to call her name in a loud, clear voice each time. Soon she will develop a conditioned response and come to you even if you are not holding the food.

This principle of command–compliance–reward works whatever behavior patterns you wish to instill, and it can be used to teach a variety of behaviors.

Teaching leash training

It is easier to teach a cat leash training than you might suppose. Start by acquiring a good nylon harness, preferably a figure-eight style. You will also need a light four- or six-foot lead. Place the harness on the cat for an hour or two every day until she becomes accustomed to it. Then attach the leash to the harness hook and let her drag it around for a few minutes each day. When she is comfortable with these new items, take her into a hallway or room in your home on the leash, and let her walk around on her own. Finally, hold the leash and lead her for short distances up and down the hall.

After a few days of practicing indoors, attach the harness and lead to your cat and take her outside. Find a quiet area without too many cars and people, and allow her to walk around. When she pulls on the leash, don't pull back. Simply hold it in place, maintaining firm resistance. She will soon get the picture and stop pulling.

Next, take a few steps forward, and coax her to follow you.

When she complies, take a few more steps. And a few more.

Never tug suddenly at a leash while you're walking, even if your cat tarries overly long at a bush or tree. Violent pulling is guaranteed to trigger terror in a cat. Always let her set her own pace.

Do a little leash walking every day. It is best if you start when your feline is still a kitten. Most cats learn this technique in a week or two, and kittens learn even faster. Many come to enjoy it.

Keeping Your Cat Well and Healthy

On the whole, cats are a healthy and hearty species. Like every creature in nature though, they get sick, they get hurt, and they have their genetic vulnerabilities. Two of the principal lessons a conscientious cat owner learns is, one, how to identify a particular physical problem when it appears, and two, how to remedy it.

Identifying Physical Problems in Your Cat

Generalized symptoms in cats that may indicate acute disease include the following:

- Vomiting, coughing, continual sneezing, drooling
- Diarrhea for more than a day or two. Constipation for more than two or three days. Be especially careful of diarrhea and vomiting in kittens. Like puppies, kittens easily become dehydrated and can die from body fluids lost in a short period of time. If your kitten shows signs of diarrhea or constipation take it to a veterinarian immediately.
- Loss of appetite; sudden and obsessive gain in appetite
- Reduced activity and energy level. Be concerned if your cat starts to isolate himself in warm, dark, out-of-the-way places such as a cellar or inside a closet. Be even more concerned if he does not respond when you coax him out.
- Intense itching, scratching, or boring into the skin with the teeth
- Black discharge, itching, and wax buildup in the ears
- Inflamed eyes, squinting
- Dramatic skin or coat change: rashes, welts, bald spots, abscesses, or color changes
- Loss of interest in cleaning and grooming
- Pale or dark red tongue and gums
- Swelling or inflammation on any part of the body, especially in the limbs and paws

- Glazed eyes and dull, lifeless coat
- Obvious signs of pain: cat yowls when standing up, sitting down, or walking about
- Constant drinking. Healthy cats absorb most of their fluids from food, and take only occasional sips from the water bowl. If your cat is constantly drinking this can be a danger sign.
- Changes in urination—straining and failure to urinate
- Sudden unfriendly or aggressive behavior—a cat hisses or spits when you try to pick her up

Cats have their own routines, and failing health quickly becomes apparent in their hour-to-hour behavior. They eat less. They sleep more. They lose interest in their surroundings. Sometimes a cat simply seems out of sorts: no particular symptoms, no bleeding or vomiting, just a sense of being "off." This condition should not be ignored. It may be the early signs of a serious ailment.

Note that cats often go to great lengths to hide their illnesses. Get to know your cat well enough so that she can't fool you in this way.

Conducting a visual checkup

From time to time cats should be given a careful visual checkup. Look for the following signs and indications:

General demeanor. Is your cat her usual energetic self? Does she seem peppy and happy? Or is she acting a bit lethargic and "off." Is she sleeping or lying down more often than usual? Does she hide an unusual amount of the time? Does she respond to you with her usual enthusiasm and alertness?

Signs of stress. Cats get stressed too, sometimes to the point of sickness. Like all of us, they grow especially anxious during times of crisis: when you move to a new residence, for instance, or when a new animal or infant comes into the house; when large numbers of people gather in your home; when a close companion pet or owner dies.

Observe: is your cat uncharacteristically restless? Is she tense and afraid when you touch or draw near? Do you detect any dramatic changes in appetite, vocalization, routine? Does she wantonly destroy objects around the house such as clothes or upholstery? Does she groom for inordinately long periods of time during the day? If so, does she do so in a nervous, anxious way? Is she suddenly refusing to use the litter box? Is she soiling in odd places around the house? Is she acting uncharacteristically aggressive? Sometimes the above behaviors are simply part of a cat's fundamental personality. If so, so be it. The time to worry is when these symptoms appear out of the blue, and then progress with a relentless consistency. Such behavior may mean your pet's stress level is becoming so great it is affecting her physical well-being. The general remedy for this problem is to remove the stressor and you remove the stress.

In some cases, for instance, time is the best healer. You have moved to a new residence, say, and now must allow your feline to get used to the new surroundings. At other times active logistical rearranging is necessary. Your four-year-old is tormenting the cat. So you keep the two of them separated. Loud street noises are frightening your cat. So you keep her in a room away from the sound. Remember, though nothing is guaranteed, if you remove the cause of the stress in a majority of instances you will remove the results as well.

Coat. Is her fur shiny and healthy looking, or has it grown listless and dull? Is she shedding more than usual? Gently pull at her fur. Does it come out in clumps? Often the only thing a cat's coat needs to spruce it up is a thorough grooming. On the other hand, if a cat sheds an inordinate amount, or if her fur starts to look excessively ragged, illness or stress may be to blame.

Eyes. A cat's eyes should be clear, alert, and focused. There should be no bulging (possible tumor) or dark, thick discharge (possible infection) from the corners of the eyes. Clear discharge may, however, be natural to certain cat breeds. Deep redness or obvious inflammation indicates conjunctivitis or infection. Be concerned if a cat's nictating membrane, the so-called haw or third eyelid, is continually exposed in the inner corners of the eyes. Continuous exposure of this third eyelid may indicate an eye injury, a wound, or infection.

Ears. Examine your cat's ears. The inner surface of the ear flap (or pinna) should be pink (but not deep red), with shiny surfaces. Be on the lookout for small, odorous, dark fragments of wax and debris clinging to the inner pinna, a possible indication of ear mites. Incessant head shaking, itching in the ear area, and bald areas behind the ears are all suspicious signs.

If such indications are found, act immediately: ear mites spread easily from animal to animal, and once they make themselves at home in the ear canal of a cat and start to multiply they are extremely difficult to dislodge. If mites are a problem, a trip to the veterinarian is in order, followed by regular ear-cleaning sessions and application of ear drops at home.

Skin. Look for signs of scabbing, rash, or raw areas where the fur has been worn away from too much scratching. Cats are prone to fungus irritations such as ringworm. If you find signs of infection or bald patches know that ringworm spores in the environment can infect both other pets and people in the household. If these symptoms appear seek immediate advice from a veterinarian concerning appropriate treatments.

Be especially on the alert for fleas and ticks. Fortunately, fleas can be seen with relative ease as they move about on a cat's fur (especially on the lighter areas of the fur). They also leave an obligingly visible trail of small pieces of dark debris behind them. Constant scratching, rashes, sores, scabs, bites, and, in cases of severe infestation, lethargy and malaise, can also be a tip-off that fleas are present. Run your hands over your cat's fur looking for live fleas—you'll see them scurrying away if they are present. Also try placing your cat on a piece of white paper. Then go over her fur with a flea comb, watching for telltale flea debris and live fleas that fall onto the paper.

Once discovered, fleas can be treated effectively with oral medications, topical drops, and insecticide preparations. Consult with your veterinarian concerning the best strategy for your cat's specific condition.

Ticks are uncommon on cats, but they are found from time to time. Like fleas, ticks carry disease. Larger than fleas, black, round, eight-legged ticks attach themselves to the warm, protected parts of an animal's body such as the stomach or neck, and here they engorge themselves on the animal's blood. The longer a tick remains on an animal the larger it gets; after several days it sometimes swells to several times its original size.

There are innumerable strategies for removing ticks. Perhaps the safest and most sensible is to simply kill the invader with several drops of alcohol, then remove its carcass with a tweezers, making sure not to leave the creature's head embedded in the cat's skin. You can also try spreading a dab of petroleum jelly over the invader. Many insecticide preparations are available for tick control. Consult with your veterinarian. (For more information on parasite control see Chapter 5.)

Bowel habits. Constipation is an occasional and often persistent problem for cats, especially older cats. If your cat continually circles inside the litter box, squats, but seems incapable of passing a stool, veterinary care may be in order. Make certain, by the way, that your cat is having trouble passing stool, not urine. The inability to urinate is more serious than constipation, and it usually constitutes a medical emergency.

Ordinary diarrhea unaccompanied by other signs such as lethargy and vomiting is also an occasional problem for cats, especially those with fussy stomachs. Cats with diarrhea sometimes fail to use the litter box and may defecate in random places around the house. Besides the obvious evidence of loose bowels in these defecation areas, recurrent signs of clinging or caked feces may also signal a problem.

If the diarrhea continues for more than a day, be concerned. Cats dehydrate quickly, and are seriously weakened by fluid loss in short periods of time. Diarrhea can also be a symptom of intestinal parasites or viral infection. If the condition fails to improve in a day or two, see a veterinarian immediately.

Digestive problems. Watch out for excessive vomiting. Not only can it indicate poisoning or serious disease, but fluids lost through vomiting produce rapid dehydration. For serious conditions, a veterinarian's treatment is advised.

Overeating and constant eating on the part of a cat may signify worms. Refusing to eat for more than two days straight is a symptom that may be related to a number of serious cat disorders, including worms, and should be reported to a veterinarian immediately.

Respiratory health. Cats are especially prone to respiratory diseases. Has your cat been coughing or sneezing? Does he seem short of breath? Is he doing a great deal of openmouthed breathing? Does his breathing seem rapid, labored, and shallow?

Put your ear close to his face and listen. When upper respiratory problems are involved—congestion, shortness of breath, wheezing— you will probably hear them. If labored breathing is accompanied by fever, pneumonia may be present. If coughing is loud and persistent, suspect asthma or bronchitis. A dry persistent cough indicates lungworm. In all the above cases, immediate medical care is required.

Note also that chronic runny nose, sneezing, and discharge from the eyes are classic signs of calicivirus or rhinotracheitis. Both are potentially serious viral respiratory diseases that require prompt medical care.

. ***Taking urine and feces samples.*** If you believe your cat is ailing but are uncertain of the problem, collect samples of her urine and feces and bring them to your veterinarian for laboratory analysis. Urine is best transported in a sterilized glass jar, feces in a clean plastic container or a plastic bag.

Common Feline Diseases

Internal parasites

Hookworm. A small, spaghetti-shaped worm that lives in the small intestine.

Cause: Hookworms are usually passed from cat to cat via contact with contaminated stool or with the milk of an infected mother. Hookworms are extremely dangerous to the health of young kittens. Infestation produces anemia, severe gastrointestinal problems, and even death.

Symptoms: These include diarrhea (sometimes bloody), weakness, anemia, lethargy, and vomiting.

Diagnosis: Identifying the parasites through a microscopic examination of stool samples.

Treatment: A course of medication, followed by improved preventive hygiene to keep cats away from contact with contaminated feces.

Tapeworm. Tapeworms are large, long worms that attach themselves to a cat's intestinal walls.

Cause: Tapeworms are transmitted directly by ingesting fleas or flea-infected mice and rats.

Symptoms: These include diarrhea, weight loss, a variable appetite, or frequently, no symptoms at all. Look for small, rice-shaped incrustations attached to a cat's anus or in its feces.

Diagnosis: Diagnosis is most often made by actually seeing tapeworm segments in the stool.

Treatment: After identifying the parasite through a stool sample a course of medication is recommended, followed by control of household flea infestations, confinement indoors, and avoidance of rats, mice, and contaminated meats.

Roundworms. Roundworms are thick white, spaghetti-shaped parasites that live in a cat's intestines.

Cause: Roundworms are transmitted to cats by eating infected rats or mice, or by contact with a contaminated litter box, contaminated food, contaminated animals, or milk from an infected mother.

Symptoms: Diarrhea, weight loss, coughing, vomiting, restlessness, potbelly, and a dry, lackluster look to the fur.

Diagnosis: Roundworms can sometimes be seen in a cat's vomit or stool. If children are in the home, keep all cats away from play areas, especially the sandbox where worms like to breed. Children can easily contract roundworm by touching dirt or cat feces contaminated with roundworms or by roundworm eggs.

Treatment: Identification from a stool sample, followed by keeping a cat indoors and away from rodents, maintaining a clean litter box, and removal of all feces from the backyard.

Coccidia. Coccidia is a single-cell microscopic protozoan that is most prevalent (and most serious) among kittens.

Cause: Coccidia is spread primarily through contact with contaminated fecal materials.

Symptoms: Diarrhea (sometimes bloody), weight loss, and lack of appetite. Pets purchased at a pet store most often suffer from this disorder.

Diagnosis: Coccidia is identified by intestinal symptoms. See those listed above.

Treatment: Identification of a stool sample and a course of sulfa drugs, then the implementation of follow-through preventive measures, such as litter box sanitation and keeping cats inside.

Toxoplasmosis. Toxoplasmosis is a microscopic single-cell parasite that lives in the intestines of cats and is transmittable to human beings. In the most severe cases it is capable of causing birth defects and brain damage to human children in utero.

Cause: Toxoplasmosis is spread among cats through eating contaminated food (i.e., infected rats, mice, and birds), and by contact with fecal matter, for which reason it is advised that pregnant women ask other family members to do litter box duty.

Symptoms: Symptoms of this disease are not usually observable in cats, and the toxoplasmosis organism may remain hidden in an animal for long periods of time. When symptoms finally appear they include weight loss, diarrhea, respiratory distress, and anemia.

Diagnosis: Toxoplasmosis is diagnosed by observable symptoms.

Treatment: A course of sulfa drugs.

Heartworm

Cause: Heartworm is caused by a mosquito-borne worm. The disease is associated with dogs, but it attacks cats as well, and it is sometimes fatal. Mainly found in warm climates such as the American South, as well as the East Coast and Mississippi Valley, cases of heartworm have nonetheless been recorded all over the country. Avoiding mosquitos and taking monthly preventive medication in areas where the parasite has been identified are both recommended.

Symptoms: Early in the disease there may be no symptoms at all. When they do appear they include coughing, labored breathing, vomiting, swollen stomach and legs, weight loss, and exercise intolerance.

Diagnosis, treatment, and prevention: Diagnosis requires identification of the heartworm parasite with a blood test and chest X rays. Treatment calls for a long course of medication and medical care. Symptoms of vomiting and coughing can often be controlled with steroids, and in many cases heartworm parasites die on their own, allowing the cat to become disease free. Prevention calls for mosquito control, preventive medicine, and always keeping a cat indoors.

Feline distemper (panleukopenia) or infectious enteritis

Cause: Feline distemper is caused by a virus that attacks the intestinal tract and white blood cells of cats. It spreads through direct contact with an infected animal or with contaminated urine, saliva, and feces. Feline distemper also attacks a number of mammals other than cats, including minks, racoons, ferrets, and other popular household pets. The disease is highly contagious, and once contracted tends to be fatal to kittens.

Symptoms: Symptoms include the sudden onset of violent vomiting accompanied by severe weakness, depression, loss of appetite, dehydration, abdominal pain, diarrhea, fever, and eventual collapse.

Treatment and prevention: Prevention for feline distemper is easy.

Have your kitten vaccinated. The shot is virtually 100 percent effective. Once the symptoms of the disease begin to express themselves, however, feline distemper is usually incurable, especially in kittens. Because it is so contagious, an infected feline is placed in isolation at the veterinarian's office, then treated with a variety of drugs, none of which are very effective. If your cat does succumb to feline distemper, immediately disinfect all contaminated articles with bleach and throw out the cat's bedding, toys, collar, dishes, etc. They all carry the virus.

Feline leukemia (FeLV)

Cause: FeLV is caused by a virus that triggers cancer of the blood and lymphatic system specifically in cats. The disease is spread through prolonged contact with infected saliva, blood, feces, and urine, and it is usually contracted by cats that live or associate with groups of cats. This fatal disease is one of the main causes of feline mortality in the United States.

Symptoms: The symptoms of FeLV are not always easy to identify, and do not necessarily reveal themselves in an organized pattern. Generally speaking, they include anemia, vomiting, diarrhea, fever, respiratory sluggishness, and weight loss.

Treatment and prevention: A preventive vaccine exists that in many cases provides effective protection against FeLV. It is highly recommended, as is keeping your cat indoors at all times. There is no evidence at the present time to indicate that FeLV is transmitted from cats to human beings.

Rabies

Cause: Rabies is such a deadly disorder that public health services consider even one reported case in a county a major threat to the entire community. The disease is caused by a virus that is present in the host's saliva and body fluids. It is communicated by a bite or by contact between infected saliva and broken skin.

Symptoms: When rabies first appears a normally friendly cat suddenly withdraws and avoids all human or feline contact. Soon she may turn hostile and aggressive, lashing out, drooling, biting, hissing, scratching, behaving in a wild and unmanageable way. Loud noises, bright lights, and sudden movements may all excite her and induce a frenzy. Or conversely, the stricken animal may become even more lethargic and withdrawn than before, suffering total loss of appetite and staring into space. Eventually the ailing cat collapses, becomes comatose, and dies. There are many possible variations on the above patterns, symptoms, and behavior, but the end result of this is always the same.

Treatment and prevention: Having a kitten vaccinated against rabies eliminates the problem of contagion entirely. Once contracted, there is no known cure for this terrible disease, either for cats or humans.

Feline infectious peritonitis (FIP)

Cause: FIP is a viral cat disease that attacks several of the animal's body systems, causing a variety of symptoms. The ailment is contagious among cats and often deadly, especially for young kittens. Currently it is believed that the spread of the disease takes place by physical contact with infected saliva and feces, or through respiratory transmission. The entire mechanism of contagion is still not entirely understood. While cats who lead an active social life with other felines are frequently exposed to this virus, many appear to develop a natural immunity on their own and remain unaffected.

Symptoms: A cat can be exposed to the FIP virus and remain symptom free for months and even years. When symptoms appear they tend to be sudden and dramatic: weight loss, vomiting, diarrhea, loss of appetite, fever, lethargy, lesions, and swollen abdomen, followed by impairment and then failure of the liver, kidneys, and other organs.

Prevention and treatment: A vaccine has recently been developed for FIP, though it is not always available, and the jury is still out on its efficacy. Once a cat begins to show symptoms, treatment with antibiotics, steroids, and immunosuppressive drugs may be tried, though none have proven universally successful.

Feline immunodeficiency virus (FIV)

Cause: Though FIV is caused by a virus related to HIV, it does not infect human beings. Like HIV, the FIV virus attacks the immune system, compromises it, and allows a number of opportunistic infections to have their way. The disease is contagious among cats, and it is most commonly spread through bites.

Symptoms: A cat with this disease tends to develop anemia plus a

number of opportunistic infections, such as gum infection, mouth
lesions, lethargy, and reduced appetite.

Prevention and treatment: At the present time there is no effective
vaccine for this disease. The disease tends to be fatal, though not
invariably. If FIV is known to be in your area, keep your cat in the
house and away from strange animals at all times.

Feline lower urinary tract disease (FLUTD)

Cause: FLUTD is, medically speaking, a series of related urinary
tract conditions, all of which tend to clog a cat's bladder with
sludgelike sandy accretions that partially or fully block urination.
This syndrome of diseases is frequently found among older,
neutered male cats. The key to successful treatment is early detection and rapid diagnosis. If FLUTD is allowed to progress
unchecked and untreated for a prolonged period of time, a cat is
no longer able to pass urine, and death from uremic poisoning
follows.

Symptoms: The most prominent symptoms of FLUTD are constant,
unsuccessful trips to the litter box, straining and crying in the box,
and blood in the urine. Check the litter box for telltale blood
stains. A cat who cannot properly pass urine meows in pain at each
attempt, and his abdomen is highly sensitive to the touch.

Prevention and treatment: Veterinarians prescribe urinary tract
medications for FLUTD, and in serious cases, catheterization and
surgery. Once the cat is healthy, he will be put on a special diet by
your veterinarian which must be followed faithfully for the rest of
his life (once FLUTD appears it tends to frequently recur if
proper preventive means are not taken). Diets low in magnesium
are often recommended. Talk to your veterinarian on this one.
Make certain your cat has plenty of fresh water at all times.

Feline viral rhinotracheitis (FVR) and feline calicivirus (FCV)

Cause: Both these related diseases are common respiratory disorders, and they are often lumped together under the title "cat flu."
Both are caused by a virus, and both are highly contagious. Any
cat that has recently been exposed to other cats at a cat show,
boarding facility, animal shelter, and so forth is a candidate for the
disease and should be checked out by a veterinarian.

Symptoms: The symptoms of both diseases are relatively similar:
sneezing, congestion, labored breathing, malaise, ulcers on the

tongue (especially for FCV), clogged nasal passageways, watery nasal discharge becoming thicker as time passes—symptoms not at all unlike those experienced by people suffering the common cold.

Prevention and treatment: While vaccinations for FVR and FCV are available and recommended, cats usually survive these ailments without them, and often the condition can be treated at home. Keep your cat warm, lubricate his nose with petroleum jelly if it dries and cracks, wipe away discharge from the nostrils and eyes, and make sure he gets plenty of fluids. Though a cat's appetite decreases in time of illness, try to get at least a few ounces of soft food into him. As with the common cold, no medicine can cure this ailment, though veterinarians sometimes give antibiotics to control the possibility of secondary infections such as pneumonia. If your cat suffers from the above or similar respiratory ailments, consult with a veterinarian for advice on home care. If the condition takes a serious turn, take the cat for professional treatment immediately.

An ounce of prevention: Having your cat vaccinated

A majority of the above ailments can be avoided entirely by making sure your cat is vaccinated.

As with dogs, very young kittens receive the disease protection they need from antibodies swimming in the colostrum of their mother's first milk, especially if the mother has received a full course of immunization. Around three or four months, however, or following weaning, a kitten loses this magic maternal protection and becomes especially vulnerable to many of the diseases mentioned above. At this time it becomes essential that she be given a full course of immunity.

When is the best time to begin an immunization program?

Six to eight weeks of age is ideal, with follow-up shots given at two- to three-week intervals until twelve weeks of age. Work with your veterinarian in establishing a vaccination schedule. The following diseases are all covered by following the proper vaccination schedules and procedures:

- Feline calicivirus
- Feline leukemia (only for cats that may be exposed to FeLV)
- Feline panleukopenia (Distemper)
- Feline rhinotracheitis
- Rabies

Vaccinations are especially important for a cat when she is being boarded, or when another cat is introduced into the household.

Finally, although the ASPCA strongly warns against allowing cats to roam out-of-doors on their own, cat owners who insist on letting cats run free should know their animal will be exposed to many more viral hazards in the wild than at home, and that for any cat who spends time outside, vaccinations are essential.

Further Cat Concerns

Hair balls

Anti–Hair Ball Tip

If your tabby is plagued with hair balls try the following method: Rub a dab or two of petroleum jelly or commercially prepared cat laxative on her paws once or twice a week. While grooming she will lick the jelly off her paws. Once ingested the jelly will keep the clumps of swallowed hair moving easily through the digestive system and then out through excretion.

When a cat grooms himself, due to his barbed tongue, he ingests large numbers of hairs at each licking that pass directly into his digestive system. Here they may become compacted, forming balls of hair that may block the gastrointestinal (GI) tract and sometimes cause constipation. To dislodge these balls a cat may cough, choke, sputter, and vomit, but alas, these ploys are not always successful, and at times hair balls grow so large and produce such major obstructions that surgery becomes the only way to remove them.

The best approach to hair ball control is a preventive one.

First, groom frequently. Careful combing and brushing removes many hairs from a cat's body that would otherwise be swallowed and compacted in the GI system. Since hair balls are formed most frequently during shedding season, groom with special care and thoroughness during this time.

Second, adding a bit of extra fat to your cat's diet may help, especially during shedding season. A spoonful of oil mixed into the soft food goes unnoticed by most felines, and helps lubricate the danger zones inside their digestive tracts.

Third, note that once a hair ball does form, commercial hair ball preparations will help purge it from the system. These preparations can also be used as a preventive. Ask your veterinarian for recommendations.

Living with a cat and an infant under one roof

Popular wisdom has it that when an infant enters the home a family should give away their cat. Cats, it is said, claw infants, knock them over, and transmit diseases.

Is this really the case?

Not very often. When problems do occur they are usually avoidable with a bit of advance preparation. What can you do to insure the safety and happiness of *everyone* in the home? Here are some precautions to take, both before the baby is born and after.

Toxoplasmosis. The moment pregnancy begins make sure all risk of toxoplasmosis is eliminated. If contracted by an expectant mother, this disease can kill the developing fetus. Precautions are simple:

1. Have all cats tested for toxoplasmosis.
2. Keep cats strictly confined in the home. Since most cats become carriers of toxoplasmosis by killing and eating live prey, confinement keeps them out of the woods and greatly reduces the risk of exposure.
3. It is now believed that gardening is a primary source of toxoplasmosis infection, as well as eating undercooked meat. Pregnant women should wear rubber gloves and protective clothing when doing outdoor work. Better yet, avoid outdoor gardening of any kind during the period of gestation.

Other steps you can take to help the infant–cat relationship include the following:

1. Make sure your cat is neutered or spayed.
2. Cats should be taught that people—and hence infants—are not toys. Never tempt a cat by wiggling your fingers or otherwise roughhousing with your hands and feet. Direct the cat's play instead to interactive toys such as a catnip mouse on a string or a feather wand. If your cat goes for your fingers and toes during play, blow a puff of air in his face, discontinue the game, and walk away. If your cat is persistent, hiss loudly at him, as cats do

to warn one another. Then wait a few minutes and resume the game. By the time your newborn enters the home all notion of batting at little hands and feet should be eliminated.

3. Set up the nursery a couple of months early. Booby trap the area around the child's room-to-be. Place double-stick tape or contact paper on the surfaces you want the cat to avoid such as the bassinet and crib mattress, the top of the changing table, the playpen and carriage. Or arrange balloons under sheets in cribs, bassinets, or carriages. The loud pop startles the cat while the sheet protects him from getting hurt. Chances are he won't venture into this area again. Another trick calls for building a false ledge out of cardboard and placing it around the crib or bassinet. The ledge extends two or three inches over the side. Then place several soda cans filled with pebbles or coins on the false ledges. When the cat jumps up on the crib or bassinet, the ledge collapses and the cans crash to the ground, making a loud noise. The cat is frightened away and does not return.

Once the child arrives the following steps can be taken:

1. Keep the door of the child's room closed at all times. If there is no separate room or if there is no door on the room to close, mosquito netting can be placed over the bassinet or crib as protection.
2. When bringing your newborn home from the hospital, first greet the cat and say hello. Let him smell the receiving blanket so he becomes familiar with the new scent. Then let him sniff at the baby.
3. In the beginning cats often do not adjust well to infants. Don't be surprised if kitty goes into hiding, sulks, or simply ignores the whole intrusion, you *and* the baby both. Allow him time to see there is no harm in the situation, and that he will not be displaced by the newcomer. Don't try to force things. Whatever your cat's reaction, find time to spend with him each day. As little as five minutes of play or grooming in the morning and evening can compensate for the changes taking place in the household.
4. Keep your cat fully caught up on all shots and medical examinations to eliminate risk of contagion for the child. Use a flea product that is safe for infants and avoid using flea collars; they are doused with a toxic insecticide that can poison any toddler who chews on them.

5. Install a cat door or baby gate in the room where the litter box is kept. This allows easy access for kitty, but makes sure baby's first sand castle is on the beach and not in the cat box.

Body language: Learning to listen to your kitty

Cats are self-sufficient creatures that seem quite capable of taking care of themselves, thank you. But don't be fooled. Though they are low-maintenance houseguests, like all of us they have their needs, their priorities, and their idiosyncracies, some of which may not be apparent at first. What's important is to tune into the signals a cat is sending you from the very start, and to pay attention to these subtleties of communication. Owning a cat is an experience in listening, watching, and waiting.

For example, study your cat's verbal signals. Hissing, of course, is pure aggression: stay away!

Then there's the feline's famous trademark, purring, a sound made by most species of cats including lions and tigers. Though often thought of exclusively as an expression of contentment, this low-throated, low-frequency rumbling is far more complex and mysterious. Indeed, scientists are still not entirely sure how cats produce this sound. Certainly cats purr from pleasure when curled up by the fireside or while being stroked on your lap. But they also make this sound when they are hungry, a signal to let you know it's time to get out the can opener. They purr when they are frightened, confused, if they want something, or if they are bored. Baby kittens purr to tell their mothers where they are located. Old cats purr when their joints hurt. Sometimes there's really no telling why a cat is purring at all.

The best way to understand the intent of your feline's purr signal is to take it in context. If there is a lot of noise going on in your den and your cat is purring, calm her down. If it's feeding time and she's rubbing up on your leg while making her accustomed sounds, she's hungry. Feed her. If you've been away at the office all day and she greets you at the door with a purr, she's lonely. Pet her.

Then there is feline body language per se. One of the qualities that make cats such highly intelligent animals is the wide range of body signals they have developed over the millennia to make their wishes and moods known to others. Examples:

- Rubbing noses, yours or another cat's, is a cat's sign of greeting and acknowledgment. The same with mutual smelling and sniffing.

- Licking, though a relatively rare behavior among cats, is a sign of greeting and affection. It is also done to mark scents.
- Rubbing against your leg or against another cat is a feline's method of marking things with their scent. Rubbing can be a gesture of affection and/or a demand for attention to a specific problem (i.e., "I want you to feed me now!"). The more insistent a cat's need, the more his rubbing will become a kind of bumping and tripping.
- Flattened ears, jutting jaw, and retracted lips revealing the teeth are displays of anger and preparation for attack. Such body language is common between cats but unusual between humans and cats.
- Blinking or closing the eyes are signs of trust. Closing the eyes says, "I am confident enough in our friendship to close my eyes in your presence without being afraid that you will harm or attack me."
- Ears pointed upright means that a cat is feeling normal and relaxed. Twitching or revolving ears shows that a cat is curiously scanning for sound.
- A tail pointed straight up means a cat is freely offering his anus for inspection and sniffing, a sign that he is happy, trusting, and feeling fine. A tail that quickly and nervously flicks back and forth signals excitement. A slowly swishing tail means a cat is alert and studying the situation. In confrontative and combative moments a swishing tail warns, "Back off or we fight!" In a casual situation, it says, "I want to be alone." On the hunt, it means, "I'm getting ready to pounce."
- An arched back is an ingenious method cats use to make themselves look large to enemies, an unmistakable sign of aggression, primarily toward other animals. This trick works in reverse as well. If human beings come across a mountain lion in the wilds, one of the best protective measures they can take is to raise their hands over their head, making them appear taller and more menacing than they are.
- When a cat turns his back to you he is often saying something along the lines of "Not interested," or "No, I don't want to do that." The same message is more blatantly transferred when he simply walks away.
- Bristling, fluffed-up fur makes a cat appear large. It denotes fear and is done to frighten enemies. When the fur stands up all over its body it means a cat is seriously frightened. When fur stands up along the back and tail it's a sign of warning: "Don't come near!"

How, in terms of body language, can one tell if a cat is permanently hostile or just temporarily upset and afraid? The key variables are context and time.

When attacked, for instance, cats may display classic signs of anger: crouching, hissing, hiding, running away, and a quick startle reflex. When the danger is over, however, they return to their placid selves. This is normal. Or again, when a new stressor appears in the household, cats instinctively seek dark, out-of-the-way, or elevated places to hide. As they acclimate themselves to the stressor, they leave these places when no one is around (at work or asleep). Eventually they feel comfortable enough to return to the household and to take part in the normal flow of life again. All this is normal behavior.

Cats display variants of these behavior patterns in a number of stressful situations. If these fear behaviors cease after a day or so it means the cat was simply upset or frightened. If they *do not* cease after a day or so, if the cat continues to act hostile or fails to respond to your entreaties (especially when you offer her food), you definitely have a problem on your hands, and help is needed. Consult with your veterinarian on the best course of action.

Last but definitely not least, it is a good idea to get into the habit of simply listening to your cat with, as it were, your inner ear. Cats are excellent communicators, but they are also extremely subtle creatures. If you open your inner ear and inner heart, they will do the same. Then they will tell you all you need—if not want—to know concerning their mood and desire of the moment.

Trust in their instincts—and in your own.

Small Furry Animals

Owning a Small Animal

Many animal lovers today are foregoing the pleasures of dog and cat and choosing the more manageable alternative of small furry mammals. The small mammals featured in this chapter come in a variety of sizes, shapes, and personalities, and not all are so very small (rabbits can exceed fifteen pounds, and ferrets sometimes have bodies as long as a dachshund). While each animal has its own advantages and disadvantages, all are proven favorites.

Hamsters

Personality profile

In 1931 the first hamster (scientific name: *Mesocricetus auratus*) arrived in England all the way from Jerusalem where at the time it was being used as part of a selective breeding program. By the late 1940s this small, furry rodent had traveled across the Atlantic into the homes of millions of Americans where it soon became the most popular of all small pets.

The reasons for the hamster's quick celebrity are easy to understand. Hamsters are inexpensive, clean, simple to care for, easy to breed, and amazingly cute. They have short half-inch tails that give them a decidedly nonrodentlike appearance, a feature that mice- or rat-phobic parents appreciate. They have large cheek pouches which, when filled with food, give their faces a chubby-cheek, merry-eye, twitching-nose look that many pet lovers find irresistible.

Behavior

Hamsters are nocturnal desert creatures. In their natural habitat they spend a great deal of time burrowing underground and building elaborate tunnel homes complete with sleeping quarters, elimination areas, and breeding chambers. Hamsters grow from three to nine inches long, depending on their species. They weigh three to five ounces, and live for two to three years.

With a gestation period of fifteen to eighteen days, hamsters breed prolifically in captivity, producing litters of five to seven babies. Fifteen species are known to exist, three of which make superior household pets (see the Breeds section below). Despite a nervous and sometimes skittish nature, hamsters can also be trained to recognize their owners in a relatively short period of time. They require little time and money and are an all-around easy-upkeep, low-maintenance pet.

Species

Of the fifteen species of hamster, the following three breeds tend to make the best pets:

Syrian hamster. By far the most popular of all hamster species, these furry, golden brown creatures are friendly, adorable, and responsive, but also solitary and antisocial as far as other hamsters are concerned. At eight to ten weeks they should be separated from their littermates and kept in a separate cage. *Never* place a Syrian hamster in a cage with other hamsters (especially of the same sex) unless you intend to breed them. Syrian hamsters come in short-haired and long-haired varieties, and exhibit a range of colors including black, white, yellow, cream, reddish brown, piebald, and gray. Note: Syrian males may kill their young if not separated quickly from the brood.

Russian hamster. Often called *dwarf hamsters*, Russians tend to be even more friendly to people than Syrians. They grow three or four inches long (as opposed to the Syrian's eight or nine inches) and come in a variety of colors including brown, opal, albino, and silver. Russians are social creatures, unlike their Syrian cousins, and males and females often cooperate to raise their young. Currently there are two types of Russian hamsters: Campbell's Russian and the winter white Russian dwarf. Both make excellent pets.

Chinese hamster. Sizewise, Chinese hamsters are long, thin, and a bit heftier than Russians. They are also slightly less prolific breeders than the Russian and Syrian varieties, but are more sociable than both, rarely fighting when placed together. Yet while opinions vary on whether Chinese hamsters or any hamster species should live together in the same cage, the more conservative approach calls for housing each hamster in a separate home to avoid fighting.

Choosing the right hamster

When picking a hamster look for an animal that is alert, clear-eyed, active, and that holds its ears nicely erect. There should be no sign of feces caked to the hamster's anal areas and no ragged or molding spots on its fur. The eyes and nose should produce no discharge, and the body should be free of open sores, wounds, and scratches. When picking up a hamster, it should sit happily in your hand without attempting to run away or bite.

As a general rule of thumb, it is better to purchase hamsters from breeders than from pet stores. Breeders tend to provide more individual attention to their animals. They make genuine attempts to keep them disease free, and they work hard to breed their stock for a friendly temperament. Pet stores, on the other hand, acquire their stock from breeding factories, then mass market them with little concern for health, appearance, or disposition. Hamsters from a breeder are more expensive than from a pet store, but in the long run the extra few dollars spent give you a considerably better pet.

Feeding and nutrition

Hamsters of all breeds should be fed a rounded diet of hamster mix and rodent pellets. Hamster mix consists of a rich conglomerate of peanuts, assorted grains, dog biscuit, and seeds. Commercial rodent pellets or dry blocks have similar substances compressed into pellet or block form. The label on both pellets and mix should tell you they contain 16 percent crude protein.

Mixes can then be supplemented every two or three days with a half-teaspoon of one or more of the following: apples, grapes, cheese, raisins, salad greens, whole wheat bread, vegetables, uncooked pasta, plus egg, chicken, or tuna fish. Small bits of dog biscuit can also be given to help wear down the hamster's sharp teeth. However, when feeding vegetables give them in small portions, as too much vegetable fiber can trigger diarrhea. Raw sunflower seeds may be fed as a special treat, but only occasionally. The rich, tasty oil in sunflower seeds quickly makes hamsters obese.

Along with this regular diet, water should be supplied every day. The best dispenser is a gravity-fed plastic water bottle with a sipping tube attached to the bottom. Secure the bottle to the side of the cage with wire or twist ties, or to the side of an aquarium with Velcro strips or a wire hanger. Set the bottle at a height that is specifically adjusted to the hamster's size and reach. Be sure to rinse and refill the bottle every day with fresh water.

Bottles are a good deal more efficient for dispensing water than dishes or bowls. They are neat, take up no floor space, are easy to fill, cannot be knocked over or spilled, and prevent contamination from food particles, fur, shavings, and feces. Be aware, though, that the lower the water level goes in a bottle the more difficult it is for hamsters to drink. For this reason, never let the water in a water bottle fall below the halfway point.

When feeding, be aware of the fact that hamsters love to pack food away in their jowly cheeks, then bury it later under the shavings. This buried food soon decays, causing unhygienic conditions and an unpleasant odor. Avoid this problem by making periodic daily checks of your pet's shavings and bedding and removing uneaten food. Finally, be careful never to feed hamsters raw kidney beans or sweets of any kind, especially chocolate, which hamsters cannot tolerate.

Housing, sanitation, and environment

Hamsters can be kept in ten- or twenty-gallon aquariums with a screened lid tightly secured on top. For a Syrian hamster living alone, a ten-gallon tank is roomy enough. For two or more Russian dwarfs together a twenty-gallon tank is best. One rule of thumb recommends that approximately twenty square inches of floor space be allowed for each hamster, with a cage height of at least a half-foot. If you do place hamsters together, observe their behavior closely and separate them immediately if fighting occurs.

Besides aquariums, wire cages are also available at well-stocked pet supply stores. These sturdy houses come in a variety of sizes and shapes, some in a simple square, others with multiple levels, climbing ramps, secret compartments, and a maze of connecting tunnel tubes. The elaborate models are certainly a great deal of fun for their occupants and a good deal more spacious. But remember, the larger and more complex the cage, the more demanding the cleaning chores. And remember too that adequate air circulation is essential in a hamster cage for eliminating urine odor and ammonia vapors. Avoid cages with poor ventilation, especially those that are closed in on all sides.

Be sure that your cage of choice comes with a solid-bottom plastic base. Avoid wire-bottom cages; they are painful on the hamster's feet. Also, be sure that the bars on the cage are positioned close enough together to keep your hamster from escaping. Russian dwarfs are expert at wiggling through bars, and they can slip out of a cage that a larger Syrian hamster would find inescapable.

Before the hamster arrives, prepare its cage in the following way:

1. Cover the floor with layers of hardwood shavings. Aspen shavings are excellent. As with all small furry animals, it is critical that the shavings not be made of pine or cedar. Both contain phenol oils that may cause severe irritations in hamsters and all other rodents as well.
2. Add the bedding. Hamsters use this material to sculpt cozy little sleeping and hiding nests for themselves. Materials you can provide for bedding include toilet paper, napkins, thin cardboard, or tissue paper torn into thin strips and placed in the corner of the cage. Hamsters will shred this material to their specifications and use it as they will. Fresh hay and grass can also be used.

Note that though many brands of commercial cotton wool bedding are sold in pet stores today, if ingested this material sometimes lodges in the animal's throat or stomach where it produces blockages, interferes with digestion, and in many cases causes death. Cotton wool can likewise get impacted in a hamster's cheek pouches, or just as harmful, the wool fibers become tightly tangled around a hamster's leg, stopping circulation, and if undetected, causing eventual loss of the limb.

Presently there is a campaign among many hamster owners and breeders to have all non–water-dissolvable brands of cotton wool bedding removed from the market. Be aware, finally, that white fluffy commercial cotton, the kind used for first aid, produces many of the same problems as cotton wool and should not be used as bedding material for hamsters.

Cleaning and hygiene

A hamster's cage should be cleaned at least once a week. Remove old shavings and replace with fresh. While cleaning, look for small pieces of food that your pet sequesters under shavings or buries in nooks. Also take advantage of cleaning time to check out your pet's droppings. Liquified or loose feces indicates diarrhea; lack of feces in the shavings is a sign of constipation. Remove the old bedding from the cage—it quickly becomes matted—and replace it with new. If your hamster lives in a glass aquarium, give the tank a major scrub at least once every six months and preferably more often to prevent molds and odors.

Toys

Hamsters are playful creatures, deriving both diversion and exercise from toys. Small cardboard boxes provide excellent hiding and nesting places. Climbing frames, cardboard and toilet paper tubes, seesaws, and running wheels are all welcome. If you do put a wheel in the cage, be sure its circumference is solid and not runged. Runged wheels can catch little legs and break them.

Especially appreciated are the elaborate plastic tubes that fit together into fantastic and rather futuristic tunnel mazes. If you plan to add this wonderful toy to the cage, be aware that these tubes are expensive and difficult to clean. Make sure that the diameter of the tubes is large enough to accommodate your pet before setting up a tunnel maze in its cage.

Handling

Despite the hamster's ever increasing popularity, there is a less advertised side to this pet that parents are wise to heed: when mishandled, frightened, or provoked, hamsters bite more quickly and more frequently than any other domestic rodent.

For this reason parents are cautioned to think twice before buying very young children a hamster. If members of a household do, in fact, choose to keep hamsters as pets, it is recommended that they use the following precautions:

- Children under six should not be allowed to handle them.
- Children over six should handle them under strict parental supervision.
- Only hamsters that are known to be friendly and docile should be picked up and handled at all, either by children or by adults.

Hamsters are nocturnal creatures. They sleep during the day and scurry around when the sun goes down. In the process they make lots of noise, perchance keeping you, your children, and everybody else in the house wide awake.

For this reason you may wish to place the cage in a daytime activity room, away from all sleeping areas. Another solution is to reprogram the animal's day–night cycle. Do this by keeping a bright light on at night in the room where the hamster lives and darkening it during the day. After a week your pet should be well programmed to your waking–sleeping schedule. Since hamsters tend to bite most when woken up from sleep, reversing their day–night cycle is an excellent way of curtailing the biting problem.

Health and disease

Hamsters are hardy creatures, susceptible to some infectious ailments from other animals (including human beings) but relatively immune to naturally occurring disease. If their cage is clean, their littermates healthy, and their diet correct, they should live out their three or four years in the best of health.

When physical problems do arise, however, they are complicated by the fact that a hamster's small size and shy nature make it difficult to recognize all the signs. Hamster owners must be especially vigilant in this regard and give their pet visual checkups every few days. Symptoms of illness include dull, glazed eyes, diarrhea or constipation, weight loss, drippy nose, runny eyes, signs of trauma, wounds, or broken bones, and intense lethargy. Irritability and an uncharacteristic tendency to bite are also suspicious indications. The following common health problems should all be referred to a veterinarian:

Skin infections: Ringworm, mange, mites, fleas, and assorted fungal infections all produce skin problems. Patchy fur, fur loss, red skin, and constant itching are signs to watch for.

Respiratory infections: Weight loss, shivering, and wheezing may indicate colds, bronchitis, or pneumonia.

Impaction of the cheek pouches: When a hamster's cheeks appear unusually protruded or lumpy this is a sign for concern, especially if the animal is not eating or appears listless and agitated. Food, grass, paper, or any number of things may be impacted in the pouches inside their cheeks. Try cleaning them out with warm water and an eyedropper. If cleaning doesn't work swab the area directly with cotton Q-tips before taking the animal to the veterinarian.

Wet tail: A common hamster disease, wet tail is a bacterial disease typified by pale, mucus-filled, bad-smelling diarrhea, feces-caked anus and tail, and a hunched-over posture when walking. Weakness, lethargy, and constant squealing may all be apparent. Wet tail is a potentially lethal disease and requires fluids, supportive care, and several rounds of antibiotic treatment. It is highly contagious, and infected animals should be quarantined from other hamsters immediately.

Malocclusion: This condition takes place when a hamster is not chewing properly, and as a result its teeth are not getting trimmed. In such situations a veterinarian's help may be necessary.

Fur loss: Sudden fur loss is caused by a number of problems including skin infection, fungus, mites, diet deficiency, and thyroid problems. If a hamster appears to be shedding excessively in patches along with normal fur loss, quarantine the animal and get medical help immediately.

Allergies: Like humans, hamsters can become allergically sensitized to a number of environmental allergens. Dust, leaves, cedar shavings, household cleaners, and grains in the diet may all trigger attacks. Symptoms include wheezing, runny eyes and nose, fur loss, and sneezing. Establish the cause by ascertaining what new environmental stressors have recently been introduced, and once found, remove them.

Diarrhea: First, make sure it's not just diet. Too many vegetables, for instance, can produce loose bowels. Keep the animal strictly on a dry mix diet for a few days. If food is not the problem, if the diarrhea persists, and/or if other symptoms such as coughing and lethargy are in evidence, seek medical help.

Rectal prolapse: Intense diarrhea or constipation sometimes causes a hamster's intestines to emerge through its anus. A skilled veterinarian can work the protruding organ back into place. Needless to say, get help immediately, and *don't* try it yourself.

Ear infections: Excessive ear scratching indicates infection. Various treatments may be required at the veterinarian according to the cause and origin of the infection.

Aspergillis fungus: Due to poor cage hygiene, aspergillis forms in patches along the body and quickly spreads to all occupants. Symptoms include choking, wheezing, lethargy, diarrhea, and skin irritations. While antibiotic treatment usually helps, reinfection can occur. Keep the cage clean to avoid the chance of this disease developing.

Sudden death: Sudden death among hamsters is not unusual and can take place due to a variety of causes including dehydration, septicemia, and chilling. Death from overheating is especially common due to the fact that when exposed to high heats hamsters are unable to sweat.

Poor nutrition: Undernourished hamsters become lethargic, thin, and lose patches of fur. This imbalance can be caused by feeding the wrong food (such as rabbit pellets) or not feeding enough food.

Gerbils

Personality profile

Since their introduction to the pet market in the early 1960s, gerbils have become one of the most popular small companion pets in America. Well adapted to human handling, they are curious, frisky, gentle, gregarious members in good standing of the rodent family. They are surprisingly and sometimes startlingly intelligent and are quite capable of learning and being trained. In Canada they have been taught to perform police-detection duties, sniffing out illegal substances at airport baggage facilities. Gerbils rarely bite and appear to show genuine affection to their owners. They are busy and active during the day (unlike hamsters), and they make excellent first pets for children.

Behavior

Gerbils come from a number of geographical places across the globe including North Africa, South West Asia, Turkey, and Central Asia. Here they live in packs of several males and seven or eight females. Highly social animals, it is recommended that in captivity owners keep more than one gerbil at the same time.

Gerbils breed quickly in captivity in litters as large as ten or twelve, with a gestation period of around twenty-five days. They are territorial creatures, bordering off their living area with a scent-marking gland located on the abdomen. They also enjoy digging and burrowing.

Though gerbils make few noises other than a small squeak, they are famous for their remarkably loud and insistent alarm call produced in times of danger by thumping their back legs. Try this experiment: With your finger or a pencil make a series of quick taps near your pet. With a little luck your gerbil may answer back with his own drum call.

Gerbils have intriguing and rather complex personalities. Like large mammals, they wash themselves with their feet like a cat, cuddle with others of their kind, especially when sleeping, and jump high in the air when startled or excited. They express hostility by head butting or pushing and mutual affection by cuddling and kissing. When happy they purr like a cat. Some gerbil owners have noted that gerbils wink one eye as a sign of happiness, submission, or, some claim, gratitude after being given a treat. Extreme gerbil fanciers even insist that if you wink at your pet, he will wink back at you. Worth a try.

Breeds

There are eighty-seven known gerbil species. By far the most popular is the Mongolian gerbil, known to zoologists as the *clawed jird*. Other species are kept as pets, but usually only by breeders or fanciers who display them at the many gerbil shows now popular throughout the United States and Europe.

Some species of gerbil are nocturnal, though the Mongolian remains awake during the day and sleeps at night. Mongolian gerbils weigh four or five ounces, and grow to be from five to six inches long. Most species live from three to a maximum of five years. They have a golden brown coat with black-ticked fur, a color pattern known to gerbil breeders as *agouti*. Other species come in a panoply of colors including black, brown, gray, slate, beige, white, ivory, pied, spotted, and even shades of lilac and blue.

Choosing the right gerbil

When choosing your gerbil from a litter, look for an animal that is friendly, responsive, and does not object to being picked up and handled. They should not be nervous or fearful around human beings. They should have bright, alert, inquisitive eyes, with no signs of discharge from the eyes or nose. There should be no wounds, scars, scabs, tufting, patches, or skin irritations on the animal's body.

As with all pet rodents, it's best to purchase gerbils from a professional or neighborhood breeder. Pet stores are usually undiscriminating when stocking small mammals and may sell diseased and/or genetically inferior pets.

Feeding and nutrition

Gerbils take well to commercial mixes, most of which contain a blend of grasses and seeds. Commercial rodent pellets also make excellent fare. If you use them be sure the labeling on the package indicates that they are balanced with 18 to 22 percent protein.

A commercial mix diet can then be supplemented with small bidaily amounts of fruits, such as apples and grapes, plus a small but daily selection of celery, brussels sprouts, turnips, fresh dandelion greens, cabbage, lettuce, spinach, carrots, cauliflower, and chicory (do *not* feed gerbils potatoes, especially raw potato). Gerbils adore sunflower seeds, but these should be given only in moderation as a special treat. Large numbers of sunflower seeds make gerbils obese. Moreover, when fed an exclusive diet of sunflower seeds, gerbils become addicted to them and often stop eating the other foods they need to balance their diets.

What about vitamins? There are no absolutes here. Some owners feed their pets liquid or powder vitamins to supplement the regular diet. Liquid vitamin supplements are added to water, powder vitamins are sprinkled in food.

Some gerbil cages come equipped with a built-in food container. If your cage is missing this piece of apparatus, any heavy-based, hard-to-tip-over metal or ceramic bowl can be used. Stay away from plastic bowls, however. Gerbils love to gnaw at—and through—them.

The feeding schedule of gerbil species differs, so it's best to take a one-size-fits-all approach and leave food down all the time. Gerbils eat less than a teaspoon of food at a sitting, but they eat several times a day. Having food set out to accommodate this need makes it unnecessary for you to go through the bowl-filling routine more than once every day.

As with all rodents, water is best provided in a gravity-feed plastic bottle with a metal drinking spout attached to the bottom. These bottles can be hung on the side of a gerbil's cage or fastened to a wall of the aquarium with tape or Velcro strips. Though gerbils rarely drink in their natural habitat, in captivity they enjoy water, often splashing, spilling, and mucking up the cage with it. You can avoid this problem by using the standard gravity-feed plastic water bottle.

Housing, sanitation, and environment

Cages and glass aquariums for gerbils can both be purchased at any good pet supply store. If you are using a preused aquarium that held fish or other rodents, give it a careful scrubbing with a disinfectant followed by a thorough hot water rinse. Bacteria and viruses linger for surprisingly long periods on old pet equipment.

If you intend to keep more than one species of gerbil always house them in separate cages. Different species do not always get along. Unless you are interested in breeding, moreover, keep males and females apart. You can tell the sex of a gerbil in the following way:

1. Female gerbils have nipples, even when they are very young.
2. The distance between the anal and urinary openings in females is a good deal shorter than in males.
3. After two weeks of age, the scrotum on males begins to develop. By six weeks it appears as a large bulge at the base of the male's tail.
4. Adult males tend to be measurably larger than adult females.

For two gerbils living together, a ten-gallon aquarium provides adequate space. If you add a third or fourth occupant, a twenty-gallon tank becomes necessary. Remember, housing too many gerbils in too small a space may cause normally placid animals to nip and fight. The standard rule of thumb is that thirty-six square inches of cage room (6" × 6") should be allowed for each gerbil.

Floor materials can be made from any hardwood commercial shavings such as aspen or coarse sawdust (not fine). Avoid shavings made from pine and worse, cedar. Both contain chemicals known as phenols that trigger health problems in rodents, rabbits, and ferrets. Also avoid sand, corncobs, and cat litter—the rough surfaces on these substrates may cause abrasions on a gerbil's face when it digs and burrows.

As for bedding, commercial cellulose is ideally suited for the job. Toilet tissue can be used too, but it's messy. Avoid newspaper. The ink rubs off and causes health problems. Avoid fiberglass batting and worse, commercial brands of fluffy cotton wool bedding. According to reports from breeders and owners, when ingested wool becomes lodged in the throat or stomach, causing blockages, choking, and sometimes death.

Sterilized antiseptic cotton, the kind used for first aid, produces many of the same problems and should also be avoided.

When choosing a place in the house for your gerbil cage, remember that gerbils are happiest living in temperatures between 60 to 70°F, and humidity below 50 percent (a dehumidifier comes in handy here, though gerbils can survive in high air dampness if they must). This means your cage should not be too near—or far—from the radiator in winter, and not too near the air conditioner or direct sunlight in summer. Areas with direct draft (such as an open window or door) should also be avoided.

Clean your gerbil's cage several times a month, changing the shavings each time. The water bottle should also be cleaned, preferably with soap and a bottle brush, and then thoroughly rinsed, removing all traces of soap. Failure to clean drinking equipment results in the growth of molds. Every few weeks give the entire cage or aquarium a careful scrub down to keep things clean and bacteria-free.

Toys

In their natural habitat gerbils spend a good deal of time curled up secretively in crevices and nooks. Like many small rodents, they have a natural need to hide.

Small, cozy hiding places are thus appreciated such as cardboard or wooden boxes, ceramic cups, ceramic or metal pots, and toilet paper and paper towel tubes. Some pet owners browse local garage sales looking for used children's toys, especially items that offer secure crawl spaces like plastic houses or trucks. Just be sure the space is large enough so that your pet doesn't get stuck. Gerbils also appreciate a few rocks arranged into small caves or shelters in the corners of the cage. Rocks make terrific climbing and frisking surfaces. So do ladders, ramps, small tree branches, and small piles of stones.

Other appreciated items include wooden blocks for gnawing, twigs and small branches, thread spools, plastic balls, connecting tubes, PVC pipe, and of course, the old standby, the exercise wheel. If you purchase a wheel for your pet be sure the tread area is solid and not runged. Runged wheels can catch and break gerbils' tails. Note by the way that some gerbils take to the running wheel and others don't, and that in general, gerbils seem to derive less enjoyment from running wheels than hamsters.

A variety of interesting and sometimes ingenious rodent toys can be found at most pet supply stores.

Handling

Gerbils are intensely curious creatures, and once accustomed to their owner's touch they seem to genuinely enjoy running along a hand or arm and checking things out. The more you handle gerbils the tamer they become. However, if picked up and held incorrectly, their tail may slough off, and in general it is best not to overhandle.

Even the boldest gerbils will run from you the first or second time you try to pick them up. But the third time, the fourth, the fifth—at each attempt they become measurably friendlier and tamer. In the beginning place a few seeds in your hand as bait, then gently scoop the gerbil into your hand. Once holding the animal, needless to say, treat him gently and with respect. A little stroking does not hurt, though at first the gerbil may think that your petting motions are an attack and he will shy away. Continue the picking-up process several times a day for a few weeks, starting when the animal is very young. Before long you will have a new friend.

Health and disease

If kept clean and in spacious quarters, gerbils remain immune to most infectious diseases. From time to time, however, it's still a good idea to give them a thorough checkup. A healthy gerbil should be energetic with no signs of lethargy or slowness. Her eyes should be clear, round, large and alert, with no discharge at the corners. There should be no signs of diarrhea, especially wet rear ends or feces caked on the anus. Fur should be clean, smooth, without any visible signs of hair loss. Appetite is normal without signs of weight loss. The animal's posture is natural with no hunching, foot dragging, or frequent rolling into a ball. Common gerbil sicknesses include the following:

Colds: The first symptoms of gerbil colds are like our own—sneezing, hacking, wheezing, dripping from nose and eyes. The animal shivers and huddles for warmth. Keep your animal warm, isolate him from the others, and consult with a veterinarian.

Respiratory infection: You'll know respiratory infections in gerbils by the sound of wheezing and labored breathing. Drug therapy sometimes helps this condition, especially with new medicines. See your veterinarian right away the moment a respiratory ailment develops.

Seizures or epilepsy: Occasionally gerbils go into a kind of spasm or fit, turning in circles, twitching, drooling. A few minutes later they resume their normal behavior. While no one is sure what causes these convulsions—in some cases it may be the result of trauma—they are neither self-destructive nor deadly. If you intend to breed gerbils, however, avoid seizure-prone animals, as the cause of this ailment is believed to be genetic.

Infected nose, eyes, or ears: Nose, eyes, and ears are all especially vulnerable in gerbils. Infected noses are red and tender. Sore eyes show discharge and redness. Sore ears result from excessive cleaning, or from mites. In most cases, antibiotic treatment is the therapy of choice.

Scent gland tumors: A disease of older gerbils, this ailment can be identified by a hard lump in the abdomen. These lumps can usually be removed by surgery. Occasionally they go away on their own.

Diarrhea: Diarrhea results from improper diet or more commonly as a symptom of infectious diseases such as a cold. If the condition continues for more than a few days see a veterinarian.

Tyzzer's disease: A bacterial ailment, symptoms include diarrhea, weight loss, ruffled, patchy fur, exhaustion, and finally collapse. This disease is often difficult to identify in its early stages. Catch it quickly though, and antibiotic treatment will sometimes helps.

Rabbits

Personality profile

Members of the biological family Leporidae (not rodents, as some people believe), rabbits are dear little creatures that enjoy human company, are gratifyingly intelligent, and make excellent family pets. Relatively clean, rabbits rarely bite, and some learn to come when called. If acquired at an early age they can be trained to use a litter box, and with a bit of guidance they are tame enough to run free around the home like a dog or cat. In all, they make excellent pets and companions.

Though rabbits survive happily indoors or out, when kept as companion animals their housing should be kept inside. Using a lead and harness, they can then be walked several times a day under strict supervision. Indeed, in city parks around the country it is becoming increasingly common to see a child and sometimes even an adult walking a pet rabbit on a leash.

Behavior

Most rabbits are social animals, living communally with others of their kind in a strictly hierarchical way. The dominant male is usually older and larger than the competition. Though he is firm in maintaining his authority and may push other males around a bit, rabbits rarely fight to the death unless under extreme duress. If you are considering keeping more than one rabbit and *not* breeding them, be wary of putting two intact males together. They fight. It's better in a mixed community to have all members neutered. Otherwise the proverbial breeding instincts of this prolific animal become quickly apparent.

The number of young borne by female rabbits varies from breed to breed. Six to nine bunnies per litter is average. Females can begin breeding as early as four months of age, and gestation lasts about a month. At maturity, rabbits weigh from two to fifteen pounds, depending on their breed. If well looked after they live from eight to ten years, though a few genetically well-endowed specimens make it to eleven or twelve, an amazing statistic when you consider that in the wild the average life span of a rabbit is less than two years. Before acquiring a rabbit it thus behooves prospective pet owners to be sure they are willing to make this long-term commitment.

Like all small mammals, rabbits exhibit an array of strange behaviors that tend to puzzle first-time owners. Each of these behaviors has a distinct message coded within it and learning to read this language is the key.

For example, when a rabbit runs circles around your feet, sometimes nipping at your ankles, she's telling you something quite personal: she's *very* attracted to you. If she rubs her chin against your arm, she's excreting scent from scent glands in her chin to tell other rabbits that you belong to her (cats do a version of the same thing). When your bunny suddenly starts to do the bunny hop, leaping up and down, this is a sign she's feeling wonderful and wants to tell you all about it. She's also doing it to exercise.

Rabbits make strange, unusual noises. Each has a definite message.

When you hear growling or clucking sounds, for example, look out: the rabbit is mad, possibly at you. What did you do?

How about stuffy nasal sounds? This means they're annoyed. Find out what's wrong.

If the rabbit hums or coos, she likes you and is feeling pleased with things in general.

The rabbit grinds her teeth in a loud and unpleasant way. Translation:

something's very physically wrong. I hurt, I'm in some kind of pain. Check her over. A trip to the veterinarian may be in order. Even worse is when rabbits emit high-pitched, sudden screams. Normally quiet creatures, a rabbit scream is a sign of anguish and terror.

Here are some other interesting patterns of rabbit behavior to look for:

- When they thump the ground with a back leg it means they are afraid, or they are warning of danger or change. Or they are letting you know this space is their territory.
- They sit up on their hind legs and look around. Nothing drastic here. They simply want a better view of what's going on.
- They run after you wherever you go in the house. They're courting you. They want you all to themselves every minute of the day.
- They scatter their droppings around the home or apartment rather than deposit them in one neat pile. They are marking off their territory.
- They lower their heads submissively in front of you and extend their necks. They want to be petted.
- Their ears stick straight up. They are alert and curious.
- They dig and scratch at you, or chew at your sleeve. Or they roll on the ground in front of you. They want your attention *now!*
- They leap wildly around the house, bouncing off the walls and furniture. They're happy. Leave them be.
- They lick you. They love you.

What about extremely aggressive behavior? Serious biting and scratching? These activities should not be tolerated. The most common cause of aggressive behavior in rabbits is sexual frustration. The best remedy is to get your pet neutered or spayed right away. Nine times out of ten neutering calms a rabbit down.

Breeds

There are currently forty-five breeds of rabbit recognized by the American Rabbit Breeders Association (ARBA). Many of these breeds are bred for style and form and are then shown at rabbit shows around the country. Among these breeds, there are four divisions: small, medium, large, and giant.

Popular small breeds (weighing two to six pounds) include the mini-rex, mini-lop, and Netherland dwarf. Medium-size breeds (weighing six to nine pounds) include the English spot, English Angora, French Angora, and rex. Large breeds (from nine to eleven pounds) include the English lop, giant Angora, and Californian. Popular supersize rabbits (twelve pounds and over) include the French lop, Flemish giant, and checkered giant.

Identifying a rabbit's breed is a complex matter and cannot be ascertained by color alone. Many rabbits appear to belong to a certain family, but are not actually purebreds. It's a complicated issue, and one we must leave to breeders, experts, and aficionados. For most ordinary pet owners the purebred/hybrid issue has little or no importance.

Choosing the right rabbit

Unless you intend to breed or show, it is best to simply choose a rabbit according to your personal preferences. Here are the three essential prerequisites to look for:

1. The rabbit's appearance should be pleasing to you and its personality appealing. When you pick her up she should like and respond positively to you.
2. Physical behaviors and characteristics are also important. For example, a healthy rabbit behaves in an active, curious way. Any signs of lethargy or extreme shyness—or conversely, hostile aggression—are danger signs. A healthy rabbit has clear, round, alert eyes with no discharge coming from the pupils. Their nose does not drip or show signs of discharge. A healthy rabbit's fur is sleek and soft. There are no signs of hair loss, bare spots, tufting, wounds, or cuts. Likewise, there is no wetness on the rear end, and no feces caked to the anus.
3. Consider whether you wish to adopt a doe (female rabbit) or buck (male). There are small but definite differences between the sexes. Male rabbits are more aggressive and friendly, females more irritable and gentle. These variations are minor, however, and in general gender differences are small.

When it comes to purchasing rabbits there are several ground rules: Mixing rabbits from different birth litters is tricky business. You'll need to house them in separate cages, and put them together only for supervised periods of time each day until they become accustomed to one another. Which they may or may not do. Don't assume they will.

Older rabbits are very territorial and almost invariably pick fights with young intruders. It's better to mix two rabbits of the same age, preferably when both are young.

Two males together often fight. Two females together usually get along—but only until breeding season when they get feisty. You may be able to determine the sex of a rabbit by turning it over, placing your finger below the anus, and pushing slightly inward. Either a protruding penis or a slit will become apparent. Sexing a rabbit is not an easy process, and lessons from a local breeder or veterinarian may be in order.

If you mix a female and a male, have them neutered and spayed.

If you are looking for a healthy, robust pet rabbit, especially a pure-bred, breeders or dedicated private owners are the experts to see. Animal shelters also have rabbits for adoption from time to time. The House Rabbit Society, a rescue and education group, may also have rabbits in need of homes.

Feeding and nutrition

The frequency and amount of daily feedings depends on a rabbit's size, age, and activity level. A twelve-pound Flemish giant rabbit obviously craves more than a small Dutch or Jersey wooly. On the average, rabbits weighing from two to five pounds require approximately an eighth to one-quarter cup of pellets a day. Rabbits six to eight pounds need up to a half a cup.

High-quality pellets are rich looking, preferably dark green. They smell fresh and do not crumble or turn to dust in your hand. The label on the product package should tell you that the contents are adjusted to from 15 percent to 19 percent protein. A count of 18 percent minimum crude fiber is also advisable, though this figure does not always appear on the package. Currently the National Research Council lists the minimum nutritional requirements for rabbits as being 14 percent crude fiber and 12 percent protein. Finally, look for the fat content. This figure should be on the label and should be no higher than 3 percent. More fat in the diet causes pets to become obese.

Rabbits are constant nibblers, and a pellet diet should be supplemented with unlimited grass or Timothy hay, and fresh vegetables. Good rabbit veggies include sprouts, green beans, cucumbers, kale, mustard greens, peas, squash, spinach, turnips, celery, carrots, brussels sprouts, broccoli, beet greens, and bok choy. A cup of vegetables per four to five pounds body weight a day is about the right amount.

Recommended fruits (one tablespoon per four pounds of adult weight) include berries, apples, mangos, plums, peaches, pears, papaya, pineapples, raisins, and melon. Grains such as oats and seeds such as sunflower can be given, but only in small amounts. Foods that disagree with rabbits and should be avoided include iceberg lettuce, corn, and avocado.

When feeding rabbits, place their pellets in a heavy metal or ceramic bowl. Water is critical for rabbits. If they don't drink they won't eat. Water should be provided with a gravity-feed water bottle. The bottle can be fastened to the side of the cage with wire or tape.

Finally, note that if you see a rabbit eating its feces from the cage floor or directly from its anus, this is a perfectly normal habit. The soft feces provides rabbits with needed nutrients and contributes a small but necessary part of their diet.

Housing, sanitation, and environment

The rule of thumb for housing rabbits is that the cage should be at least four times the size of the rabbit, and larger if the rabbit spends long periods of time enclosed.

Cages come in a variety of styles and models. Avoid those with wire floors; the wire cuts into their feet. Hard wood or plastic is better. Never place your pet's cage in direct sunlight. Keep the cage away from drafts, and maintain a room temperature of around 70°F. Cages should not be situated in basements, bathrooms, or chilly garages. Dampness and high humidity make rabbits sick.

As far as shavings go, soft wood like Aspen is ideal. Stay away from cedar shavings and pine. They may produce respiratory problems in rabbits, as well as in most other small mammals. Corncob bedding, straw, and hay all make excellent bedding.

Cleaning and hygiene

Clean the cage at least once a week, and give it a thorough scrubbing once a month. At each cleaning change the bedding and shavings, especially if they emit a strong smell.

Sanitation problems can be avoided entirely by litter training your bunny.

First, determine the area of the cage where your bunny urinates and defecates. Then place the litter box in this section with a piece of newspaper in the bottom. You can also try adding a handful of bedding with the scent of the animal's urine on it as a lure.

After your rabbit starts to use the litter box regularly and accustoms himself to its feet, place several litter boxes in different areas of the house. Then let the rabbit roam free for a few minutes each day. If he makes a mistake and goes on the floor, clean it up, then use an odor neutralizer. Or another approach: if your rabbit makes a mistake, place a litter box over the soiled area. Chances are he will return to this spot, and this time will use the provided facilities.

Now have patience. Persevere. Once accustomed to using a litter box, rabbits usually do not return to their old ways. If several clean boxes are provided throughout the home, most rabbits choose these over the floor and the rug. Spayed and neutered rabbits tend to train to the box more easily than unneutered rabbits.

For easier and safer handling, it is suggested that you clip your bunny's toenails at least once a month. When confused or angry, rabbits kick and scratch, and sometimes their claws go as deep as a cat's. In the wild, rabbits' nails are naturally worn down by contact with earth and stone. In captivity there isn't much to keep them trim, and they grow long and sharp.

Cut your bunny's nails with a regular nail clippers, the kind used for dogs and cats. As with human fingernails, trim them carefully above the quick. If you happen to cut into this sensitive pink area, styptic powder helps stop the bleeding. Use a small nail grinder for the job if you like, though rabbits may be too frightened by the noise for it to be a real option. In general, most animals do not remain still for the time it takes to trim their nails, and patience is always a necessary part of this process

Another nice way of making friends is by grooming your pet. A soft brush and small plastic comb are all that's needed for the job, though more elaborate rabbit care implements are available from pet supply houses. When grooming, brush with the fur, never against it. Make gentle, easy strokes, talking gently to your pet as you do. If she seems skittish, never force the brush and comb upon her.

As far as washing is concerned, rabbits by and large take care of their own hygiene, and rarely need bathing. This is a great blessing, as any pet owner who has ever tried to give a rabbit a bath will testify.

Toys

Rabbits are playful animals, and a few well-chosen toys not only keep them busy and exercised, but divert their sharp teeth and claws away from the furniture. Make certain that all toys are nontoxic, that they don't flake or break into small pieces when chewed, and that they have no jagged points or rough edges.

Pet supply stores sell an array of rabbit playthings that are, by and large, safe and fun. Toys you make at home are just as entertaining and a lot less expensive. Toilet paper rolls, paper towel rolls, golf balls, and rolling plastic children's toys all do the job. You may also wish to give your rabbit an old phone book or magazine to rip apart, or a hard rubber baby ring to teethe on. Small cardboard boxes with holes cut into them make nice places to hide. Be sure to rotate the toys from time to time. Like all of us, rabbits get bored.

Handling

If truth be told, though cuddly and cute, a majority of rabbits do not enjoy being picked up. Some tolerate it, yes, but the fact is that being picked up feels much like being trapped to rabbits, and all of their instincts mitigate against it.

Rabbits are extremely light-boned animals, and their entire skeletal structure accounts for only eight percent of body weight. When dropped, their bones break easily. Their instinct is thus to protect against falling by not allowing themselves to be picked up in the first place. On the other hand, some rabbits enjoy being petted, stroked, and fondled while they sit on the floor in front of you.

If you wish to accustom your rabbit to being picked up, start when she is very young. Before the lifting begins, talk sweetly to her and allow her time to become accustomed to your smell and to the feel of your hands around her stomach and back. Then scoop her up, being careful to support her hind legs with one hand and her chest with the other. Quickly set her down again. Never pick a rabbit up by her ears or dangle her in the air.

Extend the periods of time you hold your rabbit, talking gently to her the whole time and holding her securely. Most rabbits respond to this slow, patient process of pickup conditioning, and many come to like it. But not all.

Health and disease

If a rabbit's cage is cleaned frequently and the inhabitants kept away from infected animals, most rabbits live out their lives without disease. Still, at least once a month it is a good idea to give your pet a thorough physical going-over. A healthy rabbit should be responsive, energetic, and inquisitive with no signs of lethargy or depression. Her eyes are clear with no discharge in the corners or dull film over the pupils. There

should be no diarrhea, no wet rear ends, and no feces caked to the anus.
A healthy rabbit's fur is glossy and silky. There is no dry, flaking skin, or
sign of hair loss. Her appetite should be normal (rabbits nibble constantly) with no indication of weight loss. A healthy rabbit's urine is yellow, clear, or yellowish brown. If it becomes red or dark red, trouble
lurks. A rabbit's posture is erect without compromised movement or
painful joints. The pads of her feet are soft and intact, without abrasion
or bleeding.

Common rabbit health problems include the following:

Hair balls: Like cats, rabbits are prone to hair balls. These thick tufts
of hair are ingested as the rabbit grooms itself. If the balls become
too large they cause obstructions that can result in serious illness.
(Rabbits are unable to vomit and have no natural way of regurgitating the impacted hair.) Regular grooming and a high-fiber diet
both help keep this problem to a minimum. Pineapple juice
or hair ball medications such as Petromalt or Laxatone may also
be helpful for rabbits by acting as a lubricant. But be wary of pre-
scribing home treatments. If a hair ball of any seriousness develops, seek veterinary care immediately to avoid the need for
surgery.

Diarrhea: Diarrhea is a generalized symptom that may result from
poor diet, bad sanitation, or serious disease. If diarrhea lasts more
than a day or so, see a veterinarian.

Ear mites: If you see scabs or crusty accumulations in your rabbit's
ears, chances are she has ear mites. Your veterinarian will prescribe appropriate medications.

Skin problems: There are a variety of skin ailments, most of which
display in the form of patches and bald spots. One of the more serious of these conditions is fur mites. Its symptoms include fur loss
over the entire body, especially in the areas of the rear end and
neck. Mites should be treated immediately by a veterinarian.

Snuffles: Despite its cute name, snuffles is a serious disease caused
by the dangerous Pasteurella bacteria. Symptoms include sneezing, nasal mucus discharge, conjunctivitis, labored breathing, and
red, irritated nose. If snuffles develops, see your veterinarian immediately for appropriate antibiotic therapy.

Weepy eye: Discharge from the eyes may be caused by infection or
blocked tear ducts. If this condition lasts for several days and
seems to be getting worse, get professional help.

Enteritis: Symptoms of enteritis include swollen belly, diarrhea, mucus in the feces, and gurgling sounds from the rabbit's stomach. A high-fiber diet with small amounts of dry oatmeal sometimes helps, though if the condition continues it could be serious. See a veterinarian.

Wet dewlap: The dewlap is a fold of loose skin that hangs under a rabbit's neck. Lops and large breeds are especially prone to infections here. These produce raw and broken skin, plus a foul odor that emanates from under the chin. Improving sanitary conditions, replacing water bowls with a more sanitary gravity-fed water bottle, and clipping a rabbit's hair in the infected area will all help. Wet dewlaps may also be caused by dental problems, usually a malocclusion.

Heat stress: A warm weather ailment, heat stroke can be recognized when a bunny breathes rapidly, cranes her neck, has a dark disfigured skin color around her mouth, and drools. When these symptoms occur move her to a cool area, fan her, and pat her down with a washcloth dipped in cold water. Make sure her cage is moved to a cooler part of the home.

Dark red urine: A healthy rabbit's urine is yellow, clear, or yellowish brown. Urine with a red tint, especially a deep red tint, may indicate blood and hence intestinal or respiratory problems. See a veterinarian right away.

Pinworms: You will recognize these nasty creatures in your rabbit's feces, short, white, narrow little worms that cause weight loss, lethargy, and shabby, listless fur. A standard pinworm medicine like Piperazine remedies the situation in a few days. Talk to your veterinarian.

Sore hocks: Sore hocks are common in rabbits that inhabit wire-floored cages. Excessive pressure and rubbing on the hocks, or ankles, causes hair loss, redness, and finally ulcerated lesions. When sore hocks are in evidence, supply the rabbit with soft bedding and apply antibacterial medications to the sores.

Guinea Pigs

Personality profile

Guinea pigs, or cavies, as they are called after the rodent family Cavidae, compete with gerbils as the most docile and amenable of all small companion animals. First brought to North America by Dutch explorers in the sixteenth century, they came to be used as laboratory animals, but word soon got out that they made exemplary pets. And indeed, guinea pigs are extraordinarily friendly, inquisitive, low-maintenance, inexpensive, and nonaggressive. They do not require special equipment other than a cage, toys, and feeding paraphernalia. They are not destructive. Unlike some small pets, they require minimal exercise, and most members of this family enjoy being handled and even cuddled.

Guinea pigs' full, hefty size makes them easy for children and adults to pick up and hold. The strong, musky odor that pet owners complain of in other rodents is largely absent from a guinea pig cage, and unlike certain small mammals, guineas rarely claw, chew, climb, scratch, leap, squeal or—most important—bite. As an added attraction, they produce a wide assortment of squeals, snorts, purrs, and squeaks that to most pet lovers' ears is cute and appealing.

All in all, it can probably be said that among all the small furry animals, guinea pigs make the best starter pets. If carefully supervised, children as young as five years old can handle them, pet them, and help out with the cleaning and feeding chores.

Behavior

A typical life span for a guinea pig is between five and eight years. This is a long period by rodent time, and it means that purchasing a guinea pig is a commitment. If there are children in the home they should, of course, be allowed to help in the care and cuddling of these friendly animals. At the same time, the hard fact is that grown-ups will probably end up doing 99 percent of the work, and again this means that the decision to purchase a pig should come from the adult, and then only after due consideration.

Size among guinea pigs varies considerably from eight inches long to twice this size. Females breed up to five times a year, and after a gestation period of two months, they produce litters of one to six little ones. They have an especially acute sense of hearing, and are able to tune into frequencies 10 kHz higher than human beings (humans hear at 20 kHz, guinea pigs at 30 kHz). Their sense of smell is well developed, though not as highly as their eyesight, which is keen and discerning. Because their eyes are mounted on the sides of their heads, however, they have poor depth perception and fall easily from ledges.

Guinea pigs are social animals that live in herds. If you wish your pig to bond affectionately with you, keep only one pig at a time. If you prefer a less attached pet, or want your pet to enjoy the company of its own kind, two or more guineas is the way to go. But be careful of putting two adult males together: they often fight, sometimes to the death. Lessons on sexing guinea pigs are given below in the Handling section.

In terms of intelligence, guinea pigs have received something of a bum rap, most likely because their passive, nonassertive demeanor is taken as a sign of dumbness. True, guinea pigs are not at the top of the rodent intelligence curve. Rats are a good deal brighter. Still, they have an ample capacity to learn through repetition and behavioral training, and with patience they can be taught to use a litter box, recognize their keeper, and (after lots of hard work) respond to human voice commands. Though subdued, pigs are also excellent communicators, especially if their owners learn to decipher their body language. Essential noises and behavior patterns to watch for include the following:

Touching noses: A way of saying hello and giving other guinea pigs a good smell down. Sometimes pigs attempt to touch their owner's noses, an especially endearing sign of curiosity and affection.

Popcorn jumping: A very guinea-piglike activity, *popcorning* takes place when pigs suddenly and for no apparent reason leap straight up in the air, like corn kernels popping on a griddle. Don't be alarmed, popcorn jumping is a sign of high spirits and glee. A variation is when pigs run across the cage making a series of small hops. Rabbits perform a similar maneuver when happy.

Rumbling: This deep, resonant sound is often accompanied by standing on the hind legs to appear larger and more threatening. Among guinea pigs, rumbling is a method of establishing dominance over other members of the herd, or of saying "Back off, pal!" Its precise intent can only be understood in the context of the situation.

Teeth chattering: Even guinea pigs get angry. When they do they click their teeth rapidly, making a surprisingly loud and intimidating sound. If your pig behaves this way toward you be wary—it is during these spasms of teeth chattering that guinea pigs are most likely to bite.

Yawning/exposing teeth: Both activities are an overt display of aggression.

Grunting, gurgling, purring: One of the most attractive features of guinea pigs is that when happy they purr—or grunt, gurgle, warble, however you wish to describe it. Listen for this sound when you feed or caress your pet.

Neck craning: When a guinea pig stretches her neck forward she is checking out the scene. It is a sign of watchfulness and alertness to possible danger. Neck craning can also be a fear response.

Hissing: As with a cat, hissing is a sign of anger and aggression.

Frantic squealing: When a guinea pig makes a high-pitched *"wheeee"* sound it means she craves attention, usually the feeding kind. If you and your pig are on especially good terms, it may also mean she needs a hug. A more intense, alarmed squeal that sounds something like a human howl may signal dismay, loneliness, or even terror. It is a sound most frequently emitted by very young guinea pigs when they are separated from the herd or feel that they have been abandoned.

Breeds

There is a fair variety of guinea pig breeds, most of them identified by color and hair type. A sampling of popular breeds, all of which come in a range of colors such as white, black, tortoiseshell, chocolate, beige, cream, lilac, and blue, includes the following:

Abyssinian: Short-haired with whorls on their coat (these are known as rosettes). There is also a related satin Abyssinian breed.

American: Short and smooth hair. There is a related satin breed that originated in the United States.

American crested: Short-haired with a single whorl of color on its forehead.

Peruvian: Long-haired. There is also a related satin teddy breed.

Silkies: A long-haired breed (called shelties in England). There is a related satin silkie breed.

Teddy: A new breed of pig with a short, thick coat. There is a related satin teddy breed.

Choosing a guinea pig

There are many places to acquire guinea pigs including pet shops, friends, breeders, ads in the paper, shelters, and animal rescue centers. As is often the case, pet shops sometimes offer sound, healthy pigs, sometimes not. Acquiring one at these establishments is a bit of a lottery. Buying direct from a breeder has more pluses, especially if you are looking for a particular breed. Breeders are, however, more expensive than pet shops and not always easy to find. Getting your pig from friends is a good idea too, as is scanning the ads for giveaways. Occasionally local shelters have a supply of small animals to choose from, though not always. If you are bent on finding the best specimens available, you may wish to attend a local guinea pig show where especially fine guinea pigs are shown.

When choosing a guinea pig, bear in mind that guineas often sit passively and motionless in their cage. This is normal. When you approach them, however, they should immediately show a healthy interest in your presence and not object to being picked up and handled.

Guinea pigs are social creatures and should relate well with their cage mates. Observe which pigs seem most friendly and frisky, and which pigs are most curious. Be cautious when a guinea seems listless and remains separate from the other pigs. If he does not respond when you greet him and play with him, he may be sick.

Note that a healthy guinea pig has clear, bright eyes without discharge or "weeping." Their ears and nose are clean, with no sign of discharge, irritation, or redness. Their paws show no signs of scarring or infection. There should be no patches, discolorations, pulled-out tufts, or wetness on their fur.

A healthy guinea pig's droppings are firm, neither too hard nor too soft. Traces of diarrhea in the cage are danger signs. The same applies if pigs exhibit a wet rear end or feces is caked to their anus.

The skin of the guinea pig should show no wounds, scars, bare patches, scabs or signs of irritation. Whether long hair or short, their fur should be thick and healthy looking. Drab, unhealthy fur means the guinea pig is unhealthy too.

Hold the guinea pig close to your ear and listen to its breathing. Ideally, you will hear very little sound. If the creature's breath is loud and labored, he may have a respiratory problem.

Feeding and nutrition

In the wild, a guinea pig's diet consists mainly of tubers, leaves, and fruits. In captivity a pig seems quite content to live on a combination of pellets supplemented by vegetables and fruits, especially vitamin C rich fruits and vegetables: cabbage, oranges, and/or kale (vitamin C supplements are also absolutely essential for guinea pigs).

All fruits and vegetables should be as fresh as possible and given daily. Other fresh foods that guinea pigs enjoy include apple, cantaloupe, grapes, radishes, peas, Swiss chard, turnips, turnip greens, carrots, brussels sprouts, broccoli, cauliflower, celery, sweet red or yellow peppers, and whole wheat bread. Daily helpings of fresh timothy hay also provide guinea pigs with needed fiber. Fresh weeds like dandelion flowers, clover, yarrow, grass, and plantain can likewise be given. Foods to never give your pig include meat, nuts, sweets, and seeds. Some companies make yogurt treats for guinea pigs, but these should also be avoided, as too much calcium overloads a guinea pig's digestion. Finally, when purchasing guinea pig pellets, products made from timothy hay are preferable to those containing alfalfa.

Provide all food in a heavy metal or ceramic bowl, one with a broad, heavy bottom that will not easily tip. Clean these bowls regularly and carefully, as guinea pigs may defecate in them. Pellets tend to dry out quickly, and the vitamin C contained in them volatilizes. So do not remove pellets from the package until feeding time, and avoid storing them for long periods of time. It's also a good idea not to expose packages of pellets to sunlight or intense heat.

Fresh water should be dispensed to pigs via a gravity-feed plastic bottle that can be hooked to the side of the cage or fastened with Velcro or adhesive strips. Be sure to change the water frequently. If you add a vitamin C supplement to the water, be sure to change the water daily, as vitamin C loses its nourishment power within twenty-four hours. Note, finally, that like rabbits, guinea pigs eat their feces. Though not an attractive sight, this is a natural and even necessary part of their nutrition cycle.

Housing, sanitation, and environment

A guinea pig's cage should provide at least two square feet per occupant, four square feet for two occupants, six square feet for three, and so on. Avoid wire bottoms, and make sure your cage is situated in a warm, dry part of the house.

Metal cages are strong, easy to clean, and safe. Cages with a plastic bottom tub and wire top work very well. Large rodent cages now come complete with several floor levels, hiding cubbies, and stairs. Just be sure the model you choose provides adequate ventilation. In general, aquariums make poor habitats for guinea pigs. They are claustrophobic, hard to clean, and provide inadequate ventilation.

During the warm months of the year, empty plastic kiddie wading pools make ideal holding pens for guinea pigs. Pigs are poor climbers and cannot negotiate the steep sides of a pool. At the same time, the open structure of a pool provides the big sky above, plenty of elbow room below, and easy access for you and your children. Plastic pools are also easy to clean. When in use, make sure to keep an eye on your pigs at all times since they are now especially vulnerable to stray cats, dogs, and other neighborhood predators. Also keep the pool out of direct sun and avoid overheating.

As far as bedding and shavings are concerned, stay away from cedar and pine. Both may cause liver and respiratory damage in guinea pigs. Hardwood shavings like aspen make excellent bedding, as do dried corncobs and commercial brands of wood pulp bedding like Care™-Fresh straw and hay can also be used. Finally, avoid all commercial brands of cotton wool bedding. Though less harmful for guinea pigs than for hamsters, gerbils, and rabbits, the danger still lurks.

Since guinea pigs are loathe to soil their nests, a pile of litter in one corner of the cage encourages them to use this spot exclusively for excretions and makes your cleaning chores easier. Guinea pigs prefer room temperatures in the 60°F zone, but if necessary they can tolerate temperatures as low as 40°F. Be careful though: they are vulnerable to sudden changes of heat and cold and are especially susceptible to hyperthermia. There are, for instance, cases of pet owners keeping their pigs outside on a cool spring day and bringing them indoors at night into a heated house, only to find them dead on the cage floor the next morning. Whatever you do, make sure the temperatures in a guinea pig's area remain at a stable setting.

Make sure that all guinea pigs in a cage are of the same gender. Determine the sex in the following way. First, note that male pigs are more energetic and active than females. Second, note that males are larger than females and give off a strong odor when sexually aroused. Third, when you inspect a pet's hindquarters, the vulva or male genitalia should be fairly evident. Fourth, the penis in males will extrude when pressure is applied by pet owners to the genital areas.

Toys

Guinea pigs are playful animals and enjoy a variety of toys, especially those they can crawl through such as a cardboard tube or PVC pipe with elbows on the ends. In their natural habitat, pigs escape predators by squeezing themselves into small crevices in the rock. Thus any small, cozy nook like a cardboard box, oatmeal box, tissue paper carton, or plastic house toy is welcome. Pieces of cloth, patches of blankets, dish towels, and washcloths all make cozy wrap-up toys.

Adding several large stones to the habitat and arranging them into miniature caves is especially appealing. The problem is your pigs may end up spending a majority of their time holed up in these safe havens. Do be careful too that construction is sound, and that the rocks are not poised to collapse suddenly on top of your pet. Also make sure that the rocks are not piled so high that they serve as a ladder for the pigs to climb up out of their enclosure.

Before giving any toy to your pet, rub your hands over it to transfer your scent. When you reach down from now on, the guinea pigs will associate this smell with their playthings, and they will be comfortable when you handle them.

Handling

Compared to other small cage animals such as hamsters and gerbils, guinea pigs are relatively heavy and thick boned. This makes them easier to get a grip on when picking up, but also more vulnerable to dropping. Even a tumble of a few feet for a guinea pig can cause broken bones or worse. It is thus imperative that children handle guinea pigs only when closely supervised by parents, and children under five years of age should not handle them at all.

When lifting a guinea pig, cup one hand beneath his bottom and steady his head and back with the other. Then lift. Talk calmly and reassuringly to him as you perform the maneuver.

If you want the guinea pig to bond with you, make a habit of handling him at least once a day. The more handling the better, and the more familiar your touch becomes. Remember though, some guinea pigs—not many, but some—do not take well to handling and prefer to be left alone. If this is the case, honor their needs.

Your guinea pig also responds well to grooming, but only if you start the practice when he is young. Short-haired pigs should be brushed at least once a week. While you brush inspect the fur for lice (an affliction guinea pigs are especially prone to) and skin irritations. Long-haired guinea pigs require more frequent brushing than short. If their hair becomes too long and tangled, or if they trip over their own coat and drag it through the litter, a serious trim may be in order.

A pig's nails also need periodic trimming. One effective method is to place the guinea pig on a tennis racket, with feet and toenails poking through the webbing, then trim away. Another is to wrap the pig in a towel and hold him firmly while clipping each nail. Use an ordinary fingernail clipper for the job, and be careful to take only the very tip off each nail. Whatever you do, avoid cutting into the quick. In many cases, it is best to take a lesson or two in this tricky process from a breeder or veterinarian before trying it on your own.

Guinea pigs tolerate water fairly well, and baths are sometimes in order, especially when debris or feces is caked to her hair. Fill a plastic container with an inch of warm water. Using a mild pet shampoo, lather her coat, rinse thoroughly, and dry with a towel. Blow-dryers tend to generate too much heat for pigs and should be avoided.

Health and disease

If a guinea pig's cage is clean and his diet balanced, he will most likely remain fit and well. Still, problems do occur, and indeed, guinea pigs tend to be more susceptible to infectious ailments than most other small pets. Periodic checkups are thus always in order.

When examining a guinea pig, look for signs of dull, glazed eyes, diarrhea, constipation, weight loss, runny nose or eyes, signs of trauma, wounds, or broken bones. Lethargy and irritability are all early signs of sickness.

Sick guinea pigs segregate themselves from their mates and huddle miserably and listlessly in a corner of the cage. Sick pigs stop eating entirely, and this is a serious sign. To stay healthy a pig must eat all the time. Even a day without food can result in death.

The following health problems should all be attended to immediately:

Respiratory ailments: A bit of sneezing is normal for guinea pigs— both dust and dirt in the cage can trigger it. Guinea pigs that cough and sneeze constantly, however, may have a cold or a more serious respiratory ailment such as pneumonia. If these symptoms are accompanied by lethargy, loss of appetite, and a runny nose or eyes, take your pet to a veterinarian immediately. Meanwhile, make sure the cage is in a warm part of the house far from dampness and drafts.

Diarrhea: Dehydration is a dangerous condition for guinea pigs and can kill them in a few hours. The cause may be something as simple as diet—too many vegetables or the introduction of a new food. Or it can be a symptom of a far more dangerous ailment. In either case, immediate attention is required.

Lice: While a certain amount of scratching is normal for pigs, excessive scratching is usually a sign of lice or parasites. Examine your pet's fur for signs of infestation, bare spots, or rash. The best remedy for lice is a commercial powder or medicine recommended by a veterinarian.

Discolored urine: A healthy pig's urine has a milky white tinge. If the urine is extremely white your pet has too much calcium in her diet. If her urine is red, this is probably caused by blood, often from bladder stones. A veterinarian's attention is needed immediately.

Seizures: Guinea pigs occasionally suffer from seizures. They shake, salivate, roll over on their backs, then regain their balance and go about their business as if nothing happened. In many cases this behavior is normal. If excessive, seek a veterinarian's care.

Bumblefoot: When a guinea pig's foot swells and shows slight redness it probably has a condition known as bumblefoot. Commonly seen in obese guinea pigs who are housed on wire-bottom cages or who sleep on abrasive bedding, the sores from bumblefoot should be treated with antibiotics, and a softer bedding should be provided.

Enteritis: Enteritis is the number one cause of death among guinea pigs. Symptoms include loss of appetite, a low-grade temperature, lethargy, and dehydration. Caused by parasites, infection, antibiotic toxicity, impactions, or contaminated food, enteritis responds fairly well to appropriate medical treatment.

Ferrets

Personality profile

Though ferrets are thought of as unusual and exotic animals, according to one authority they are presently the third most popular large pet in the United States, after dogs and cats. While this may or may not be the case, and while it is actually illegal to sell them in certain parts of the country, it is accurate to say that Americans are discovering the joys of ferret ownership at an ever-increasing rate, and that many of the misconceptions concerning these fascinating and affectionate animals are being dispelled.

Ferrets are not rodents, as some people believe, but members of the Mustelidae, a zoological family that fits somewhere between dogs and cats (with an emphasis on the dog). First cousins to the weasel and polecat, second cousin to the skunk, ferrets are exceedingly resourceful, certainly the most intelligent of all species featured in this chapter, and the only predator. If treated with affectionate care they make delightful pets.

Most obvious of a ferret's virtues is their love of fun and play, a quality they maintain throughout their lives. Inquisitive, determined, friendly, independent, cuddly, fantastically energetic, ferrets can be trained to perform many of the acts we take for granted in a dog or cat such as coming when they are called and using the litter pan. Like dogs and cats, they are high-maintenance pets, requiring an investment of time, money, and attention. Just be sure to handle these furry energy balls with care, to supervise them when they are around children, and to keep them away from children below the age of seven. And though a bit nippy at times, the consensus is that ferrets are safe, friendly, and agreeable companion animals.

Behavior

The average household ferret grows to be about fourteen or fifteen inches long, weighs three or four pounds when mature (females are smaller and lighter than males), and lives from six to ten years. They come in a variety of shades including albino, white, sable, brown, cinnamon, silver, chocolate, and mixed colors. Interestingly, ferrets change color with the seasons, becoming lighter in the wintertime (perhaps to blend into the dried vegetation), and darker in the summer (perhaps to become one with the foliage). For some ferrets fur color lightens as they age or when they become ill.

Ferrets are social animals and prefer sharing their cage with at least one of their kind. Ferrets will not languish away from lack of company as some animals do, especially if you play with them on a daily basis. Indeed, regular interaction with ferrets ultimately causes them to think of *you* as their cage mate.

If you do keep more than one ferret, separate them by sex. You can tell the males and females apart by inspecting the ferret's belly, halfway between the tail and bottom of the rib cage. Here you will see a protrusion if the animal is male, and if not, check the ferret's anus for an opening with a tiny flap of skin. If the flap is visible it's female.

Some other points to note about ferret behavior:

- Ferrets emit a distinctive musky smell. If you find his odor offensive, neutering reduces the problem substantially, as do frequent cage cleanings and shaving replacements. Look into Ferret Sheen powder too. In many cases it is reputed to reduce ferret odor.

- Spay or neuter your ferret, both for breeding control purposes and for better health.
- If you have allergies, ferrets make excellent pets. They are hypoallergenic, which means they almost never cause allergy problems, even in the highly allergic.
- Ferrets bite most frequently when they are startled or frightened. Always move slowly around your pet and never make sudden lunging motions in his direction.
- Though ferrets are criticized for sleeping so much during the day, they are not nocturnal creatures by nature, and sleep only because they are bored. If members of your household are at home for at least part of the day, ferrets easily adapt to human time cycles.

Choosing the right ferret

Ferrets have distinct, recognizable, and in many cases charming personalities. A majority of them are cheeky characters who will give you hours of fun and amusement. Before purchasing a ferret, however, spend a bit of time with each candidate. You will find them all to be surprisingly different.

A healthy, happy ferret is full of play, curiosity, and nerve. He's everywhere, looking at everything, all the time. If not—be careful. A lethargic ferret is usually a sick ferret. On the other hand, if the animal seems too aggressive, this is not a good sign either.

Physically, a healthy ferret has bright, inquisitive eyes without discharge or mucus in the pupils. His whiskers are straight and perky, and his ears and nose are clean, with no signs of discharge, irritation, or redness. His paws show no signs of scarring or infection. Examine the ferret's backside as well. His anus should be dry and uncaked, and there should be no signs of diarrhea in the cage.

As far as the coat is concerned, a ferret's fur should show no holes, tufts, signs of skin irritation, bare patches, discolorations, or wetness. Whether long hair or short, his fur should be sleek and healthy looking. A drab, unhealthy-looking coat of fur usually means the ferret is unhealthy too.

As with dogs and cats, you will need a number of pet-care items for the proper maintenance and housing of your new pet. A roomy, well-ventilated cage (not a glass aquarium) can be purchased from most animal supply stores. You will also need bedding, shavings, toys, a litter box, food, water bottle, food dish, and a good supply of kitty litter. More on all this below. Also, ferrets require regular vaccinations and trips to the veterinarian, making a roomy, well-constructed pet carrier a necessary investment.

Concerning where to acquire ferrets, there are a variety of sources. Shelters sometimes offer ferrets for adoption, as do ferret rescue groups and private owners. Pets offered at these sources are usually mature animals, and this has certain advantages. Older ferrets are past the biting stage, which is a plus. Moreover, if a ferret is raised by attentive persons, she is likely to be litter trained. Adopting from a shelter is less expensive than buying from a pet store or breeder, and you are doing the animal kingdom a kind turn in the process. Ask your veterinarian for the name of a ferret club, rescue group, or shelter in your area. Or use a search engine on the Internet, typing in "Ferrets, adoption" or "Ferrets, pets" as the key words. Also see www.petfinder.com.

Breeders are another good source for ferrets, as are ferret owners and fanciers. Ads in local newspapers or on bulletin boards at schools and supermarkets sometimes bring results. Last on the list are pet stores, which often carry inferior and sick animals, and which are rarely a safe bet.

Feeding and nutrition

Ferrets do well on commercial feeds that are especially formulated for their nutritional needs, especially those varieties balanced for a protein level of between 32 to 38 percent (check the label). Being carnivores, their feed should not include more than 4 percent fiber.

Ferrets receive optimum daily nourishment from small amounts of food eaten on a frequent basis. It is thus important always to keep their food bowl available and filled. Use a heavy metal or ceramic bowl to avoid messy accidents—ferrets are great spillers—and hang a plastic gravity-feed water container to the side of the cage with tape or Velcro strips. Clean both bowl and container every day.

Housing, sanitation, and environment

Ferrets are long-bodied and energetic, and their cages should be roomy. A cage that measures approximately two feet by three feet by two feet high is about right, though larger would be better. As with other exotic pets, the choice of cages is vast, as a visit to a well-stocked pet supply store shows. Cages with several floor levels, hammocks, ramps, stairs, tubes, and small hiding places are favorites among ferrets and are referred to as "condo" cages. These make the best and most ac-commodating cages, unless you intend to build your own.

Before purchasing a ferret cage, be sure there are no sharp edges on the bars, and that the bars are narrowly spaced—one and a half inches is the maximum width—to prevent escape. Stay away from aquariums. Ferrets are so active they can shatter the sides of a glass enclosure. Choose a cage with a plastic or metal bottom. The comfort level inside can be increased by covering the bottom with newspaper, blanket, or old sheets.

For bedding, the usual warning to avoid pine or cedar applies. The phenol oil in both woods, and especially in cedar, may cause a variety of respiratory problems in ferrets. Aspen wood is preferable and available at most pet stores.

Ferrets enjoy being warm and snuggly while they sleep. A small dog or cat bed in the cage, or a friendly blanket, accommodates this need. As far as climate is concerned, ferrets prefer cool over hot. Their ideal temperature is between 55 and 70F°. Temperatures above 90°F make ferrets sick and in some cases kill them. During the sultry days of sum-mer make all efforts to keep your ferret in an air-conditioned room.

Cleaning and hygiene

Clean your pet's cage and shavings at least once a week and give the cage a major washing and scrubbing every month or so. Rugs, blankets, sheets, bedding, and so on should be laundered on a regular basis.

How often a ferret should be let out of her cage depends on whether or not she is litter trained. If she is not, training is in order.

Start by procuring a litter box. Fill it with a half-inch of litter and place it in a corner of the cage. For sanitation's sake you may wish to place an old sheet or newspaper under the box to absorb any mistakes. Ferrets are clean animals by nature and do not like to soil their nests. Chances are they will begin to use the box on their own as soon as you put it in the cage. After a few weeks regular use makes litter training a habit.

If your ferret makes repeated mistakes, take a piece of her feces and place it in the litter box. The smell establishes an association in her mind between the box and defecation. Next, when your animal is about to defecate—typical signs include crouching and huddling in a peculiar way—pick her up and place her in the box. Ferrets are very bright; they quickly get the picture.

Except for brief playtimes during the day, keep your ferret confined to her cage until she's trained. Once you are confident that all lessons are learned, allow her to roam in one room of the home, then another, keeping an eye on her during this time. For most ferrets the process of litter training takes a couple of weeks. Once training is mastered you can allow your pet to roam the house for a few hours a day. But be warned: ferretproofing is essential.

This means keeping all household poisons and poisonous plants out of reach (see Chapter 5), and all cabinets, closet doors, drawers, nooks, and crannies shut. Ferrets wiggle into the smallest places, and their sleek, long bodies allow them to squeeze through spaces less than two inches in diameter. At the same time, an exploring ferret is neither as careful nor as graceful as a cat. Be sure to take all breakable objects off the shelves. Also, be careful of exposed phone and electric wires; both make attractive gnawing materials. Most important, check for small holes in the walls or doors. While ferrets are Houdinis of escape, once on the loose they quickly become disoriented and lost.

Toys

Ferrets consider pretty much anything a toy. A cardboard roll, a piece of PVC pipe, a tissue box, a branch from a tree, a block of wood, a children's toy—it's all the same to them. Do not, however, supply ferrets with playthings made of rubber or plastic. Both materials break into pieces when chewed on, and if swallowed they can cause blockages in the animal's intestines. Most pet supply stores carry a wide range of safe, ferret-oriented playthings.

Handling

As with any pet, begin handling your ferret when she is young to accustom her to your feel and smell. Baby ferrets almost always nip. This is normal, but all the more reason for keeping young children away. If your pet continues to bite into adulthood it's time to train this nasty habit out of him.

Start by letting your ferret out of the cage. Allow him to sniff around and give him a treat to win his confidence.

Now pick him up in the following biteproof way: Make a V shape with your index and middle finger. Clamp this V over the ferret's neck and pick him up, the V-shaped fingers of one hand on his neck, the other hand supporting his body. Trapped in the crossbars this way, it becomes impossible for your ferret to nip. Keep him in this position for a while, allowing him to wiggle and squirm, and talking to him lovingly. The moment he tries to bite say loudly, "Stop biting!" then put him in his cage and walk away.

Lesson: The moment the ferret starts to bite the fun stops.

Repeat this process over and over and be patient. Patience is the key. After a few weeks your ferret will come to realize that biting ends the fun, and she will start behaving herself. As a supplement to the process, some ferret owners cover their hands with bitter apple spray or paste (available at pet supply stores). Ferrets hate the taste of bitter apple and avoid biting anyone who carries this smell.

Health and disease

Ferrets should be given the same degree of medical attention that is afforded a dog or cat. Regularly scheduled visits to the veterinarian are a must—your veterinarian will advise you here—and vaccinations are necessary for both rabies and canine distemper (ferrets are immune to feline distemper). Though ferrets do not transmit rabies any more commonly than other animals, they are definitely on the list of potential carriers and should be vaccinated at around twelve to sixteen weeks of age. For canine distemper, the first shots are given at six weeks, followed by boosters at eleven weeks and fourteen weeks.

An important factor in ferret health is spaying/neutering, especially among females. According to one estimate, approximately 90 percent of unspayed, unbred females die within a year, usually of anemia. For females, therefore, spaying is mandatory, and it is best done before the animal goes into her first heat. Ideal spaying time is around six months. Neutering for males, meanwhile, reduces odor, stops urine spraying, calms aggression levels, and controls biting and nipping. Neutering and spaying, in short, are highly recommended for both sexes.

A healthy ferret has clear eyes with no film or discharge on them, no lumps or swelling along his throat or body, a sleek coat, stiff, unbroken whiskers, hindquarters free of caked feces or wetness, and no signs of sneezing, coughing, or respiratory disease. His foot pads are soft and pink without bleeding or abrasions. His ears are clean and pink with no black spots or waxy debris from ear mites. By nature, ferrets are constantly in motion, sniffing, wiggling, inquiring, playing. A ferret that sits passively, slumps all day, or is unusually lethargic is probably a sick ferret. Bring him to a veterinarian immediately.

Common ailments among ferrets include the following:

Adrenal tumors: Adult ferrets over three years old frequently suffer from adrenal tumors. Early symptoms include hair loss on the tail, sides, and abdomen (hair on the muzzle tends to remain intact). The skin thins and weight loss is common, with the ribs gradually becoming prominent. Diagnosis of this serious disease requires laboratory work, and treatment usually involves surgery.

Insulinoma (hypoglycemia): Ferrets commonly suffer from low blood sugar—hypoglycemia. Caused by a tumor in the pancreas, early symptoms include weakness, lethargy, and disorientation. As the tumors grow, ferrets salivate, make strange chewing motions, and drag their rear legs. Treatment options vary according to the age of the ferret and the clinical signs involved. Medication and surgery are often indicated.

Diarrhea: Blood may appear in the ferret's runny stools, and it sometimes leads to rectal prolapse. This condition is often caused by viral bacterial parasites.

Flu: Ferrets are susceptible to certain of the same flu germs that infect human beings, and the symptoms are surprisingly alike: sneezing, labored breathing, runny nose, conjunctivitis (red eyes with thick discharge), malaise, and lack of energy. Like most colds and flu, they run their course in a week or two. During this time be sure and keep the patient warm (but not hot), well nourished, and hydrated.

Gastrointestinal blockages: One of the most common of all ferret problems is the ingestion of foreign objects such as marbles, fruit pits, sponges, or pencil erasers. Symptoms vary according to the object swallowed, then manifest themselves in a range of reactions, such as constipation, vomiting, appetite loss, and collapse. Treatment for blockages often involves surgery.

Ear mites: Ear mites are extremely common in ferrets and can be identified by the small pieces of dark, waxy debris that form in the ear. Initial treatment by a veterinarian includes a good ear cleaning, then medication that is administered at home.

Hair balls: Matted hair often becomes impacted in a ferret's throat or stomach, creating a hair ball. Weekly treatment with a medication called Petromalt prevents these balls from forming and helps the animal pass them when they do form. Regular brushing helps to eliminate loose hairs that are ingested while grooming.

Canine distemper: Perhaps the most fatal of all ferret diseases, canine distemper in the early stages includes fever, loss of appetite, apathetic behavior, and runny discharge from the eyes and nose. Eye membranes turn red and eyelids swell shut. Although diagnosis of canine distemper can be made, no treatment is available, and mortality rates are almost 100 percent. This ailment can, however, be prevented by timely vaccinations.

Rats

Personality profile

Certainly no animal has been more despised and vilified by the human race than the common rat. This is ironic, as these rodents make entertaining, responsive, and affectionate household pets for grown-ups and children alike.

Domestication began several hundred years ago in Europe and in Japan, where the creatures that we know today as "fancy" rats were gradually bred. These species are regularly bought and sold among enthusiasts today, sometimes for surprisingly large sums of money, and they are displayed at a variety of fancy rat shows around the United States and Europe.

The first thing to realize about rats in that not all rats are the same.

Many live in the woods, in the swamps, in your cellar, and your garbage cans. But these are not the animals you will adopt. Rats sold by breeders and pet stores are different, a separate breed known as domestic brown or Norway rats (*Rattus norvegicus*). This species has been bred for centuries as a pet and as a show animal, and it appears to have an instinctive and genuine liking for human beings. If given proper attention a Norway rat will bond with its owners almost as faithfully as a dog or cat, and with patience, it can be trained to perform tricks and become part of the household.

Since rats are so sensitive, resourceful, and intelligent, they require a good deal of attention and affection, and as far as small animals go they are considered something of a high-maintenance pet. If you do decide to adopt one or more of these cute furry creatures, be prepared to give your pets at least an hour a day of playtime, petting time, and affection time. If pet rats do not receive this quality attention, they often become sulky and withdrawn.

Behavior

Domestic rats are bred in a variety of colors including brown, gray, white, black, and pied. They grow from seven to ten inches long (not including their tails), and weigh about a pound and some ounces, depending on the species.

In the wilderness rats live in large groups and are exceedingly social. This tendency to colonize carries over to domestic housing where groups tend, by and large, to get along in harmony. Two or more rats in a cage will keep each other company when you are out of the house. The exception are two or more male rats who sometimes push and shove among themselves, and occasionally indulge in serious brawling. If you do intend to adopt rats, make sure to keep the males apart. To sex a rat, lift the tail and observe the rear end. Females have an evident vulva; males have evident testes.

While rats are often companionable with other animals in the house, the family dog, or the family cat, there are many tales of friendly canines, and far more commonly, friendly felines, suddenly turning and attacking their erstwhile rodent friends. Even large birds like parrots have been known to peck and bite a curious rodent. In general, it is best to keep rats separated from all other pets in the house.

Rats are relatively clean creatures, defecating and urinating in one small area of the cage. Their cages rarely generate objectionable smells unless they go uncleaned for long periods of time. Males do, however, spray urine during mating season, and residues get smelly. For this reason, pairs of female rats are often preferred as pets over mixed pairs.

Rats have keen smell and hearing, but poor eyesight. They are prolific breeders, with a gestation period of twenty-one to twenty-eight days. They become fertile as young as five weeks, which means that if you have several young specimens in your cage, it is best to separate the males from the females before they begin to breed.

Rats have a life span of around two years, though some make it to three.

Choosing the right pet rat

If you are lucky enough to find a pet rat at a shelter or rat and mouse rescue society, this is your best bet for adoption. Ask your veterinarian for the address of the nearest shelter that handles small animals, or access a search engine on the Internet under "Rats, rescue." Pet stores usually carry rats in abundance, and there are breeders in every state. If you simply want an entertaining companion, pet stores can sometimes be an acceptable source, but only if their levels of sanitation and care are high. For rats that you intend to show, breeders are a better bet.

When choosing a pet rat look for animals that are active, curious, energetic, and friendly. When you put your hand into their cage they should not immediately run away. At the same time, be wary of lethargic or sick-looking rodents.

Physically, wet rear ends or feces caked to the anus are bad signs. Diarrhea in the cage is a major danger signal: stay away. Healthy rats have sleek, thick, glossy coats. Their fur lies evenly throughout and is not matted or standing up. There are no wounds, patches, bald spots, scabs, or skin irritations. Healthy rats also show no signs of discharge or mucus build-up in the eyes, ears, or nose. They do not cough, sputter, wheeze, or rattle.

Feeding and nutrition

Though rats are omnivores, commercial rat pellets provide a majority of the nutrition needed and are available at most pet supply stores. Dog food kibble can be used in a pinch, but *only* in a pinch. Stay away from cat kibble entirely.

This basic pellet diet can then be supplemented with small, daily amounts of vegetables, whole grains, and fruits. Especially appreciated are lettuce greens, dandelion leaves, peas, carrots, cooked beans, corn kernels, broccoli, and tomatoes. Be careful though not to serve beans, brussels sprouts, potatoes, and red cabbage in their raw state; always serve them cooked. In the grain department, give whole wheat bread, pasta, dog biscuit fragments, rice, and cereal. For fruit, rats enjoy apples, cherries, bananas, grapes. Seeds and nuts, however, are oily and fatty, and should only be given occasionally, a seed or a nut at a time. Foods to avoid include citrus fruits, chocolate, cookies, potato chips, and junk foods in general.

If you want to make your rat or mouse's menu even tastier, the following nutritious recipe can be given in lieu of ready-made feeds:

1/3 part cooked whole grain rice
1/3 part crushed barley or oats (or porridge oats)
1/3 part millet or cockatiel seed
1/4 cup molasses

Optional additions to this mixture include sprinklings of brewer's yeast flakes, wheat germ, and a drop of cod-liver oil.

Rats must eat continually, and their feed bowls should be full twenty-four hours a day. Use a heavy metal or ceramic bowl, with a plastic gravity-fed water bottle attached to the side of the cage with hook, tape, or Velcro strips.

A word to the wise. Avoid hand feeding rats through the bars of their cage. Instead, open the cage door and place the food directly inside. If fed through the bars of a cage, rats soon come to equate anything that comes to them through the bars as food—including your fingers.

Housing, sanitation, and environment

There are a variety of commercial cages on the market today for rats, a majority of which make excellent homes. Two small rats of different sex can be happily kept in a fifteen- or better, twenty-gallon glass aquarium, though some rat fanciers prefer metal wire cages. The better wire models contain solid metal shelves for climbing, ramps, and removable plastic pan bottoms for easy cleaning. Interestingly, studies show that rats are calmer and brighter when raised in complex, entertaining cages filled with items that challenge their intelligence such as toys, passageways, tubes, partitions, wheels, rocks, and climbing levels.

When choosing a cage, the doors should swing open easily and be large enough to accommodate both your hand and the rat. The shelves and levels should all be reachable and easily cleanable. If the cage is made of wire mesh, be sure the mesh openings are not too wide. Small rats and baby rats can squeeze through surprisingly small spaces. The bottom pan of the cage should be deep enough to hold ample litter, plus adequate amounts of bedding.

As far as bedding is concerned, the usual warning is posted to avoid shavings made of pine, or worse, cedar. Both contain phenol oils that may be harmful to most rodents and to rabbits and ferrets as well. Pine and cedar both may cause liver damage, shortening a rodent's life span and causing a good deal of pain. Shredded aspen, shredded paper, and pelleted bedding all make excellent sleeping and cuddling quarters for rats.

Cleaning and hygiene

Keep the bottom of your pet's cage filled with approximately one inch of bedding, and replace the shavings every three to five days. Once every week or so give the entire cage a careful cleaning with soap, water, and disinfectant.

Keep a rat cage out of direct sun and away from radiators and drafty parts of the house such as windows and doors. Never keep a rat cage in the basement. Though rats often call human cellars home, domestic species are vulnerable to dampness and tend to languish in dark, airless spaces.

Toys

Small rodents are not choosy about the objects they make into toys. Anything that spins, rolls, bounces, turns, and amuses does the job. Ladders, shoeboxes, cardboard boxes, toilet paper rolls, paper towel rolls, PVC pipe. PVC elbows (or the commercial transparent pipe that connects together to form labyrinths), running wheels, old clothes, plastic toy houses, toy cars, wooden blocks, and ramps all make excellent objects of play.

Some rodent fanciers like to make the setting inside a cage naturalistic as well as entertaining. Do this by adding piles of small pebbles, rock caves, tree branches, hay, stones, or a small box filled with soil or peat moss for digging. Be warned that this last item can get messy and should be changed on a regular basis. Also be alert to the fact that running wheels should be made of solid materials. Otherwise long tails and little legs get caught in the spokes.

Handling

To lift a rat, scoop it gently into your hand, positioning one hand under its chest, the other behind its front legs. (When a rat is first becoming accustomed to this routine you may wish to place a free thumb under its chin to discourage biting.) Apply just enough pressure to hold the animal securely.

If pet rats are familiar with your smell and the rhythm of your movements, they will usually come to you with enthusiasm and speed. The more they are handled the more happily they respond. Some rats even come when called.

Start handling when a rat is young and handle him for a few minutes every day (morning, noon, and night is best). If your pet is allowed to run free in your home for a period of time each day, be aware that rats mark their territory with small drops of urine. Either protect all your furniture and rugs with towels, plastic, etc., or avoid the furniture problem entirely by ratproofing a special section of your home, then confining your pet to this area during exercise and free-run sessions.

Health and disease

The first step in ensuring good health in rats is to acquire them from reputable sources. One sick rodent in a litter quickly infects the others. When this happens you will not be the first rodent owner to find a stock of once healthy creatures sick and dying before you. Ask your veterinarian for recommendations.

While rats are generally healthy creatures, they are also vulnerable to several opportunistic diseases. Conditions requiring immediate medical attention include the following:

Blood in the urine: Blood in a rat's urine indicates infection, most likely bladder threadworms, or in females, a uterine infection. Have the condition checked immediately.

Hair loss: If your pet has nonspreading patches of hair loss, especially around the eyes and muzzle, parasites, mange, or ringworm are probably to blame. Have these ailments treated with the proper medication before they spread to other rats in the cage.

Diarrhea: Diarrhea can be the symptom of serious disease, or simply the result of dietary problems. Foods that most commonly produce loose bowels include crispy greens, namely lettuce, cabbage, brussels sprouts, kale, and broccoli. Try removing these foods from the menu. Stress is also a cause of diarrhea, and like the stress itself, the condition usually passes in a day or so.

Red or brown tearing: Rat owners panic when they see red or brown secretions forming in their pet's eyes or staining their nose and paws. But don't worry, this condition is usually normal, and it is due to a naturally secreted substance from glands behind the rat's eyes. At the same time, dark tearing at times can be due to a virus, bacteria, or plain stress. If the condition persists see a veterinarian.

Sialodacryoadenitis: Symptoms of this highly contagious disease include restlessness, obsessive blinking, rubbing of the eyes, swelling of the neck, and sneezing. When these symptoms appear there is not much you can do except separate the sick rats from others in the cage. In some situations, this condition is a result of poor chewing due to overlong lower incisor teeth. Trimming the teeth can help.

Pneumonia: A contagious ailment that affects rats and mice alike, pneumonia symptoms include the usual respiratory syndrome: sneezing, sputtering, coughing, red nose. As the disease progresses equilibrium is thrown off in the inner ear, and a strange head tilt results. Mice and rats squint in a strange way, and there is visible discharge from the eyes. Treatment for this ailment is sometimes successful if caught early, though the outcome is never predictable.

Obesity: Rats have a tendency to become enormously and sometimes ludicrously overweight, a condition encouraged by owners who provide all the temptations: oily seeds, nuts, an overabundance of fatty foods, and junk foods like candy, donuts, cake, and french fries. The remedy is simple: remove all junk foods and oily seeds from your rat's daily menu. Remember, as with all of us, being overweight tends to shorten a rat's life expectancy.

Mice

Personality profile

The first thing to realize about mice (known as *Mus musculus* to zoologists) is that all mice are not the same. Like rats, there are the many wild varieties dwelling in fields, woods, and attics, but only one common species kept as pets, with a variety of breeds.

Mice are frisky, friendly, and playful animals that quickly accustom themselves to human company, especially if adopted at an early age. They are relatively easy to keep and are as intriguing to watch as they are to handle. They come in a variety of attractive colors, and their fur differs from species to species. For example, rex mice have curly coats; long-haired and hairless mice need no description.

Once you become acquainted with each member of your mouse community, moreover, you may be surprised to discover that each mouse exhibits a distinct personality of its own. This personality comes complete with individual likes, dislikes, habits, and eccentricities, a feature that makes pet mice endearing as well as interesting.

Mice have been bred for many centuries, both for show and companionship, and they are well adapted to human ownership. Not quite as intelligent or responsive as rats, mice are nonetheless surprisingly bright and enthusiastically loving. They rarely bite unless threatened.

Behavior

Among mice fanciers a distinction is made between pet store mice and fancy mice. The latter are bred for exhibition. They are larger than pet mice, have bigger ears and eyes, and are more docile. Both breeds, fancy and pet store variety, come in a number of colors, markings, and patterns, including white, brown, gray, black, silver, coffee, sable, striped, pied, and spotted. There is also the so-called albino mouse with its pink eyes and lack of skin or coat pigment.

Mice have a keen sense of hearing and smell, but like rats their vision is poor. Babies should not be separated from their mothers until they are weaned at four or five weeks.

The average size of a pet mouse is three to four inches, with tails measuring almost the same length. Life expectancy depends to a great extent on genetics and species. An average mouse life span is from one to three years.

Mice are sporting by nature, often playing a kind of tag among themselves. When they shake their tails at one another however, be careful. As with a rattlesnake, the message is, stay away!

Frisking among mice can also turn into fighting. While it is often difficult to tell the two behaviors apart, there are indicators to look for. As a rule, for instance, mice at play tend to be quiet, while battling mice squeak loudly, run frantically in circles with their fur fluffed up, and leap at each other with their tails angrily twitching. When fighting, one mouse may relentlessly chase the other or pick on it. If you discover scratches or blood on a mouse's body, this is a telltale sign. Fighting often takes place immediately after a mouse cage is cleaned when the occupants are jostling to reestablish personal smell zones.

Like rats, mice of the same sex—especially males—will sometimes fight, and it is best to separate the sexes within a colony as soon as their gender can be distinguished. See the section below on Handling for information on sexing mice.

Choosing the right pet mouse

Healthy mice are energetic, bright, and inquisitive. When you put your hand into their cage for the first time they should appear curious rather than frightened. If you try to pick them up, they should not try to bite you. They should appear calm, curious, and friendly. Be wary of a mouse that sits passively in the corner of its cage or that appears listless or droopy. Chances are it is sick.

Physically, wet rear ends or feces caked to the anus are signs of disease. Stay away from any mouse that has diarrhea in its cage. A healthy mouse displays a sleek, bright, glossy coat, with no patches, scabs, bald spots, or rashes. Fur should be dry, have an even lie, and not be matted, or standing up. A healthy mouse has absolutely no mucus drip from its eyes, ears, or nose. Its eyes should be clear and inquisitive. There should be no signs of respiratory illness such as sneezing, wheezing, sputtering, coughing, or chest rattling.

Feeding and nutrition

Mice enjoy standard rodent pellet mix with its assortment of different grains. You can then supplement this basic diet with a variety of common kitchen grains, such as whole grain rice, whole grain bread, millet, barley, and oats (especially porridge oats), but avoid wheat; it is a reported troublemaker for some mice.

Along with grains, mice eat small amounts of fruits and vegetables, though these should constitute no more than 15 to 20 percent of their diet. Best in this department are peas, broccoli, carrots, and apples. Some mouse owners give their pets citrus fruits, though many experts warn against this practice on the grounds that the acidity in citrus fruits irritates a mouse's delicate digestive system. If beans are given, they should be soaked and cooked before serving.

To the above diet, mice owners can also add a little brewer's yeast once or twice a week, and provide vitamin and mineral supplements as needed. Talk to your veterinarian about your pet's needs in this area. Be cautious, however, about feeding seeds to mice, especially sunflower seeds. The latter are overly rich in fat, and too many can make mice obese. Save your seeds for special (and occasional) treats.

Foods not to feed mice include chocolate, corn, wheat, and especially peanuts. Peanuts are extremely fatty, low on nutrition, and (some mouse fanciers report) may cause skin rashes.

Finally, do not forget to give your pet an adequate daily supply of water. Water is best supplied in a side-of-the-cage, plastic, gravity-feed water bottle equipped with hook, holder, and sipper tube. Be sure to clean the bottle and tube every day. It tends to clog frequently in mice cages.

Housing, sanitation, and environment

Providing pleasant housing and a comfortable environment for mice is essential for the well-being of any community. Mice do well in enclosures made of glass, wire, or stainless steel. Avoid wood. It is easily gnawed through and absorbs urine smells.

As far as size goes, a twenty-gallon tank or a wire cage approximately two feet long, one foot wide, and one foot high will accommodate four or five (or more) mice quite nicely.

Wire cages provide excellent ventilation plus good climbing surfaces and a pleasant airy, open feeling. They are not always as escape-proof as you might wish, however, so if using a wire cage be sure that the bars or mesh are close enough together to provide a safe surface. Otherwise mice can slip through, or even worse, slide halfway through and become lodged. If you can slide a finger through the mesh, your mouse can probably slide through it.

Glass tanks allow for less ventilation, have no climbing surfaces on the sides, are not always easy to clean, and create a closed-in feeling for the inhabitants. At the same time, they are sturdier than wire cages, virtually escape-proof, tend to smell less than wire cages, and generally provide owners with a better view of their mouse community. If there are other pets in the house such as cats, a glass tank with a heavy screen on top provides far better protection than the open and vulnerable wire cage.

Once your mouse community is adequately housed, you will want to create a pleasant and challenging environment inside the cage with appropriate cage furniture. Like rats, mice are intelligent creatures that require plenty of diversion and exercise to keep them content. Mice that are raised in an active environment with climbing facilities and toys tend to be brighter and better adjusted than mice brought up in barren environments.

Especially appropriate in a mouse cage are shelves arranged in levels for climbing. Also appreciated are ladders, nest boxes, cardboard boxes with holes cut into them for crawling in and out, pieces of wood for climbing and gnawing, and connecting lengths of PVC tubing for tunnel running. It is also a good idea to arrange a number of small crawl-in spaces throughout the cage so that each mouse can have its own hiding place. See the section on mouse toys for further suggestions.

For bedding, choose a clean, nontoxic material that is absorbent and easy to replace. Shredded aspen (or most other hardwoods), shredded paper, and pelleted bedding laid on the floor an inch or so thick are all recommended. As usual, avoid shavings made of pine, or worse, cedar. Both contain phenol oils that may be harmful. Pine and cedar can also cause irreparable liver damage, shortening a mouse's life and causing it a good deal of pain.

Cleaning and hygiene

Good hygiene in a mouse cage goes a long way toward keeping all inhabitants healthy and happy. Clean the cage at least once a week and change the shavings and bedding every few days. Avoid exposing mice to loud or sudden noises or extreme changes in temperature. Avoid drafts. Make sure the room is well lit but not bright and that ventilation is adequate.

Mice are relatively clean animals, and they usually defecate in isolated areas of the cage. They can often be seen grooming and licking themselves and each other like cats. Some mice owners give their pets a bath from time to time, though this is unnecessary and a bit tricky. Do, however, change the bedding in your mouse's cage every three to five days, and clean and disinfect its cage, toys, and furniture once every week or so.

Toys

Besides the amusements and exercise devices mentioned above, mice appreciate cardboard rolls, toilet paper tubes, cardboard boxes, large PVC tubes and elbows, climbing wheels, egg cartons, small cardboard cartons, rocks, and small children's toys. Needless to say, make sure none of these toys has sharp edges.

Wooden toys are also coveted by mice, but they quickly take on urine smells and must constantly be washed. Some mice fanciers give their pets wooden bird toys as well, but the same caveat applies—they smell—along with the fact that they are usually gnawed to a nub within several weeks.

Handling

As a rule, mice bite only when terrified or in pain. Nonetheless, caution is appropriate, especially when you and the mouse are not well acquainted.

Mice are best picked up by gently scooping them into the palm of your hand and gripping them lightly. Do not make any sudden movements or noises while handling. Allow the mouse enough time to sniff you and to get the message that you are friend, not foe. The more a mouse is handled, the more tame it becomes. Handle it three or four times a day, a few minutes each session, and it will quickly come to consider you a friend.

If you wish to determine the sex of your mouse while handling it, proceed in the following way.

Grip the mouse by the tail and gently turn it upside down, supporting its head and chest with your free palm. Examine the area at the root of the tail. If the mouse is more than four weeks old, either a vulva or a pair of testicles will be evident. If you are going to keep mice, it is a good idea to learn the art of sexing them as soon as possible. The process is not difficult, and practice makes perfect. Once you are able to tell the sexes apart by sight, it becomes a good deal easier to separate males from females and thus maintain order and tranquility within your mouse community.

Health and disease

By and large mice are healthy creatures, but like rats, they have a tendency to develop opportunistic diseases. Conditions requiring immediate medical attention include the following:

Allergies: Mice sneeze, cough, sputter, develop red eyes, and have difficulty breathing when affected by allergies. Prevention is the key. For example, allergens often lurk in a rodent's bedding. Try changing to another brand or variety and avoid sawdust and hay. Ammonia in urine that has been sprinkled around the cage floor can trigger allergic reactions in mice. Clean the cage more often.

Also, certain foods trigger allergic symptoms. To correct this problem, remove one food from your pet's standard menu for a day or so. Then observe: are allergic symptoms lessened? If not, a day or so later remove another food from the diet, then another, until the offending food is identified. A second related method is to feed your pet a baseline of hypoallergenic foods—that is, foods the animal tolerates—then every day or so add a food that you suspect may be causing the problem. When and if the animal shows allergic symptoms, you have found the culprit.

Diarrhea: Diarrhea may be an indication of serious disease in mice caused by bacteria, viruses, or parasites. More commonly it is simply the result of faulty diet. Foods that most frequently produce loose bowels in mice are crispy greens, namely lettuce, cabbage, brussels sprouts, kale, and broccoli. Remove them from the menu for a few days and look for improvement. Stress also causes diarrhea, and like the stress itself, this condition usually passes in a day or so.

Skin allergies and parasites: Skin diseases in mice are triggered by two factors: allergies to food and parasites. With the former you must experiment. Vegetables or fruits rather than grains are usually the offenders. Try changing your pet's diet, removing or adding one food at a time until the problem is identified (see Allergies above). If nothing improves by altering the diet, chances are the problem is due to fur mites. Unfortunately, parasites are difficult to identify and diagnose, and usually require a veterinarian's expertise.

Mouse pox: A disease exclusive to mice, mouse pox symptoms include diarrhea, inflamed eyes, swelling of the legs, disordered fur, and lethargy. Affected mice crouch and hunch in a peculiar way, appearing sick and miserable. There is a tendency toward self-mutilation through obsessive grooming. Presently, there is no known cure for this disease.

Tyzzer's disease: Tyzzer's disease is usually associated with gerbils, though mice are susceptible as well. A bacterial ailment, symptoms include weight loss, diarrhea (sometimes), ruffled fur, extreme apathy, and sudden collapse. Though this disease is difficult to spot in its early stages, if caught quickly antibiotic treatment sometimes helps.

Barbering: Mice are frequent and sometimes incessant groomers. Using teeth and claws, they gnaw at themselves and their friends night and day. When nervous or afraid they may also overgroom, sometimes biting holes in their own or others' fur, a phenomenon known as *barbering*. This condition can be identified by small, bare patches on a mouse's fur, but with an absence of irritation or sores on the skin itself. Usually this phenomenon is a result of stress or sudden fright. Is something in the mouse's environment upsetting it or scaring it? Try to find the specific stressor, then eliminate it. If one mouse incessantly barbers others, and environmental changes do not improve conditions, you may have to separate the offending mouse from the rest of the community, at least for a while.

Pneumonia: A contagious ailment that affects rats and mice alike, symptoms of this disease include a range of respiratory reactions. Mice sneeze, cough, and develop red, runny noses. If the ailment goes untreated, their inner ear is affected and equilibrium is thrown off. A peculiar tilt of the head results. Mice and rats also squint in a strange way when afflicted with pneumonia, and they show large amounts of fluid buildup around the eyes. If caught in the early stages, treatment for this ailment is sometimes success-ful, though the outcome is far from predictable.

Tumors: Mice are prone to tumors as they age. Every month or so you can search for small lumps on the body. If you find any have them checked by a veterinarian.

10

Birds

What Kind of Bird Do I Want?

When we enter the realm of companion birds we arrive at a brightly plumed and colored universe teeming with a variety of species, sizes, temperaments, songs, and diversions. Yet in the beginning, more than 150 million years ago, these bright, ethereal creatures descended from ungainly reptiles, some of which could fly, some of which could not. Along the way they developed one feature that few other creatures besides insects and bats possess—the ability to fly. This, plus a feature that *no* other animal can boast of—feathers.

Currently the world counts around eighty-five hundred species of birds, and ornithologists are discovering new varieties every year. Some experts estimate that there are at least one thousand species of avian forms still to be discovered.

For millennia, people have kept birds as pets. The ancient Egyptians bred rare African species and practiced falconry for more than two thousand years. Among the ancient Greeks owning an exotic bird was a sign of wealth and prestige; it meant that you had traveled a great deal and had plenty of money. Alexander the Great himself is said to have been a bird fancier, and is reputed to have been the first traveler to bring parrots from the East. Even today in rural parts of Pakistan and Afghanistan it is common to see old men and young children walking through the village square carrying pet finches and canaries in brightly colored, hand-decorated cages. Birds are universally admired and universally loved.

If you are in the market for a companion bird, deciding which variety best suits your tastes may seem a challenging prospect. There are, as we have seen, thousands of species, including three hundred species of parrot alone.

But be of good cheer. Through centuries of trial and error, the most congenial companion birds have been identified, bred, and domesticated. The choice is still a wide one, yes, but it is not unlimited, and it basically falls into a manageable number of categories. In this chapter we will introduce you to the birds that are most likely to match your lifestyle and to fit your tastes and needs in a pet.

Determine your personal preferences

What kind of bird most tickles your fancy? Would you enjoy owning a bird that talks or one that sings? What about both? Or neither? Do you intend to handle your bird regularly? Or are you content to listen to it sing and watch it hop happily around its cage?

BIRD LONGEVITY GUIDE	
Bird	*Average life span*
Parrots	10–50+ years depending on type
Finches	5–10 years
Budgerigars (parakeets)	10–20 years
Canaries	10–15 years
Lovebirds	8–10 years
Cockatiels	10–25 years

What about size? Is a bird that sits on your shoulder what you're looking for? Or would you prefer one that perches puckishly on your finger? Should your bird be beautifully plumed and feathered? Or is appearance secondary? Does color matter? Head and feather configurations? Do you intend to breed your bird? If so, do you have the space, knowledge, and equipment to do so, plus the time it takes to perform this most demanding task? What about longevity? Some types of parrots live for forty or fifty years. If you decide to purchase such a bird in your middle age, there is a chance he will outlive you. You then need to consider in advance who will assume the caregiving duties should this happen.

Before you purchase a bird and take on the responsibility it entails, a project that can go on for a lifetime in some cases, it is therefore suggested that you familiarize yourself with the types of birds that are available, learn a bit about bird care in advance, and appraise the different candidates firsthand.

Start by reading books and magazines about the birds you're interested in. Look at pictures. Ask around. If you have friends who own canaries, cockatiels, parakeets, etc., probe their owners concerning the pros and cons of each. Join a bird club. Visit breeders and rescue groups. Become familiar with the selections. Quiz proprietors concerning the positive and negative characteristics of different birds. Find out how much time and attention each species requires. Learn how long different birds live, how large a cage they require, how much noise they make, how clean or dirty they are, their health needs, how they cope with children and other pets, what foods they eat, and in what quantity. Check out the style and costs of available cages, feeding equipment, toys, exercise, and enrichment needs. Become informed, learn the essentials, be prepared, *then* make your decision.

Though there are many ways of classifying pet birds, the varieties you are most likely to bring into your home can be classed into two convenient categories:

1. Larger birds, mainly members of the parrot family
2. Smaller birds, specifically finches and canaries

Included in the first category are birds that tend to be social with human beings. Some of them talk, and most respond to training and handling. Ranged in this category are primarily members of the parrot family: cockatoos, parakeets, cockatiels, lovebirds, conures, and more.

Birds that are less social with humans are included in the second category, specifically canaries and finches. These gentle creatures are prized for their beauty, their cuteness, and their wonderful song. They are less expensive than birds in the first category and also less socially interactive. We will become thoroughly acquainted with members of both categories in the sections below.

Pick a bird that best fits your home and lifestyle

While looking for a bird that fits comfortably into your personal style of living, the following factors should be considered:

How much space are you prepared to allot to your new pet? Big birds require big cages. Small birds have more humble needs. Where in your house do you intend to keep the cage? The bedroom? Living room? Do you intend to let the bird roam about free, or will she be constantly confined to a cage? If the bird does roam free, is your home secure? Are there visible escape routes such as open windows, doors, vents, chimneys? If so, be sure to close them off before allowing a bird out of its cage.

Both large and small birds need plenty of light, but you should avoid direct sunlight. A cage set near a window, but not in front of it, is ideal. Make sure air circulation is good and that the cage is away from drafts (which means not too near the front and back door, especially in the winter).

Household poisons—detergents, soaps, paints, varnish, sealers, glue, waxes, lye-based cleaners, ammonia (and its fumes), cigarette smoke, chlorine, hair dye, toothpaste, petroleum products, car exhaust, drugs and medicines—are all extremely toxic for birds and should be kept in closed cabinets, containers, or drawers. The same goes for foods; seemingly harmless treats such as soda drinks or chocolate can make a bird very sick.

Birds should be automatically barred from all cooking areas. Otherwise you will have to be continually watchful of hot stoves and ovens, boiling water, gas fumes, and burned food (caged birds kept in the kitchen may suffer from grease-generated smoke). Be especially vigilant if you cook with nonstick Teflon or Silverstone pans: when heated to 530° or higher they emit a gas that is incurably deadly to many varieties of birds; same with self-cleaning ovens.

Aerosol hair sprays are another substance highly toxic for birds. Never discharge them in a bird's vicinity. The same goes for insect sprays and aerosol polishes. Watch for lead-based paint on doors and windowsills. Large birds love to chew wooden frames, and the lead in some older paints is poisonous. If you allow your birds to roam free, confine their winged activities to one room of the house, and make sure this room is birdproof and minus all of the above temptations.

Birds can be messy, especially large ones. Chunks of food, droppings, and feathers often escape the confines of the cage and are deposited on shelves or mantels when birds move about freely. To avoid this problem, clean the cage often and place it in a convenient location. Also, allow the bird access only to parts of the home that are birdproof. If your bird is particularly messy, spread newspaper under its cage.

Before you purchase a bird that squawks loudly or sings continuously, be sure your neighbors are factored into the picture. In private houses this is not much of a problem. But families next door in an apartment building don't always appreciate birdsong as much as you. Complaints can follow, then landlord trouble, then worse. Some bird owners have actually been taken to court for disturbing the peace with their pet's continual "jungle noises." Nip this problem in the bud by discussing the situation with your neighbors *before* you buy the bird. Work out the details to both your satisfactions, then be sure to place the cage in a part of the house or apartment that is farthest from your neighbor's ears. Trees and plants placed near the cage may help muffle the sound.

Are there children in the household? If so, sensible precautions should be taken. Talk to your children beforehand. Tell them about the bird. Explain that it is a delicate, sensitive, sometimes aggressive creature that needs attention and care, and it should not be played with or harassed. Explain that large birds from the parrot family have extremely strong beaks, and they are capable of inflicting serious bites.

Indeed, it is best to stay out of harm's way entirely by not adopting a large bird until your children are old enough to deal with this complex creature. If a large bird is already part of your family when a child is born, or if for some reason child and bird are already under the same roof, keep all unsupervised children a good distance from the cage. Handling should be done *only* under close adult supervision, and then only on special occasions. Keeping small fingers out of the cage seems an obvious caveat, perhaps, yet it is one that is ignored surprisingly often by heedless children and distracted parents.

If you travel a good deal of the time, or if you are out of the house all day and sometimes into the evening, you may wish to adopt an undemanding, low-maintenance bird such as a canary or finch. Larger, more intelligent species are extremely needful of human attention and affection. When deprived of these attentions, they may become neurotic and destructive. Once a bird develops these habits, it takes a great deal of time and training to change them. Birds are social creatures, and unless you can provide constant companionship, they need the company of other birds. As a rule, smaller birds are easier to keep in pairs than large.

Follow these important guidelines when choosing a bird

The first prerequisite for adopting a bird is to make sure it is healthy.

If possible, take the bird out of the cage and inspect it. Make sure its breast bone is not too prominent or protruding, a possible sign of weight loss and disease. Check for any signs of mites. A healthy bird is active and energetic. It preens a good deal and often stands on one leg with the other tucked up and under it. Unhealthy birds stand on two legs much of the time and sometime lose their balance. They sit too still for too long a time, appear droopy with half-closed eyes, and do not respond spiritedly to the stimuli surrounding them.

A healthy bird's eyes are clear without traces of redness, swelling, or discharge at the corners. It breathes silently and does not sneeze or cough. Its beak has a firm, well-aligned, shiny look, without white crusts or scale caked to it. Its feathers are sleek. They are not plucked, patchy, fluffed-up, or dull. Its feet are smooth with no sores, swellings, or cuts, and its claws are all intact (beware of missing claws—damaged feet mean birds cannot sit comfortably on a perch). There should be no sign of feces on the bird's vent (the area below its tail). Its droppings are dark green with specks of white, well formed, and cylindrically shaped or coiled.

In all, a healthy bird is clean, bright-eyed, peppy, and social.

When choosing a particular species, novice bird owners are best advised to start their adventure with hardy, easy-to-care-for birds such as zebra finches and parakeets.

Cockatiels and canaries are a bit more demanding.

Lovebirds are next on the list.

Finally come larger members of the parrot family. These should be adopted only by people with patience, experience, money (parrot cages are expensive and so is their upkeep), plus an inclination to care for a pet whose intelligence level is on a par with dolphins and chimpanzees, and whose nature is sensitive, individualistic, demanding and—often— exasperatingly eccentric.

Where are the best places to buy a bird?

As with any pet, there is no one definitive best or worst place. Some pet owners inherit birds, some purchase them from pet stores, some adopt from shelters or from friends. All things considered, it is safest to purchase birds from a breeder and least safe to buy one from a pet store. The quality of birds at a reputable breeder tends to be excellent, and chances are you will get a healthy specimen that has been hand-fed. Hand-fed birds tend to be especially comfortable when handled by human beings, exceptionally affectionate, and responsive.

Your local veterinarian may know the names of different breeders in your area, and in which types of birds they specialize. The Association of Avian Veterinarians (see appendix for address) is also a good source when shopping around. They maintain statewide lists of sources for different birds and can help track down your bird of choice. Also try getting in touch with bird rescue groups in your area.

When examining a species of bird that takes to handling, get hands-on about it. If the bird sits happily on your finger or palm, that's a good sign (when examining a parrot for the first time it's always wise to use a glove). Avoid birds that seem terrified of human contact or sit apathetically when you reach for them. Be especially wary of discount birds at pet stores or even at a breeder.

Types of Pet Birds

Three types of birds are most often kept as domestic companions in the United States and Europe: hook bills, hard bills, and soft bills.

Hook bills: Members of the parrot family, they have hard, hook-shaped bills, and powerful mandibular muscles used for chewing, cracking nuts, and opening seeds.

Hard bills: These include finches and canaries. These small, colorful birds have long, tapered bills engineered for pecking and dislodging seeds and for poking into trees in search of insects.

Soft bills: Birds such as the mynah bird, though often thought of as parrots, belong in a separate grouping. Unlike their hook-billed cousins, they cannot crack nuts and seeds. They derive most of their nourishment from soft foods such as fruits, berries, small insects, and grubs.

While the biological organization of bird orders, families, and species is an intriguing subject, for our purposes it is more convenient, if slightly less scientific, to avoid complex soft bill–hard bill designations and to organize the pet birds you are most likely to own into two convenient and basic groups: large birds and small birds.

Large birds

With a few exceptions, birds that talk and squawk are members in good standing of the parrot family. Native to all continents on earth except Europe and the polar regions, capable of learning hundreds and in some cases thousands of words, canny, amusing, beautiful, feisty, boasting a longevity rate that sometimes exceeds that of their owners, parrots are among the more responsive and evolved forms of life on earth. As pets, they rank with dogs and cats in both intelligence and loyalty. And like dogs and cats, they require substantial investments of time and emotion if the relationship is to prosper. Before bringing one of these amazing creatures into your home certain facts and caveats should be reviewed and kept in mind:

Parrots that live alone require the constant companionship of human keepers. Without day-to-day and sometimes hour-to-hour attentions these sensitive birds default into a variety of unpleasant habits such as feather picking, screeching, biting, and depression. Be advised: when you own a parrot the parrot owns you.

Unless raised together, parrots and other domestic pets don't always get along. If you already own a menagerie of dogs, cats, smaller birds, and whatever, it may be the better part of valor to consider acquiring a parrot at some later date.

A parrot's constant chattering can be a double-edge sword, amusing to you, a nightmare for friends or neighbors. Before you commit to a talking, squawking household citizen, be sure the walls of your apartment are thick, and that other members of the household share your avian enthusiasms.

Parrots need plenty of elbow room, which in this case means an area of your home or apartment to walk or hop around in safety. Be sure that you have the space to accommodate these movements, and that you are prepared to do a bit of serious birdproofing before the fun begins.

Some parrots live to be fifty years old or older. If you are already middle aged, and if you intend to acquire a long-lived, relatively young parrot, remember that after the bonding takes place this loving creature will be as loyal to you as your trusty dog. The sudden shock of then losing its beloved keeper can send the parrot into a depression from which it never fully recovers. And who will take care of the bird should you, in fact, pass away?

There are no easy answers to these unpleasant questions, of course, but they should nonetheless be considered beforehand and contingency plans be made in advance.

So much for the negatives; the rest is all good news. The talking birds profiled below are all bright, funny, responsive, and accessible, and all make excellent companion pets:

Budgerigars, a.k.a. Parakeets. A perennially popular companion bird that has been selectively bred into a number of eye-poppingly beautiful varieties, parakeets come originally from Australia where vast flocks can still be seen darkening the sky.

A parakeet's basic diet consists of fruit, grain, vegetables, and seeds. Parakeets live well in a cage by themselves or with one or more companions. Indeed, if your cage is large enough and if you have the inclination, the more parakeets under the same roof the merrier. Note, however, that if you intend to teach your bird to speak, it should be kept separate from others of its kind. The moment it pairs up with another parakeet its willingness to talk declines.

The best time to buy a parakeet is around six weeks of age. Hand-feed it in the early days and it will bond to you 100 percent. Parakeets come in a variety of interesting colors including albino, slate, gray, pied, tan, brown, cinnamon, opaline, red, and violet. The most common parakeets (and the least expensive) are yellow, blue, and green and are referred to among owners as "normals."

Regarding temperament, parakeets are gentle creatures that if properly trained and cared for rarely nip. Their mild temperament makes them ideal first pets for children or for anyone who wishes to sample the pleasures of bird owning. They take great pleasure in sitting on their owner's hand or shoulder and enjoy hopping freely about the house from chair to table. Remember, if you intend to build a relationship of any type with your bird, it is essential that it be let out of its cage for at least an hour a day.

As far as talking goes, there appears to be a wide range of abilities among different species of parakeet. Some have learned to say as many as a thousand words. Others, no matter how well loved and trained, never get the hang of it. Most parakeets, with persistence, can learn to say a respectable number of words, and even if they don't, they still make adorable, cheerful, and low-maintenance companions.

Cockatiels. In the past several decades cockatiels have increased in popularity among the bird-buying public, for good reason. Intelligent, willing talkers, fond of humans, and highly trainable, cockatiels represent a step up from parakeets in size, intelligence, and responsibility. Like parakeets, cockatiels hail from Australia where their natural habitat is low grassy land, usually near water. In the wild they are nomadic, flying in pairs and flocks, the latter sometimes growing so large that they pose a threat to local crops.

Cockatiels come in shades of yellow, green, brown, and white. The most common color combinations are gray with yellow head and beak and a circle of orange or red on the cheeks. Cockatiels grow twice as large as their parakeet cousins, reaching lengths of twelve to fourteen inches, and they live from ten to twenty-five years. Though common wisdom claims they should always be purchased in pairs, this is not true at all, and in fact, solitary cockatiels make the best human companions. For optimum training results, start with a young bird and hand-feed it from an early age. In general, baby parrots of any kind that are hand-fed make the most congenial and trainable adult pets.

Cockatiels are a sturdy, healthy bird that require a straightforward diet of commercial seed mixture supplemented with sunflower seeds and dark leafy greens (like spinach or kale) plus peas, carrot tops, celery, and corn. Unlike other parrots, they are not enthusiastic fruit eaters, and may turn their noses up at it entirely. On the other hand, cockatiels enjoy freshly picked roadside weeds such as plantain, milk thistle, dandelion greens, and chickweed, all of which grow abundantly in most parts of the country. Important for their digestive health too is grit and cuttlebone. The calcium in cuttlebone is especially essential during breeding season when it helps mother cockatiels produce strong-boned broods.

As far as personality goes, it is hard to beat a cockatiel. The best of them are bright, perky, funny, overtly affectionate little fellows that love sitting on the shoulders of everyone in the family, and that walk from room to room with a peculiar Woodstock waddle that is hard to resist. As talkers they are a quick study. Their call is a bit shrill, it is true, but in compensation they produce a beautiful song. In general, cockatiels are gentle and friendly creatures that make excellent pets.

Lovebirds. While some of the nine species of lovebird are relatively new to the West, others have been kept as pets for four hundred years.

Among many bird aficionados, lovebirds are considered to be the most beautiful of all small parrots. Diminutive yet stocky, gentle but tough (many tend to bite), these fascinating fliers come originally from the savannas of Africa and Madagascar, where they were once nomadic, and where, before being bred into a number of dazzling hues, their original color was a surprisingly drab shade of green. Today color mutations are highly prized by collectors, and you can expect to pay far more money for a variegated or rainbow-tinted specimen than for a plain monocolored bird.

Lovebirds grow to lengths of four to seven inches, depending on the species, and they have a considerably varied life span stretching from ten to thirty years. If you intend to train your lovebird it is best to acquire it at a very young age and to hand-feed during the early months of life. In general, lovebirds are happier and healthier when kept in pairs.

Biologically speaking, lovebirds are divided into two categories, dimorphic and monomorphic. A lovebird is dimorphic if the male cock is visibly different in coloration from the female hen. Madagascar, Abyssinian, and red-faced lovebirds fall into this category. A lovebird is monomorphic when the cock and hen have similar colorings. Species of lovebirds that are monomorphic include Fisher's, Nyasa, black-cheeked (all of which have a ring around their eye), black-collared, and the most popular and common of lovebird species, peachfaced (all of which are without eye rings). The peachfaced lovebird is common, yet quite colorful.

Lovebirds thrive on commercial seed mixes. Supplement this diet with a daily array of fresh greens, cereals, safflower seeds, carrots, fruit, and corn. With their finely tuned balance of seed, grain, and vitamins, pellets are also a good bet, if you can find them. High-protein dry baby food and millet spray are likewise appreciated, and many experts suggest that you provide a feed that is vitamin fortified. Lovebirds are lusty eaters and really appreciate both quality and variety in their foods.

Though they are naturally active and love to hop, flap around, and play with toys, lovebirds can also adapt to surprisingly small spaces. A cage measuring three feet high, wide, and long provides ample room, though a larger space is always appreciated. Temperamentally, lovebirds are curious, fun-loving, bright, and full of charm. Though far from being champion talkers, with perseverance some can be taught a few words. Lovebirds make a high, shrill sound that some find annoying and others endearing. In almost all cases hand-reared lovebirds take readily to training.

Conures. Conures are highly intelligent, affable birds that take well to training and interact easily and pleasantly with human beings. Originally from the savannas and hills of Central and South America, they tolerate other birds fairly well except during mating season when they attack any being—human, bird, or otherwise—that attempts to approach their nest.

Conures come in a number of varieties, with a wide distribution of colors among them, some of which are fascinatingly beautiful. The white-eared conure has a unique spray of white and black semicircles decorating its neck and upper chest. The blue-winged conure boasts a rainbow of off-white, black, and green semicircles on its breast. The sun conure shows dazzling yellow feathers with subtle spots of orange on its body and around each eye.

Conures are medium-size parrots. They measure anywhere from nine inches (the white-eared conure) to twenty inches long (the blue-winged conure). They enjoy a variable life span from ten to twenty-five years, and they live happily in a cage that is three feet long, two feet high, and two feet wide. For diet, they thrive on standard commercial seed mix or seed pellets. To this diet you can add cereal, cheese, pine nuts, fresh corncobs, hard-boiled egg yolks, insects, fruit, millet spray, and dark greens such as spinach and kale.

Very playful and easily hand trained, conures have one drawback that some people mind and others don't: they're loud, especially certain species such as Jendaya and sun conures. But not to worry. If you purchase conures at an early age their shrill voices can be modified by exposing them to a medley of mellow sounds. Some conure owners play their pets tape recordings of small bird chirpings or of soft, beautiful singing. The conure modulates its voice in imitation of these sounds, and soon imitation becomes habit.

Cockatoos. Cockatoos are relatively large birds that come from the eastern climes of Indonesia, New Guinea, and Australia. Perhaps the most affectionate and loving of all parrots, those that are hand-fed when young adore being caressed, petted, played with, and even wrestled with by their human companions. They also have a powerful "flock urge," an instinct that is equivalent to the pack urge among dogs. This means that anyone who takes on the responsibility of acquiring one of these loyal creatures must be prepared to contribute at least several hours a day to care for it and keep it entertained. Indeed, cockatoos need to be part of the family, like a dog or cat. If left alone for long periods of time in small cages, the cockatoo is the most likely of all parrots to become withdrawn, destructive, screechy, and eventually feather pick. In this sense, cockatoos are among the most demanding and needful of all large birds.

Cockatoos are divided into five genera, with seventeen species among them. The members of these species sometimes appear considerably different one from the other. For example, the lesser sulphur-crested cockatoo measures twelve inches long. The Moluccan cockatoo has an attractive head crest, while Major Mitchell's cockatoo has a crest as large and colorful as that of a Native American chief.

A cockatoo's crest, incidentally, is an excellent barometer of its moods, standing straight up, sliding back, moving up and down warily, as the emotional situation warrants. Pet cockatoos boast shades of pink, orange, white, and yellow, with most of the high color located in the wings and crest, and the rest of the body displaying various shades of peach, salmon, and white.

Cockatoos require a lot of elbow room, and they do poorly in small, cramped cages. It is difficult to say just how large a cage they require, though four or five feet high, wide, and long is not excessive. Among creatures in the parrot kingdom, they are not the best talkers, or the worst, and with proper training acquire a respectable vocabulary.

As far as diet is concerned, commercial seed mixes or pellets are both acceptable, and should be supplemented with fresh fruits, vegetables, pine nuts, grapes, pineapple bits, sunflower seeds, millet, wheat, oats, corn, and berries. Cockatoos also need a cuttlebone in the cage for calcium, a mineral block, and a large piece of wood to appease their insatiable chewing habit.

Finally, if you do purchase a cockatoo, it will be for life. Many members of this family live to be thirty-five years old or more, and a venerable old Moluccan cockatoo named King Tut from the San Diego Zoo made it to one hundred.

Macaws. Macaws come originally from Mexico, Central and South America, and, before they were overhunted there, from Cuba and the West Indies as well. In the wild, they live both in small family groups and in large flocks, moving nomadically about in jungle and savanna-type landscapes.

Like most parrots, Macaws come in a variety of colors depending on species: the red and blue green-winged macaw, the blue and red scarlet macaw, and the green, blue, red and green military macaws are typical. The standard macaw diet includes commercial pellets or seed mixtures supplemented with apples, berries, pears, grapes, raisins, pasta, bread, carrots, corn, green vegetables like broccoli and kale, seeds, and nuts.

Macaws are hardy birds that live for amazingly long periods of time, some making it to sixty or seventy years. Among the largest of parrots, the scarlet macaw measures over thirty-four inches, the military macaw is twenty-seven inches. There are smaller species too. The foot-long Hahn macaw and the red-shouldered macaw, for instance, are scarcely larger than a cockatiel.

While its size variation is great, the personality of the macaw remains more or less the same across species: affectionate, sensitive, intelligent,

with a very loud, sometimes harsh voice, and limited talking and mimicking skills.

Macaws are social creatures but they can be temperamental as well,
especially when not receiving the attention from their keepers that
they need and expect. Their enormous hooked beak is employed in defense and aggression alike, and their claws are something fearsome. A
macaw's beak can snap a finger in two, generating three hundred
pounds per square inch. Though they rarely put these weapons to
work against people they trust, it is better not to keep a macaw in a
house populated by children, especially children so young they don't
know there's anything wrong with jabbing their finger at the bird's eye
or beak.

The African grey. When gazing at illustrations of R. L. Stevenson's
great sea yarn, *Treasure Island,* note that the parrot perched on the
shoulder of the villain, Long John Silver, is usually an African grey cawing out "Pieces of eight, pieces of eight!" These charming and attractive
birds measure a little more than a foot long, and have been the pet of
choice among British seamen back to the time of Sir Francis Drake. In
many ways they are the classic parrot of story and lore.

Shy, kindly, intelligent, sometimes unpredictable, inclined to give
their affections to one person only, African greys by almost unanimous
acclaim are the best talkers among all talking birds. Indeed, scientists
now believe that greys not only mimic human speech, but understand
the fundamentals of language itself. According to several studies, greys
not only reproduce certain sounds, but are able to understand their
meanings as well.

Living from thirty to fifty years, greys require a roomy cage, lots of
toys to keep them from getting bored, and plenty of time climbing
around your rooms.

The Amazon parrot. Coming in many sizes and shapes, Amazons
are excellent talkers. Methuselahs among birds, they sometimes make it
to fifty years or older, and they are among the most popular of all parrots. They are gentle, fun-loving, easily tamed creatures, and if hand-fed
from infancy make wonderful companions. At the same time, Amazons,
especially adult males, can be unpredictable. They sometimes tend to
be biters, for which reason they are best kept away from children.

Though not enormous as parrots go—their average length is from
eleven to fifteen inches—they require a relatively roomy cage and
plenty of time spent flying around outside it. If confined for too many

hours of the day, they become unhappy and bored, and should always be provided with a large repertoire of toys and bird gadgets to keep them busy. Amazons can also be destructive, and their call is particularly loud and piercing.

Amazons are among the hungriest of parrots. They have a tendency to become overweight, and their diet should be carefully planned, preferably with a veterinarian's input. Some bird owners work out special eating regimes to make sure their Amazon is adequately nourished but not overfed.

Poicephalus parrots. More on the small size than the large as far as parrots go—poicephalus parrots measure from nine inches to a foot long—these congenial characters come in a variety of interesting and colorful species. They are small enough to hold comfortably in your hand, and they can be accommodated in a conventional medium-size parakeet cage. They thrive on pellets or a good-quality seed mixture of sunflower seeds, safflower seeds, pine nuts, oats, hemp, and millet. These should be supplemented with beans (black-eyed peas, butter, harvest) and assorted vegetables such as cabbage, sprouts, shredded carrots, and broccoli.

Some favorites among the poicephalus parrots are the black and green jardine parrots, distinguished for their endearing mellow whistles and chirps; the turquoise and grey Meyer's parrot, also a pleasant whistler; the especially popular Senegal parrot, known for its friendly nature; and the grey parrot and the yellow parrot.

Though not talented talkers, poicephalus parrots can learn human sounds if enough time is spent at the task. Sometimes resistant to training, sometimes not, individual birds of this species differ widely in their training receptivity and, for that matter, in their general personalities.

Pionus parrots. Short, square, popular birds that originally come from South America, pionus parrots make good talkers when trained by experienced keepers, and they are a joy to have around. They play easily, take well to hand training, and are considerably less high-strung than many other parrot breeds (some bird fanciers find them a little *too* placid).

Cage size for the pionus should be large enough to accommodate a swing, perches, and perhaps some branches from nature—two feet tall, three feet wide, and two feet deep is generally adequate. As for diet, the pionus thrives on a pellet diet supplemented with vegetables such as shredded carrots and sweet potatoes.

Measuring nine inches to one foot long, there are eight species in the pionus order, five of which are sold in the United States. The small white-capped pionus is blue and green, and has perhaps the sweetest nature in this group. The dusky pionus is especially sought after, perhaps because it bears such a striking resemblance to a hawk. The most common and easily attainable variety is the Senegal parrot.

Pionus parrots are well known for producing a peculiar kind of wheezing or whistling sound that causes owners to think they have been struck with a wicked case of asthma. The bird is then rushed to the veterinarian where it is discovered that this sound is made by all pionus parrots when frightened or stressed.

Mynah birds. Mynah birds are not members of the parrot family at all, but are related to the humble starling, which they resemble more in shape than in color and personality. Birds of this genus originally come from India, Thailand, the Philippines, and the Indonesian islands, where they are adaptable denizens of forests, jungles, and coastal areas alike.

The most popular species of mynah, and the one you are most likely to find for sale, is the greater hill mynah. These sleek, black creatures with their glowing scarlet-colored bills and distinctive white feathers measure anywhere from ten to nineteen inches in length. Not as long-lived as parrots, a mynah can reach forty years, though twenty is more the average. They are an affable and popular bird, if a bit mysterious; we know far less about soft-billed birds than about other domestic birds. Many mynahs are illegally imported into this country from Southeast Asia, where they are sold on the black market, a dangerous proposition. Always buy captive domestic-bred birds. These make wonderful talkers, or we should say mimics, as they seem able to copy just about any sound in the world including car horns, computer keyboard clicks, and crying babies. They also make friendly companions who adore sitting on the shoulders of their owners and giving pecklike kisses. Hand-raised captive birds make the best talkers and form the closest attachments.

Inside their cages mynah birds are hoppers, not climbers, which means they need plenty of floor space: a cage four feet wide by three feet deep is the minimum, with a small birdhouse inside for privacy. They are physically clean creatures, though messy with their food and water, and quickly become unhappy if not given a daily bath. As for diet, they are soft-billed birds, which means they cannot crack nuts and seeds. They thrive on commercial mynah bird pellets, and these should be supplemented with tasty soft foods such as banana, papaya, guava, mango, pear, plus bread slices, salad greens, hard-boiled egg yolk, and baked sweet potato. Raisins, grapes, apple, and dates can be given sparingly as treats.

Small birds

Small birds are less friendly than large and, generally speaking, cannot be tamed. They are kept mainly in the home for their beauty, their perkiness, and for their lovely song. Who, indeed, has not enjoyed the warbling of a canary, or the sight of two colorful finches sitting demurely side by side in a cage?

Small birds are generally cheaper to purchase than large. They are easier to maintain, and since they do not require much social interaction with humans, they demand less emotional commitment than larger birds.

Finches. It is estimated that members of the finch family make up approximately *one half* of all the birds on the planet today. Even canaries, though classed separately for our purposes, are actually a kind of finch. Indeed, the rule of thumb is, if it looks like a finch it probably is a finch.

A small, delicate bird measuring four or five inches long and weighing less than an ounce, finches are found on almost every continent and climate in the world. Coming in a dazzling variety of colors that imitates the rainbow, they live for seven to fifteen years, and are subdivided into several hundred different species. Zebra finches are probably the most popular species and the easiest to care for. Other popular species include the society finch, orange cheek, silver bill, spice, and java rice.

Finches crave the company of at least one, and preferably many, of their own kind, and they should always be kept in pairs as a minimum. Easily frightened and a bit fragile, most finches pine away when alone in a cage.

Though finches do not sing in a melodious way like canaries, their chirp has a pleasant, congenial ring to it. Their incessant daytime chatter, many people insist, is akin to listening to soothing background music, or being lulled by the calm sounds of flowing water.

In terms of personality, finches are perky, chirpy, gentle, and ever active. Don't expect a finch to come when you call it or to hop on your finger, however. That's not part of their biological agenda (though there are occasional exceptions). Not exactly unfriendly—finch owners talk of feeling a palpable communion when talking to their birds and looking them in the eyes—it is still a rare finch that shows direct signs of recognition or makes overtures of friendship.

While finches enjoy cage room, they are comfortable in a small to medium-size cage. At a minimum, cages should be four times a finch's wing span, and seven times their length from head to tail, with the bars of the cage spaced no more than a half-inch apart. Like most birds, finches thrive on pellets or commercial finch feed mixtures. This diet can be supplemented with fresh greens several times a week, plus slices of raw apple and orange, millet spray, boiled egg yolk, and live food such as mealworms.

Canaries. For many years the cheapest and most common cage bird in America—up till the 1970's they were sold at five-and-dime stores for a few dollars apiece—canaries have increased in price and rarity as the years have passed. First introduced to Europe during the 1400s by the Portuguese and Spanish, the canary's popularity quickly soared, and within a few centuries they were a common sight in the windows of every city of Europe.

Members in good standing of the finch family, canaries are generally a bit larger than finches, measuring three or four inches in length. They live from seven to fifteen years. Though svelte and lovely to look at, and though available in a limited but charming group of colors, the canary's predominant attraction is its sweet, bubbling song, a sound that has soothed and thrilled listeners for centuries. When picking out your canary at the pet shop, pay special attention to the quality and the timber of its warble. If it sounds good to you now, it will sound even better when you get it home. And remember, *only male canaries sing.*

A canary's cage size should be at least three times the length of its wing span or seven times its length from head to tail. Like finches, it is a rare canary that can be trained to interact in any sort of complex way with human beings. Even simple feats like sitting on your finger or eating from your hand are rare.

Plain commercial canary seed is the main item on a canary's menu, supplemented with an assortment of soft foods such as shredded carrots, apple slices, romaine lettuce, cabbage, sprouted seeds, and fresh weeds such as dandelion greens and shepherd's purse. When feeding fresh foods to canaries clean the food thoroughly first. Canaries are sensitive eaters, and the slightest chemical contamination can make them sick. Along with the standard seed mix, a good supply of calcium and minerals should also be available (it can be given in the form of baked, sterilized eggshells), along with a cuttlefish bone fastened to the bars of the cage. Canaries need a constant supply of pure water as well. Drinking water should be changed once every twenty-four hours, and twice a day during the summer months or when a female is growing chicks.

One word of caution. Avoid stressing a canary in any way when it is molting. Canaries are highly vulnerable at this time, and even a short car ride or bus trip from the store to home can make them fatally ill.

Housing for Pet Birds

Like all of us, the place where a bird lives is his castle, his survival post, and his home. It is the single most expensive purchase you will make for your new pet and the most important.

When acquiring a cage, purchase the largest and sturdiest model you can afford. Metal is traditionally the material of choice, though in the past few years glass-enclosed vitrines have come back in style and make serviceable homes for some species. Cages composed of wood are best avoided. Even small birds chew on the bars and eventually bore holes. Also avoid inexpensive cages made of composite woods: the formaldehyde added to these mixtures is a slow poison to practically every species of bird.

Like all animals, birds need plenty of elbow room, at least enough to hop comfortably from perch to perch, and preferably enough to do a bit of wing flapping, if not actual flying. Stay away from fancy decorative and antique cages, however, even if they appear roomy and solid. They are almost always built for appearance rather than utility, and are usually very difficult to clean.

Optimally, a cage should be four times a bird's full wing spread, or alternately, seven times its length from head to tail. A cage should never be so confining that a bird's wings touch opposite sides of the cage when extended. Also make sure no sharp edges, loose wires, rusty metal, or pointed protrusions are in evidence. To prevent cage-induced accidents, the width between the bars in a cage should be no larger than the width of a bird's head. Be especially careful of rubber in a cage, even rubber toys. When chewed, rubber is toxic to many domestic species.

Among small birds, parakeets need a relatively tall cage for climbing on. Canaries and finches require more horizontal room for hopping and flying. Larger birds like Amazons and macaws need appropriately roomy living quarters, and here one should not economize. A spatially restrictive cage exerts a profoundly negative effect on birds, especially the larger parrots. It can trigger depression, overeating (and hence obesity), and highly aggressive behavior that may be aimed at you, or other birds, or both.

As far as very large birds go, like cockatoos, you will need a cage measuring three or four feet high and several feet across. Inside this roomy home a large tree branch is fixed to one corner for sitting, and in the other corner (in parrot cages) a wooden bird house is located for hiding and sleeping. Plastic shower rings or a thick piece of rope dangle from the top bars as a diversion. Feeding dishes are made of heavy-duty metal or ceramic, and perches are one- or two-inch-thick dowels. Parrot cages are large, solid, built from strong biteproof materials, and are correspondingly expensive. Floor stands are fine if there are no children or other pets in the house.

Hang the cage at least four feet or more off the ground, away from all drafts and damp floors. Cages for large parrots and cockatoos are usually quite large and should not be hung at all. Place them on a table or secure base instead. Many come on wheeled carts.

The ideal room temperature for a domestic bird is around 70°F. Birds require a minimum of a half-hour a day sunlight for maximum health and vitamin D production. Without this exposure soft bones and rickets may result. At the same time, avoid leaving a bird in direct sun from morning to night. A few hours a day, preferably in the morning, is more than adequate. Full-spectrum light, the kind used for plants and plant terrariums, makes a good substitute for sunlight if direct daylight is not available. During the summer months, as a special treat, you may wish to hang your feathered friend's cage outside and let it commune with the great outdoors for an hour or so. Just be careful not to place the cage in a location where it is exposed to strong breezes. Be sure to keep all cage doors tightly locked.

After the cage is purchased and set up, install two or three sturdy perches arranged at intervals of different heights throughout the cage. For larger birds, a T-shaped perch should be set up for comfortable seating outside the cage, with food and water close by. In the appropriate location, a large bird with clipped wings may be allowed some exercise in the backyard foliage. Or if you have room, consider building an outdoor flight cage.

Perches are an extremely important piece of equipment for birds. They allow hopping, exercise, and a place to stand and socialize with other birds. Perches made of wooden dowels are more natural and tree-like than the plastic variety. Wood provides large birds with a good chewing post, and smaller birds with a surface to rub and polish their beaks. Some bird owners place real tree branches in the cage, criss-crossing the ends through the bars. Just be sure to wash and disinfect all wooden perches every few months. Also, avoid using perches that are covered with sandpaper or abrasive surfaces. Once quite popular because of the firm foot hold they provide, abrasive perches rub away at a bird's tender feet (imagine what it would be like standing on sandpaper all day long in your bare feet), and over time produce open sores and eventually lameness.

Most small cages come complete with a removable and easily cleanable bottom grate. If this accessory is missing, find a cage that has one. As far as sanitation is concerned, the bottom of a cage should be lined with paper or plastic. Avoid wood shavings in the bottom, as birds choke on them. Also stay away from gravel paper—it roughs up a bird's feet—and kitty litter, which may be accidentally ingested and produce stomach blockages.

Bedding placed at the bottom of the cage can be made from shredded corncobs or empty paper bags. To control dampness and the invariable molds and spores that follow, change all bedding material on a regular basis, preferably daily.

Cage liners are easily fouled and begin to smell if left unchanged for even a few days. Leave yourself reminders. Food dishes should be checked daily for seed hulls and other waste. Every week or so make a thorough inspection of the cage frame, wiping droppings and feather fragments from the bars, removing debris, and checking for damage or irregularities to the frame. Every two or three weeks clean the entire cage, soaking toys and perches in a disinfectant solution to eliminate the spores and bacteria that inevitably build up over time.

Food and Nutrition

When we say that someone "eats like a bird" the analogy is a poor one. There are few creatures in nature that eat *more* than birds or as often.

This constant need on the part of birds to eat means that providing adequate nutrition is one of a bird owner's more important and demanding tasks. Unlike human beings, the avian digestive system requires outside help to process its food. Part of this help comes in the form of gravel or sand, which the bird ingests with its seeds and that serves as a kind of mortar and pestle in the bird's gizzard, pulping the food, and facilitating digestion and absorption. For this reason, commercial bird grit—that is, fine-size river gravel containing plenty of quartz particles—is often placed in the bottom of the cage and/or in a container hanging on the side. Grit, however, is not absolutely necessary for domestic birds, and some experts caution against providing too much of it. Talk with your veterinarian or breeder concerning the appropriate amount of grit to use for your bird's specific needs. Don't, by the way, mistake digestive grit for grit made from shell fragments or cuttlebone. Both are excellent forms of calcium, but the latter does nothing to help the digestion process.

Different domestic birds require different diets, and you will want to get a full briefing on the varieties best suited to your pet at the time of purchase or adoption. Any good pet supply store carries a variety of commercial seed mixtures blended for different birds. A majority of these mixtures are composed of seeds and grains—oats, maize, hemp, linseed, peanuts, pine nuts, sunflower seeds, millet, and more. To this basic menu a supplementary assortment of soft foods is added at home including fruit, pasta, bean sprouts, commercial egg biscuit mixtures and greens. Grapes, peanuts, apples, lettuce, bread dipped in fruit juice—as well as insects, such as mealworms and aphids—all may be part of a bird's daily diet. Cuttlebone or calcium blocks in the cage help your bird get its daily quota of calcium (if your bird doesn't chew on the bone directly, scrape a little into powder and sprinkle it over the feed every few days). Beware, however, of rhubarb and avocado—they are poisonous to many species. Other substances to avoid include food that has been fried in grease, heavily salted food, junk foods in general, and food which contains alcohol. Especially beware of alcohol—a single teaspoon can kill a large bird. Again, confer with the breeder or pet store concerning the most appropriate diet for your particular pet.

Still another nutritional source for birds are commercial pellets. The best of these manufactured food products contain more nutritional value than ordinary bird feed, and birds appear to love them. Pellets are good, too, because they leave no seed hulls and because they prevent birds from picking out their favorite seeds and leaving the rest.

Since birds are such voracious eaters, food containers in the cage should be kept filled to the brim. Plastic containers make acceptable seed dispensers for smaller birds such as finches and canaries, but for large birds whose powerful beaks can rip apart a plastic container in a matter of days, metal is preferred. As a rule, it's a good idea to remove uneaten bits of fruit and vegetable remains from the cage after three or four hours. Soft foods tend to spoil quickly. Supplementary soft foods such as fruits or vegetables should not be mixed in with seed mixtures, but are better placed in a separate container to the side.

How can you tell if your bird is being improperly nourished? Poorly fed birds tend to have poor feather color, to pluck their own feathers, and to have a tired, droopy look. Fortunately, this problem often stems from nothing more than a lack of proper vitamins and minerals. Talk to your veterinarian about the use of bird supplements and about which changes he or she recommends to your bird's basic diet.

The Art and Science of Bird Care

If the chores required for birds' health are neglected, even for a few days, they quickly become sick. Most important in this regard are consistency and quality of care. The following activities are all part of the day-to-day, week-to-week upkeep regime required of responsible avian hobbyists.

Bathing

If you have a birdbath in your backyard, notice the joy with which the feathered denizens in your neighborhood splash and preen. Birds love to get wet. Water refreshes them, cleans them, removes feather dust. And just like birds in the wild, domestic birds need their daily baths.

Basically, there are three ways to bathe a bird.

First, if you own a large bird that trusts you, and that you know enjoys being exposed to direct streams of water, turn on the shower, bring the bird into the bathroom, place it in the shower, and let it do the rest. Some bird owners bring their birds into the shower with them, though this can get tricky and is not necessarily recommended. During the summer months the spray from a hose or lawn sprinkler is a welcome treat for some birds. Pet supply stores sell special hose appliances for cleaning and spraying larger birds.

A second less dramatic method is to fill a plastic spray bottle with lukewarm water, hold it about eighteen inches away from your bird, and spray a fine mist in its direction. Most birds respond by splashing-like movements, peeping or cawing cheerfully, and flapping their wings. If your bird is frightened by the spray, cease and desist, then proceed to the third cleaning method of choice.

Simply fill a bowl halfway to the top with lukewarm water and place it in the cage. The bowl should be large enough to allow a bird to hop and splash around comfortably, heavy enough to avoid tipping. Place the bowl in the bottom of the cage, then allow the bird to do the rest. Commercial birdbaths that attach directly to the cage door are also available at most pet supply stores.

Allow the birdbath to remain in the cage for an hour or so, then remove it before the occupants start to drink the dirty water. After a bath some birds—not all, but some—enjoy being exposed to the warm, dry heat of a blow-dryer. Set the heat level to warm and give it a try. Remember that a wet bird is a vulnerable bird, especially in the colder months. For the first half-hour after bathing keep it in a warm room away from breezes and drafts.

Bathe your bird three times a week and more if possible. Morning and afternoon are the best times for the task, as they allow a bird's wings to dry by nightfall.

Grooming

Most birds spend a majority of their day preening, cleaning, and secreting a special oil onto their feathers from their so-called preen gland, located near the tail. Clean creatures by nature, you can help their spiffing-up process by clipping their nails with a fingernail clipper (or toenail clipper with larger birds).

For many birds the simple act of hopping from perch to perch wears their nails down to an acceptable length. Nonetheless, the nails on inactive birds sometimes grow so lengthy they become a danger to its balance and to other birds in the cage. You will know it's time to take out the clipper when the front and the back nails on the foot have grown so long they're touching.

If you are new to bird keeping and skittish about doing the trimming yourself, bring your bird to a veterinarian for basic trimming lessons. While you're at the doctor's ask if a beak-trimming session is in order as well. Though the beaks of most domestic birds are worn down naturally by the rigors of climbing, scratching, eating, and rubbing against cuttlebone, in some cases beaks grow too long and interfere with eating.

Molting

Most birds grow a new set of feathers approximately once a year. Molting season is a special time for birds. Don't worry if your pet is unusually quiet, pensive even, or behaves in frightened and eccentric ways.

In a bird's world, feathers perform a multitude of important physical and psychological functions, including providing warmth and camouflage, attracting mates, asserting dominance, making nests, and, well, just looking good. To lose this crowning glory appears to be both a trauma to birds and a terror, hence their withdrawn behavior.

During molting season, make sure your bird is kept warm, well fed, and tended for. They are particularly vulnerable to chills and disease during this time. For most birds, molting season lasts for several weeks.

Covering at night

In nature when the day ends birds seek the protection of a heavy branch or a canopy of leaves. You can provide your pet with an approximation of this avian security blanket by covering the cage ten to twelve hours at night with a lightweight fabric or commercial cage cover. Cage coverings bring darkness to a cage in the midst of a lit-up house and help birds to sleep. They discourage squawking and talking in the middle of the night, an annoyance that even the most dedicated bird lovers prefer to avoid. And of course, cage coverings keep birds warm and screen them from drafts. Some birds such as finches prefer to sleep in nests.

Relieving boredom

Like any confined pet, birds need a bit of frolic to break the monotony. A bored bird is an unhappy bird, and their actions prove it. Does your bird pick listlessly at its feathers all day long? Does it make repeated rocking motions for long stretches of time while standing on a perch? Does it chew at its toes? Does it behave in an overtly and inappropriately aggressive manner? Has it stopped singing, playing, and interacting with other birds in the cage?

If so, it may be sick. More likely, it is simply bored out of its mind.

Part of this void can be filled with your attentions (more on this below). The rest is filled by the toys you provide. Anything that swings, reflects, shines, makes noise, rolls, or can be climbed on or pecked at makes a good bird diversion. Ladders, mirrors, seed balls, swings, bells, and wood block toys are all available at pet supply stores. A cuttlefish bone fixed to the side of a cage allows birds to sharpen their beak and to get needed exercise in the process. Larger birds require large, complex toys to challenge their minds. See the section on parrots for particulars.

As far as making toys for your pet, the choice is wide. Just be sure they are safe. A set of keys tied to a piece of string has kept many a bird fascinated and on the move, as have open paper bags left in the bottom of the cage. Large birds appear to enjoy chomping on chewy rope, Nylabone, or a rawhide toy just as much as dogs. They enjoy shredding up old paperback books and newspaper. They roll paper tubes, climb into cardboard boxes, and adore old magazines and cardboard six-pack containers. They especially relish fresh corn on the cob and dried cobs, the former to eat, the latter to rip up and toss around. As with children, the best toy is one that challenges the intelligence, and at the same time entertains and engages.

Allowing a bird out of its cage

Like all living things, birds need a quota of daily exercise to remain cheerful and fit. Assuming their cage is large enough, and that there are enough toys and diversions to keep them hopping, smaller birds usually get all the exercise they need inside the cage. Larger birds, and especially birds that interact frequently with humans, are a different story. If kept permanently confined, large birds become overweight, listless, and ultimately angry and depressed. They need to move around the home for an hour or two a day, both to exercise their wings and to let their spirits soar.

First, make sure that your parrot, cockatoo, or larger bird has its flight feathers trimmed before giving it freedom to roam the house. Your veterinarian will do this job for you, and/or will show you how to do it yourself. Many larger birds with clipped wings actually engage in walking, gliding, and climbing more than actual flying.

Once a bird's wings are clipped, the best way to prepare for its release is to designate one, or at most two rooms in the house or apartment as free-flight zones, and then set about birdproofing these areas.

Before you allow your bird to roam freely around the house, do a bit of birdproofing. Check the layout of your house for potential trouble spots. Electric and phone wires, for example, are eager attractions to avian eyes and should be tucked away carefully before your bird is given its freedom. Beware of large picture windows. Birds take one look at them, think they see the blue sky of freedom, and head into the glass at fifteen or twenty miles per hour. The same goes for mirrors and other reflecting objects. Birds think they've found a friend and fly smack into them. Remedy this situation by keeping the window blinds closed and curtains pulled when your bird is free.

If you have clothing, furniture, food, or fragile display treasures that don't take well to bird droppings and flapping wings, store them in a safe place. All windows and doors should be closed, along with small places that inquisitive avians may wander into—closets, cabinets, fireplaces, boxes. Pull the curtains on all windows to discourage birds from flying into the glass.

Floors should be uncarpeted and covered with a commercial sealer against stains and droppings. Exposed electric wires are always a temptation, and are best kept out of sight. If a door or window ledge is covered with paint containing lead, paint over these areas before allowing the bird access. Lead is one of the most deadly substances to birds. In some areas of the world, even the relatively small amounts of lead contained in car exhaust contribute to the extinction of certain avian species.

Note that a surprisingly large number of common plants, leaves, vines, and flowers are poisonous to birds; so many, in fact, that one wonders how birds in the wilderness survive at all. A partial list of bird-unsafe plants includes the following:

Amaryllis	Cherry tree leaves	Impatiens	Plums
Anemone	Crocus	Iris	Priveterinarian
Apple seeds	Daffodils	Ivy	Rhododendron
Azaleas	Delphiniums	Jasmine	Spider plants
Bleeding heart	Dieffenbachia	Lily of the valley	Virginia creeper
Boxwood	English laurel	Mistletoe	Wisteria
Buttercups	Foxglove	Morning glory	Yews
Calla lily	Holly	Philodendrons	

Quite a list, and there are more. So don't take chances: keep all cut flowers, house plants, vines, and potted trees out of the free-fly room.

Once the coast is clear, open the door to your birdcage and allow her the luxury of leaving whenever she chooses. Some birds, especially parrots, are often happy to simply climb out of the cage and perch on top, surveying their domain like eagles. Further activity is not on their agenda, and if this is the case, so be it. Other birds may take off and fly excitedly around the room like, well, like prisoners let out of a cage. Though these initial acrobatics seem to go on forever, birds *do* eventually get tired and return to their cage.

Keep the door of the birdcage open at all times while it is out and flying around. Most tame birds, after they have flown for a while, work up an appetite and return to the cage on their own. Close the door when this happens and end the exercise session for the day.

In some instances, of course, birds do not return to the cage of their own accord, especially in the beginning when they're growing accustomed to the heady feel of freedom. When this happens, turn off the lights and make the room as dark and quiet as possible. The bird takes this as a sign of night, and thinks that it's now time to go to sleep. It will sit quite still and may even tuck its head in its chest. At this point carefully creep up, gently cup the bird in your hands, and place it in the cage. It is not a good idea in general, incidentally, to let canaries and finches out of their cage at any time. Confine these outings to the larger birds.

In some cases a bird may simply refuse to return to the cage. When this occurs, you must catch it by hand.

If the bird is large and uncooperative, a heavy-duty set of work gloves are a must, especially if it tends to become easily upset and frightened. Whatever you do, do not move too quickly when approaching the bird. Avoid all jerky motions. Try never to force the issue. Gentleness is the key. Finally, before you allow a bird to fly free from its cage, make sure it is trained to walk onto a dowel. Use the dowel to carry the bird back to the cage.

If all other catching methods fail, a net, or for parrots and larger birds, a towel can be used. But only as a last resort. Nets and towels frighten birds and sometimes get tangled, causing physical harm. It is better to remain patient and cool and allow the bird to return to the cage on its own accord.

Training

Almost all large birds and some small ones—parakeets in particular—can be trained to talk and to respond to your commands. The training process begins by building a relationship with the bird and letting it get to know you. Don't allow a day to go by without making friendly personal contact. Feed the bird, water it, talk to it, stick your fingers in the cage, open and close the cage door several times each day, keep it company. Though it is sometimes difficult to see, birds gradually learn to recognize people, and eventually they come to like and trust them. It just takes persistence.

After a few weeks of getting to know your new friend, hand training begins.

Open the cage door and v-e-r-y s-l-o-w-l-y insert your hand, speaking softly and reassuringly as you do. In the beginning, lure the bird to you with a little treat, a piece of vegetable or fruit. Encourage it to move toward your finger or hand and to use it as a perch. If you prefer, use a stick instead of your finger.

Once your hand is close to the bird, press your finger lightly against its chest. This slight pressure forces it to either hop backward or onto your finger. Since most birds hate hopping backward, the outcome is usually a foregone conclusion. For cockatiels and parakeets, a protective glove can be worn, though it is not mandatory. When working with parrots and large hooked-bill birds, a heavy protective glove is recommended, especially in the early stages of training. Some parrot trainers start by using a wooden dowel or broomstick, then progress to hand training when the bird becomes trusting and tame.

During your first attempts at all this your bird will, of course, flutter away excitedly and hover in the corner of its cage. This is to be expected. You'd do the same if a gigantic hand tried to grab you. So be persistent. Use a gentle voice, offer food, move slowly, keep at it. In time your frightened friend will come to realize that standing on a human finger is a kind of adventure, and that nothing bad comes of it. In fact, it's sort of fun. Different, anyway.

As with all animal training, the most important assets you as trainer bring to the process are patience and perseverance. Ten or fifteen minutes a day is enough time, but you must be consistent. Missing even a day or two sends you back to point zero in your bird's mind. The process from A to Z will take weeks and sometimes months. But the end result is worth it—a tame, friendly family member who sits on your shoulder, flies freely from person to person, and even watches television with you or walks behind you when you pass from room to room.

For further specifics on bird training talk to your breeder or veterinarian, and read every book you can find on the subject. There is much valuable information currently offered on the Internet as well. Go to your favorite search engine and type in "Birds, Pets, Training." You may be surprised to see just how much essential training information is out there for the asking.

Teaching your bird to talk

First, of course, you must be sure that the species you own is, in fact, a talker. Finches and canaries are kept predominantly for their song and appearance and do not have the vocal apparatus to mimic human speech. Some of the smaller parrots such as the Senegal or blue-headed, are technically able to copy speech, but are not very talented in this department. While there are exceptions, males tend to learn speech better and faster than females, and younger birds pick up talking skills more efficiently than old.

Which birds are the best talkers?

The short list includes the cockatiel, conure, African grey, cockatoo, macaw, Amazon, and other more exotic members of the parrot family.

But while all these creatures are biologically capable of this amazing feat, this inherent ability by no means assures that they will in fact talk. For the truth is that while most talking birds are perfectly able to talk, some won't. In the end it is a matter of the individual bird.

Certain parrots, for example, adapt to talk training with great alacrity and soon demonstrate a wide and sophisticated vocabulary, mimicking sounds they pick up from the environment such as barking dogs or telephone rings as well as human phrases. Others learn a handful of simple words—*Hello there! Good night, ladies! Watch it, pal!*—and stop here, never advancing to more sophisticated sentence structures. Still others remain silent no matter how long or diligently they are coaxed.

There are no guarantees.

All this said, the actual process of teaching a bird to speak is relatively simple.

At the beginning of each lesson remove all distractions from the cage and surrounding area such as toys, food receptacles, other people, pets, a turned-on radio or TV.

Once quiet reigns, say the word or phrase you wish your feathered pupil to learn. Pause a moment or two to let the sound sink in, then repeat. Don't stand too near the cage when you speak. In fact, you may wish to remain out of the bird's line of vision entirely.

At first your bird will sit on its perch and look at you as if you've lost your mind. You repeat the words and repeat and repeat. But no dice—only silence. Day follows day. Then, after two months, say, or six months, or even longer, just as you're about to throw in the towel and assume you have a nontalker on your hands, suddenly, like a bolt from the blue, out it comes—*Polly want a cracker!* The first word has now been spoken; the dam has broken. Soon other words come in torrents, and the more a bird talks the more its capacity to learn increases. Indeed, once your parrot starts its mimicking shenanigans it is hard to turn them off: Names, jokes, insults, ad slogans, John Wayne imitations, Bronx cheers—the sky's the limit. With a talking parrot, what goes in eventually comes out. Congratulations: you now have a talking bird.

Perform the word training session every day for a minimum of ten or fifteen minutes (thirty minutes a session is better). Do it twice daily if possible at the same time. During the rest of the day repeat the word whenever you happen to pass by the bird's cage, speaking in the same volume and tone. One school of thought has it that parrots are most receptive to talking lessons from seven to nine in the morning, and seven to nine at night. Another has it that the room should be kept as dark as possible during each learning session to cut down on distractions. Some people record their own voice on a tape recorder and play it back to the bird. From all reports, this system works just about as well as the real thing. If you go this route, divide the lessons, some done in person, others with the taped message. If your time is limited, you may also want to purchase tapes and CDs from your pet supply store designed by experts to teach birds how to speak.

Introducing a companion bird to the cage

If your bird is lonely and you decide to find a mate, the process of introducing the new bird can be tricky.

Start by keeping the two birds in separate but nearby cages for a week. Living together but separate in this way allows them to become accustomed to each other's sight and sound and encourages them to form the habit of communicating across the room.

When the day comes for placing them in the same cage, keep a close eye on the proceedings. If there is going to be any scrapping or commotion it will usually be initiated by the in-residence avian fighting to protect its territory.

Smaller birds such as finches and parakeets tend to accept company quickly. Canaries are best kept alone. Parrots and other large birds may be contentious when first introduced, especially if they have lived alone for long periods of time and are especially attached to their human keeper. In such cases the newcomer parrot is viewed as a rival for the keeper's affections, as well as an invader of home ground. All you can do in this situation is keep an eye on things, especially during the first week or so, and make sure the birds do not seriously attack each other. In some cases two birds will simply be incapable of living together under the same roof. When this occurs it's best to segregate them and leave it at that. If both birds are then kept in separate cages in the same room, some amount of company is afforded, and the loneliness quotient is correspondingly reduced.

A word on banding

Bird owners new to the avian world often wonder what the small metal band wrapped around a bird's leg really is. In fact, this band is your bird's personal identification. If you look closely at it you will see letters and numbers printed on its surface. These figures comprise your bird's personal ID code. Write them down and keep them in a safe place. If your bird is stolen or escapes, this code will help you get him back.

Bands come in two varieties: open bands and closed.

Closed bands are solid unremovable rings with no splits or breaks along the surface. They are made of metal, usually aluminum, and display abbreviations for local bird organizations or breeders such as "ALB," "AFA," "NCS," "SPBE." Closed bands are placed on a bird's leg during the first or second week after birth.

Open bands are made of plastic, aluminum, or wire, and are often fashioned in bright colors. They can be removed at any time, and have a break in the surface, indicating that they were placed on the bird's leg a few months or even a year after its birth. If you are contemplating buying an exotic bird, and if the bird has an open band on his leg, be careful: an open band may indicate that the bird was raised out of the country, illegally imported, then banded once arrived. Make all appropriate inquiries before purchasing such a pet.

Communing with your bird

Day-to-day care for a pet bird can be a rewarding and even meditative experience. Talking to a bird, feeling her presence on your shoulder, standing quietly next to her, singing along as she bugles out her morning greeting, all these activities bring a satisfaction that is difficult to explain to nonbird owners. Even with small birds like finches and canaries, a wonderful and sometimes magical rapport can develop over time, as any inveterate bird owner will agree. This magic, however, comes only to those who are willing to work on the bonding process with serious intent.

Start by spending quality time with your bird at a set hour each day.

Talk, sing along, dangle objects outside the cage, play the radio, hand-feed him, interact with him. Encourage other members of your household to do the same. The important thing is to make your presence known and to let the bird become familiar with your voice, appearance, touch, and ways.

Birds that adapt to hand and shoulder sitting should be handled every day without exception. Some large parrots need as many as two or three hours a day. Indeed, unless large birds are given the attention and affection they need, they can become neurotic and even hostile. As far as spending quality time with pet birds goes, the more the better.

When you leave home

Though some pet birds, especially songbirds, appear not to notice your presence to any extent during the day, you might be surprised to find out how aware of you they really are, and how much they miss you when you're suddenly not there. On those occasions when you and the occupants of your household must leave home for more than a day or so, you will want to make sure your birds are well tended to, and that the delegated bird sitter provides plenty of quality attention and care in your absence.

Before departure, provide the bird sitter with a written list of duties including information on feeding and feeding schedules, watering, bathing, exercise, and medicines. Make sure the sitter knows where you will be on any given day. It is also a good idea, if possible, for the sitter to spend an hour or two getting to know the bird before you leave.

If you choose to board your bird, check out the boarding facility first. Be sure the premises are clean, bright, roomy, operated by a concerned staff, and have proper facilities for taking care of birds. Before departure, give the boarding facility all necessary information concerning your bird's diet, health problems, idiosyncracies, and needs. Provide them with a phone number where you can be reached (cell phones are excellent in this regard), plus the name and number of the veterinarian who cares for your birds.

Keeping Your Bird Healthy and Fit

Symptoms of sickness

Unlike dogs, cats, and even small furry animals, it can be difficult to identify sickness and disease in birds. Still, there are telltale indications, and a practiced eye knows the signs. The following physical and psychological symptoms may all be evidence that your feathered companion is ailing.

- The single most common behavior pattern of sick birds is to fluff out their feathers. This odd-looking maneuver is done quite purposefully. It creates small air pockets in a bird's feathers that trap body heat and serve as a kind of insulating device to hold in warmth. When you see birds indulging in obvious feather fluffing, the message is, something has gone wrong with my body's thermostat, and I am now attempting to regulate it on my own.
- Sick birds tend to compulsively pick at their feathers. Birds are easily infected by mites, especially in the area around the bill. When signs of pitting appear in the cere area (the area surrounding the beak) this can be a tip-off. Mites not only torment birds, but in some cases make them sick. If signs of mites appear, get medical help immediately. Once mites are well established, they are notoriously difficult to remove.
- The feces of sick birds tends to change in color and consistency. Be on the alert for unusually dark or watery droppings. Be worried too if this condition continues for more than a day or so. Any signs of blood in the feces are always cause for immediate concern. Diarrhea in birds is recognized by an increased accumulation of runny droppings in the cage. Constipation is indicated by dramatically fewer droppings, and when birds use their bills to pick continually at their vent areas.
- A sick bird's eyes are often red, puffed up, watery, dull, glazed, half-closed, or dripping with secretions.
- A sick bird's feathers tend to fall out. Their plumage is continually damp and unhealthy looking. Sick birds pick listlessly at their tails. If the number of feathers accumulating in the bottom of a cage dramatically increases over a short period of time, this may be a telltale sign.
- Sick birds sometimes make sudden jerky movements with their tail or entire bodies. They shiver and shake uncontrollably, often in the corner or bottom of the cage.
- Sick birds tend to slump quietly and nonresponsively on a perch. Or worse, they sit inertly on the floor of the cage, appearing lethargic and disinterested in everything around them. They ignore the sights and noises they normally seem to enjoy. Sitting quietly for long periods of time with eyes closed is also a danger signal.
- A sick bird's song, talking, or squawk is often weakened. (When larger birds stop talking or squawking, however, this may simply indicate boredom and frustration, not disease.)

- There is a marked decline in the bird's appetite and thirst level.
- The bird is constantly sniffling, coughing, or sneezing. When a bird keeps its bill open and its head back, this is a probable sign of respiratory congestion, equivalent to a stuffed nose in human beings.

Human Health Alert

A recent medical warning has been issued to people with severely suppressed immune systems, advising them to avoid close contact with pet birds. A fungus called *Cryptococcus neoformans* is found in the droppings of canaries, parrots, parakeets, and pigeons; when dry, these droppings form dust clouds that can be inhaled. The cryptococcal fungus has no negative health effect on birds or on healthy human beings. Individuals with compromised immune systems, however, such as those with AIDS or lymphoma, or people who have received organ transplants and are presently on antirejection drugs, may be vulnerable. Once contracted, this fungus is known to cause meningitis and perhaps other serious disorders. If you fall into one of the above categories, caution is the watchword as far as keeping pet birds is concerned.

Preventive medicine

As always, prevention is the best cure. The following stay-healthy tips will help keep your bird out of harm's way.

Many bird ailments are airborne. Make sure the circulation in the bird's room is adequate, and that fresh air is always available. If there are many airborne contaminants in your house, such as chemical fumes or debris from dried wastes, use an air purifier. Be careful of air conditioners around birds, however. During hot weather, sudden blasts of cold air can give birds a chill. Indeed, keep birds out of drafts in general, but maintain good air circulation in the home.

Bird diseases are brought into the home via contact with people, objects, and animals. If you have recently visited a pet store, walked in the woods, attended a circus or animal show, visited a farm, touched garden manure or chemical wastes, spent time with friends who own animals, or been in contact with other pet birds, wash your hands carefully before touching your pet.

If your bird is prone to colds, make sure it receives adequate amounts of vitamin A and C in its daily diet. Vitamin deficiencies make birds vulnerable to bronchial problems and viral ailments.

Avian digestive systems are notoriously fussy. If their food is even a little spoiled or dirty, it can wreak havoc. Always give your bird clean, fresh feed. Use food and water containers that have a hood over the feed area to shelter the contents from feathers, droppings, and airborne contaminants. If possible, feed your bird organic, unsprayed greens, fruit, grains, and vegetables.

Change the paper at the bottom of your bird's cage on a daily basis, and give its cage a thorough cleaning and disinfecting at least once a month. Dirt and bacteria build up over time and cause disease. These simple preventive measures alone can save your bird's health, and life.

If you travel with your bird or take it to bird shows, keep it away from contact with other birds and steer clear of areas that contain dangerous chemical or biological contaminants.

Keep your bird's habitat warm and dry, away from drafts, damp floors, and fans. In the wintertime avoid exposure to open doors and windows. Birds catch cold easily.

Be sure there are no harmful toys or jagged objects in a bird's cage. Birdproof your house thoroughly (see above) before allowing birds to fly free. Accidents do happen, and when birds break a leg or tear a wing proper medical care may or may not be close at hand.

Check up on your bird as many times as possible during the day. Scan its living area for signs of trouble. Vigilance pays.

Veterinarians trained in avian medicine are uncommon, and it is a good idea to locate available medical resources in advance. Neighborhood bird clubs and breeders will know of local practitioners who are skilled in bird care. Write down their names and phone numbers and have this information at the ready should trouble occur. There are many cases where a sick or wounded bird died simply because its keepers took so long to find a qualified veterinarian. Be prepared. You can also find an avian veterinarian near you through the American Association of Veterinarians' (AAV) website (see Appendix).

Get to know your bird's habits. Study them. Become familiar with its song, its voice, its way of eating, its movements, its elimination and sleeping patterns. Become finely tuned to its day-to-day disposition. This familiarity helps you recognize problems quickly when and if they occur.

Treating a sick bird

Avoid playing doctor. If your bird develops any of the above symptoms, serious problems are at hand, and time is of the essence. Turn the job over to a trained medical expert at once.

If veterinarian service is not immediately available, the first rule of bird care is to keep the bird warm and dry. During the winter months be sure a sick bird's room is adequately heated. A bird's body temperature is high to begin with, around 102°F. In time of sickness it quickly loses this heat, especially if it is a small bird. Until you get medical help, a warm room is a must. Some bird owners find that hanging a lightbulb over the cage maintains the right balance of warmth and dryness. Infrared heat lamps are also useful, but be sure not to place them too near the cage.

During times of sickness, keep your bird as clean as possible. If there are secretions or liquids on its feathers, wipe them off immediately. These secretions are often infectious. If other birds are in the house, keep the ailing bird quarantined in a "hospital cage." Allow no contact between sick and healthy birds until all medical problems are cleared up.

Avoid store-bought medicines for your bird, such as over-the-counter bird antibiotics sold at pet stores. And don't listen to what well-meaning friends tell you concerning home remedies. Birds are highly delicate creatures, far more delicate than most other pets, and what cures one species may kill another. Get professional help in the early stages to avoid later complications.

Common Bird Ailments

Bronchial disorders

Bronchial diseases are common among birds and can be recognized by listening to the sound of a bird's respiration. Any signs of labored breathing or wheezing is a danger signal and should be taken seriously. If the weather is hot, heavy breathing may be a bird's version of panting, a reaction brought on by heat exhaustion or heat stroke. Both conditions are potentially lethal. In a few cases, respiratory ailments are caused by mites that live in the bird's air sacs. Whatever the cause, intensely labored breathing is always reason for concern.

Newcastle disease

Produced by a virus, Newcastle disease affects all birds and is potentially fatal. Spread through respiration and cage droppings, symptoms include nervous disorders such as convulsions, neck twisting, tremors, and paralysis. Diarrhea and labored breathing also occur. If symptoms appear, take your bird to the veterinarian immediately.

Colds and pneumonia

Cold symptoms in birds are surprisingly similar to those suffered by human beings. They include the familiar sneezing, coughing, runny eyes, runny nose, fever, and slight malaise. The best strategy when these symptoms appear is to keep your bird warm and let the cold cure itself, as it usually will. If symptoms worsen after a day or two, seek medical help.

Pneumonia, on the other hand, is a serious ailment that kills birds as efficiently as it does people. Unlike colds, pneumonia is a bacterial disease and can be treated with antibiotics, but only if you catch it early. In the beginning, the symptoms of bird pneumonia are much like those of a cold, only worse. Any indication of heavy breathing difficulty, coughing, and lethargy should be watched carefully.

Diarrhea

As in many animals, bird diarrhea can be a separate condition but is more likely to be a symptom of a more serious ailment. If your bird develops diarrhea for a day or so, then seems better, everything is probably fine. If the condition persists for several days, there can be a variety of causes—fumes in the air, chemicals, or a specific diagnosable disease. If loose or dark feces continues for several days, your bird is most likely sick. Get medical help. Before panicking, however, make sure the problem isn't due to something simple like poor diet or the fact that your bird is eating something it shouldn't.

Parrot fever

Parrot fever or *Chlamydia psittaci* is caused by a bacteria that affects most birds, especially cockatiels, cockatoos, and budgerigars. Highly infectious to humans as well as birds, the disease is spread through feces-contaminated food, water, and respiration. Symptoms include labored breathing, weight and appetite loss, and loose, greenish-colored stools. Afflicted birds may sit passively for hours in their cages with eyes closed, sometimes twitching or making strange twisting movements with their heads. Any bird showing symptoms should be taken to a veterinarian's immediately for blood tests and X rays. Be aware that humans are vulnerable to infection by *Chlamydia psittaci*, and that its effects can be extremely serious. Caution in handling is strongly advised.

Iron storage disease

Primarily affecting toucans and mynah birds, iron storage disease primarily affects the liver. Sometimes fatal, symptoms include diarrhea and lethargy. This ailment can be diagnosed with laboratory liver tests.

Coccidiosis

The prime symptoms of this contagious intestinal disease caused by parasites include appetite loss and runny feces. This highly infectious disease is spread by contact with the feces of other birds. If a cage is shared by several occupants, contagion can be avoided by keeping the interior of the cage meticulously clean.

Mites

These pesky creatures tend to settle on the bird's face and claws. Scaly face mites produce a crust around the bird's beak and eyes. Your veterinarian can diagnose this condition and prescribe insecticide lotions for treating it. Parakeets are especially vulnerable to mites.

French molt (BFD)

A disease of the feathers that strikes baby birds, symptoms include extreme and unexplained feather loss, especially in the areas around the tail. While the cause of French molt is a mystery, the disease appears to be passed on by mother birds to their young.

Accidents

No matter how thoroughly you birdproof your home, accidents do happen. The most common, perhaps, is when birds slam into mirrors or windows, smashing their heads and sometimes giving themselves severe fractures or concussions. When and if these collisions occur, take the bird to a veterinarian immediately. If the bird goes into convulsions, this may be a sign of brain damage. Talk to your veterinarian about what to do next.

Even for less serious accidents such as broken bones, professional treatment is still needed immediately. The bone must be set and cast, and in some cases pins are surgically inserted. Broken bones are quite obvious in birds, causing them to favor one leg, and to hop pathetically around the bottom of the cage.

In case of bleeding wounds, it is a good precautionary policy to keep a pet styptic pencil on hand. Styptic stops bleeding and to some extent disinfects wounds. If pet styptic is not available, a human styptic pencil, the kind applied to nicks when shaving, does just as well. One teaspoonful of alum mixed in a pint of water and applied to the wound accomplishes the same result. Dab the solution onto the wound with sterilized cotton. If blood is spurting, apply pressure as you would with a human wound until the bleeding stops. During the healing period, keep the wound clean and disinfected to avoid infection.

11

Fish

The Subtle Magic of the Fish Tank

There are pets, and then there are pets.

Some greet us at the door with a wagging tail and a newspaper in their mouths. Others rub up against our legs and sleep on the pillow beside us. We wrestle with our animals on the floor or hold out a finger for them to perch on. Some eat from our hands or from the community bowl. Most of them know us the minute we walk into the room.

But not always. A majority of pets are responsive, yes, but not all. Some are on the passive side. And the most passive of all are fish.

For the most part, people do not keep fish to play or interact with, but to look at and enjoy. They keep fish to admire; to savor their amazing displays of color and shape; to learn the lessons of pond, tropical waters, and freshwater lakes; to care for them, feed them, clean their tanks, keep them healthy, nurture them, and to then relish the truly sublime and restful sight of these beautiful creatures gliding contentedly back and forth in their underwater homes. Keeping fish is a contemplative, even meditative form of pet care.

And fish have their charms, too.

Some owners will tell you that the relationship between human and fish is not all one-sided; after a while your little swimmers come to recognize you, to know your shape and movements through the aquarium glass. Owners tell stories of how their fish greet them each morning with open mouths and flapping gills. Fish, they will tell you, have their own language, and their own interactive intelligence. They know when it is time to be fed. They know morning from night. They nibble harmlessly at your finger, and some claim this is as much from affection and recognition as from hunger. Fish make few demands. They are quiet and well mannered. You won't get asthma from their gills, or sneezing fits from their feathers. They do not bite; they never complain. For children, they provide ideal introductions to the mysteries and delights of the underwater world; they teach as they entertain.

Fish, in short, make fitting pets both for those who have other animals at home but who wish to add something more exotic to the mix, as well as for those who treasure living things but who do not have the time or inclination to care for more complex, demanding animals.

This chapter introduces you to the world of fish keeping as a hobby. It provides the basic information you will need to purchase an aquarium, set it up, maintain it, and stock it with an interesting and easy-to-care-for selection of fish.

The focus in this chapter is on freshwater tanks and tropical fish. Saltwater aquariums, the kind filled with ocean swimmers and marine life, make a remarkably fascinating hobby, perhaps one of the most fascinating hobbies in the world. Yet to set up and successfully maintain a saltwater tank requires years of experience and expertise, *plus* a great deal of money, *plus* plenty of room in the home and time to spare. If you have a hankering to own a saltwater tank, it is strongly suggested that you first begin with the freshwater varieties, learn all you can about this fascinating branch of aquarium keeping, then work up from there.

Setting Up the Aquarium

Here is a general list of the items you need to get your tank up and running. Some fish supply stores sell ready-made kits that contain most of the materials mentioned below. But be careful: expert fish hobbyists warn that these kits contain bottom-of-the-line materials in every category. They advise you to spend a few more dollars and, with a knowledgeable friend or trustworthy dealer, to handpick the items you will need for your future aquarium. We will discuss the items featured on this list in detail in the sections that follow:

1. A glass-sided fish tank
2. A hood or tank top
3. An aquarium stand
4. A filter
5. An air pump
6. A heater, preferably the submergible kind
7. A light source, preferably the kind that comes built into the tank top
8. Gravel for the bottom of the tank
9. An assortment of aquatic plants
10. Accessories:
    - Decorations—scenic photographic backdrops, rocks, figurines, sunken ship models, plastic plants—your choice
    - A siphon or gravel vacuum for cleaning debris in the bottom of the tank
    - Algae scrubbers for removing algae from the sides of the tank
    - Commercial dechlorinating liquid
    - Buckets and towels
    - Wire brushes for cleaning the filter and filter tubes
    - A net (Forget trying to catch fish with plastic containers or cups—it's almost impossible.)
    - Fish vitamins
11. An assortment of tropical freshwater fish to form a community tank

Tank

The tank or aquarium is *the* basic piece of tropical fish equipment. Serving as a home for your fish and a diorama for you, tanks should be chosen for their appearance, size, durability, and quality of construction. Make it a rule of thumb: always purchase the best quality tank you can afford. A solidly built, well-proportioned aquarium is the foundation of all successful tropical fish hobbying. Don't skimp on this one.

What size tank should you start with?

For beginners who simply want a small display aquarium stocked with a few brightly colored fish, a ten-gallon tank is adequate. But for those who wish to become actively involved in tropical fish hobbying, a standard twenty-gallon aquarium is preferred. These provide a relatively large, dramatic display area, and at the same time are small enough to maintain easily.

Larger tanks, the thirty-, forty-, and fifty-gallon variety and up, are also attractive and hold many fish. But they also require larger, more expensive filters and a good deal more looking after. In the beginning the ASPCA recommends that you start with a twenty-gallon tank, get your sea legs, and master the principles of aquarium art. Once you know your way around a tank and are certain you want to take on the extra work, a larger setup is then feasible.

Most tanks are plastic frame constructions with glass sides. Beware of tanks that are too tall or too narrow. If a tank looks oddly proportioned and out of balance, it probably is. The tanks you are likely to encounter at a fish supply store come in standard sizes: 2.5 gallons, five gallons, ten gallons, twenty gallons. While the most popular shape is rectangular, there are also hexagon designs that fit well in corners, as well as custom sizes and designs. Some tanks are made from a new material, polycarbonate, that can be molded with rounded corners. Beware of Plexiglas sides in a tank, however: it scratches easily.

When choosing an aquarium, weight must be given equal consideration along with external dimensions. Fish tanks weigh a great deal, even the smallest models. Note the following chart:

Tank size (gallons)	Dimensions (L × W × H) (inches)	Weight empty (lbs.)	Weight full (lbs.)
10	$24^1/_4 \times 12^1/_2 \times 12^3/_4$	21	170
20	$30^1/_4 \times 12^1/_2 \times 12^3/_4$	25	225
30	$36^1/_4 \times 12^5/_8 \times 16^3/_4$	43	345
40	$48^1/_4 \times 12^3/_4 \times 16^7/_8$	50	455
50	$36^7/_8 \times 19 \times 19^5/_8$	100	600

The figures in this chart are for relatively small aquariums. Larger models hold up to 150 gallons of water, and weigh around 350 pounds—*when empty!* The figures presented above, what's more, measure only the weight of the actual tank and its water load. Once the aquarium is set up this weight increases by as much as 20 or 30 percent from added gravel, rocks, filter, heater, base, and accessories.

It is, therefore, wise to go the drawing board in the beginning so that you do not have to return to it later on. Decide in advance which tank size best suits your needs and tastes, which room in your home will hold the tank, and where in that room the tank will go.

When considering these choices, remember that aquariums are best kept away from sources of direct daylight (or worse, direct sunlight) such as a window, door, or skylight. When exposed to direct light for even a week the inner surfaces of fish tanks act as a kind of petri dish, culturing layer upon layer of algae. The slimy green rugs that result are not only unsightly, but they are difficult to remove, even if you happen to have the right scraper tool. After scraping they then tend to grow back in record time. Direct sunlight also makes it difficult to control the temperature in a tank and to keep it fixed at a specific reading.

Yet another reason for placing aquariums in low light areas and using artificial light is that artificially lit tanks tend to look better than tanks lit by ordinary daylight. What's more, when situated near a direct source of light, the thick plate or double glass in a tank filters out the ultraviolet rays that are so important to a fish's health. Artificial light, on the other hand, and specifically full spectrum fluorescent light, provides ultraviolet rays in abundance.

While many tank kits come complete with artificial light attachments on the lid, this is not true across the board. Be sure and ask whether full-spectrum fluorescent lighting facilities are included in the package when purchasing your setup.

Exactly where in the room should your tank go? A location that affords easy viewing angles is best (arranging a tank too high, too low, or behind other pieces of furniture defeats its purpose as a display piece). If possible the tank should be situated conveniently near an electrical outlet. If it sits too far from this key spot you may be forced to deal with nests of extension cords stringing halfway across the room. You will also be cleaning your tank frequently, and will want to leave as much maneuvering room around it as possible. Place the tank in a part of the room that affords easy access from all sides.

Finally, there is the tricky matter of selecting a stand to hold your tank.

A 1×12-inch piece of pine board may make an excellent support for bookcases. But remember, the weight of these books is distributed along the entire length of the shelf. A fish tank concentrates all its weight into one small area, and this density of weight places an enormous stress on otherwise strong supports.

It is thus mandatory to make sure that the substructure holding your tank is built to bear the weight. Most commercial tanks come with optional four-legged stands or heavy bases, and both are recommended. By substructure we mean not only a table or shelf, but in the case of an especially large tank or an entire wall of tanks, the floor joists as well.

Sounds improbable, perhaps, but there are reports of fish hobbyists setting up so many aquariums in one part of their room that the floor bowed. In a few cases floors have actually caved in, creating quite a surprise, no doubt, for the neighbors downstairs!

Finally, note that since water is a powerful conductor of electricity, and since aquarium care involves a great deal of contact with wet surfaces, it is important that all electrical wires be in good condition, well shielded, and plugged into a power strip with a fuse.

Preparing and maintaining the tank water. For fish, water is air. It is atmosphere and environment. If the chemical balance of this water is off, your fish is off too. If the balance is far off, your fish dies.

Before you begin this hobby, therefore, it is necessary to acquaint yourself with the basic principles of water care.

Filling the tank. Water care rule number one: the water level in a tank should always be even. To accomplish this feat, place a spirit level on top of the tank before filling it and check for balance. If there is a disequilibrium, place shims under the tank or tank stand. Keep working with the shims until the water level is even. The idea is to nip trouble in the bud now, before the tank is filled. Balancing water levels later on when the tank holds twenty or thirty gallons of water can cause the tank to crack and is strongly discouraged.

Next, clean the tank carefully, then begin filling.

Transport water to the tank by hand with a clean carrying vessel such as a watering can or plastic bucket, or use a rubber hose connected to a nearby faucet; pet stores carry special indoor aquarium hoses built for this purpose. If you intend to place a decorative background on the back of the tank's exterior such as a photograph or colored foil, now is the time to set it in place.

Always fill a tank *in situ*—that is, when the tank is located in its permanent location. Never fill a tank in the sink or bathtub, then try to lug it to the stand. Chances are you will spill half the contents before you arrive, and in the process split your seams (and perhaps the tank too—assuming you can lift it in the first place). If for some reason you must move your tank from room to room, *always empty it first*.

Defective tanks are uncommon but they do come along. It is best to give your new aquarium the once-over at this time rather than later on when it is full of fish, and when even a small leak can ruin your day. Generally speaking, if your tank does not leak within the first twenty-four hours it is probably not going to leak at all.

Finish filling the tank a day or so later.

Determining water quality. Once the tank is filled, the quality of the water becomes your next concern.

What determines water quality?

Three things: whether the water is hard or soft, whether it is alkaline or acidic, whether it is clear or dirty.

In some parts of the country, for instance, tap water is soft, in other parts it is hard. This varying mineralization affects the water's pH—the balance between an alkaline environment and an acidic one.

As a general rule, soft water tends to be acidic (think of vinegar), alkaline water hard (think of salt). Tropical fish owners measure this all-important balance factor using a commercial pH kit. The scale in these kits runs from 1 to 14. Anything below a pH of 7.0 on the measuring scale is acidic, anything above it is alkaline. A count of 7.0 is neutral. Generally speaking, a pH of between 6.5 and 7.5 is best for most tropical fish, although certain fish require a more specific range of pH/soft-hard balance. Moreover, if the water you are filling the tank with contains chlorine, you may want to add several drops of a commercial chlorine remover, available at many fish supply stores.

Remember that if you fill your tank with totally clean, even chemically purified water, contaminants from the air, your hands, or the environment will still dirty the waters. And, of course, fish themselves manufacture toxins through ammonia wastes released as part of piscine metabolism.

Fortunately, the water in a tank purifies itself via a natural biological process known as the *nitrogen cycle*.

In a nutshell, the cycle works like this. A bacterial species in the water known as *Nitrosomonas* converts deadly ammonia wastes into a less dangerous nitrogen compound called *nitrite*. Then another natural bacteria in the water, *Nitrobacter*, takes over, converting the nitrites into a still more harmless substance known as *nitrate*. These nitrates in the water then serve a useful purpose in your tank's ecosystem, fertilizing and nourishing plant life.

The most effective way to encourage this cycle in your own tank is to remove and replace 10 to 25 percent of the water load as frequently as possible. Once every one or two weeks is ideal. Follow this easy-to-do rule and your aquarium will remain free from excess wastes of all kinds.

Note, finally, that the toxic presence of ammonia and nitrite in a tank is especially significant during the first few weeks when the tank is being established, a condition referred to as *new tank syndrome*. Once you get through this initial ripening and balancing, the nitrogen cycle clicks in and starts to run on its own, with better performance all around. This wonderful cycle of self-purification and self-feeding takes a while to get into full swing, however, which is why the water in a new tank should be allowed to season for a few weeks before populating it with fish. When the time comes to purchase fish, moreover, they should be added to the tank only one or two at a time every few days.

While waiting for the water to ripen, consider visiting your local pet supply store and asking about commercial water test kits that measure ammonia levels and pH balance. These kits are largely underutilized by fish owners, but they are a useful resource, and relatively inexpensive. You can also "seed" your new tank with helpful bacteria in these early stages by adding water taken from a friend's tank, or from tanks in the pet store where you purchased your fish.

Cleaning the tank and replacing the water

No matter how elaborate or powerful, don't assume that your aquarium's filter removes all pollutants. It doesn't. The process must be helped along with frequent water changes.

How often should water in a fish tank be replaced? Twice a month is acceptable, but once a week is better. Start the process by purchasing a siphon hose from your fish supply store, then every week or so siphon off around 10 to 25 percent of the water from your tank, and replace it with fresh water. Never remove all the water from a tank, by the way, not even to do a major cleaning. Again, 10 to 25 percent at each cleaning is adequate.

If your replacement water comes from the tap, allow it to sit in a bucket for twenty-four hours before adding. A twenty-four-hour "ripening" period eliminates most of the chlorine. A quicker method is to procure water conditioner from your local pet store and pour a capful into the replacement water. Water conditioners neutralize chlorine and other harmful chemicals on contact. They also improve the quality of tank water and protect fish against disease.

While you're in the process of replacing the water, clean the glass walls of the tank to eliminate algae buildup. Pet stores sell special abrasive pads and scrapers for this job. Be careful though not to remove all the algae in the process. It is best to leave bits of this organic material along the walls of an aquarium so that the fish can "graze" here for plant-based food.

While cleaning, you will also want to "vacuum" the gravel at the bottom of the aquarium with a siphon. Activate the suction in the siphon, then move the mouth of the tube along the bottom to suck up debris.

Your fish supply store proprietor will show you how to use this important device. Newcomers to the tropical fish hobby are often amazed at the amount of wastes and uneaten food drawn up by a siphon, even after just a week's time. Moral: if there is a single secret to maintaining a healthy fish tank it is this: clean your tank regularly, and replace 10 to 25 percent of the water at least once every one or two weeks.

Filter and air pump

Though some tropical fish can survive in tanks where the water is unfiltered, many cannot, and all prosper from living in a medium of pure filtered water.

A water filter in the tank serves several essential purposes. It continually cleans and freshens the quality of the water. It removes grit, uneaten food, waste products, and suspended particles that contribute to turbid conditions. It balances the gas exchange between the water inside and the air outside, thus improving respiration for the inhabitants. And it keeps the otherwise static water moving in gentle currents and ripples, a refreshing plus for all the tank's occupants including its plant life. Finally, by creating constant motion, filters eliminate temperature pockets in the water (too hot, too cold), thus helping to maintain an even temperature throughout the tank.

There are two types of filters: box filters and undergravel filters.

Box filters. Box filtration works by mechanically drawing water up from the tank into the filtration box, then pushing it through a filtering medium such as activated charcoal or polyester glass filters. This medium removes suspended particles and solid wastes from the water, then pumps the cleaned and aerated water back into the tank.

When using box filters, be warned: filtering mediums often become clogged after a few weeks' use, and must be washed and/or changed on a regular basis. Though some box filters are located inside the tank, the trend today is toward box filters that fit on the outer edge of the tank, and that can be flushed and brush cleaned with relative ease.

Undergravel biological filtration. This is an ingenious system that uses the cleaning action of live bacteria to purify tank water naturally, using the tank's gravel as a filtering medium. In a biological filtration system, water is mechanically circulated through the gravel with an air-pump or power head via a series of perforated plastic pipes set under the gravel. The bacteria that live in the gravel break down the wastes as the water passes through it, thus keeping harmful nitrogenous levels safe, and transforming wastes into nontoxic substances and mineral salts that are beneficial for plant growth.

Air pumps. Fish "breathe" under water by taking oxygen in through their gills and discharging carbon dioxide in exchange. This means that a certain amount of oxygen must always be present in an aquarium. Without adequate oxygen supplies, fish will literally suffocate.

Today many commercial filters automatically supply the bubbles and/or wave currents necessary for stirring up the surface of the tank's water. This stirring of the waters encourages an exchange of oxygen and carbon dioxide between the water and the atmosphere and helps aerate the tank. Filters that produce bubbles also provide viewers with a pleasant aesthetic. Contrary to popular opinion, the tiny bursting bubbles generated by a filter or air stone do not release oxygen directly into the water. They serve to agitate the water, which then expedites the gas interplay of water and air.

In a very large tank, or when a filter does not provide adequate aeration, oxygen must sometimes be added artificially by means of a bubble-producing air stone located at the bottom of the tank, and driven by an air pump. Air stones can be purchased from any fish supply store, and come in a number of shapes and capacities. When setting up an aquarium, consult with the personnel there concerning the best type of aeration setup for your particular tank.

Heating

For optimum water temperature control, use a well-made, high-quality commercial heater. The most common heaters are tube-shaped glass immersion models that contain a coil of resistance wire wrapped around a ceramic stem. These devices operate by means of an internal thermostatic switch that turns on an electric heat coil when the water temperature drops below a certain preset level. The temperature settings within the coil can be controlled by turning an adjustment knob on top of the heater.

Most immersion heaters fasten onto the side of an aquarium, turning on and off as needed all day, and giving out a warm, reassuring orange glow that is visible from across the room. To make sure the water temperature stays at the desired degree in your tank, purchase a small, inexpensive floating thermometer, place it in the tank, and check the readings regularly to make sure everything is on target.

When first adding a heater to your tank, start by setting the temperature to a low reading. Then, using the thermometer as guide, work your way to the desired temperature by making a series of incremental upward adjustments. In a large tank this process may take several days.

How strong a heater do you need for your aquarium?

Heating needs are rated by wattage. The standard convention is: 5 watts of energy are required for every gallon of water in the tank. To heat a twenty-gallon tank, therefore, a heater that puts out 100 watts is needed. Many people, it should be added, find 5 watts per gallon excessive, and maintain that 3 watts per gallon provides more than enough heat for their aquarium.

Plants and fish in a tropical aquarium both require water temperatures that approximate warm tropical waters. Around 74 to 84°F is the tolerance spectrum, depending on which species you keep. Within this broad range, between 76 to 78°F is the preferred temperature for most tropical fish.

Once the appropriate temperature level for an aquarium is established, keep it stable. Sudden rises or drops in temperature shock fish and plant life alike and under certain circumstances kill them. Anything above a 2°F fluctuation during a twenty-four-hour period is harmful.

A point to note when choosing tank heaters is that inexpensive models invariably contain low-grade thermostatic controls and thus break more frequently than better made brands. Be especially wary of "bargains" in tank heaters offered by pet stores as part of their introductory tropical fish package. It is always better in the beginning to spend a few extra dollars for quality equipment.

Lighting

Since fish, like most other animals, require light to live (just as aquatic plants require light for photosynthesis), the standard starter aquarium package comes complete with an artificial lighting system. This system often includes two small 15- or 20-watt incandescent filament bulbs built into the reflector.

For many fish owners this basic system is satisfactory. Incandescent light has a great deal of illumination power. It shows off fish and plant life beautifully, if a bit unsubtly, and makes the tank appear bright and attractive.

Like regular household bulbs, however, incandescent bulbs do not last very long, and they generate enough extra heat to raise the water temperature higher than you might wish it to go. Delicate aquarium flora do not take well to incandescence, and in some cases incandescent lights are actually harmful to species of plant life.

The solution to these limitations is to substitute full-spectrum fluorescent lighting for incandescence. Some tank covers come equipped with these long tubular fluorescent lights. Others do not. In the latter case you may wish to purchase a separate tank cover for your aquarium that comes with a fluorescent fixture built in.

The advantages of fluorescent light are several, though it sometimes takes a few weeks or months for its virtues to become visible.

Though more expensive than incandescent, fluorescent bulbs last a great deal longer than incandescent, and they are far more efficient with electric current. Many fluorescent bulbs are specially adapted for aquatic plant life, which means the plants in your aquarium will thrive as never before. Fluorescent bulbs come in several interesting colors, and the light they generate is more aesthetically pleasing than incandescence— more muted and colorful, more artistic and mysterious.

If you have any doubts concerning which type of lighting to use in your tank, visit your local pet store and observe both varieties. Then decide.

How long should an aquarium light remain on every day?

Fish require alternating periods of light and dark. Ten hours of light a day and the rest in dark is the figure usually suggested, though your own waking and sleeping schedule is probably just as valid a measuring stick. That is, when you get out of bed in the morning, turn the aquarium lights on. When you go to sleep at night, turn them off. Despite the hours-of-light timetables you may find in books on tropical fish, nothing more complicated is usually needed.

Gravel

Commercial gravel can be purchased at any fish or pet supply store in its original stony tones. If you prefer, colored and even multicolored are also available. Grain sizes vary from around 1–5 mm. Coarse gravel allows better circulation for undergravel filters. Fine gravel works well with box filters.

Many fish hobbyists introduce gravel into their aquarium before adding the water. Others find it more pleasing to terrace and rake the gravel after the tank is filled. There are no set rules.

The same is true for decorative rocks. Some tank owners arrange the rocks before the water is added, others after. Either way you do it, a thorough washing of *all* decorative materials is first required, and preferably two or three washings. Place the gravel and rocks in a bucket, and let the tap water run over them for a few minutes, stirring vigorously. Drain, dry, then repeat the same procedure an hour or so later. Keep washing the materials until the rinse water becomes clear and all traces of grit and dirt are removed.

Aquatic plants

The many uses of aquatic plants. Plants and fish are natural partners. They look attractive in the same setting, and they need one another if a harmonious ecosystem is to exist within the tank.

Plants also serve a number of uses in a tank, which may not be immediately evident.

Fish, for example, are naturally cautious creatures, and aquatic plants provide them with excellent hiding places. Fish are hungry creatures and take delight in nibbling leaves. Plants, on the other hand, live off the carbon dioxide exhaled by fish, and help keep the tank water clean. They also do their part in the photosynthesis cycle, exhaling oxygen and aerating the waters. And, of course, even the most humble water plant improves the aesthetics of an aquarium.

There are two basic types of aquarium plants: those that root in the gravel at the bottom of the tank and those that float freely on top.

Rooting plants propagate by sending out runners along the bottom of a tank that eventually become autonomous and develop into new plants. Floating plants display trailing roots that are very picturesque, but which sometimes grow so thick and tangled they require periodic cutting back.

Rooting plants are classed into two further categories, stemmed and stemless. The first category has an obvious stem at the center, usually with leaves growing along it and branching off it. Stemless plants are, as the term describes, stemless, with all leaves growing in clumps directly from the base of the root.

Planting. Before adding plants to an aquarium, rinse them off under tap water for a minute or two, then remove all dead or dying leaves. If you find eggs or tiny snails sticking to the foliage, scrub them off immediately.

Next, dig a small hole in the aquarium gravel. Wrap the plant's roots around your finger to compact it, then firmly insert the plant into the hole, letting the upper part of the root remain slightly exposed above the gravel line.

Once inserted, pull the plant up slightly, helping its roots to comfortably branch out into the substrate. Then press the gravel firmly around the base.

If the plant has particularly shallow roots, or if it constantly uproots itself and floats to the surface, fix it to the bottom by obtaining commercial anchoring devices from a fish supply store, and winding these around the base of the plant. Do not use lead anchors, as these leach harmful metals into the water.

While arranging plants, be careful of bunching them too closely together, and be sure all plants in the tank have at least some access to light, artificial or otherwise, from above.

Finally, as far as the planting process for specific aquatics goes, different species have different environmental requirements, and it is always helpful to confer with a fish breeder or knowledgeable pet store proprietor concerning the best planting methods for each.

How many plants should you keep in a twenty-gallon aquarium?

There is no set number, and usually, the more the merrier—up to a point. Certainly you do not want so much flora in your tank that it hides the fish. At the same time, a few meager green wisps floating here and there look silly by themselves in a big tank, and for mysterious reasons do poorly when isolated in this way. In general, it is best to start with three or four different, fast-growing plants, then work up from there, adding or replacing plants as need and appearance demand.

Maintaining your aquatics. It is important to check aquarium plants on a regular basis. Some flora spreads quickly in the tank and needs constant trimming. Other flora starts to brown or lose its leaves after just a few days. Why? Not enough light, perhaps. Or too much light. What about temperature? Is the water in the tank too hot or too cold for your particular species of plants? Is the pH too acidic or too alkaline? Chemicals in the water may be causing the trouble. Or you may not be changing your water frequently enough. Perhaps the filter is clogged or dirty. Or the plants are being choked out by other, more aggressive varieties. Perhaps their leaves are being nibbled by fish.

If you cannot determine why a certain plant is doing poorly, and if none of the above solutions solve the problem, consult with your local fish breeder, veterinarian, or tropical fish store expert.

What species of plants will go best in your aquarium?

Through the years a select number of aquatic species have been identified as the easiest, most attractive, and most affordable plants for freshwater aquariums. The following species fall into this category: they are inexpensive, attractive, accessible, and friendly to one another and to their fish neighbors.

Recommended low-light aquarium plants

Cryptocoryne affinis: Cryptocorynes are large, shrublike, highly decorative plants that are attractive enough to become the center point of any tank. A deep green foreground plant with pointed leaves and red undersides, *Cryptocoryne affinis* is one of the few aquatics that thrives in subdued light.

Cryptocoryne willisii: Cryptocoryne willisii is a pale, green-leaved plant with long, narrow, and wrinkled leaves that reach heights of eight inches in the tank. It is adaptable to many water conditions, including low light, and is very attractive when planted toward the back of a tank as backdrop.

Recommended moderate-light aquarium plants

Acorus (Japanese rush): A moderate light plant with long, spiky leaves. There are many varieties of this aquatic. Some are tall growers, others are dwarfs.

Anubias lanceolata: An unusual plant with heavy, shiny leaves that grow on short stems. This plant tolerates surprisingly small amounts of light, though it prefers moderate lighting.

Echinodorus: The so-called sword plant, echinodorus has long, sharp, pointed leaves that grow fifteen inches and higher.

Sagittaria: The so-called arrowhead plant is highly adaptable, attractive in both foreground and background plantings, and has long, straight green leaves.

Recommended moderate-to bright-light aquarium plants

Bacopa: A bog plant, this aquatic has bright green oval leaves and thick, fleshy stems that grow and branch widely apart. A fragrant plant, it is best planted in clumps. Bacopa tends to become stringy after a while and requires frequent trimming.

Ceratopteris thalictroides: Known as *water sprite* or *Indian fern*, this plant is an aquatic fern that roots well in gravel, grows happily in artificial light (as long as there is plenty of it), but must be carefully managed. If not trimmed regularly it grows several feet high.

Hygrophila polysperm: A simple, long-stemmed plant with bright green, ovate leaves, Hygrophila polysperm is attractive when placed in any part of the aquarium.

Limnophila: An import from Asia, this round-leaved, vivid green water lily–like plant is a surface floater. It grows slowly and adds a real touch of beauty and class to any tank. With enough light it periodically sends out beautiful bluish-white flowers.

Ludwigia: Commonly called red ludwigia and green ludwigia, this grouping of pale green and red plants with wide-leaf stem is a bog plant, not a real aquatic. It nonetheless does reasonably well in aquariums as background foliage, but only if there is plenty of available light.

Riccia fluitans: A commonly used floating plant, this attractively tangled green aquatic must be regularly thinned and cropped. It makes a nice decoration just about anywhere in the tank.

Accessories

Decoration.   Now that you have your tank, filter, heater, gravel, and plants in place, it is time to consider tank decor.

Some fish lovers are purists as far as furnishing their tank goes, and prefer a minimalist look. Others are artists who enjoy sculpting an environment, arranging the gravel into interesting mounds and terraces and placing porcelain figurines, underwater castles, and pieces of driftwood along the aquarium floor.

For those who follow the second course, rocks offer a special enhancement to any underwater tableau. Most pet shops carry a number of models to choose from—lava rocks, granite rocks, and colorful striated rocks with holes in them for your fish to swim through. Underwater rock gardens can be arranged into caves, terraces, tunnels, megaliths jutting up like a miniature Stonehenge. Some fish fanciers use silicone sealant to glue the flat side of rocks directly to the aquarium wall. This way a number of interesting overhang effects can be achieved.

For fish owners who wish to avoid the sometimes tedious upkeep of aquatic plants, plastic substitutes never decay, look amazingly lifelike, and are absolutely nibbleproof. Check the surfaces and contours of all plastic plants before purchasing, however, to make sure they are not too sharp.

A final note: If you do decide to place decorative objects inside your tank, especially natural objects like wood and rocks, be sure to wash each one of them thoroughly before adding.

Other accessories

Nets: A necessity when removing fish from a tank. Though it was mentioned earlier, it should be said again: do not try to catch fish with a cup or container. Not only is this method ineffective, but the hard edges of a plastic or ceramic container can damage the fish.

Water temperature thermometer: A mandatory piece of equipment for any tank. Check your water temperature at least once a day.

pH kit: Mandatory for keeping your water at the right alkaline-acid balance. Use this kit frequently.

Water conditioner: Useful for dechlorinating fresh water. Some people add water conditioner to their tank every few weeks as a general health aid for fish.

Tank glass scrapers: Useful for removing algae from the aquarium walls.

Plant tongs: When planting, tongs allow aquarium owners to position plants with precision.

A siphon tube with hand pump on one end: A necessary piece of equipment for removing water from a tank, and cleaning sediment from the gravel.

Aquarium brushes: An excellent tool for scrubbing hard-to-reach places in your setup such as the filter box or the inside of a plastic tube.

Buckets and towels: For general cleanup work.

Visit your local pet or fish supply store and talk to the proprietors about your particular aquarium needs. See what he or she recommends. Remember, you do not have to purchase every piece of aquarium equipment on the shelf when you are beginning this hobby. Work at it for a while, watch, and learn. Soon you will know precisely which tools you really need, and which ones you don't.

The Art and Science of Adding Fish to a Tank

Once the aquarium tank is filled and furnished, the equipment bought, and the plants in place, wait a week or so for the water to ripen. Then you can begin the pleasant process of adding fish.

When purchasing fish, make sure that your dealer removes them from the tank carefully and places them in a plastic bag filled with water taken from the fish's original environment. Some pet stores have an apparatus for adding oxygen to the bag, a procedure that looks something like inflating a balloon. With oxygen in the mix a fish can remain inside a bag for an hour or two without suffering harm.

Once home, place the bag on the surface of the water in your tank. Allow it to float freely for an hour or so, or until the water temperature in the bag equalizes with the water temperature in the aquarium. You may wish to open the bag as it floats and add a small amount of water taken directly from the aquarium. In this way your new pet is introduced to tank water conditions with a minimum of stress.

Finally, open the bag and let the fish swim into its new home.

When adding new fish to an aquarium, it is a good idea to follow some precautions.

1. Add fish to a new tank s-l-o-w-l-y. One or two fish a week is enough. No hurry here. Creating a community tank is a science. You cannot hurry the process.

2. Do not place too many fish in the same tank. Overcrowding is a primary cause of stress and disease. The general rule of thumb is one inch of fish per gallon of water in each tank. In other words, a twenty-gallon tank will comfortably accommodate twenty one-inch-long fish or ten two-inch-long fish. Note that during the first month of setup you may notice the water in your aquarium is turning a bit cloudy. This simply means that the good bacteria are proliferating and taking hold. Do not be alarmed. Cloudy water in the beginning is a good sign.

3. Mixing fish of various sizes in a tank can sometimes be a problem, sometimes not, depending on the aggression level of each fish. Consult with your dealer concerning which species of fish are compatible, and which are not. Certain tropical fish are beautiful to look at but highly aggressive, and they will chase and bite other fish. Some fish eat smaller fish. And so forth. Find out all you can about the aggression level of different fish *before* adding them to your aquarium. When shopping for fish, always tell your vendor: (a) how many fish you already have in your tank, (b) which species you own, and (c) how long you have owned them. If well informed, this information will help vendors advise you concerning which new varieties of fish to add and which to avoid.

4. If a certain type of fish is too aggressive for a community tank but it still captures your fancy, consider establishing a separate tank exclusively for members of this fish group. Note, though, that

some fish are even aggressive with members of their own species. Ask for help in this area.

5. Purchase fish of the same type in sets of three, preferably one male and two females at a time (your dealer will, hopefully, know how to tell the difference). This combination reduces male-on-male rivalry. Schools of a single colorful species tend to look handsome when kept together in a tank.

6. During the first few months of operation the mortality rate in an aquarium often tends to be high. Fish seem to die for no observable reason. The best antidote for this problem is to hold off adding new fish for a while, and to take the following steps:
   - Avoid overfeeding.
   - Make regular water changes.
   - Test your water frequently.
   - Keep the water temperatures at the proper levels.
   - Be sure the filter is working correctly, and that the water is adequately aerated.
   - Check regularly for ich and other fish diseases (see section on fish diseases below).
   - Be sure you are performing all tank-maintenance rules by the book. When your aquarium seems to be functioning properly, be sure to add just a few new fish at a time, and to avoid species that are known to be problematic and/or delicate.

Feeding Time

The first and last rule of feeding fish

First, last and always: *beware of overfeeding.*

No other mistake is more common among first-time aquarium owners, and few mistakes are as harmful. Novice fish owners especially fall into the "hungry little fish" syndrome. They watch their finned friends swim about the tank eagerly searching for food, and decide that the poor little creatures are starving and desperately need to be fed. Owners then shake food flakes lavishly onto the surface of the water, thinking they are doing their fish a good turn.

The result is that the fish overeat and promptly get sick. Or they eat until full, then allow the uneaten food to drift to the bottom of the tank where it quickly rots, turns to sediment, and finally to garbage. Uneaten food then becomes the primary cause of water pollution in the tank.

The irony is, spoiled food sediment is also one of the easiest pollution problems to avoid: simply do not overfeed.

Feeding schedules

Even if no food is available, fish still spend their entire day looking for it. This search is a necessary form of physical activity for fish. It forces them to breathe properly, and to exercise: to swim, dart, burrow, hunt. The less food there is in the tank the more exercise fish get looking for it. So again, as far as feeding goes, moderation, moderation, moderation.

How often should fish be fed? And in what quantities?

For a ten-gallon tank filled with, say, ten fish, a modest pinch of dried food sprinkled onto the surface of the water two or three times a day (morning, afternoon, and evening is best) does the job, especially if combined with a once- or twice-a-week feeding of live food such as brine shrimp or tubifex worms. As far as fish food goes, less is more.

What is the best type of food for your fish?

Most commercial tropical fish foods are excellent, especially for the types of fish that are likely to stock a beginner's aquarium. Be aware, though, that while most commercial brands have a hefty shelf life, they surrender a portion of their nutritional value over time and when left sitting too long they spoil. If you own a modest-size tank it is better to purchase small containers of food frequently than one large container that lasts for years but spoils in months.

As far as live foods go, these are optional: not absolutely necessary, but highly appreciated and very nutritious. Most fish supply stores carry a stock of such treats. Typical are tubifex worms and bloodworms. These come coiled in somewhat smelly clumps and are dropped directly onto the surface of the water. In a minute or two there is scarcely a worm left swimming. Those that do manage to wiggle their way to the gravel floor are soon scavenged by bottom feeders.

Brine shrimp, known universally to children as sea monkeys, are another favorite food, available at pet stores in both adult and egg form. These eggs can be kept in a dry place for a surprisingly long time, then activated in salt water and made ready for feeding. Other interesting varieties of worm and insect food also come in freeze-dried form: mosquito larvae, worms, shrimp. Check these out at your local supplier.

Keeping your fish well fed when you leave home

The sensible thing to do when traveling is to ask a friend, neighbor, or relative to care for the fish-feeding chores while you are away. Write down all instructions for the feeder in a conspicuous place, and make sure he or she has the necessary information concerning your whereabouts, phone number, and address.

When visiting your local pet store ask about long-term feeding equipment. There are plenty of feeding devices to choose from, including automatic food dispensers, slow-dissolve food cakes, food rings, tablets, and more. Finally remember: though tropical fish are enthusiastic eaters, the members of any well-nourished tank can easily go several days without eating anything at all if they have to. Some experts even believe that an occasional fast is good for fish health. If you are going to be away from home for a few days at most, and your fish feeder gets the measles at the last moment, don't panic. Your fish will survive.

Choosing Fish for an Aquarium:
A Catalog of Good Starter Fish

The first thing you may notice when choosing fish at the pet store is that the more interesting, colorful varieties often seem to be the most expensive. This is not always the case, however, though it takes some education before you learn the ropes concerning how to identify the beautiful fish that are also hardy and inexpensive.

All things considered, your best strategy is to put yourself under the tutelage of a knowledgeable expert. This person can be a friend or neighbor who keeps fish, or it can be the proprietor of your favorite fish supply store. People who work at tropical fish specialty stores are often avid fish fanciers, and many have encyclopedic knowledge of the subject. "I learned more in a ten-minute conversation with one of the salesladies at the pet store," one person told us, "than by reading a dozen books on fish care."

Under such tutelage, you will soon discover that there are wonderful-looking fish that come at surprisingly low costs, and pedestrian-looking fish that sell for hundreds, even thousands of dollars. You will learn which fish are difficult to maintain and which are easy. You will learn about starter fish, standard color fish plus variants (marble, albino), live bearers and egg layers; about fish that attack other fish, and fish that are peaceful as lambs; about fish that never stop moving for a moment, and fish that rarely move at all. You will learn about bottom feeders and top swimmers; transparent fish and fish with a fluorescent glow; fish with fantails, spotted bellies, and bulbous eyes; fish with colorful fins; fish that hide all day in the reeds; and fish that dart to the surface the moment you approach the tank.

Fish, fish, fish. The choice is vast and appealing, and anyone beginning this wonderful hobby has many treats in store. The fish listed in the sections below are mostly easy to care for, inexpensive, hardy, and available at a majority of fish supply stores. Again, however, nothing beats the advice of an expert. Whenever you have questions, consult with your local tropical fish supply store or with your favorite hobbyist.

Angelfish

A large and attractive fish, some mature angels grow to lengths of a half-foot long. Prominent in a tank with other fish, they are striped, have a roundish, disk-shaped body with long anal fins, and feathery dorsals that look as much like plumage as fins. There are silver angels plus varieties of black, marble, and zebra, some varieties with longer fins.

Relatively large, angelfish require plenty of elbow room, which means they need a tank at least twenty inches high and at least fifteen gallons, or better, twenty gallons of water. They enjoy having plenty of plants and vegetable matter in their vicinity. While Angelfish make gentle and amiable companions when swimming with fish their own size, they quickly eat very small fish and stray fries. At the same time, their long, trailing tails make a handy target for fish that nip.

Barbs

When you enter the world of barbs you enter a universe all its own. One encyclopedia of tropical fish dedicates thirty pages to describing the various barb colors and kinds.

A barb's average size varies considerably. There is the two-inch-long cherry barb, the six-inch-long banded barb, the seven-inch-long T-barb, all of which are extremely peaceful in a community tank. Barbs are, however, best kept in small schools of three or four; when placed one at a time with other kinds of fish, males can get nippy.

A sampling of popular barbs includes the following:

Rosy barb: The rosy barb grows about 3½ inches and longer and has a silvery color punctuated with pink. The males are brighter and more colorful than the females. Because they are easy to keep, rosy barbs are one of the most popular of all aquarium fish.

Cherry barb: A delicate, cute, and colorful little fish, cherry barbs are shy and sometimes withdrawn, preferring to hide behind foliage than swim in plain sight.

Clown barb: Growing to around four or five inches, the clown barb is a peaceful fish that likes to dig in the gravel for food. A bright silver color with a few thick stripes, it does well with a variety of other fish in a community tank.

Striped (zebra) barb: Originally from the warm waters of Malaysia, striped barbs are what their name states, picturesque zebra-stripe fish that grow around four inches long. They are extremely active, constantly on patrol, and require a fairly large tank.

Tiger barb: Probably the most popular of barbs, this enchanting fish literally has tigerlike stripes on an orange-tinted white body. It grows to be a little over two inches.

Betas

Popularly known as Siamese fighting fish, these beautiful fantail creatures come in a variety of wonderful glowing colors and are often the most striking fish in the tank. Because of their supposed aggressivity, however, betas are often kept isolated in small individual bowls. Though it is true that a beta will fight others of its kind, especially male against male, and though they may tear at each other's fins, they rarely go for the kill. Moreover, most aquarium owners find that betas actually mix very well with other fish in a community tank, and that they are gentle and well mannered when other betas of the same sex are not around.

Unlike most other tropical fish, betas do well in a tank without filtration, just as long as the water is changed regularly. They are hardy creatures that enjoy tubifex worms and brine shrimp, and grow to be from 2½ to 3 inches long. Colorwise, they are available in dark reds and metallic blues and greens, peach color with red fins, and occasionally, albino.

Betas are among the most beautiful of tropical fish, the least expensive, and the easiest to maintain. Like all other fish, however, they need their room. The custom of confining them to a tiny bowl is unnecessary and harmful to their well-being.

Catfish

Catfish make a wonderful addition to any community tank. They come in a variety of forms, sizes, and personalities, and spend almost all their time scavenging the bottom or sides of a tank, often at night, eating garbage that other fish won't touch, and generally minding their own business. Catfish are inexpensive, plentiful, gentle, and great fun to watch.

Try, for instance, a pair of aeneus catfish. The bodies of these peculiar creatures are armored with scale plates against attack from larger fish, and they have tentacles (barbels) around their mouths which, like all catfish, give them a distinctive and amusing muttonchops whiskers look. Coming in several color variations, aeneus sit for hours at the bottom of a tank apparently doing nothing, then suddenly they burst into motion, eating, wiggling, digging, dancing. Then, just as suddenly, they return to their motionless position. At times an aeneus may also hide in the tank and be difficult to locate.

Another favorite catfish is Adolfo's catfish, a small silver creature with a spiky fin. An excellent scavenger, its habit of digging in gravel is intriguing to watch. The same for suckermouth catfish, sometimes known as plecos, which slide along the glass walls of aquariums like living vacuum cleaners, sucking up algae and any available green stuff they can get their mouths over. Stripetail catfish, whiptail catfish, and armored catfish are all popular. Or try the really zany and exotic black-bellied upside down catfish that literally spends a majority of its life, as its name states, swimming upside down.

Since catfish tend to be drab in color and bizarre in appearance, they are often neglected or even excluded from aquariums. At best they are looked on as oddities and valued for their utility rather than decoration. At the same time, there are fish keepers who breed this fascinating species exclusively, and who find them to be among the most interesting, attractive, and engaging of all aquarium fish.

Danios

Long, with horizontal stripes or patterning, danios are favored for their energy, their sleek swiftness in the water, and because they are easy to keep and maintain.

Most popular is the giant danios, a four-inch-long swimmer that evolved over the eons in India where it still grows as long as a half-foot in the wild. Its body is decorated with two long gold stripes on a blue background (or some say two blue stripes on a gold background). Preferring others of its kind, danios make a gorgeous sight when swimming in a school.

Giant danios eat whatever you give them, but you better give them plenty. They have hardy appetites. Being relatively large, giant danios require a twenty-gallon and preferably a thirty-gallon tank to thrive. They are not terribly sensitive to water conditions, and are relatively immune to many fish diseases. Giant Danios and rainbow danios also do well in cold water.

Other types of danios include the pearl danios, leopard, blue, spotted, and especially the zebra, popular for its high energy and easygoing personality. All are pleasantly colored, well liked by fish hobbyists, and easy to maintain, especially when kept in groups of five or six.

Goldfish

Probably the best known and most popular of all aquarium fish, goldfish belong to the carp family, and are natives of the Orient, especially China, Japan, and Thailand. Here even today, they are prized for their striking appearance, and for their legendary value as symbols of longevity (goldfish in captivity have been known to live a quarter-century and perhaps longer).

Since goldfish are cold-water dwellers and do not require a great deal of maintenance, they are popular for use in ponds, fountains, and ornamental pools. To date, well over one hundred new varieties have been bred.

Goldfish basically come in two varieties, single tail and twin tail. Of the two, single-tail fish are less striking in appearance, but a bit easier to keep, and make ideal pets for beginning aquarium keepers. Among them are the common goldfish, found in several shades of color, as well as the orange comet goldfish. The bristol shubunkin bears a graceful fantail and a fascinating color pattern, starting as orange in the head regions, moving to gray in the middle, and ending a darker gray and black at the tail.

Among twin-tail goldfish, the bubble-eye and celestial are without dorsal (top) fins, and are noted for their huge protruding eyes and round stomachs. The fantail goldfish is a pleasant orange color, the veil-tail a striking white, sometimes with stripes on the head or the base of its tail. Even more exotic is the granda goldfish with its large bumpy head, elaborate tail, and speckled orange-and-gray body. Also fascinating is the all-black, bulbous-eyed moor, as well as the lionhead with its black-tipped twin tails and large, imposing orange head.

A well-equipped goldfish tank should include a variety of aquatic plants, all well anchored to the tank's substrate of gravel. Goldfish are tireless foragers, and will easily uproot any poorly seated plant.

Goldfish are relatively "dirty" fish and require constant water filtration. Avoid using undergravel filtration units, however. External box filters are always the filters of choice in any goldfish tank. Foodwise, goldfish are omnivorous eaters, gladly devouring either goldfish flakes or live insects, worms, and especially small crustaceans. Be careful, however, not to overfeed, and to clean the tank at least once every one or two weeks.

Rasboras

A member of the carp family, rasboras are hardy swimmers that get along well with almost all members of a community aquarium, and they are among the easiest of tropical fish to maintain.

Coming originally from Thailand and the Malay Peninsula, rasboras are thin, silver-colored fish, tinged with subtle shades of red, green, and brown. They can be purchased in several popular varieties including the scissortail rasbora, the red-striped rasbora, the harlequin, red-tail, and pygmy. The size of rasbora species differs substantially from the one-inch-long pygmy to the 4½-inch-long scissortail.

Lively swimmers, rasboras are most comfortable kept in schools and most often seen swimming toward the top of the tank, searching for food particles. They prefer plants that live on the water's surface and that are large enough to use as a hiding place. Rasboras will eat commercial fish flakes but far prefer live foods, especially insect and insect larvae. In fact, regular feedings with live food are a necessity if your rasboras are to be kept healthy and content.

Gouramis

One of the most popular of all starter fish, and one of the easiest fish to maintain, gouramis mix with just about any species, making them excellent occupants for all community tanks. They are enthusiastic eaters and appreciative of occasional live foods. Their one drawback is that over time they tend to outgrow small tanks, sometimes reaching lengths of a foot or more.

Fish in the gourami biological family are sometimes called *labyrinth* fish due to the labyrinth-shaped organ located in their head regions. This unique piece of breathing equipment allows these fish to inhale air directly from the atmosphere if necessary, a handy survival mechanism when the water level runs low. Gouramis come in a number of interesting varieties as follows:

Dwarf gouramis: The smallest of the species, growing only two inches long, they are subtly blue-green colored and extremely gentle.

The honey gourami: The same size, nicely amber colored, and quite peaceful, sometimes to the point of timidity.

Blue gouramis: These fish grow to be six inches long and come not only in blue but amber and whitish silver.

Kissing gouramis: Growing to almost a foot long, when two kissing gouramis are kept in a tank together they can occasionally be seen pressing their lips together in what appears to be an affectionate fish kiss, but which is actually a male-to-male dominance challenge.

Thick-lipped gourami: Untrue to its name, this fish does not have particularly thick lips, though from a certain angle its rectangularly shaped mouth gives this impression. Thick-lipped gouramis grow about three inches long, have few distinctive markings, and are unusually inquisitive and lively.

Swordtails

One of the most popular of tropical fish and a member of the live-bearing toothcarp family, swordtails are named for their long, sword-shaped tail that males sport to attract members of the opposite sex.

Bred in a number of colorful strains, swordtails come in red, piebald, silver, yellow, lovely mixes of orange and yellow, and many other combinations. They are perhaps the fastest of all backward swimmers, and often indulge in elaborate mating dances that are fascinating to observe.

Swordtails grow from two to four inches in length, depending on the variety. They are jumpers, which means that if your aquarium lid is not kept in place they may jump out of the tank entirely.

Swordtails take enthusiastically to commercial flakes, but they also love fresh food, especially brine shrimp. Be careful though: swordtails have ravenous appetites and will overeat. Don't overfeed.

Finally, swordtails are also among the more disease-prone of popular fish and should be watched carefully for spots, lethargy, and frayed fins.

Guppies

One of the most loved and best known of live-bearing tropical fish, guppies are attractive, hardy, and easy to breed. The females are larger than the males, measuring around two and a half inches, but they are mostly plain monochrome in color (the exception being certain fancy female types that come in subtle shades of color and with exotic fins). The distinctive fanlike tail fin, however, plus the wonderful array of rainbow colors that make this species so popular mostly belong to males. Interestingly, no two males guppies are ever quite the same in coloration, another feature that makes guppy breeding popular among hobbyists.

Guppies enjoy both live and commercial foods, and they seem to eat just about anything you give them. Most of the time they make good communal fish, though they may chase a slower fish around the tank from time to time, and older fancy guppies are known to eat very small competitors.

Guppy raising is a separate hobby of its own, and tropical fish enthusiasts often collect and breed their guppy families in several tanks. If you keep guppies segregated from other kinds of fish, a pinch or two of sea salt in the tank improves their mood. Don't let the pH in the water fall below 6, however, or the guppy's caudal fin will become ragged.

The molly

In the same family as guppies (life-bearing toothcarps), mollies are natives of Central America and the American South. They grow over four inches long and live for several years. Most popular among them is the black molly, a jet black swimmer with a graceful fan-shaped tail fin and small, daintily white-tipped dorsal fins. Black mollies usually (though not invariably) mind their own business in a community tank, and they tend to do best in the company of other mollies.

Mollies like their water hard and on the warm side—no lower than 77°F. If healthy, they join with catfish and other scavengers to keep the algae population in the tank under control, and are thus a useful as well as decorative fish to have in the tank.

Platys

Also a member of the live-bearing toothcarp family, platys are sometimes referred to as *moons*. They come originally from Mexico and Central America, and they are closely related to the swordtail, which hails from the same areas of the world. Beginning aquarium keepers sometimes mistake platys for goldfish, though platys are warm water fish, not cold water, like goldfish, and biologically they are derived from a different line.

Growing approximately two inches long, female platys tend to be longer than males, but males are more colorful, sporting a variety of shades of orange, red, and black with small, low dorsal fins, and a small but attractive back fin. Platys are active swimmers but quite peaceful in a communal tank. They also make excellent breeders.

Hatchets

A marvelously unusual-looking fish, the hatchet is a South American swimmer that displays svelte, winglike dorsal fins, and a large curved and dropped stomach that is hatchetlike in shape.

Hatchets require large swimming spaces and a low pH. They enjoy gliding along the top of the water, and they jump so well that if the tank cover is not kept firmly in place they may leap out entirely, and onto the floor. For many hobbyists hatchets make a peaceful and attractive addition to the community, especially when grouped in schools of four or five in relatively large tanks. Hatchets take well to commercial flake foods, but require liberal amounts of live foods as well to thrive.

Most popular among hatchets are the silver hatchet that grows to lengths of three and a half inches, and the marbled hatchet, a striped olive-colored fish that is about half the size of its silver hatchet cousin.

Loaches

A long, agile fish that is indigenous to Southeast Asia, loaches come in a variety of interesting colors, have underslung mouths and "whiskers" much like catfish, and also like some varieties of catfish, they are essentially bottom dwellers.

Active but relatively peaceful, loaches are shy when first introduced to a tank and may spend a good deal of time hiding, emerging only at night. Once they feel confident in their new surroundings, however, they come out from behind the rocks or plants at all hours of the day, and appear to enjoy the life of a community tank.

Especially popular among loach varieties is the clown loach, a striking, relatively large fish that grows to lengths of seven or eight inches. Its three black stripes encircle its svelte, light orange body.

The orange-finned loach is another large member of this group, reaching lengths of seven to eight inches. Its body is steely gray with delicate fins of orange or yellow.

The fascinating Pakistani loach comes, as its name states, from Pakistan and parts of India. With its long silver body and Y-shaped stripes, it reaches lengths of 4½ to 5 inches at maturity.

Much appreciated in community tanks is the dwarf loach. A handsome black and white spotted fish, it is relatively small as far as loaches go (2½ inches at maturity) and is often purchased in groups of three or four to form a school.

The chain loach, another smaller member of the group (in fact, the smallest) is strikingly marked in a yellow, brown, and white chain-link pattern and is extremely social with other members of its species.

Tetras

Coming mainly from Africa and South America (they are in the same family as piranhas), tetras have long, fancy fins and tiny teeth that are no threat to humans but can do damage to other fish. There are many species of these prolific fish. Most are no longer than two and a half inches, though the splashing tetra and Congo tetra sometimes grow three inches or more.

The cardinal tetra has electric blue stripes that stretch horizontally along a deep red body, making them one of the lovelier sights in any aquarium.

The flame tetra is a striking creature with dark vertical stripes overlaying a pink body. Flame tetras are friendly, communal fish that can be easily bred.

The neon tetra is much like the cardinal tetra in appearance. Its glowing blue-green, red, and silver coloration is a shade less impressive than that of the flame.

The black tetra is actually more gray than black. A common and hardy swimmer that prefers to inhabit the middle of the tank, it thrives in schools and in community tanks.

The silver-tipped tetra is likewise hardy and similarly prefers the company of other tetras.

The glowlight tetra has an orange stripe down its side that indeed seems to glow, adding a beauty to the community tanks it prefers.

The head-and-taillight tetra with its compact, diamond-shaped body is less showy than the glowlight but equally peaceful.

The bleeding-heart tetra is a subtle but striking-looking fish. It is a popular community swimmer that bears a single, deep red spot on its side.

The diamond tetra comes with shiny speckles on its side. When it swims it truly appears to be made of hundreds of tiny, flashing diamonds. The diamond tetra goes well in community tanks, but needs more elbow room than most other tetra varieties.

The Congo tetra is a lovely orange and bluish striped fish that is decorative but extremely shy. It should be kept in at least a twenty-gallon tank that contains other peaceful fish.

The lemon tetra with its flashy, yellowish green coloration adds a touch of drama to any tank.

Tetras look best when swimming in schools. To thrive, they require relatively soft, slightly acidic water with a pH below 7.

Maintaining the Health of Your Fish

Insuring fish health

There are three main strategies you can take to ensure the health of your tank.

Prevention. Clean your tank once every week or so, replacing approximately 10 percent of the water each time. Change the charcoal in your filter on a regular basis. Make sure your fish receive proper nutrition (especially be careful of overfeeding). Be certain there are not too many fish in your tank, that water temperature is within the acceptable ranges for your particular species of fish, and that the filter is strong enough to keep the aquarium clean.

Cure. If there are signs of disease in a tank, immediately isolate the sick fish, then talk to your veterinarian about appropriate medicines. A wide variety of medications are available for common fish diseases such as ich. Sometimes—not always, but sometimes—these preparations remedy the problem.

Be prepared in advance. The best way to spot sickness in a fish tank is to be well informed concerning the possible dangers. Sometimes the problem is simply the wrong combination of fish. When this is the case, certain of the residents need to be relocated to a separate tank.

Talk to your veterinarian or members of your local fish club about the best combinations for your community tank, and about how to identify potential health hazards. Read books on fish care. Seek the advice of experts. Visit or join a club.

Perhaps the number one way fish contract disease is through infection received from a new fish recently added to the tank. Even fish from clean, well-managed pet supply stores may carry contamination, and there are simply no watertight guarantees. At the same time, this danger can be reduced considerably by taking some precautions:

1. Talk to other tropical fish hobbyists. Ask which stores and dealers they recommend and which stores and dealers they suggest that you avoid. Where tropical fish purchase is concerned, word-of-mouth referrals are the best.

2. Check out the dealer before you buy. Is the store clean? Is the staff knowledgeable? Does the staff seem mainly concerned with profits, or are they genuinely interested in and informed about their stock? Are there many dead or sick-looking fish floating around in the tanks?

3. Do you see a number of tanks in the pet store with blue- or green-colored water? If so, beware: colored water means that medicine has been added, presumably because the fish inside have ich, velvet, or some other infectious disease (more on ich and other fish diseases in a section below).

4. Beware of buying cheap fish at wholesale prices from bargain sellers. Cheap fish are often sick fish. Stores that specialize in this commodity sell in volume and have little time to practice quality control. At best, you take your chances, and in general it is better to stay with suppliers you know and trust, even if their fish cost a few more dollars.

5. Quarantine any new fish in a special holding tank for a week or two before adding them to your aquarium. During quarantine keep the fish under strict observation, checking for spots, lethargy, and quirky behavior. If there are any signs of sickness, the fish should be kept away from all community tanks.

6. Before you add a new aquatic plant to your tank, carefully clean and disinfect it first. The bacteria and/or eggs on a new planting are common causes of infection.

7. Give your fish frequent visual examinations. Check them out, every day if possible. Be on the lookout for white spots, symptom

of the most common of all freshwater fish diseases, ich. For details see the section below on fish diseases.

8. If fish show signs of ill health, remove them from the aquarium immediately and quarantine them in a second "hospital" tank (the same holding tank you use to keep new fish before adding them to the main aquarium). You can medicate the ailing patient now without worrying that the medicine will affect the other fish (certain antibiotics that cure ailing fish can sicken or kill healthy ones).

9. Keep your tank as clean as possible. Scrub the glass frequently. Change the water. Flush the filters and replace the filter mediums often. Avoid sediments and pollution created by overfeeding. Dirty tanks breed sick fish.

10. If you are worried about bacterial or viral infection in the water, pet supply stores sell chemical water purifiers that protect against diseases like ich. Ask your dealer for recommendations.

11. It has been estimated that 75 percent of all sickness in a community fish tank is a result of stress. It is good preventive practice to reduce stress in a tank whenever you can. Stress among fish can result from overcrowding, poor water conditions, overly aggressive fish in the tank, and insufficient swimming room.

12. Make sure that your fish are properly fed and nourished. Do not mix unfriendly fish in the same community tank. If you see that a certain fish is constantly chasing and harassing another fish, place them in separate tanks. Provide plenty of plants for extra oxygen and as a place for shy fish to hide. Monitor water temperature regularly, and avoid sudden ups and down of temperature. Make sure the pH remains stable and check for ammonia levels. Avoid moving fish from one tank to another. Keep chemical sprays and harmful household substances away from the tank. Turn off the light over the tank for at least eight hours every night. Make certain the filter is clean and properly functioning. Keep all aquatic plants trimmed back so that they don't take over the tank. Avoid putting too many fish in a tank: overcrowding is a sure ticket to stress—and disease.

| \multicolumn{4}{c}{**Suggested Maintenance Schedule for a Freshwater Aquarium**} |

Job	Daily	Weekly	Monthly
Feed fish	Dry food 2 times or 3 times a day. Feed small pinches of food—only as much as the fish can eat at one sitting. Do not allow any extra food to float down to the gravel.	Optional: Live food once or twice a week	
Check pH	Once a day *during* the first few months	Once a week *after* the first few months	
Change water		Every one or two weeks	
Check water temperature	Every day, especially in the winter time		
Clean gravel		Vacuum with a siphon every one or two weeks.	
Plant maintenance		Remove dead leaves and stems.	Thin out and trim all plants when they become too thick.
	Check every day to make sure the flow is even and the filtered water is clear.		Replace filter medium.

Job	Daily	Weekly	Monthly
Health and welfare	Make sure fish are healthy and not fighting among themselves. Check their fins, mouth, and gills for fungus or damage.		

Symptoms of disease

Tropical fish are relatively fragile creatures, and even when well cared for may suddenly—and mysteriously—turn up ailing. Many fish diseases are incurable, most perhaps; but some can definitely be treated and many prevented. As usual, the keys are preventive care, early identification, and rapid treatment. General symptoms in fish that may signal sickness include the following:

- White spots on the body, or a whitish blue coloration
- Lethargy and unusual slowness of movement
- Signs of fungus around the gills
- Signs of damaged skin or shredded fins
- Constant hiding
- Rapid gill movement
- Lack of appetite: The fish shows no interest in food for several days.
- Impaired swimming: The fish sinks, floats, flits wildly, swims sideways or upside down, rubs awkwardly against the side of the tank, or constantly flicks its tail against objects in the water, as if to scratch its skin. The fish floats on its side, or upside down. Or it swims and/or floats at a strange angle, sometimes backward or tilted toward the side.
- The fish's stomach is swollen and distended; the fish's fins are frayed or deteriorated.
- The fish holds its fins flat against its body rather than keeping them erect and outspread.
- The fish shows signs of blemishes, sores, white or black spots, or ulcers around the fins, body, and mouth.
- The fish's eyes are clouded or have a whitish film over them.
- The fish's gills pump especially fast.

Dealing with specific fish diseases

If any of the above symptoms appear in your tank, take heed. These symptoms are most likely due to one of the following common tropical fish disorders:

Dropsy. The predominant symptom of dropsy is bloating or stomach distension. The fish's eyes, even its entire body, swells to such an extent that the fish resembles a balloon about to pop.

Less contagious than many fish diseases, dropsy appears to favor certain species, gouramis and platys among them. Current opinion is divided concerning what causes this disease and whether or not it is ultimately curable. At the first sign of infection, some experts urge removing the fish from the tank and disposing of it. Others maintain that a rigorous course of antibiotic treatment can in some instances effect a cure.

Fin rot. This disagreeable and all too common ailment often strikes fish that are already sick with another disease. It also affects fish whose immune systems have been compromised by long periods of stress brought on by changes in water temperature, movement from one tank to another, dirty water, poor nourishment, and so forth.

Caused by both a virus and bacteria, the symptoms of this ailment include a frayed and disintegrated look around the fins and an overall "rotted" look. If the condition does not clear up on its own after a few days, purchase a good commercial antibiotic from your fish supply store. Treatment for fin rot is much the same as for fungus (see below).

Fungus. Another common freshwater fish disease, fungus or *saprolegnia*, is a slimy, cottony clump of fibers that hangs on the infected areas of the fish, often around the mouth where it adheres to open sores. Fish that are constantly nipped at or that fight frequently with other fish tend to develop fungus on their wounds.

Fish with fungus should be placed in a hospital tank. Add two teaspoons of salt to the water. If the fungus does not go away in several days add another teaspoon of salt. If still no cure, ask your supplier for a good commercial medication.

Ich. Sometimes called *white spot*, ich (an abbreviation for *Ichthyophthirius*) is perhaps the most common of tropical freshwater fish diseases. Its predominant symptom is a rash of pinhead-size white pustules that cover the skin, especially the area around the gills. These pustules are approximately all the same size and shape. Sometimes they are confined to the gill area alone. Fish with ich often swim quickly and hysterically around the tank, rubbing themselves against objects to relieve the itching caused by the spots.

Triggered by a parasite that burrows deep into the fish's skin, if unchecked, ich quickly covers the fish's entire body, and death results. Ich is highly contagious, and if the ailing fish is not removed from the tank immediately the disease is likely to spread to the other inhabitants.

Ich tends to first enter a community with the introduction of a new fish. It is also theorized that the ich parasite remains dormant in many fish, and that it is activated only when there is a sudden change in water temperature—one more reason to keep the water temperature in your tank even.

As dire as the above scenario seems, however, if ich is caught early it is usually curable.

The first thing to do is to isolate the sick fish in a hospital tank. Increase the water temperature in the tank to around 80°F, and keep the thermostat at this setting. If your fish is alive after ten days, and the white spots are gone, consider it cured.

Commercial preparations for ich are available at fish supply stores and tend to work quickly and well. If you have questions about ich, consult with a veterinarian or with a knowledgeable dealer.

Oodinium (velvet). Sometimes called *velvet* or *rust*, the major symptom of this common ailment is an amber coloration that first appears around the dorsal fin and soon spreads to the rest of the body. Fish infected in this way often swim with a shimmy kind of motion.

Velvet is more difficult to cure and more persistent than ich. Quarantine the infected fish immediately in a hospital tank and raise the water temperature to around 80° F. The old-fashioned way of dealing with this ailment is to drop several pennies into the tank, and allow the copper that is leached into the water to cure the disease. While this method often works, if you have the ways and means to get to a pet supply store it's more efficient to purchase a commercial antibiotic medication such as Chloromycetin that is specifically designed to treat this disease.

Pop eye. Pop eye or *Exophthalmia* is characterized by a bizarre protrusion of one or both of the fish's eyes. Caused by hemorrhaging behind the eye, this condition is often brought on by simple stress. Fish that have been moved from one tank to another are especially prone to this condition.

Treatment for pop eye consists of isolating the fish in a hospital tank. Raise the water temperature to around 80 °F., then with a medicine dropper, add one drop of ammonia for every gallon of water in the tank. A twenty-gallon tank thus requires twenty drops of ammonia. Allow the fish to remain in the tank for three or four hours, then add new water to the tank and keep the fish under observation. When it shows signs of improvement return it to the tank.

Reptiles and Amphibians

Why Have Reptiles or Amphibians as Pets?

There are many answers to this question. The one you're most likely to hear from reptile and amphibian fanciers is that reptiles and amphibians are *interesting*.

Interesting to look at, interesting to handle, interesting to talk about and think about, interesting to learn about and show to others. They are interesting for scientific reasons and social ones as well. They make excellent conversation pieces, and they are invariably spellbinding to visitors, especially children. Indeed, to have a turtle or snake sharing your household is to have a window into worlds that are infinitely remote from our own, worlds of the swamp and the jungle and the cave. Though it is true that as pets reptiles and amphibians are low on the companionability scale, they are arch survivors in the long-time battle of the fittest, and from this perspective are worthy of both study and respect. To own a reptile or an amphibian is to own a tiny living remnant of our own infinitely remote evolutionary past.

Which reptile or amphibian should you own?

In this chapter, four categories of reptile and amphibian are covered in detail: snakes, lizards, and turtles (reptiles), and toads, frogs, and salamanders (amphibians).

Other more exotic creatures might be added to this list, but these are often endangered and sometimes dangerous. The four categories profiled below include the scaled and webbed animals you are likely to find at pet stores, and are likely to want to own.

Telling reptiles apart from amphibians

There is always the perennial question: what is the difference between a reptile and an amphibian? Though most of us studied this topic in tenth-grade biology, the particulars blur.

In a nutshell, amphibians are biologically defined by the fact that they lay their eggs in water, and that in the process of becoming adult their young undergo a transformation from one physical form to another (think of a pollywog turning into a frog).

As babies, amphibians are born and bred in ponds and streams. Once reaching adulthood they say good-bye to their watery cradles, crawl to the closest sandy shore, and spend the rest of their lives on land.

Physically, amphibians are cold-blooded, which means that their blood temperature goes up or down in a constant attempt to adjust to external temperatures. Their skins are moist but not scaly (think of a frog).They breathe with gills in the larval stage and with lungs once they are grown and living on land.

Reptiles, on the other hand, though similar to amphibians in some ways, have considerably different physical makeups and breeding habits. Some lay eggs like amphibians, others give birth live by incubating their eggs inside their bodies until ready to hatch. Reptiles that give birth live are known as *viviparous*; those that deposit their eggs in the earth are *oviparous*.

Physically, reptiles are dry skinned (or slightly moist), terrestrial (with a few exceptions), scaly (mostly), and cold-blooded (always). In the larval stage amphibians breathe with gills and develop lungs as adults; reptiles breathe with lungs from birth to death. Reptiles range widely in size from the two-inch lizard to the ten-foot crocodile, to the thirty-foot anaconda, and are found in practically every part of the world. Amphibians are considerably smaller, most of them the size of a frog or toad.

Choosing a reptile or amphibian as a pet

When searching for reptiles and amphibians, first determine whether you will acquire the animal from a breeder, shelter, rescue group, or pet shop. If you do plan to go the pet store route, know in advance that most of these establishments do not specialize in exotic animals, and that their knowledge of reptiles and amphibians is usually meager. You may luck out, of course, and find a salesperson well versed in these areas. More likely, you will be forced to rely on your own knowledge to help you make the choice, and/or the knowledge of friends or experts.

When viewing the reptile or amphibian for the first time, examine it carefully. Danger signs include scratches, cuts, mite infections, deformities, crusted eyes and nose, feces caked on the vent areas, wheezing or clicking sounds, and an overall sense of lassitude and lethargy. If you make sudden motions near the animal it should try to scurry away. If it sits there indifferently and does not react, it is probably sick. Keep looking.

When choosing an amphibian or reptile, think of the same practical issues you might face with any other pet: where in the house will I keep the animal? How much room will it take up? If there are children in the house, is the pet dangerous? Friendly? Indifferent? Does it smell? Does it make a lot of noise? How much does it cost to purchase and then to maintain it? Who in the household will oversee pet-care duties? How long does the animal live? How many years am I physically, financially, and emotionally prepared to watch over it?

Do some comparison shopping at several pet stores. Ask around. Be informed and take your time. If you find salespersons who seem to know their stuff, establish rapport with them and pick their brains. Let the search be a learning process as well as a buying trip.

What about providing health care for reptiles and amphibians?

Finding veterinarians who specialize in reptiles and amphibians, or who are at least well versed in their management, can be a challenge.

Start by calling the veterinary offices in your area and asking how much experience they have in caring for lizards, snakes, turtles, frogs, and the like. Find out what special training they have in these fields, and specifically with what type of exotic animals they feel most comfortable. Some veterinarians know a bit about snakes but nothing about lizards, or vice versa. Ask if the veterinarian belongs to the Association of Reptilian and Amphibian Veterinarians (ARAV). Find out if he or she stays in touch with local reptile organizations and societies.

If your local animal doctor is not comfortable treating reptiles and amphibians, locate a veterinarian near you who has expertise in this area by contacting the ARAV. (The contact address is provided in the Appendix.)

When purchasing your reptile or amphibian, educate yourself ahead of time concerning its environmental needs. Snakes and lizards are especially sensitive to extremes of heat and cold, and require precise environmental temperature controls. Some are better off at 70 to 85°F, others at 85°F to 95°F. Each reptile and amphibian also has its specific humidity needs. Jungle creatures require high humidity; desert creatures require low humidity. A hiding cave in a snake or lizard's tank is a great psychological support and often a boon to the animal's state of health.

There is also the matter of heat distribution throughout the cage. Reptiles have no internal mechanisms to regulate body temperature, and their bodies take on the temperature of their surroundings. This means that if a reptile is unable to move about freely in its tank, or if it cannot make the transition from more heat to less heat and then back again, its health may suffer.

For this reason experts caution against distributing hot rocks evenly throughout a reptile's tank, as was once the practice. Instead, they recommend that pet owners create *thermal gradients*, by positioning a heat lamp in one section of the creature's living space, and leaving the other sections cool. This arrangement provides reptiles with a hot spot to glide into and out of when the spirit moves them. Just be careful not to make the hot spot *too* hot.

Nutrition is always an important factor in maintaining reptile and amphibian health. Make sure your pet is being given the proper type of food in the correct amount, including fresh and live foods when appropriate. Water should always be available for snakes during molting season. Check the nutrition sections below for reptile and amphibian nutrition specifics.

Note that reptiles are prime carriers of the dangerous disease salmonella, a painful and occasionally fatal gastric disease that is contagious among human beings. Avoid this problem entirely by washing your hands after *every* direct contact with a reptile and amphibian and with its habitat. While cleaning enclosures, moreover, be sure not to touch your face or exposed skin parts (of other people as well as yourself), and keep reptiles in a separate part of the home away from all places where food is handled and prepared. If you stick to this routine your chances of contamination are almost nonexistent.

Finally, there are two key questions one must ask oneself before acquiring an amphibian or reptile as a pet: Do I *really* like this animal? Do I really *want* this animal?

If the answer is yes to both, then proceed. The following sections will guide you through the choices and techniques required for finding the right snake, lizard, turtle, or toad of your dreams and effective ways for maintaining it.

Reptiles

Snakes as pets

Few animals evoke such a mixture of fascination and fear in people as snakes. For thousands of years humankind's myths have portrayed these creatures as both demon and sage, devil and god. Some people even argue that animosity toward snakes is genetically built into the human unconscious, the idea being that our natural survival mechanisms steer us away from potentially dangerous animals.

Perhaps. Yet ironically, both at home and in the wild snakes are timid, retiring, and resourceful creatures that when brought into human environments take up a modicum of room in the home, are colorful and sometimes even beautiful, live for many years, and in a majority of cases are docile and well behaved. Although one would not typify snakes as being either emotional or responsive, many dedicated snake owners claim their pets recognize them when picked up and that they demonstrate their own subtle form of affection and attachment.

Of the approximately four thousand species of snakes inhabiting the earth, only eight or ten adapt well to captivity. Those that conform to human environments appear to enjoy being touched and handled, and, with some exceptions, get on well with other snakes.

Yet snakes have their own needs and idiosyncracies too. They can, for instance, be expensive and time consuming, especially the rarer breeds, and many take careful nurturing in the beginning to get them on track.

If you are interested in acquiring a snake as a pet, it is recommended that you become thoroughly informed on the subject before making a commitment. Start by finding out how large the snake in question eventually grows (you may be surprised). Find out what the snake eats and in what quantities; what its cage requirements are; how much space it needs; how well it lives with other snakes; and what it costs to buy and maintain. Talk to other snake owners concerning safety issues and how well your particular snake adapts to handling. Attend meetings of "herp" clubs ("herp" for *herpetology*, the study of amphibians and reptiles), and talk to the "herpers" there about your questions. A highly specialized and often complex hobby, snake owning should be well researched in advance and should never be approached on a casual basis.

Snake biology. With a few exceptions, snakes are born from eggs. Once hatched, they take around two years to reach maturity. In the protected environment of captivity they live an average of twelve to fifteen years, though there is considerable variation in this area. The python and boa, for example, have a considerably longer life expectancy than the garter snake and water snake. Some Burmese pythons live to be thirty years old.

Eons ago, herp experts tell us, snakes moved about on a primitive set of legs. Today they travel the earth and water by undulating their bodies or by using their ribs to push themselves along the ground. Snakes are found throughout the world and are able to survive in a variety of climates and terrains. Some are native to underground burrows, some to trees, some to desert and mountains, some to water and caves. Most are prettily colored and many highly so. Unlike a majority of animals that use their coloring as camouflage, however, the often gaudy coloration found on the backs of snakes is designed to stand out boldly against the blacks and browns of the earth, a warning to potential enemies rather than a disguise to elude them.

Snakes use their tongues as navigational devices, operating halfway between our sense of smell and our sense of hearing. A mysterious radar is at work that allows them to sense prey from vast distances and to blaze trails over the most hostile terrains. Like most other reptiles, snakes also shed their skins as they grow. During the shedding period they are especially helpless, and some even become temporarily blinded by their half-shucked skin. Indeed, snake experts urge owners not to bother their snakes during this sensitive time and to keep them as quiet and protected as possible.

Buying a snake. A point on which all herpers agree is this: unless you have government sanction, never attempt to bring a snake into the United States from another country. Many species of snakes are on the endangered species list today, and overcollecting has dramatically raised their chances of extinction. There are numbers of laws on the books governing snake control, both on a federal level and statewide. All these rules and regulations are targeted at achieving two basic goals: to protect the snake buyer from the snake, and to protect the snake from the snake buyer.

Unwitting buyers can, for example, purchase an expensive imported snake from Africa or South America, sometimes on the black market, only to discover that the snake is sickly, or that it does not fare well in human surroundings. Snakes uprooted from natural habitats rarely survive the first few months of captivity, and even if they do, the strange new environment makes them surly and neurotic. And of course, particularly poisonous snakes can bite and sometimes kill heedless owners.

Unscrupulous snake buyers, meanwhile, go to heroic lengths to acquire rare and exotic specimens from foreign places, frequently at the expense of that country's snake population. Laws designed to prevent such ecological and moral disasters are extremely complicated, especially when problematic snakes, such as pythons and poison vipers, are involved.

Some species of snakes can be kept as pets if they are bred in this country, but not if they are kidnapped from the wild. Others are forbidden entry into the United States no matter where they are raised. Some species are protected within their own country by the Convention on International Trade in Endangered Species of Flora and Fauna (CITES), but not in other countries. Others can be imported to the United States only if the buyer obtains an exemption. To complicate this exemption option, laws governing them differ from state to state and municipality to municipality. A snake that is legal in Montana may be illegal in Georgia, and vice versa. If you have questions concerning the legality of keeping a particular species of snake consult with your local Fish and Game Department, or with your local Department of Health.

The second point all snake hobbyists agree upon is that pet snakes should always be acquired from a known and reliable source. People who go into the woods or into their backyard, collect a garter snake, and place it into a tank—a practice which is definitely not advised—should be prepared for the fact that their pet will languish in captivity. And be warned: snakes from the wild carry disease. They may be injured, deformed, or otherwise unmanageable. Better to stick to the beaten path as far as snakes go, and acquire your pet from a reputable rescue group, or shelter, or from contacts with a local herp club.

Breeders and pet shops also do—or should—guarantee that their snakes are free of disease or malformation. Be sure to get this assurance in writing.

Of the two sources, stores and breeders, breeders are probably the better way to go. But there are problems, the most obvious being that breeders are difficult to locate, and hence prices tend to favor the seller's market, with fees on the high side. What's more, the demand for certain types of snakes is often so great you may find yourself put on a waiting list for several months.

At the same time, you are also most likely to acquire the fittest and most attractive snakes from breeders. And since raising snakes is the breeder's business, most people in this profession are veritable encyclopedias of help and advice.

How to recognize a happy, healthy snake. While the temperament and appearance of snake species differ, there are universal features to look for when purchasing. These include the following:

1. The snake's eyes should be clear and focused. When you reach down to pick the snake up there should be movement in its eyes to show it is aware of your presence. Snakes with dull glazed eyes that fail to respond to local movement may be sick or dying.
2. The snake's body should show no abdominal bulges, kinks, or backbone irregularities.
3. The snake's skin should be firm without any blemishes, cuts, or abrasions. Beware of scars; these may be signs of a serious injury in the past. Watch for skin lesions, missing scales, and loose skin. Also check the snake's skin closely for mites.
4. The areas around the snake's mouth should be free of mucus or bloodstains. If the snake's mouth is constantly open beware of respiratory disease or mouth rot.
5. The snake's vent should be clean and clear.
6. The snake should occasionally flick its tongue, especially when you examine it.
7. The snake should have a good "feel" in your hands—well rounded, solid, plenty of muscle tone, not too fat or thin, strong, generally well constructed.
8. The snake should appear to be comfortable and relatively unafraid as it slides and slithers through your fingers. Be wary of aggressive or unreasonably irritable specimens.

Housing. Different snakes require different types of housing depending on their size, temperament, and breed. For small snakes a glass aquarium with cover and light on top and perhaps a small heater is adequate. The aquarium floor can be covered with a variety of substrates including moss, tree bark, carpet, cut clay beads, earth, rocks, straw, wood chips, astro-turf or whatever materials are natural to the snake's environment in the wild. Avoid using cedar shavings; they are poisonous to some snakes. Be careful too of gravel in the tank, even aquarium gravel with its rounded stones; it irritates the snake's skin, and constant contact may cause abrasions on its delicate belly.

Sizewise, the rule of thumb is that a snake's home should provide approximately one half of a square foot of space for every foot of snake's length. A tank 36 by 18 inches is suitable for snakes up to six feet in length. For larger snakes, one quarter of a square foot of space per foot of snake's length is adequate.

In actual practice, a twenty-gallon tank is usually large enough to hold most small snakes. When choosing an aquarium, get the long size as opposed to the high or wide. A hinged, screened top or sliding Plexiglas or glass side is preferable. Even small snakes need all the crawling room they can get. Be sure the tank top is tightly sealed at all times. If your snake is an agile climber, a weight placed on the lid will stop it from pushing its way up and out to freedom.

For larger snakes more elaborate and expensive cages are needed. These come in innumerable sizes and prices, and vary from the homemade wooden crate variety to the slick commercial glass-sided, sliding door models. Whichever model you choose, be aware that snakes are escape experts par excellence, and they will take advantage of the smallest hole or chink in a cage to wiggle free. If you are the owner of a large snake such as a python or boa constrictor, talk to your breeder or pet shop staff about the most appropriate housing for your particular breed.

Many varieties of snakes like it hot, especially desert dwellers such as gopher snakes. Eighty degrees is about right. Other snakes from temperate areas prefer a climate in the sixties, and overheating can cause sickness and lethargy. The issue of proper temperature control is further complicated by the fact that most snakes neither require nor particularly like large amounts of light. Sometimes a fluorescent bulb is all that's necessary.

One good trick in this regard is to set up the lighting and heating sources in such a way that snakes are provided with hot spots they can crawl into when they need warmth (place a lightbulb in one corner of the tank, for instance), and cool spots for when lower temperatures are desired (a cave or rock overhang in the other corner of the cage provides adequate shadow and shade).

Known as *thermal gradients*, these adjacent cold and hot zones provide the cold-blooded snake with some degree of control over its body thermostat as the environmental temperatures around it rise and fall. Use an incandescent lamp positioned on the rim of the aquarium for best effect, or try combining the incandescent lamp with a full-spectrum fluorescent. Experiment with different wattage and light types to determine the best setup. Avoid ultraviolet lamps, however; unlike other reptiles, snakes do not require ultraviolet rays, and overuse discolors their pigmentation.

When a steady heat source is required for heat-loving snakes, a heating pad under the tank provides uniform warmth. Or consider installing a ceramic heater, the type that screws directly into light fixtures.

In general, establishing proper heat and light gradients in a snake's cage is a tricky matter, and it's a good idea to talk with your veterinarian, breeder, or pet store staff concerning the best climate control setup for your particular type of snake.

Feeding your snake. All snakes are carnivores, subsisting on living creatures of one kind or another: insects, fish, frogs, mice, birds. Since snakes are cold-blooded, the heat they generate internally is not needed to maintain a fixed body temperature. A snake's metabolism thus operates differently from that of warm-blooded mammals, and their digestive systems, unlike the ones we know in our own bodies, have the luxury of breaking down nutrients in the food s-l-o-w-l-y. For this reason, snakes require a considerably different feeding schedule than other pets. Once a week or once every two weeks is average, though there are variations.

Some snake species, for example, require food every three or four days. Others can go months without getting hungry. Feeding schedules depend on the size of the snake, its age, species, and individual predilections. Note too that snakes lose their appetite when shedding their skins. During this time they usually avoid food altogether. Beware, too, of feeding snakes cold food. They tend to dislike cold food and to avoid it.

Which type of food do snakes like best?

Animal owners accustomed to feeding a pet standard canned or kibble-size food several times a day often find it troubling to adjust to a snake's habit of swallowing prey live on the spot, then not eating again for a week or two while their victim is slowly digested. Feeding live food to snakes, however, is not mandatory, and in most cases pet snakes are content with prekilled prey. In fact, the habit of feeding snakes live food such as mice, then leaving the cage unattended, may result in the prey turning on the predator, biting it, and causing the snake a good deal of damage. In general, it is advised that snake owners feed their pets prekilled food.

A majority of domestic snakes prefer a diet of small rodents, especially mice. For larger snakes, rats are the food of choice. As far as the size of feeder rodents goes, the general rule of thumb is that a feeder mouse or rat should be approximately the same size as a snake's head. Some serious snake owners maintain rodent breeding farms to make sure their snakes receive fresh fare at every feeding. For the individual snake owner, a single mouse a week, preferably a newborn mouse, does the trick for young snakes. As snakes then grow older and larger their appetites grow with them, of course, and the amount and size of their meal must be adjusted.

Most pet stores carry a selection of mice and rats that are raised exclusively as snake food, then killed and frozen. Ask if your pet store carries frozen feeder mice. Frozen rodents are easy to handle, require no upkeep, and are ideal for snake owners who find live feeding too difficult a task. Frozen mice have almost as much nutrition in them as the live variety, and are a good deal less expensive. Some pet owners even buy frozen mice in gross, then keep their stock in the freezer until feeding time. If you do feed your snake frozen mice, however, avoid keeping the mice in a freezer for too long a time. After two or three months they tend to lose much of their nutritional value.

Note that certain species of smaller snakes such as garters and water snakes require a special diet of small amphibians, worms, crickets, or goldfish. Talk to your veterinarian and pet store owner about the best type of food for your particular species of snake. Note too that some snakes fix on one type of food, usually the one they were raised on, and refuse to eat any other. If this is the case, ask your suppliers what type of food your snake was fed on before you acquired it.

Water. Snakes are suction drinkers, and they test water quality through their sense of smell. They thus require fresh water on a regular basis, especially after eating. Even the dry and desert-living varieties need a certain amount of wetness to stay healthy, especially when molting. Supply your snake with a bowl of fresh water every day.

Snakes enjoy soaking, and they sometimes curl up in the water bowl, remaining there for hours at a time. The water bowl should be large enough to hold the snake's entire body, and sturdy enough not to tip over when it wiggles about contentedly. The more broad based a bowl is and the lower its rim the better.

Change the water in the bowl once a day if possible. If a snake is molting be absolutely sure it has a constant water supply. Many snakes use their water bowl for elimination purposes, thus providing another persuasive reason for keeping it clean. Salmonella is a lurking threat with reptiles of any kind. Be sure and carefully wash the water and food bowls at least once a day, then wash your own hands. Keep a separate set of sponges and scrubbers for the purpose. *Never* use the same sponges or cleaning implements for your dishes that you use for cleaning a reptile's bowl. Finally, note that the digestive systems of reptiles are sensitive to dishwashing liquids and soaps. When cleaning their bowl bleach is better, or better still, soap or disinfectant designed for cleaning reptile cages, an item usually carried by local pet suppliers.

Shedding. Snakes periodically grow new skins and shed their old several times a year. During this period they often behave in eccentric ways. They may, for instance, stop eating and become lethargic and withdrawn. They sometimes turn surly and unfriendly. Shedding is a very vulnerable moment for a snake, and owners should do all they can to make their pet's environment quiet and unthreatening. As a rule, older snakes shed their skin less frequently than young. The entire process usually takes from eight to fifteen days.

Several days before shedding a snake's eyes begin to become opaque. During this time it is best to keep all food out of its cage. The snake then passes through the skin-denuding process. This ordeal is over in a week or two, and the snake then returns to normal. To expedite the process a large bowl of water should be available to snakes at all times, and the humidity level should be kept high.

During the opaque period a snake also becomes blind, a condition responsible for many of its behavioral changes. A few days before the actual shedding process takes place a milkiness and dullness appears. At this stage it is a good idea to provide the snake with a rock or other rough surface for sloughing off dead skin. Ordinarily this skin comes off in one piece (make sure the old eye caps are sloughed off in the process). If this skin does, in fact, come off in patches, take the snake immediately to the veterinarian. There may be a medical problem.

Some snake owners help the shedding process along by placing their snakes directly into a bowl of warm water for ten or fifteen minutes at a time. Water relaxes snakes and helps then loosen their skin.

Tips on handling snakes. Despite their leathery feel and stoic demeanor, snakes are delicate creatures, especially smaller ones, and knowledge of proper handling is a must. Take note of the following techniques:

- Always hold a snake with both hands, one hand positioned at the neck just below the head, the other toward the back. Always avoid picking up a snake by its head or by its tail only.
- While holding, allow snakes to undulate freely through and about your hands at will. Never try to hold a snake immobile or pin it down.
- Do not handle a snake for at least a day after it has eaten. Handling can disturb digestion.
- Except for placing it into water, do not handle a snake while it is shedding its skin.
- Keep handling sessions brief, no more than a few minutes at a time. Always avoid overhandling. Being touched by humans is an unnatural experience for snakes, and too much hands-on time can cause them to become agitated and even sick.
- Keep young children away from snakes. If children insist on touching a snake, adults should hold the snake while children pet it. Supervision is essential.
- Most pet snakes do not like to bite and usually must be provoked, even goaded, into the act. Remain calm when handling a snake and avoid rapid movements. The main causes of biting are gripping a snake too firmly and making threatening movements near its head. Remain calm and the snake remains calm too.

Although a snake cannot actually be "trained" or taught "tricks," it does grow accustomed to its handler and to its surroundings. When familiarity sets in snakes tend to become docile and even—perhaps this is stretching the sense of the word—"friendly." They eat from their owner's hands, slither through their fingers in a relaxed way, and make no attempt to escape when set on the floor. The most important element in "training" is to handle a snake a little while each day until it comes to know you and the members of your household. As far as snakes are concerned, familiarity breeds content.

Snakes are common carriers and breeders of salmonella bacteria. Always wash your hands after handling a snake, and make sure children follow suit. Never—*never*—kiss a snake or any other reptile, for that matter, and never bring it close to your mouth or let it breathe in your face. When food is in the area, keep the snake at a respectable distance. When washing dishes, keep the snake's food and water bowls separate from your own.

If you are bitten by a snake, do not panic. Assuming it is not poisonous and its fangs are not too large, chances are the bite will be superficial and will cause no harm. Hold still until the snake withdraws, then immediately tend to the wound, washing it thoroughly and applying a disinfectant. If the wound becomes discolored or if it is slow to heal, check with your doctor immediately. Infection and salmonella are always a possibility with snakebites.

Types of snakes

Out of the hundreds of species of snakes that crawl our planet only a few take kindly to captivity. Those that do adapt to the human world, however, do so with great style and even apparent pleasure. Despite a snake's lack of emotional give-and-take, herp fanciers often have wonderful and sometimes surprising stories to tell concerning their pet's level of responsiveness.

When acquiring snakes, one should adopt a snake *only* if it is raised in captivity. Never take a snake from the wild. Consult with your local snake rescue group, or with a herp fancier, for help finding captive snakes that have a healthy background. Know also that though snakes raised in zoos under optimum conditions often set impressive longevity records, snakes raised in captivity usually have a considerably shorter life span.

The following section features a representative selection of the most popular snakes currently available.

King snakes. Among the most popular of pet reptiles, kings adapt well to captivity and are among the most amiable of snakes. Natives of Mexico and the United States, they grow to be around four feet in length—some longer than this—and live for twenty years and occasionally more. Among their seven subspecies, the chocolate brown California king snake is perhaps the most popular and the most accessible at pet stores and from breeders. The Eastern king snake, a bit more difficult to find at pet suppliers, is the largest of the species, occasionally reaching lengths of six feet or more. The Florida king is brownish with yellow or cream-colored scales.

King snakes are opportunistic eaters and easy to satisfy in the food department. They thrive on mice and tend to get hungry after about a week. Kings are persistent escape artists as well, and when in captivity spend much of their time searching for punch holes or loose-fitting lids to push through. Aquariums for king snakes should have high impenetrable sides and well-secured tops.

King snakes also like to be warm. Between 77 and 85°F is the right approximate temperature. They prefer at least one hiding place in their tank, preferably beneath several large rocks set one on top of the other to form a cave.

Milk snakes. Actually a kind of king snake, milk snakes are different enough and interesting enough to warrant their own place on the selection list. Their odd name derives from the old wives' tale that they latch onto the udders of cows and suck their milk, and also from the fact that they are frequently found in dairy barns feeding on rodents. There are actually cases of farmers killing these innocent creatures to prevent them from "draining" their dairy stock.

Red or brown with white or black stripes, depending on the subspecies, milk snakes live from twelve to fifteen years, prefer a dry environment in the tank, and thrive on a diet of frozen mice. Like other king snakes they appreciate a supply of rocks in their lair, both to stretch out on and to hide beneath.

Milk snakes are found across the entire United States, and are sometimes known as *house adders* or *checkered adders*. They are friendly, easy to care for, gentle, and after acclimating to their surroundings, they appear to genuinely enjoy the company of humans.

Rat snakes. One of the larger domestic snakes—they sometimes reach lengths of seven feet—rat snakes come in several subspecies including the Everglades, the trans pecos, and the Asian. The trans pecos is probably the best known and most popular of the group, though all three members have friendly temperaments and make amiable companions as far as snakes go.

Not long-lived when compared to the average snake longevity scale—most survive twelve years or less in captivity—rat snakes come in a variety of flashy reds, black, pinks, and yellows, and are remarkably impressive when stretched out to their full length. They prefer an especially dry substrate and enjoy plenty of elbow room in their tanks. Foodwise, rat snakes are a *constrictor*, which means in the wild they squeeze their prey to death. When in captivity, however, the rat snake readily adapts and is more than pleased to dine on a steady diet of prekilled mice. Rat snakes are among the most popular of all pet snake varieties.

Corn snakes. A type of rat snake—don't worry, designations and subdesignations get confusing in the snake world, and sometimes it is easiest to simply refer to variant snakes of the same species with different names—corn snakes are indigenous to the southern United States and come in a variety of color patterns including orange, gray and red with brownish patches.

A medium-size snake, corns grow from three to four feet long and occasionally longer. They do well on a diet of live or frozen mice, and like other rat snakes, they are friendly and gentle. Strong on appetite, juvenile corns eat as often as twice a week, and adults eat at least once a week.

The corn snake is a nocturnal hunter, and the light source over its tank should be dim and unfocused. Some people simply keep corns near windows and dispense with artificial lighting entirely. Never place corn snakes in direct sunlight. The indirect light of day more than meets their needs.

Pine, bull, and gopher snakes. Biologically and temperamentally, pine, bull, and gopher snakes are closely enough related to speak of as a trio. Native North Americans all, pine snakes populate a long swatch of the East Coast running from New Jersey to Florida. Bulls and gophers are found in the Midwest and West.

Bull snakes can be recognized in the wild by their five- to six-foot length and their attractive coloring of earth tones—browns, beiges, brownish yellow, and deep browns. Pine snakes are mostly brown and black, or white with dark blotches. They grow to lengths of six feet and occasionally longer. Gopher snakes are approximately the same size and are mostly light brown, dark brown, and cream, sometimes with various dark or rust-colored blotches.

All three snakes in this category are constrictor-type hunters, with voracious but not picky appetites; most are content with a diet of mice. An amusing side benefit of owning any of these three snakes is the loud sound they make when annoyed, a result of an extrusion of skin located in the throat that amplifies air into a crackling hiss on the out breath. Though intimidating to the uninitiated, this noise is a bark, not a bite (indeed, these snakes rarely bite at all), and for all intents and purposes the pine, bull, and gopher snakes make congenial, picturesque, and easy-to-care-for pets.

Garter snake. For many people who are brought up in rural or even suburban settings, garters are often the first snakes encountered in the wild. A native of North and Central America, garters are active foragers and require ample living room in relatively large glass tanks.

The common garter snake can be identified by horizontal light and dark stripes (of many possible colors) running along its back and flank.

The checked garter has long cream-and-white stripes attractively inter-spersed with checked black spots.

Inside the home, room temperature is usually fine for garters, with the ideal comfort zone ranging between 68 and 86°F. Garters enjoy a thermal gradient in their tanks as well, with one end relatively cool and the other artificially heated to allow for basking (see pages 370–71 for information on thermal gradients).

Garters thrive on crickets and goldfish and require a large supply of water, both for drinking and for bathing. When setting the bowl in the tank, be sure to place a water-absorbent covering beneath it. A wet sub-strate causes chafing along the garter's belly, which soon produces blis-tering and sores. Garter snakes grow up to three feet in length in captivity, and make hardy and interesting pets.

Pythons and boa constrictors. Large exotic snakes like pythons and boa constrictors (plus other varieties of anaconda) are for experi-enced snake handlers *only*. Both types of snakes require a strong snake-proof enclosure: even for baby pythons a fifty-five-gallon tank is just about minimum size. After a few years, owners must then build their own large glass and wood houses, or purchase a commensurately sized shelter for many hundreds of dollars. Both types of snakes require lavish supplies of mice, then rats, then rabbits, and eventually chickens to sat-isfy their appetites.

Boas and pythons are constrictor hunters. There is nothing wrong with this if your snake is two feet long. But how would you feel about having a fifteen-foot serpent that thinks you're a chicken, attempting to squeeze you to death as you wrap it fondly around your waist? Fatalities are rare in this department, but they do happen. Also know that zoos will not be interested in adopting a boa or python once they outgrow your home, budget, and commitment.

Last on the list of red flags, be aware that both pythons and boas are prone to a variety of strange diseases, some of which are extremely con-tagious to human beings, and worse, to parasites.

The list of caveats goes on, but you get the point. Pythons and boas are for expert and highly knowledgeable snake owners only. Don't let anyone sell you a bill of goods to the contrary.

Caring for a snake's health

Most of the serious ailments that a pet snake is likely to suffer from are not treatable at home, and must be referred to a veterinarian who specializes in reptiles. Snakes are hardy, long-lived animals, however, and most pet owners need not worry too much in this area, just as long as they provide bottom-line health measures such as adequate food and water, a clean, roomy cage, right amounts of light, a lack of overcrowding, and a controlled temperature. General symptoms in snakes that may signal sickness include the following:

- Skin lesions and blisters
- Red or yellow spots around the mouth
- Lethargic or withdrawn behavior
- Signs of mites (Look for crawling spots along the animal's skin.)
- Unsuccessful or half-finished skin shedding (Improper molting occurs when a snake is not growing properly, which in turn is caused by poor nutrition or lack of proper cage hygiene.)
- Signs of loose, greenish diarrhea in the tank

Snake diseases. Typical pet snake ailments include the following:

Mites: Snake mites live directly on their victim's scales where they lay eggs. These quickly hatch, perpetuating the infestation cycle. Unlike some species of mites, snake mites can be easily seen with the naked eye. It is a good idea to check your pet's entire body once a week for signs of infestation. Look for the mites themselves, small and brown, as well as a telltale grayish powder or dust around the eyes. These are mite droppings. Mites can usually be controlled by hanging a pest strip in the cage. Your veterinarian can advise you on which brands are best. Another method of mite control is to immerse the snake in lukewarm water up to its head for five to ten minutes twice a day, literally drowning the mites off its body.

Salmonella: Though it causes a painful gastrointestinal disease in human beings, salmonella bacteria is a common intestinal flora for many snakes. When handled a snake can easily pass this bacteria on to human beings. Moral: Always wash your hands after cleaning and handling.

Mouth rot (infectious stomatitis): Early symptoms of this highly contagious bacterial ailment include red spots on the gums and excessive mucus. Other symptoms may include a yellow spot in the mouth that generates a thick, viscous substance. If untreated, mouth rot eventually prevents snakes from eating. At the first sign of this disease, immediate veterinary care is recommended.

Improper skin shedding: There are times when a snake is not able to complete the process of shedding its skin. Occasionally improper skin shedding is the result of a disease or of a poor state of health. More commonly, it is due to overly dry conditions with lack of adequate humidity. Be sure your shedding snake has a large bowl of water in its tank, and that the surrounding humidity does not go below 50 percent.

Worms: If a snake's feces is green and watery, examine it for worms. Do-it-yourself home worming tablets are available from most veterinarian offices.

Respiratory disease: Snakes are vulnerable to a variety of bacterial and viral respiratory infections. Symptoms consist of listlessness, bloating, weight loss, excretions of mucus around the mouth, and open-mouthed breathing with wheezing sounds. In some cases of respiratory disease, the tines of a snake's forked tongue are stuck together. Respiratory ailments can be fatal, so act quickly. At the first sign of infection seek a veterinarian's advice and care. Keep the animal extremely warm, dry, and draft-free until help is available.

Lizards as pets

When lizards are spoken of most people picture the two-inch-long green variety skittering around the floors of pet store aquariums. In fact, there are more than three thousand varieties of lizards in this world, and they vary dramatically in shape, size, color, and habits. Some are practically as large as crocodiles; others are small as worms. Some eat meat, others eat vegetables, and some eat both. Lizards live in forests, deserts, mountains, swamps, trees, and holes in the ground. Some come out only during the day, others only at night. Most live on land, though one species in the Galapagos Islands lives its entire life in the sea. On the whole, lizards prefer warm climates, but even here there are exceptions.

A bit less exotic than snakes, and in some ways less problematic, the same reasons for owning snakes applies to lizards as well: they are interesting, educational, independent pets that make great conversation pieces, are fun for children, and bring us into a world far different and more primal than our own.

Lizard biology. On the evolutionary chart, ancestors of the creatures known today as iguanas and geckos originated during the Triassic period some 200 million years ago, making lizards among the oldest and the most successful orders of animal on earth.

A reptile in good standing, lizards are biologically related to snakes and are sometimes referred to among scientists as "snakes with legs" (only a herp expert, for instance, would know that the slithery, four-foot-long glass lizard is not a snake).

Cold-blooded, with a darting tongue and scaly skin that is regularly shed, a lizard's manner of locomotion is the main biological characteristic separating it from its serpent cousins. Though legless specimens like the glass lizard and red worm lizard do exist, a majority of lizards possess four stubby appendages that pump like little pistons when active and propel their bodies along the ground at remarkably high speeds. Some varieties of lizards have feet that are capped with claws. Others have feet studded with suction cuplike disks or hairs that afford them remarkable climbing agility. In Indochina and India, first-time travelers are often taken aback when they regularly discover lizards of one variety or another skittering up and down the walls of their high-priced hotel rooms or hanging upside down in the marble bathrooms.

A majority of lizards are insectivorous and require a large daily supply of live crickets, grasshoppers, and flies. Though not necessarily thought of in aesthetic terms, many lizards are in fact decorated with marvelous arrays of iridescent spots, stripes, and patterns, and as a group they are among the most colorful and handsomely ornamented animals on earth.

In the intelligence department smaller lizards like geckos and anoles are modestly endowed and cannot be trained to any extent. Larger members of this group, however, such as iguanas and chuckwallas can be surprisingly interactive with humans. Some even know their names and come when called to dinner. Generally speaking, certain of the larger lizards—not all, as we shall see, but some—make responsive, if somewhat stoic, companions.

Buying a lizard. In terms of habits and temperament, it does not make a great deal of difference whether a lizard is male or female, though males can sometimes be overly territorial. This is a good thing, as lizards are notoriously difficult to sex, even for herpetologists. If you do plan to keep more than one lizard in a tank, be sure to include lizards that are comfortable together in the same environment and that are approximately the same size. Cannibalism is not unknown in lizard colonies, especially when big critters are mixed with little ones. If both lizards turn out to be male, be sure that one lizard is not bullying the other or keeping it from the food.

When shopping for lizards, examine the animal carefully, both from a physical point of view and from the point of view of activity level and responsiveness. Features to look for in a lizard include the following:

1. Are the lizard's eyes clear and unclouded? Is there any watery discharge from the eyes or nose? If so it may be sick. Is the skin clear? Are there cuts, burns, scratches, discolorations, abscesses? Old scars may indicate old disability—be careful. Does the lizard's skin fit smoothly over its body, or does it hang in lackluster folds? Lizards with inordinately baggy skin are best avoided.

2. Are the lizard's vent areas caked with feces, mucus, or urine? Does it dribble or spot in any way? If so, it's probably sick. Do all the animal's limbs move freely and easily when it walks? Is there any distortion, disfiguration, or undue protrusion to its limbs, head, bones, or tail? Are its nails and claws intact?

3. Watch the animal carefully as it crawls around the tank. Does it move with unencumbered ease? Does its energy level seem substantial? When prodded, does it instantly react and take off? Are there any indications of lameness or wounds to its limbs?

4. Check for small black or orange moving dots on the lizard's body, especially around its neck and dorsal areas. Any sign of living beings on the skin is probably an indication of mites. Avoid infested animals. Not only are the mites harmful to lizards, but they quickly infect others in a colony.

5. Does the lizard seem alive and awake? When you approach it does it tense up and go on a kind of all-systems alert? If so, that's good. Beware of lizards that sit there dully when you prod them or hang like lumps when you pick them up. Dullness and lethargy are signs of disease. A healthy lizard is a sensitive and responsive lizard.

6. As with snakes, do not purchase lizards that are imported from other countries. Some species may be endangered. Others, because the lizard is not brought up in captivity, never adapt to human households and prove to be hostile and even dangerous pets. Many lizards bite, even small ones, and some inflict wicked scratches. Still others transmit diseases that can affect you and your household.

7. Before purchasing a lizard from either a pet store or a breeder ask to see the documentation on where the animal comes from and where it was raised. If you have any questions or doubts about the legality of a lizard's background, it's best to go with these doubts, and to do your shopping elsewhere.

Housing. Provide living quarters for a lizard that to some degree reproduce its native environment in the jungle, desert, or mountains.

For small lizards, a glass-sided aquarium with a well-ventilated, well-sealed top does the job. But be careful: even small lizards are tenacious escape artists and can unseat surprisingly heavy tank lids. They are expert at finding the tiniest holes or crevices to crawl through. Once a small lizard has escaped onto your living room floor or behind the curtains you may never see it again, and if you do, you may spend a day or three trying to catch it.

A ten-gallon aquarium provides romping room enough for two or three geckos or other small lizards; a twenty-gallon aquarium accommodates four or five (one rule of thumb states that five gallons of tank size should be supplied for every lizard inhabiting the space).

For some lizards, especially those from tropical climates, temperature control is necessary, and an external heating source mandatory. Ultraviolet light may also be required, as it is for many reptiles. Ask your supplier about lighting needs at the time of sale. (A mail order source that sells a variety of lighting equipment especially for reptiles and amphibians, including ultraviolet lighting equipment, is included in the Appendix.)

For lizards that need lots of sun in their natural habitat, light from a basking lamp should be provided several hours a day. Contrarily, some lizards are nocturnal, and too much light is damaging. A lamp timer is a good investment for lizards that require a set number of light hours and dark hours each day. A timer takes care of the light cycle problem when you must leave home for a day or two as well.

Another important temperature concern is establishing thermal gradients in a lizard's tank.

Thermal gradients are provided by maintaining different temperatures in different parts of the tank. For example, a heat-providing light is placed at one end of the tank, a shadowed crawl space at the other. Reptiles are cold-blooded animals and their body temperatures are controlled by environmental conditions. Thermal gradients provide them with some degree of control over these conditions and should be part of every lizard colony setup.

For floor-covering substrate there are a number of materials to choose from. If you keep desert lizards, sand and rocks do the trick; for jungle lizards, use moss and greenery with living plants to add moisture and atmosphere. When taking inventory at your local pet supplier you will no doubt find an assortment of reptilian tank items to choose from: reptile bedding and litter, lizard litter, litter bark, terrarium moss. You can add interesting objects from your kitchen and garden to the mix as well such as flower pots, crawl-in children's toys, cardboard boxes, rocks, and pebbles. Be sure to clean these items thoroughly before they come in contact with your lizard colony, but avoid using petroleum-based cleaners such as Lysol when doing the job.

If you wish to make your reptile's cage attractive as well as functional, think of adding decorative props such as driftwood, branches, photographic backdrops, hollow crawl-through logs, basking stumps, and—this is important—small rock caves or boxes with small openings in them for lizards to hide in and hang out in. Some pet stores carry corner cage waterfalls complete with miniature pumps and recycling water flow. Others offer large, complex climbing platforms. If you do opt for elaborate props, however, remember that these tend to become soiled as the weeks go by, and you will be obliged to disassemble them and clean them on a monthly basis.

For larger lizards a larger enclosure is mandatory. If using an aquarium, a hundred-gallon tank is not too large, even for baby iguanas or chuckwallas. As the animal grows, its home must grow with it, and eventually you will need to purchase a large professional enclosure or build one yourself. As with smaller lizards, a substrate of sand or soil goes into the tank, along with an external heat source plus recreational facilities such as rocks, crawl spaces, tree branches, and pieces of wood.

Feeding. Lizards fall into four eating categories: insectivore, herbivore, carnivore, and omnivore. As they grow and mature, their taste in foods may change. Some juvenile lizards, for example, start out as insectivores, enjoying a diet of crickets and flies, then become herbivores at maturity.

Diets for large lizards vary according to species. Giant members of the lizard group such as monitors and Chinese water dragons are carnivorous, and they require a daily supply of rats. Desert iguanas are herbivorous and thrive on dark greens, soft fruits, flowers, cactus, and grasses. Omnivorous chuckwallas are happy with vegetables, fruits, plus a daily supplement of crickets and worms.

When in captivity, lizards require vitamin and mineral additives, especially for the much needed calcium supply. A variety of these supplements is offered at pet shops. Vitamin powders or sprays can be sprinkled or sprayed on the food before feeding, or they can be fed directly in supplement form. If you feed your lizards insects that you catch yourself, be sure they have not been exposed to pesticides in your area. The breeder or supplier you purchase your lizard from will presumably have the feeding information and supplies necessary for your particular pet.

Water. As with any reptile, make sure your lizard has adequate daily water rations, and that its water bowl is heavy based and difficult to tip over. The bowl should also be large enough for the lizard to climb into should it care to take a bath or a soak. Some lizards like and even require frequent wetting.

Salmonella is a lurking threat with reptiles of any kind. Be sure and carefully wash a lizard's water and food bowls at least once a day, and keep a separate set of sponges and scrubbers for the purpose. *Never* use the same sponges or cleaning implements for your dishes that you use for cleaning a reptile's bowl. And always wash your hands before and after these chores, Finally, note that the digestive systems of reptiles are sensitive to dishwashing liquids and soaps. When cleaning their bowls a bleach is better than ordinary soap, and better still is reptile soap that you purchase from a local pet supplier.

Shedding. Like snakes, lizards shed their skins periodically. You'll recognize when the time comes by the fact that your pet looks like it's wearing a suit of clothes that's gone ragged and is disintegrating on its body.

When shedding time rolls around a lizard may alter color or otherwise exhibit odd behavior and strange physical changes. Lizards with moveable eyelids, for example, will puff out their eyes just before the skin dropping begins. Others become withdrawn or immobile.

When the shedding process starts do not by any means try to help it along by pulling at the animal's skin. Lizards know instinctively how to rub themselves against objects in their environment to get the job done. You can help some lizards out, however, by making sure that a large bowl of water is always nearby. Larger lizards especially like to soak themselves during shedding time, and these dips help their skin slip off more easily.

Tips on handling lizards. The best rule for handling small lizards like anoles is: don't. Or at least don't do it very often.

No matter how hard you try, it is extremely difficult to hand-train small lizards, and in the process overhandling can injure their delicate legs and heads. If and when you do pick up small lizards, don't panic if their tails go awry in a strange way, or even fall off entirely. A lizard's tail is segmented into sections that snap off easily when tugged at. This feature is natural to their order, and is a form of self-protection when predators nip at them from behind. If you happen to witness a lizard under attack notice how their yanked-off tail continues to jump and wiggle around on its own for several minutes after it is severed, a wonderful contrivance of nature designed to confuse predators into mistaking the tail for the body. The real lizard, meanwhile, escapes, and soon grows back a new tail.

Larger lizards take to handling more readily, but some species bite, and a few bite frequently and with lethal precision. As far as large lizards go, it's the better part of valor to know fully what you're getting into before attempting regular handling. All things considered, large lizards are an area of pet keeping that is probably best left to experienced and knowledgeable herp collectors. Certainly it is not advisable to purchase an iguana or other large lizard as a starter pet.

Again, lizards, like turtles and snakes, may be breeders or carriers of the salmonella bacteria. Always wash your hands immediately after handling, and make sure children do the same. Never—*never*—kiss a lizard, or any other reptile, and never bring it close to your mouth or let it breathe in your face. When food is in the area, keep the lizard at a respectable distance. When handling eating utensils, keep the lizard's water and food bowl well away from your own dishes.

Types of pet lizards

Green anoles. Anoles are small lizards, cute, fast, and fascinating to watch as they change colors and skitter about. Anoles perform this stunning act of aesthetics in order to blend into their surroundings, to camouflage themselves from enemies, and perhaps most of all, as an expression of mood. Enclose them in a cluster of green leaves and see what happens. Move them to a bed of sand and watch again. Fun. Because of these color changes, anoles are mistaken for chameleons, though the two are entirely different creatures.

Though there is no guarantee, some reptile fanciers claim that anoles can be trained to take food from their owner's hand. It is worth a try, though you will have to start the process when the animal is young, and then keep at it for some time. Anoles prefer a diet of live insects, especially mealworms or crickets which can be procured from pet stores or, if you're adventurous, gleaned from surrounding fields or even from your own backyard.

Anoles prefer that their cages be kept on the warm side, say between 80 and 85°F, so be sure a heating device is set up. High humidity is important too. Keep a few plants in the cage to provide humidity and mist them frequently with a sprayer. Anoles get their daily water supplies by drinking condensed droplets from the leaves of plants. In the wild anoles are thus frequently found in tall grass, on trees, or among shrubs and vines.

Chameleons. There are more than one hundred species of chameleon in the world, a majority of them coming from Africa, Southeast Asia, and the Middle East. All share the well-known characteristic of changing color.

When hiding in leaves, for instance, a chameleon turns leaf green. When scurrying along a tree or across the earth it takes on a brownish hue, while among yellow flowers it is yellow.

Blending is not the only reason for a chameleon's color change, however. Such sudden alterations take place in response to a number of environmental stimuli such as a loud noise, a sudden light, a rise or drop in temperature, or simply as a result of fear. The ability to assume different hues at will, moreover, is not exclusive to chameleons, and is actually a characteristic shared by several other lizards.

In size chameleons range from an inch to two feet long. Some large specimens have three "horns" on their head, giving them an exotic look, not unlike that of the prehistoric triceratops. While different size chameleons require different size tanks, smaller chameleons are comfortable in a ten-gallon aquarium with a screen top. New tank models that are manufactured specifically for chameleons with all sides made of screening are also available, but are not always easy to find. Since most chameleons are climbers, they appreciate a tree limb or two in the tank. Many species also enjoy having a hot basking spot in their tank, supplied by concentrated heat from a reflector lamp, and they generally prefer temperatures in the tank to be between 80 and 90°F. Chameleon setups also require a unit for supplying ultraviolet light (such as a full-spectrum fluorescent lighting unit that emits energy in the UV-B wavelengths). Consult with your supplier concerning your pet's specific needs in this department.

As far as diet is concerned, chameleons usually prefer insects, especially the ubiquitous cricket. Relatively slow-moving, chameleons dine on insects that they catch with a dart of their remarkably long, quick tongues. A knoblike protrusion at the end of this appendage traps the insect; the tongue then retracts inside the mouth, and the insect is eaten. Chameleons make intriguing and affordable pets, and several varieties can be purchased at most pet stores.

Geckos. Geckos are tropical lizards. They populate forests and jungles from the Mediterranean to India, and come in a rollicking variety of attractive forms and colors. Mainly insectivorous, they enjoy crickets and flies as a main course, and in some cases they are known to dine on tiny mammals such as baby mice. A gecko's meal should be supplemented with reptile vitamins including hefty supplies of calcium.

Mainly nocturnal, the leopard gecko, which grows up to eight inches and requires a dry, desertlike environment in the tank, is perhaps the most tameable and easy to keep of the group. The Madagascar day gecko, growing eight or nine inches long, is known for its spectacular appearance, green with red streaks, and is one of the few geckos that stays awake in the day and sleeps at night along with its human keepers. The tokay gecko is striking and easy to care for, but one of the more aggressive members of this group.

Most geckos prefer temperatures above 80°F, along with daily doses of ultraviolet light delivered by means of a full-spectrum fluorescent lighting unit (see the Appendix for source). Sand or gravel are both acceptable substrates in the bottom of the tank. Like most lizards, geckos need nooks and crannies for hiding, for making their strange cheeping sound, and for self-cleaning (they have the amazing ability to lick their eyeballs with their tongues). Be sure and provide an arrangement of rocks, plants, tree branches, and/or cardboard boxes in the tank with crawl holes cut into the sides. Geckos have special gripping hairs growing on their toes that give them acrobatic climbing abilities. They can easily scale the sides of any glass tank. A well-secured lid is a must for covering any colony.

Geckos breed easily in captivity and are sociable animals in general, though in their relationship with humans minimal handling is best. Males sometimes come to blows, but the worst that happens in such confrontations is a severed tail left wiggling in the aftermath.

Skinks. Skinks are small, long, snakelike lizards that propel themselves along the ground with mighty little legs. Some varieties bear their young live like mammals. Skinks constitute the largest of all lizard families, and come in a variety of sizes. The Western skink, for instance, makes a shy, small pet at five inches long, while the Australian blue-tongued skink is far feistier, befitting its length of two feet or more.

Depending on the species, skinks live on insects, small mammals, and/or fruits and vegetables. Many enjoy table scraps such as bite-size pieces of chicken or fish. Special reptile pellets are also available for skinks from pet suppliers. Like most reptiles, they also need regular supplements of vitamins and minerals, and especially a liberal daily supply of calcium. Plenty of water is a necessity, and it should be changed every day.

Depending on the species, sand, soil, or a mossy substrate is a requirement in the cage. Be sure to have a well-weighted top over the tank as well. Skinks will escape given any opportunity.

Most skinks prefer warm temperatures of at least 80°F.

Iguanas. Owning one of these fascinating and demanding pets is a quantum step up from keeping a terrarium full of four-inch-long geckos or anoles. Don't get the wrong idea, iguanas are among the most responsive and likable of pet lizards. It is just that they put hefty demands on both your time and pocketbook, and they can be temperamental and aggressive at times. Once you adopt an iguana and undertake its care and management, turning back is nearly impossible. As any herp fancier will tell you, trying to find a home for a mature six-foot-long reptile is as challenging as climbing Mt. Everest. Having an iguana, in short, is a major commitment similar to owning a dog or cat.

To begin, you will require a large cage to accommodate your new pet. Iguanas, and lizards in general, are roaming animals that require plenty of space for climbing and running. As a rule of thumb, a large lizard of any kind requires a space roughly twice as long as its body length, and preferably longer. Forget about using glass aquariums for this purpose. Only the largest are sizeable enough to hold a growing iguana, and large glass models are not only expensive but, not having the most discriminating vision, iguanas can injure themselves by ramming up against their glass walls. Wire cages or combination cages of wire and wood are best. Talk to your supplier about the options and brands.

Coming from an equatorial climate, iguanas like it hot, preferably 82–87°F. Thermal gradients are essential for their survival, and at least one basking spot should be set up in their cage using an incandescent bulb with a reflector (be sure to place a screen between the animal and the bulb; iguanas often burn themselves on lightbulbs). A full-spectrum lighting unit that emits ultraviolet light is also necessary; without it iguanas wither and die. Fluorescent ultraviolet light tubes are available from most pet stores or from mail order suppliers (see the Appendix for the address of an ultraviolet unit distributor).

Along with artificial light, iguanas need a certain number of dark hours at night, and they become stressed if denied this rest. Cover their cage at night and allow this cover to remain in place for at least eight hours.

Let your iguana out of its cage at least once a day and encourage it to roam around the room. Climbing creatures by nature, they appreciate a thick branch for climbing on in their daily exercise. Iguanas take well to taming, and if handled at least a half-hour a day they become docile with everyone in the household.

Do be careful of their claws, though. Iguana nails are razor sharp. While your reptilian friend may not mean any harm when it reaches out to pat you with its paw, you may still end up with several bloody scratches. Trim your iguana's nails at home with a regular nail clippers when it is young. As the creature matures, doing this at-home clipping becomes increasingly problematic. Though some intrepid owners employ the guillotine variety of cutter used to trim dogs' and large birds' nails, the more conservative route is to take your pet to the nearest veterinarian for a professional trimming job every few months.

When feeding time comes around, reptile pellets sold at pet supply stores contain all the nutrients the average iguana needs. Supplement these pellets lavishly with turnips, leaves, and flowers (avoid spinach, lettuce, and cabbage) plus a liberal sampling of pears, bananas, grapes, strawberries, cantaloupe chunks, alfalfa, acorn squash (the pulpy parts), hibiscus flowers, sprouts, peas, grated carrots, zucchini, tomatoes, sweet potatoes, and green beans. A little bran cereal or wet dog kibble can also be added. Vitamin and calcium supplements are recommended, along with small amounts of brewer's yeast sprinkled on top of the day's portion.

One small but important point to note about iguana nutrition is that iguanas should be fed in the late morning after they have a chance to warm up. If fed at night when they have cooled down, their digestion becomes prolonged.

Chuckwalla. Chuckwalla lizards are native to the prairies of the southwestern United States, and they prefer to do their hunting in high, rocky country. When threatened by danger they have the strange and surprising ability to crawl into small crevices and inflate their bodies like balloons, wedging themselves into tight spots in the rock and making it impossible for predators to dislodge them.

The average chuckwalla grows to about a foot in length, large enough to qualify as a "walkable" pet, small enough to remain unintimidating. Being denizens of the desert, their tank should have at least one-hundred-gallon capacity for moving room, and it should simulate a desert environment as closely as possible. Chucks prefer their humidity very low with desertlike temperatures (from 85 to 105°F). A heating pad placed under the tank helps in this regard. Be especially careful of exposing the chuck to sudden drafts, cold outdoor breezes from doors and windows, and dramatic fluctuations in temperature.

Chucks also require long stretches of direct light, say twelve to fourteen hours at a time, and plenty of ultraviolet rays. (See the section above on housing for information on artificial light in reptile tanks.) Three inches of clean playground sand provides a solid substrate for chucks and helps them feel at home, as do flat rocks for basking and artificial "cave" formations for hiding and inflating themselves (just be sure the rocks can be dismantled in case your pet gets itself too well dug in). A cholla cactus skeleton or two adds atmosphere. A large, clean bowl of water should always be kept filled and in the tank.

Dietwise, chuckwallas are mostly herbivorous, though they occasionally dine on crickets and worms. As a daily diet they prefer reptile pellets along with servings of dark leafy greens (dandelion, collard, mustard, turnip), carrots, parsley, squash, orange peppers, tomatoes, soft fruits (like bananas and pears), flower heads (hibiscus, rose, geranium, nasturtium), cactus meat, and prickly pear. Complement these with a good multivitamin plus daily supplements of calcium.

Chucks are among the most responsive and pleasant of large lizards. With plenty of contact they come to know their handlers and respond to them in kind, sometimes in surprisingly intelligent ways.

Caring for a lizard's health

Like most reptiles, lizards are naturally tough creatures and rarely turn sick in the wild. When in captivity, however, their immune systems are less active, and they become more prone to disease. Still, most lizard owners find that if they provide proper tank accommodations, handling, hygiene, and nutrition, their pets stay healthy and happy all their lives. Again, it is a question of sanitation, environment, and care: appropriate food and water, a clean, roomy cage, proper lighting and humidity, and thermal gradations.

Symptoms that may indicate disease in a lizard include the following:

- Dull, apathetic behavior. The lizard seems half-asleep much of the time. Even when prodded he does not move.

- Mites crawling on the skin, also signs of mite infestation such as small, brown droppings on the body.
- Frothy mucus around the mouth and nose.
- Spots on the skin and any kind of skin discoloration, welt, sore, or abscess.
- Labored, rattling, or open-mouthed breathing. Respiratory disease in a lizard will sometimes cause him to make a strange bark-like sound.

The ailments lizards are most likely to come down with include the following:

Respiratory infections: Reptiles in general are prone to a variety of respiratory infections, many of which present in the same way, and lizards are no exception. Symptoms include weight loss, decreased appetite, bloating, bubbly mucus at the mouth, and especially gaping, open-mouthed breathing, sometimes with an audible wheezing or barking sound. The lizard's head is often raised at a peculiar angle to facilitate breathing. Respiratory disease is difficult to treat in lizards and requires veterinarian treatments with antibiotics. Be sure to keep the animal warm and dry while it is convalescing.

Mites: Mites live directly on the lizard's skin. They lay eggs there and these quickly hatch, perpetuating the infestation cycle. Check a lizard's entire body once a week for signs of infestation. Look for the mites themselves and for their droppings. Mites can be controlled by hanging a pest strip in the lizard's cage. Your veterinarian will advise you on which brands are best for the job. Another method of pest control is to immerse the lizard in a bath of lukewarm water up to the head for around five to ten minutes twice a day. This way you literally drown the mites off the lizard's body. (Note that certain desert lizards are not bathers and will not take to this method of treatment.)

Rectal plugs: A rectal plug is any type of food or object that gets lodged in a lizard's digestive system. A fairly common problem among reptiles, you will know it is happening when your pet stops eliminating or eliminates in sparse, infrequent amounts. The method of choice for opening a rectal plug is to soak the lizard in lukewarm water for fifteen to thirty minutes a day, and then work the plug out with an oiled cotton swab. Considering the delicacy of this operation, the job is probably best handled by a veterinarian.

Turtles as pets

The humble, ancient, and beloved turtle. Hero of so many myths. Character in so many comic strips. First pet for so many animal-loving children through the ages. There is, perhaps, no creature that is less demanding and better behaved as a pet; no animal that asks so little of its keepers and of the hands that feed it. Yet though they are stolid and independent, turtles have their own beguiling ways about them, and of relating to human beings. Over the months and years, a rapport often arises between human and reptile that is both tangible and touching. Like all creatures on this earth, turtles have their own story to tell; and for those with the patience and ears to listen, it is one worth hearing.

Turtle biology

The earliest turtles evolved over 175 million years ago, predating most of the large dinosaur species that followed. As one of the more successful products of animal evolution, early turtles developed into two major branches, the land-going variety (tortoises), and the sea-going variety. This division remains unchanged today.

The main identifying feature of the nearly three hundred species of turtles in the world today are their picturesque boxlike shells that afford them protection and privacy, and out of which protrude four stumpy legs attached to a soft inner body. From a distance this shell appears to be a hard, seamless encasement. Closer inspection reveals many plates of bone joined together into a single solid covering, which is then fused directly onto the turtle's backbone, shoulder, and hips. Capable of withstanding enormous shocks and weights, this shell is so ingeniously constructed, and is made of such resistant materials, that when certain species of turtle die their shells remain hard and intact for literally thousands of years.

Being reptiles in good standing, tortoises and aquatic turtles alike lay their eggs on land, sometimes in batches of 150 eggs or more. These eggs hatch according to varying timetables, then produce an army of young turtles, some of which, should they survive their many bird, mammal, and reptile predators, live to be more than one hundred years old. Indeed, turtles and tortoises are among the longest-lived creatures on the earth.

And speaking of which, what exactly is the difference between a turtle and a tortoise? *Is there* a difference?

Yes and no.

For linguistic purists in both Britain and America, a turtle is a shelled reptile that lives in the water, swims well, has webbed feet, and is a carnivorous or omnivorous eater. A tortoise is a shelled reptile that lives on land, cannot swim, has thick, stumpy legs with unwebbed feet, and is primarily a herbivore. Dictionary definitions notwithstanding though, all reptiles with shells are classified in the same group, and it is well within the realm of scientific accuracy to refer to tortoises and turtles under the same umbrella title of "turtle."

Buying a turtle

Unless a herp fancier resides in your area, or your local shelter and animal rescue society have turtles on hand to adopt, you will probably do your turtle shopping at local pet stores. When assessing the quality of a supplier, refer to the sections on acquiring pets in Chapter 1. Here we quote a section from this chapter that is especially pertinent.

> The most potentially problematic of all reptiles acquired from pet shops are turtles. Because they are so abundant in the wild and simple to catch, they are easily scooped out of local rivers and swamps, then smuggled in as stock to pet stores. Very young, small red ear sliders, the kind sold years ago with decals on their backs, are still sold illegally in some parts of the country (the federal law states that suppliers cannot sell a turtle until it grows to be four inches long). But beware: wild turtles are breeders of disease, especially salmonella, and should be avoided, especially by children who often handle pets, then put their hands into their mouths. When purchasing a turtle from a pet store be certain it is disease free, American born, and raised in captivity from birth.

In the long run, whether or not the specimens you find at your local pet supplier are healthy or sick depends on the integrity of the store itself. If you already have a good experience purchasing animals here, if the store is clean, the stock of animals bright and healthy looking, the staff well informed, and their return and guarantee policies fair, chances are the turtles they sell will be healthy and strong as well.

As a rule, turtles are on the inexpensive side, and except for an initial outlay for tank and equipment, are relatively cheap to maintain. For more exotic turtles, be prepared to pay a hunderd dollars or even higher. When examining turtles for purchase, make sure a turtle's eyes are clear and unclouded. Its eyelids should be intact, not swollen or distended. If the lids are distended this may indicate disease or lack of vitamin A. There should be no secretions in the corners of the eyes or mouth.

Healthy turtles should behave in an energetic and alive way. When you touch them they instantly react, pulling into their shells. If turtles do not respond to being handled they are probably sick.

Examine the turtle's underside. There should be no discolorations, chipping, cuts, abrasions, or suspicious markings. The shell should feel firm and intact when you squeeze it. No conspicuous cracks, broken edges, or soft spots should be in evidence. Next, examine the turtle's underside for mites or other parasites. Even the smallest of these creatures are visible and volatile, moving from place to place on the turtle's body with great quickness. Though mites are curable, it is usually better to avoid infected specimens when purchasing and to find one that is fully healthy.

Finally, are all the turtle's limbs in place? Are the toes all there? Does the turtle have both eyes? Are there telltale scars on the body, indicating previous accidents or mistreatment? Are there lumps on the turtle's legs or neck? Is the turtle making gasping or wheezing sounds?

Housing. Some turtles live on land and some in the water, and never the twain shall meet—at least not in the same tank. In order to get it right from the start, be sure to know what kind of native habitat your new turtle is from, whether it is a land turtle, a water turtle, or a turtle that prefers a bit of each. Then set up the tank accordingly.

For aquatic turtles, a twenty- or thirty-gallon aquarium makes good housing, preferably the long, low models. Fill the tank with enough water so that the turtle can entirely submerge itself and swim around comfortably without constraints. While depths should generally be at least two times the length of the turtle's body, the precise amount of water depends on the species of turtle.

As a rule, painted turtles, map turtles, and sliders are all comfortable in deep water, while box turtles are not adept swimmers, and prefer shallow depths. All turtles need to leave the water at some point in the day to dry and bask, so a rock or two placed in the middle of the tank and set low enough to the surface for the turtle to crawl up on at will is a must. Also useful is a gradient of aquarium gravel that starts low in the water and rises gradually above water level to form a dry embankment. It is important for turtles to climb fully out of the water to bask in the light each day, so be certain all rocks in their tank are accessible and that pebble gradients are not too steeply banked. To keep the water in the tank clean and well aerated, some turtle owners use a filter, though changing the water every few days makes filters generally unnecessary.

For tortoises or land turtles, a wooden box or twenty-gallon aquarium offers adequate shelter. Fill the bottom of the box or tank with shredded newspaper, peat moss, aspen shavings, or dried corncob bits as a substrate. A few well-positioned rocks serve as turtle hiding places—like all reptiles, turtles need their privacy—and for basking purposes.

For both land and semiaquatic turtles, a source of light and warmth is necessary, not only for staying warm but to catalyze proper calcium metabolism.

A few hours' direct sunlight is best in this regard. If sunlight is not available, a full-spectrum daylight-simulating 150-watt bulb focused over one part of the tank, preferably on a dry rock for basking, is ideal. Keep the light temperature around 85 to 90°F. Thermal gradients are useful, providing heat at one end of the tank and a cool area at the other. Like most reptiles, moreover, a majority of turtles require ultraviolet rays along with their quotient of daylight. These can be supplied by means of a full-spectrum fluorescent lighting unit that emits energy in the UVB wavelength. (See the Appendix for information on where to find ultraviolet lighting equipment.)

Finally, sanitation and hygiene are a critical part of proper turtle husbandry. The water in a turtle's tank should always be clean. As a rule the water should be changed weekly or whenever it turns cloudy or dark. Once or twice a month, turtles should also be removed from their tank, placed in a safe holding area, and the aquarium glass scrubbed, the gravel drained and cleaned, the rocks cleaned, and utensils washed.

Hygiene also extends to feeding, and the most important rule here is don't overfeed. Uneaten residues quickly rot, and nothing turns a turtle's water foul more quickly than rotting food. If you feed your turtle live fish parts or chopped liver, feed tiny amounts at a time. When these are eaten feed a few more. If any part of the fresh food goes uneaten for more than an hour or so, remove it immediately.

Feeding your turtle. Aquatic turtles are primarily carnivorous. Semiaquatic species that live partly on land, partly in the water, are primarily herbivorous. Land tortoises are entirely omnivorous. A standard diet for the more common pet turtles includes commercial turtle food, mealworms, soft dog food, raw shrimp, crickets, goldfish, guppies, fish bits, chopped liver, and earthworms. Supplement these items occasionally with fresh fruits and vegetables such as apple, bananas, grapes, peaches, berries, carrots, romaine, kale, dandelion leaves, and other dark greens. When feeding fresh food like fish, be sure and chop it into fine bits before giving it to your pet. Turtles have small mouths, and most have no teeth.

Turtles require plenty of calcium for healthy shells and bones. Reptile vitamin supplements are recommended, especially those that are strong on vitamins D and A. The rule of thumb with a turtle's diet is, the wider the variety of food turtles eat the healthier they become. Be careful though of overfeeding: most adult turtles require two or three feedings a week at most. Babies and juveniles can be fed every other day.

If your turtle is a poor eater and turns its nose up at the daily fare, the problem may be sickness, but more likely it is due to the fact that the temperature in its tank is too low. Warm the tank up a bit by placing a heating pad underneath or by bringing the overhead light source closer to water level. You should see an increase in your pet's appetite within a day or two.

Water. The water in an aquatic turtle's tank is not only the water it swims in; it is also the water it drinks. Be sure it is changed frequently. Turtles are not the most sanitary animals in the world, and their lairs should periodically be put in order.

For land turtles, a majority of the water they need is taken in via their food. At the same time, land turtles become dehydrated if a source of water is not kept on hand as a supplement. Not only will turtles avail themselves of this extra water, but they will immerse themselves in the water bowl from time to time. Even the most dedicated land-going members of the turtle family enjoy a good dip.

Serve the water to your turtle in a nonmetal bowl one or more times a day. The bowl should be large enough to accommodate all the turtle's soaking needs. Keep the water temperature lukewarm and the depth shallow. Remember, this water will be used for elimination as well as drinking, so the bowl should be removed and cleaned each day with dispatch.

Tips on handling a turtle. Turtles, even the cleanest, may harbor and breed salmonella bacteria. Immediately after holding a turtle, wash your hands and make sure your children do the same. Never kiss a turtle (or any other reptile), and never bring it close to your mouth or let it breathe in your face. During meal preparation or mealtime, keep your turtle away from all food areas. When washing or handling dishes, keep the turtle's utensils a good distance from your own.

Otherwise, handle turtles as you would any other small, vulnerable creature. Do not make sudden, violent motions. Keep loud, abrupt noises to a minimum. Move slowly and be respectful. Do not grasp too hard, never shake, and avoid hanging the creature upside down or putting it through acrobatics (turtles especially dislike being rolled on their backs—the weight of their intestines compresses their lungs, a potentially dangerous situation). Pick them up with one hand under their stomach and the other steadying the top of their shell. Be gentle.

Over time, with careful and tender handling, a turtle will come to know you and even come running (well, walking or swimming) when you approach its tank.

Types of turtles

Of the almost three hundred species of turtle, a select handful make good pets. Some are simply too large or too sensitive to fit into a home environment. Others pine away in captivity. And though reptile purists may object, pet owners are advised to stay away from the snapping variety, especially if children are in the house. Snappers are bright and interesting creatures, but they can yank out sizeable pieces of flesh when they bite, and of equal importance, it is generally prohibited to remove snappers from the wild. Avoid them.

The following varieties of turtles all make friendly and easy-to-care-for pets.

Painted turtle. A purely aquatic turtle, painted turtles are native to the United States, have attractive green and yellow markings, and grow to be about seven inches long at maturity. Their tank should contain plenty of swimming room, with at least one and preferably two basking rocks. Be sure to keep the water clean and the surrounding temperature between 75 and 80°F.

Painted turtles happily eat commercial turtle food, though some experts recommend this basic diet be supplemented with fresh foods. A standard feeding regimen for painted turtles includes 25 percent commercial turtle pellets, 25 percent live goldfish and guppies, and 50 percent plant material such as kale, turnip greens, and dandelions. In general, the young require more protein in their diets, while adults require more plant material. Painted turtles are inexpensive and plentiful at most pet stores.

Map turtle. Like the painted turtle, map turtles are native to the United States, especially the southern parts. Males of the species attain six-inch lengths at maturity, females grow just under a foot long. Maps are an aquatic turtle that require a full tank of crystal clean water, with a rock or two projecting for basking, and temperatures around 75 to 80°F. Like painted turtles, maps require frequent water changes to stay healthy.

Maps subsist on a diet of feeder goldfish and guppies and very small amounts of dog food or cat food, plus vegetables and dark greens like kale, turnip greens, and dandelions. Pieces of raw fish, chopped liver, and snails are all appreciated.

Slider turtle. Perhaps the most common and inexpensive of pet turtles, the aquatic slider is a native American that at maturity grows to lengths of eight inches or more (red-eared sliders are known to grow almost a foot long). Green and brown in color with a reddish stripe on their heads, sliders are active, intelligent little creatures that need a good depth of water to swim in, an appropriate basking surface to crawl on periodically, and temperatures between 75 and 80°F. If properly cared for they will live for twenty-five years or more in captivity.

Feed your slider the usual turtle favorites: feeder goldfish and guppies, dog food and cat food tidbits, raw fish bits, chopped liver, snails, and dark greens like kale, turnip greens, and dandelions.

Box turtle. A terrestrial land-dwelling turtle—and hence technically a tortoise—box turtles have brown-spotted, rounded shells and walk the earth with stumpy feet and little toes (as opposed to the webs of aquatic turtles). They are small as far as tortoises go, reaching only around a half-foot in length, and they are natives to the southern states from Texas to Georgia.

A box turtle's diet is omnivorous, consisting of earthworms, slugs, vegetables, fruits, and berries. For those who are interested, an easy way to sex box turtles is to remember that males have red eyes and yellow or orange spots on their heads, females have brown eyes and no yellow or orange spots on their heads.

Turtle gender and health

Turtles are relatively easy to sex. The female has a flat plastron (bottom of the shell). The plastron on a male is more concave, making it easier for the male to mount the female at breeding time.

As far as turtle health is concerned, clean water, controlled temperature, proper light, frequent tank cleanings, and a nutritious, all-round diet will go a long way toward keeping your pet well and fit. Make especially sure that the turtle's vitamin A intake is adequate.

Signs of ill health in turtles include clouded eyes, lethargy, impaired swimming or walking, secretion from the eyes and mouth, soft spots on the shell, and white fungus discolorations of the skin. To determine if there are signs of mites, look for tiny crawling creatures along the bottom of the shell.

Turtles are difficult to treat at home. At the first sign of disease, veterinarian care is usually required.

Amphibians

Amphibian biology

Approximately 400 million years ago a group of intrepid seagoing vertebrates resembling fish more than frogs crawled onto dry land for the first time and established, as it were, a beachhead. Others followed as the millennia crept ahead, and before many more eons had passed the continental regions of the planet were colonized with walking, breathing beings destined to evolve into the familiar classes of reptiles and mammals we now see around us. Without this bold evolutionary step by amphibians, we might all be swimming in the sea today.

Still, some of the ocean-going creatures that first strayed onto land did not adapt well to a terrestrial environment. So nature allowed them a compromise: spend part of their life in the water, part on land. The name *amphibian* is thus derived from the Greek word *amphi* meaning "both."

The most common amphibians, and the ones you are most likely to keep as pets, are the four-legged varieties: salamanders, frogs, and toads. Together they comprise the two major amphibian orders, Anura (without a tail—i.e., frogs and toads) and Caudata (with a tail—i.e., salamanders). A third order, Gymnophiona, has fewer species, most of which are blind, limbless, wormlike, and not well suited to be pets.

Amphibians begin their lives in the water as larvae or tadpoles. They swim and seek food, taking in air through a set of external gills. After weeks of underwater life the great metamorphosis begins: the amphibian's legs start to grow, a set of lungs develop similar to those of mammals, and eventually a migration to land follows where in many cases amphibians live out the remainder of their days.

Yet there are few absolutes with amphibians. Some varieties crawl onto land, live here for a while, then return to the water in the later stages of life to die. Still others, especially frogs and toads, live in the driest parts of the world, deserts and prairies, where at different stages in life they manage to find a small body of water to be born in, to swim in, or to die in. Some simply absorb the water they need from dampness in the environment, or from rain. Though there are no varieties of salt-water amphibians we know of—which is strange when you think that amphibians came originally from the sea—the approximately twenty-five hundred species that populate the earth today are found on every continent except in the Arctic zones.

With a few exceptions (such as the West African giant frog that grows a foot long, and weighs as much as a dog), amphibians are small and light. They have limbs rather than fins, shed their skins periodically, capture their prey with tongues rather than teeth, and like reptiles, are cold-blooded. Their skins are a miracle of nature, an organ unto itself that helps the lungs to breathe (and in the lungless salamander the skin actually *does* the breathing), absorbs water, keeps the body moist, and serves as a highly sensitive touch receptor.

Just below the surface of this remarkable covering runs a network of glands that produce mucus to keep the skin lubricated, and in some species it secretes irritating substances that make the frog or toad decidedly unsavory tasting to enemies. Among certain frog and toad species, a highly toxic substance is also manufactured on the skin that kills predators on contact.

Unlike reptiles, amphibians have no scaly or armored coverings to protect them from predators, and, with few exceptions, no poison to inject into their enemies. Most amphibian survival tactics are thus based less on strength and intimidation, more on camouflage, wily tactics of evasion, and, as we have seen, making themselves indigestible for potential enemies.

There are few among us who as a child did not catch toads or salamanders, place them lovingly into a shoe box surrounded by rocks and grass, and keep them as pets. For many of us, they were our *first* pets. Which is why amphibians are still enjoyable animals to have in the home, even for grown-up pet lovers. Though we do not recommend kidnapping them from the wild—many amphibian species are endangered today—those raised in captivity make excellent low-maintenance pets, especially after the initial purchase and setup procedures are completed. They are interesting, educational, and just plain fun to look at in their tanks and cages.

Buying amphibians

Chances are you will purchase your amphibian from a local pet store. Before you make your choice, consider the fact that the quality of pet store amphibian stock varies enormously depending on the store's policies and management. Some pet suppliers order screened and healthy frogs, toads, and salamanders. Some don't. It is advisable to check out the store's reputation ahead of time with friends and local veterinarians, and to know who you're dealing with.

When screening and evaluating a frog, toad, or salamander at the pet shop, examine the animal carefully. Its eyes should be clear, unclouded, and free of all excretions. The animal should appear alert and aware. When you reach into the cage to pick a frog or toad up, they should try to hop or crawl away. Nonreactiveness on the part of an amphibian does not mean it is friendly; it means it is sick. Frogs, and toads especially, should have hair-trigger responses: the second you touch them they are in the air. If a frog or toad does not respond in this way when touched it is probably a sick frog or toad.

Healthy amphibians should be sound of structure and limb. Avoid animals with broken, twisted, or odd-looking limbs. The one exception to this rule is salamanders, which lose their tails and sometimes even their legs as a matter of course. If you do see a salamander you like but it is missing an appendage, you do not necessarily have to worry about the creature's health—chances are the limb will soon grow back—though you might ask yourself (and the supplier) how the accident happened in the first place

The amphibian's skin should be firm without any wounds or abrasions. Beware of scars. These may be signs of a serious injury in the past. All vent areas should be clean and clear of feces. Last but not least, the amphibian should have a good "feel" in your hands—solid, energetic, not too fat or thin, strong, generally well constructed and healthy.

Cage and habitat. A ten- or twenty-gallon glass aquarium tank makes an ideal frog, toad, and salamander home. To accommodate amphibians like toads that live mainly on land, place a layer of sterilized store-bought soil on the bottom of the tank, then cover it with a layer of vermiculite or potting soil. On top of this substrate place an inch or two of peat moss (or perhaps an inch of sterilized topsoil), a rock, a wooden branch or block, green growing things like small ferns, your choice of decorations, and if you wish a layer of green moss. In one corner of the tank, place (and always keep filled) a water bowl, both for drinking and for adding humidity to the tank, then place a screened lid on top.

For aquatic amphibians, a sloped underlayer of several inches of gravel with several inches of water on top and scattered rocks for climbing and hiding does the trick. Some tropical species of frogs require their water be warm, dechlorinated (use a water conditioner or allow the water to stand twenty-four hours before adding to the tank), and a small heating attachment may be necessary.

As for temperature, most amphibians like it cool to temperate. Around 68 to 85°F. is ideal. In most cases room temperature does the trick, unless, of course, one's home turns extra cold during the winter, in which case an external heating unit may be needed.

Keep the tank well ventilated, shaded to simulate a forest environment, and place it away from direct heat and light sources such as sun through the window or wintertime radiators. Since they do require some light during the day, a full-wave fluorescent bulb over the tank delivers the appropriate amount of rays. Keep the light on for seven or eight hours a day, then turn it off at night. If you own a tropical amphibian, a tropical frog, for instance, warm temperatures and bright, incandescent lighting may be necessary. Again, consult with your source of purchase concerning the best setup for your particular pet.

Amphibians tend to be messy, and their tanks should be thoroughly cleaned at least once a week. Remember again, these creatures carry salmonella. A good hand scrubbing is always necessary before and after cleanup. Do research before mixing or housing more than one species of amphibian as well to ensure safety. Also avoid mixing frogs and toads together in a single tank. Some frog species are toxic to others. Some cannibalize one another. Some simply have entirely different needs.

Feeding amphibians. With a few exceptions (see below) the basic amphibian diet consists of insects. Indeed, except for certain poisonous varieties of spiders, amphibians eat practically any bug that crosses their path. Endowed with highly sensitive motion-sensing equipment, the moment something flies, crawls, hops, or swims past them they're off, tongue flicking, jaw opening, jaw closing—end of story.

This almost exclusive preference for insects makes feeding amphibians a relatively easy job. Well-stocked pet supply stores all carry a variety of amphibian insect treats such as flies, white worms, and the old standby, crickets. Some owners prefer to catch and raise their own insects, and this is fine, just as long as they have the time and patience. You might consider dusting these insects with a good amphibian-oriented vitamin supplement. Remember though, a frog or toad eats an awful lot of insects in a short period of time, and you may have to work overtime to keep the larder filled.

Besides insects, larger frogs enjoy pinkies, and aquatic frogs happily devour mealworms and brine shrimp. But be careful: overfeeding can produce intestinal blockages. Most pet stores sell specially blended vitamin preparations that supplement regular insect diets. Add these to small tidbits of meat, or sprinkle them over insects before feeding. And don't forget to keep supplies of fresh water in your pet's cage at all times. Amphibians with damp skin also enjoy daily mist sprays from a spray bottle.

Don't be concerned, by the way, if your pet turns up its nose at dinner now and then. This is amphibian biology at work. Like reptiles, amphibians are built to go for long periods of time without food, especially creatures like frogs and toads that sometimes sit silently for days waiting for their prey to wander by. If your pet decides to be choosy now and then about eating, this is normal. On the other hand, if it avoids food for two weeks or longer, health troubles may be brewing, and a veterinarian's advice is necessary.

Handling amphibians. Amphibians are not your ordinary touchy-feely type of pets, and, in fact, tend to be far better off if not touched at all. The reason for the hands-off policy is not just that amphibians are shy and reclusive. It is due to the fact that part of their oxygen delivery system works through their skin. When people handle frogs or newts, the oils and salts on the human hand coat this skin, sometimes clogging the creature's delicate breathing mechanisms.

Frogs and salamanders, as you have also no doubt noticed, are slimy to the touch. This slippery coating is produced by mucous secretions that cover the creature's skin and provide protection from infection and disease. If pet owners overhandle their amphibians, constant contact wears away at this protective layer, ultimately resulting in compromised health for the animal.

Amphibians, therefore, are much like fish—look, enjoy, wonder, but don't touch.

If you do handle your frog, toad, or chameleon on a regular basis, be sure to wash your hands first to protect the animal. Careful washing will remove salts and oils, and the residual moisture left over helps prevent erosion of the mucous surfaces.

When finished, wash your hands again immediately, this time out of self-protection. Like their reptilian cousins, amphibians carry salmonella.

Frogs and toads

Chubby frog. An impressively colored frog with mahogany brown tones and cream-colored bands along its side, the chubby is a voracious eater and expects a large daily supply (and wide variety) of moths, crickets, grasshoppers, et al. Sometimes a bit noisy—owner reports vary here—and generally peace loving, the chubby has the habit of digging into the ground and hiding itself. Avoid handling these frogs if possible; they produce sticky slime secretions that can be difficult to remove from the hands.

European tree frog. A popular breed of semiaquatic frog, you must provide your European tree with plenty of moisture and misting, plus warm, humid room temperatures. A deep green in coloration, they are small as far as frogs go, growing no more than one and a half inches long. Be sure and add several branches plus leafy greens to their tank.

White tree frog. Growing to four inches in length, hardy, chubby, white trees are easy to care for and make ideal starter pets. Natives of South America, they are among the longest lived of all frog species, sometimes making it to twenty years. They enjoy having lots of plants and branches in their tank, along with high humidity, and a thorough misting at least once a day. Never mix white tree frogs with smaller species—the smaller species may end up as a meal.

Red-eyed tree frog. A popular and easy-to-care-for species, red-eyed trees come originally from Central and South America. Their striking red eyes and bright green and blue skins make a stunning sight in the tank. Nocturnal and basically tropical, they require high humidity and temperatures around 85°F during the day and no colder than 65°F at night. Good swimmers, they appreciate a large water dish in the tank, along with plants, moss, twigs, rocks, and aquarium gravel in the bottom of the tank. Red-eyed trees are great climbers, so be sure and keep the lid on their tanks tight at all times. They prefer an arboreal-style tank, taller than wide, with many live plants to crawl on.

Asian floating frog. Asian floating frogs have become popular among pet owners in the past few years, both because they are cute and because they are relatively easy to maintain. While Asian frogs spend a great deal of time floating on the surface of the water (as their name implies), they also require a tank setup known as a *half-and-half*, an arrangement that supplies dry spots for the frog to crawl up on such as plastic plants, rocks, and so forth. Nutritionally, Asian floating frogs require a diet of insects, mostly crickets, and preferably those dusted with vitamin supplements.

American green tree frog. Among the most popular of pet frogs, the green tree frog is grass-green color, sometimes with cream-colored lines along its jaw and sides. Adaptable to room temperatures, they nonetheless enjoy a bit of heat now and then, and owners sometimes recommend the use of a fluorescent tube over their tank. Easy to feed, they are hardy and alert.

Fire-bellied toad. Named for their attractively colored orange bellies with black spots, fire-bellied toads require several inches of water in the tank along with graded gravel as a land habitat. Great hoppers, be sure to keep the top on their tank. These creatures are extremely sensitive to chlorinated water, so add a few drops of water conditioner (or let the water stand twenty-four hours) before adding it to the tank. Fire-bellied toads also need plenty of rocks and hiding places for privacy. Like many toads, their skins are slightly toxic, so always wash your hands after contact.

Fowlers toad. A large yellow-and-green-spotted toad, Fowlers grow up to five inches in size and let out a loud mating croak, sometimes described as "the bleat of a sheep with a cold." They are nocturnal creatures and are delightful additions to any outdoor pond. They are found in nature throughout much of the United States east of the Mississippi, from Lake Michigan to the Gulf Coast.

European green toad. An adaptable and congenial pet, this green and brown species is active, hardy, and grows up to four inches in size. It happily eats just about any insect you give it, and is sometimes described as one of the more "intelligent" frogs and toads by amphibian owners in the know.

American tree toad. Native of the eastern United States and southern Canada, the American tree toad measures from two to four inches, feeds on insects, and is primarily nocturnal. Many pet owners catch them in the wild, though this is not a recommended practice, as it can become the road leading to extinction. Remember, the animals you purchase at pet stores are specially raised as pets. Avoid trapping animals in the wild.

Colorado River toad. Green-and-cream-colored, the Colorado River toad is a nocturnal animal that grows up to six inches in size. It both hunts and sings loudly at night, and it can be a noisy companion if kept in your room while sleeping.

Frog and toad health concerns

As with reptiles, there are not a lot of animal professionals who specialize in amphibian care and health. Assuming that you are attached to your frog or toad and are willing to pay the veterinarian fees, you may still have to do some asking around, first with your regular veterinarian, second with herp clubs in the area concerning where to find a doctor who specializes in, or at least who has a working knowledge of, amphibian medicine and disease.

In general, frogs and toads should be kept cool and moist. Keep temperatures constant, avoid too much direct sunlight, avoid overcrowding in the tank and make sure to clean the tank at least once a week. If a frog or toad is ailing, remove it from the tank immediately and place it in isolation. Amphibian diseases are usually contagious, and infection can spread from one colony member to another in record time. Common ailments that strike frogs and toads include the following:

Fungus: Amphibian fungus presents as a red inflammation on the surface of the skin. Try bathing your pet in a bath treated with several drops of 2 percent Mercurochrome for five minutes each day. If no improvement results after three or four days, consult a veterinarian.

Spring disease: Symptoms include yawning, lethargy, skin discoloration. Spring disease is usually fatal. All you can do is isolate your pet in a hospital tank, keep it cool and fed, and hope for the best.

Malnourishment: If a frog or toad appears to be abnormally skinny and lethargic, and if its bones appear malformed, it may be suffering from lack of important vitamins and minerals in its diet. Increase the variety of foods you feed it, and obtain a good amphibian vitamin and mineral powder from your pet supplier. Calcium deficiency is probably the most common cause of malnourishment among amphibians.

Red leg: Triggered by a common parasite, red leg causes the skin to redden, especially around the area of the thighs and underbelly. The creature appears apathetic and lazy, and usually loses its appetite. This condition can sometimes be helped at home by bathing your pet in a 2 percent solution of copper sulfate every day for a few minutes over a two-week period. Your veterinarian can recommend antibiotic treatment, if necessary.

Wounds: Frogs and toads are fragile creatures and frequently show mysterious signs of cutting and bruising, even when you cannot isolate the cause. If a frog or toad shows a wound, isolate it in a hospital tank and let nature take its course. Often it will recover on its own.

Salamanders

Eastern red salamander. Relatively large at six or seven inches, the Eastern red is a quite active amphibian who subsists on insects of all kinds and tends to be shy. You will often find it hiding beneath a rock or piece of wood in the tank. Be sure and keep its environment shady, cool, and damp. Eastern reds dry out quickly, and when they do the dryness can kill them.

Common newt. The humble newt is one of the first pets many of us adopted from under stones and in the woods as children. Fascinating not only for the fact that they change forms several times in their life (they actually go back to the water when they reach maturity rather than leave it), newts are fascinating as well because they change colors so frequently and subtly to blend into their environment. Growing from three to five inches long and happy to subsist on a diet of crickets, flies, and most other small insects plus tubifex worms, newts are inexpensive, low-maintenance, and interesting first pets for children.

Red eft newt. Cute, small (about three inches), low maintenance, and surprisingly hardy, the red eft is actually a young version of the red-spotted newt (all these stages get confusing). Keep reds damp and provide lots of interesting crawl spaces for them in the tank—rocks, ledges, moss platforms, wood bark. Make sure to give them fresh water daily. When feeding, besides their usual insect diet, newts of all variety will gobble small crustaceans, tubifex worms, and even small tidbits of fish and liver.

Northern dusky salamander. A dark brown amphibian that thrives on small insects, a Northern dusky grows from four to five inches long, and requires a cool, damp environment in its tanks. If the temperature goes over 75°F in the room, they become endangered. Their delicate moist skin must stay damp constantly. They need fresh water daily and a diet of small insects.

Salamander health concerns

Most important, keep them cool. An overheated salamander is soon a dead salamander.

Cage sanitation is critical for maintaining the good health of your pet. Salamanders are vulnerable to a wide range of bacterial and viral ailments, and a clean cage is the best form of prevention. Salamander skin is also extremely sensitive to touch. If their delicate surface covering is even slightly damaged or bruised, this can lead to breathing problems and disease. Avoid handling whenever possible. When transporting, be especially careful.

Another important step you can take toward preventing disease is to avoid unsanitary overcrowding in a salamander cage. When contact becomes too close, members of a 'colony often become irritable and stressed, and they turn on one another. Worse, an incurable disease known as amphibian leprosy may result, especially if overcrowding is accompanied by overly dry tank conditions. Leprosy is probably lurking when salamanders develop bloody spots under their skin surface, lose all signs of appetite, and show peeling skin and rot at the ends of their legs and tails. When and if this fatal ailment strikes, isolate the sick salamander immediately, clean the tank, and if possible thin out the population of the original colony, distributing them into two or more new community tanks.

If your salamander appears lethargic, has glazed or swollen eyes, strange spots, colorations, blood splotches, or white fuzz (fungus infection) on its skin, it is most likely ailing. Place it in a separate tank, keep it separate from others in the colony, and give the community tank a thorough cleaning to rid it of bacterial deposits left by the sick salamander. There are many highly contagious diseases among amphibians, and ailing members of a community should always quickly be removed and segregated.

As far as specific diseases are concerned, most of the frog and toad disorders mentioned above are common to salamanders as well. Of special concern with salamanders is to avoid placing two or more aggressive males in the same close quarters. Two males almost invariably fight and inflict mutual damage. Sometimes the aftermath can be messy. But take heart. These ingenious creatures have the power to regenerate body parts. If a leg or tail is damaged in a tussle between salamanders, if it is dangling precariously, and if you have the heart for it, slice the limb off cleanly, then allow the creature's body wisdom to do the rest. Usually the limb grows back in a few weeks.

Appendix

Chapter Two: Home Is Where Your Pets Are

To obtain the ASPCA's booklet on toxic plants and pets, write:

ASPCA National Animal Poison Control Center
1717 South Philo Road, Suite #36
Urbana, IL 61802

Chapter Four: Traveling with Your Pet

For more information on pet sitters and the services they provide contact:

National Association of Pet-Sitters
1200 G Street
Washington, DC 20005
(800) 296-PETS

Pet-Sitters International
418 East King Street
King, NC 27021
(880) 263-SITS

For information on pet guest policy at leading hotel chains call the following numbers:

Best Western (800) 458-7500
Econo Lodge (800) 553-2666
Four Seasons Hotels (800) 527-4727
Holiday Inn (800) 465-4329
Hilton Hotels (800) 445-8667
Howard Johnson (800) 446-4656
Hyatt Hotels (800) 233-1234
Inter-Continental Hotels (800) 442-7375
Marriott Hotels (800) 228-9290
Sheraton Hotels (800) 325-3535
TraveLodge (800) 578-7878

For websites offering information on travel with an animal and moving to a new residence with pets see:

www.usps.gov
www.aaa.com
www.takeyourpet.com

Chapter Five: Keeping Your Pet Healthy

For comparing pet insurance prices, services, etc., start with the following insurers. Call and ask for their brochure.

National Pet Club
(800) 738-2582

Veterinary Pet Insurance
(800) 872-7387

Premier Pet Insurance
(877) 774-2273

Websites that provide useful general information on pet insurance include the following:

www.drlarrypetvet.com/health-petinsurance.htm
www.tailchaser.org

For information on alternative medicines for pets contact the following:

International Veterinary Acupuncture Society
P.O. Box 2074
Nedorlund, CO 80466
(303) 258-3767

American Veterinary Chiropractic Association
623 Main Street
Hillsdale, IL 61257
(309) 658-2920

American Holistic Veterinary Medical Association
2214 Old Emmorton Road
Bel Air, MD 21015
(410) 569-0795

National Center for Homeopathy
801 North Fairfax Street, Suite 306
Alexandria, VA 22314
(703) 548-7790

A website directory featuring a list of veterinarians who practice alternative medicine is available on the web from the American Holistic Veterinary Medical Association Directory at:

http://www.altveterinarianmed.com/associat.html

Chapter Six: Saying Good-bye

Grief counselors at the ASPCA can be reached via the following beeper number twenty-four hours a day. Dial (800) 946-4646, then type in the number 1407211, plus your phone number. The pager will prompt you through the process. Whoever is on duty will call back as soon as possible.

The following institutions offer free pet loss support hotlines:

Tufts University School of Veterinary Medicine
(508) 839-7966
Hotline hours: 6 P.M. to 9 P.M., Monday, Wednesday, Friday. Leave a

message and your call will be returned (outside Massachusetts call-backs will be made to you collect).

Virginia-Maryland Regional College of Veterinary Medicine
(540) 231-8038
Hotline hours: 6 P.M. to 9 P.M., Tuesday, Thursday. Leave your name and number. A volunteer will call you back.

Animal Medical Center of New York
(212) 838-8100
Hotline hours: Follow directions on the voice menu, and/or leave a message.

St. Huberts Animal Welfare Center (New Jersey)
(973) 377-7094
Hotline hours: Follow directions on the voice menu and/or leave a message.

Cornell University Veterinarian School (New York)
(607) 253-3932
Hotline hours: 6 P.M. to 9 P.M., Tuesday, Wednesday, Thursday. If you call after hours, leave a message and a volunteer will call you back.

University of Pennsylvania Veterinarian School
(215) 898-4529
Hotline hours: Leave your name and number on the answering machine. A volunteer will call you back.

Chicago Veterinary Medical Association
(630) 603-3994
Hotline hours: 7 P.M. to 9 P.M., Monday through Friday.

University of Florida
(352) 392-4700, then dial 1 (as instructed by the voice menu), followed by extension number 4080. Leave your name and number. A volunteer will return your call during hotline hours.
Hotline hours: 7 P.M. to 9 P.M., Monday through Friday.

For helpful information and resources related to grief work with pets, get in touch with the Delta Society, a group that specializes in animal bereavement:

The Delta Society
321 Burnett Avenue South
3rd Floor
Renton, WA 98055-2569
(206) 226-7357

The following website specializes in placing testimonies and written memorials to pets:

www.in-memory-of-pets.com

Chapter Ten: Birds

For information on buying birds contact:

The Association of Avian Veterinarians
P.O. Box 811720
Boca Raton, FL 33481

For finding a veterinarian near your place of residence who specializes in medical treatment for pet birds, contact the following organization on the web:

www.aav.org

Chapter Twelve: Reptiles and Amphibians

For finding a veterinarian near your place of residence who specializes in treating pet reptiles and amphibians, contact the following organization:

Association of Reptilian and Amphibian Veterinarians
c/o Wilbur Amand, D.V.M., Executive Director,
P.O. Box 605
Chester Heights, PA 19017

A mail order source that sells a variety of lighting equipment for reptiles and amphibians, including ultraviolet lighting equipment, is:

Big Apple Herpetological
90-1 Colin Drive,
Holbook, NY 11741
(800) 92-APPLE, Fax: (516) 419-1058

4/21/14.